D1594068

SOLDIER
OF THE PRESS

SOLDIER
OF THE PRESS

Covering the Front in Europe and North Africa, 1936-1943

HENRY T. GORRELL

Edited with an Introduction by **Kenneth Gorrell**

Foreword by **John C. McManus**

UNIVERSITY OF MISSOURI PRESS COLUMBIA AND LONDON

Library of Congress Cataloging–in–Publication Data

Gorrell, Henry T., 1911–1958.
  Soldier of the press : covering the front in Europe and North Africa, 1936–1943 /
Henry T. Gorrell ; edited with an introduction by Kenneth Gorrell, foreword by John C.
McManus.
     p. cm.
  Includes bibliographical references and index.
  Summary: "This memoir by United Press war correspondent Henry T. Gorrell
provides eyewitness accounts from the battlefields of the Spanish Civil War and the war
fronts in Greece, the Balkans, the Middle East, and North Africa during World War II"—
Provided by publisher.
  ISBN 978–0–8262–1851–3 (alk. paper)
  1. Gorrell, Henry T., 1911–1958. 2. World War, 1939–1945—Journalism, Military—
United States. 3. World War, 1939–1945—Personal narratives, American. 4.
World War, 1939–1945—Journalists—Biography. 5. Spain—History—Civil War,
1936–1939—Journalism, Military—United States. 6. Spain—History—Civil War,
1936–1939—Personal narratives, American. 7. Spain—History—Civil War, 1936–1939—
Journalists—Biography. 8. United Press Associations—Employees—Biography. 9. War
correspondents—United States—Biography. I. Gorrell, Kenneth. II. Title.
  D799.U6G677 2009
  940.54'21—dc22   2009004261

∞™ This paper meets the requirements of the
American National Standard for Permanence of Paper
for Printed Library Materials, Z39.48, 1984.

Designer: Stephanie Foley
Typesetter: FoleyDesign
Printer and binder: The Maple-Vail Book Manufacturing Group
Typeface: Century Old Style

To my wife Beatrice
In memory of my father
—H.T.G

CONTENTS

FOREWORD

by John C. McManus

I N WORLD WAR II, there were two kinds of war correspondents—those who reported the war from the safe distance of rear areas, and those who risked life and limb on the front lines as veritable participants. Hank Gorrell was definitely of the latter variety. From the Spanish Civil War through World War II, he saw more than his share of war, certainly more than most reporters. Many times, he came close to getting killed. From the considerable distance of a subsequent century, his writings remain perceptive and fresh. He never quite attained the fame of Ernie Pyle or Ernest Hemingway—to name just a couple of his well-known acquaintances—but it was not for lack of insight. Hank understood the geopolitical realities of his time as well as any other writer. He also never lost sight of the human story in war.

His manuscript, edited by his relative Kenneth Gorrell, following many years stored in a family attic, offers a long-overdue fresh perspective on the war. Hank takes us on a fascinating stroll through the war in the Mediterranean, from his days with the Loyalist Army during the siege of Madrid during Spain's Civil War to his coverage of the Greek campaign in 1941, to his experiences aboard an American B-24 Liberator during a bombing raid on Naples. These were momentous events indeed. The Spanish Civil War set the stage for World War II, as future antagonists tested weapons and doctrine. Later, the German conquest of Greece established Nazi domination of southern Europe. The war in North Africa, fought between 1940 and 1943, foiled Axis designs on the Middle East, and foretold a turning point in favor of the Allies.

Hank was there for all of it. His description of the Allied retreat from Greece in 1941 is both heartbreaking and spellbinding. His ill-fated romance with a Nazi spy only adds flavor to an already spicy brew. He captures the North Africa campaign so well—the seesaw, tank-dominated combat, the heat of the desert, the indomitable spirit of the British soldiers he befriended, the naive newness of the Americans, the arrogance of Axis leaders, and the elusive, yet tangible sense that perhaps the Allies were gradually turning the war in their favor. All of this oozes from the pages. Hank somehow found a way to combine the historian's hindsighted accuracy with the journalist's on-the-spot reportage. He tells us what the war looked like, sounded like, and felt like.

Hank wrote this book two years before the war ended, yet his work is remarkably prescient and accurate. He vividly weaves his personal adventures into the larger fabric of events, and he never commits the journalistic cardinal sin of making himself larger than the story he is covering. Kenneth's balanced editing only adds to Hank's story, sprinkling important footnotes throughout the text, but never intruding too much on Hank's clean, informative prose.

After the North Africa campaign, an exhausted Hank took a brief sabbatical in South Africa, where he met and married Beatrice Moser. As if rejuvenated by his nuptials, he returned to the war, covering the Normandy invasion at Utah Beach, the triumphant Allied liberation of Paris—entering the great city alongside Pyle—and the nightmarish Battle of Hürtgen Forest in the fall of 1944. By the end of that terrible battle, one of the worst and most wasteful in American history, Hank had seen enough of war. He came home to the United States, eventually resigned from the United Press, settled into the Washington, D.C., area with Beatrice, and started his own newspaper.

Sadly, he did not live a long life. He died in 1958, leaving Beatrice to raise their three young children. During the war he had suffered from a variety of maladies including malaria, which no doubt took their toll on him later. More than that, though, he was haunted by his wartime experiences. Anyone with even the slightest familiarity with post–traumatic stress disorder (PTSD) can recognize, just by reading Hank's book, that he manifested many symptoms of this combat-induced emotional problem. In fact, careful reading of his Spanish Civil War chapters reveals that he was already suffering from those symptoms at that early stage of his career. It is probably safe to assume that his PTSD did nothing good for his physical health. Indeed, his short life was probably the price he paid for his front-row seat to history.

Because he did not enjoy the name recognition of a Pyle or a Mauldin, he had trouble after the war finding a publisher for his fine book (until now that is). Regrettably, he never wrote in book form about his experiences covering the war in 1944. The earlier writings will have to suffice. His book now stands alongside other prominent books in the field, such as Pyle's *Brave Men*, Ralph Ingersoll's *The Battle Is the Payoff*, Mauldin's *Willie and Joe*, as well as the excellent works of Jack Belden, H. R. Knickerbocker, and Don Whitehead to name just a few of Hank's prominent colleagues. Like them, he has given us a priceless window into World War II.

EDITOR'S NOTE

RECOGNIZING THE HISTORICAL SIGNIFICANCE OF Henry Gorrell's unpublished manuscript—a time capsule from 1943—I focused my editing primarily on verifying the factual information he presented (dates, places, people, events). Where appropriate, I added titles and first names for officials from the war years who might be unfamiliar to the modern reader and harmonized the spelling of places (e.g., "Beirut" replaced "Beyrut").

Henry's handwritten changes were included in the editing where time had not rendered them unreadable. Occasionally, to maintain the flow of the narrative, I removed or reordered some material or added a few words. This was done sparingly. One recurring editing challenge required knitting together words separated by gaps created by military censors. Though each page bears multiple censors' stamps approving its release, more than a dozen pages are missing words, sentences, or even entire paragraphs, carefully removed with a razor.

SOLDIER
OF THE PRESS

OZYMANDIAS OF EGYPT

I met a traveler from an antique land
Who said: Two vast and trunkless legs of stone
Stand in the desert. Near them on the sand,
Half sunk, a shatter'd visage lies, whose frown

And wrinkled lip and sneer of cold command
Tell that its sculptor well those passions read
Which yet survive, stamp'd on these lifeless things,
The hand that mock'd them and the heart that fed;

And on the pedestal these words appear:
"My name is Ozymandias, King of Kings:
Look on my works, ye Mighty, and despair!"

Nothing beside remains. Round the decay
Of that colossal wreck, boundless and bare,
The lone and level sands stretch far away.

—*Percy Bysshe Shelley*

INTRODUCTION

by Kenneth Gorrell

I F YOU GROW UP IN AN OLD HOUSE WITH LARGE, DARK ATTICS, it's almost a certainty that you will spend time sifting through boxes in cluttered corners in the hope of stumbling across a treasure or two. As a child raised in an old New England farmhouse that had been in my family for generations, I often prowled the attics and the barn in hopes of finding some long-forgotten item. An old coin, a map, a lost copy of the Declaration of Independence—I didn't know what I might find, but my childhood self was convinced that one of my relatives must have left behind some valuable trinket awaiting my discovery.

Over the years I found old photographs, usually unmarked, of unrecognized faces. A few letters, books, scraps of clothing, and personal mementos in steamer trunks rounded out my collection. Then I came across an original manuscript written by a United Press correspondent titled "Eyewitness." It was a firsthand account of battles from the Spanish Civil War to the North African campaigns of World War II, dated 1943.

The manuscript—more than four hundred double-spaced pages—was typewritten, and had handwritten corrections. It was marked with censors' stamps testifying that U.S. and British military personnel had found no objectionable information on each page, though some pages were missing a few lines or even entire passages. They had been cut out with a razor to remove objectionable bits.

"Eyewitness" had been written by Henry Tilton Gorrell, a contemporary of the great Ernie Pyle. Henry was my grandfather's cousin, and he had left the manuscript with their aunt, who at the time owned the family farm that she eventually left to my grandparents. The manuscript had remained in a trunk in the attic, forgotten, for decades.

As an adult, I revisited the manuscript, driven by an interest in military history developed during my years as a naval officer. Reading the story typed on paper fragile with age, I came to recognize that I had, in fact, discovered treasure in the attic. Henry's story was not only riveting— tragic, hopeful, romantic, thrilling—it was well told. This distant relative had experienced years of warfare close up, all the while armed only with a pad and pen, manual typewriter, and his wits.

I did not know why Henry's book had never been published, but I knew that it should be published. It deserved to be. In a very real sense, I felt obligated to complete this book's journey from the mountains of Spain and the vast desert wastes of North Africa to the hands of historians, journalists, veterans, and general readers interested in exploring the best and worst of human nature as only war can reveal. No one could ask for a better guide than Henry Gorrell.

The Internet made my job of self-appointed editor easier. Henry had been a professional journalist for a major wire service, and his many news dispatches from the war years, printed in national and international newspapers and magazines at the time, were accessible to me without having to leave home. His precise reporting included the names, ranks, hometowns, and other personal details of the many fighting men and civilians who crossed his path in battles on land, sea, and air. Some were famous; most were not. But a surprising number were mentioned in articles, newsletters, and other postings from across the intervening decades now archived in the Internet. While some of their life stories ended in battle, others continued well into the postwar years. I had the privilege of speaking with one man, now in his nineties, who fondly remembered Henry—or "Hank" as he was commonly known— confirming and embellishing the details of the harrowing story recounted in chapter 23.

This book (renamed, but otherwise true to the original) covers Henry's experiences from 1936 though early 1943. While his manuscript was then sent to the States for safekeeping, Henry was sent to Europe to continue reporting the news. Though already a veteran correspondent who had witnessed much bloodshed and suffered deprivation alongside battle-hardened soldiers, he was to see far more. But after the Battle of Hürtgen Forest, he had reached his limit. He had thought he had reached it before, and touched on his feelings in his memoir, but this time he knew he was through. The year was 1945, and he had spent the better part of nine years in and around the front lines of some of the most deadly combat of the twentieth century. Henry, now married and with a daughter, returned home a few months before VE Day. He resigned from United Press a month after Germany surrendered.

Between these events, Henry wrote an article for the *Saturday Evening Post* that was published in the May 19, 1945, edition. Titled, "We Psychos Are Not Crazy," this article proves that his keen powers of observation could be applied to the world inside his mind as well as to the world around him. For all to read, Henry tells of his mental struggles in clean, honest prose. He is reporting, and it seems not to matter to him that, unlike in his war dispatches, the subject of the story is now himself. He begins:

> The medicos have done the fighting man no favor by applying to him the term "psychoneurotic." That's the bad word of this war, for it automatically suggests to most people that a fellow is crazy. I, for one—and I guess I've suffered from war neurosis, off and on, since a day in 1936, in Spain, when I was captured by Franco's Moors—would much prefer either "battle fatigue" or restoration of the World War I term, "shell shock."

Henry tells the reader that he writes this article because, "I feel that I can be of service to the fighting man who doesn't get a chance to express himself." He describes the condition as one in which " . . . a man in the firing line will crack suddenly, to the extent of hugging his head between his knees and crying like a baby. Such a man has done his best, but he has folded up inside and is incapable of going any further."

The good news, he explains, is that the condition is usually not that severe, and that " . . . in many instances, without himself registering a complaint, a soldier will be pulled out of the line and sent to a rest camp. For this, he can thank his superior officers or his battalion chaplain." Assuring the *Post* readers that "It may be of comfort to some of the thousands of so-called psychoneurotics now back in the United States to know that I have snapped myself back four times from this condition," he goes on to describe the circumstances and experiences that led to his own mental distress. Many of those tales are fully reported in this volume.

Henry ends his article on a positive note, confirming that while the suffering is real, a returning soldier can overcome it. "Let him have some quiet and understanding, and he'll grow out of it and will be able to face the future, no matter how tough it is." Henry was very much a part of the Greatest Generation both in his actions and in his thoughts.

Though a journalist reporting facts, Henry clearly supported the cause of freedom. His sympathies are with the poor Spanish peasants fighting against geopolitical forces beyond their understanding. In what would become World War II, he supports the Allied cause, but reports faithfully the few triumphs and many setbacks of British forces before the United States entered the war. He sometimes describes the German and Italian enemy using ethnic slurs (which I have retained here). But "spin" was not in his lexicon. He was an "embedded reporter" at a time when such a construction would have seemed redundant. Nowhere is that more clearly demonstrated than in Henry's actions which resulted in the award of the Air Medal.

Presented to Henry personally by Major General Lewis H. Brereton, then commander of the U.S. Army Air Force in the Middle East, the medal citation reads in part,

> While participating in a bombing mission, Mr. Gorrell displayed extreme gallantry in conduct under fire. During his mission, enemy aircraft were encountered and in combat two enemy aircraft were shot down. For several hours Mr. Gorrell rendered vital aid to a seriously wounded member of the crew. Mr. Gorrell's action undoubtedly saved the life of this soldier.

Henry saved the life of an airman in a B-24 strafed during a raid on Navarino Bay, Greece. In presenting the award, General Brereton declared his courage "typical of representatives of a free press fighting for a free world." I can think of no higher praise for a journalist.

This book goes to print in the year that Henry would have celebrated his ninety-eighth birthday. He didn't live even half of those years. After the war, Henry and his family settled on their farm in Virginia. He and his wife, Beatrice, founded the newspaper *Veterans Report*, raised three children, and tended the farm. Henry had found his "quiet and understanding." But it didn't last. While working on a tractor he suffered a stroke. Months later, he died in his sleep, in 1958, at the age of forty-seven.

During the war years, Henry was touted by United Press as one of their exclusive, professional journalists putting his life at risk to bring the news to the home front. And that he did: from Spain, to the Balkans, Greece, Palestine, Egypt, and Libya, he filed countless reports that appeared in major daily newspapers across the globe. But the unique insights and eye for detail that he brought to his memoir more than six decades ago are presented here in their entirety for the first time.

As I edited this book, I connected with members of my extended family. The author's grandson, Timothy Schwilm, first contacted me when he found my name and his grandfather's name on a Web site where I had quoted Henry for a newspaper article. Tim shared my dream of having "Eyewitness" published, and put me in touch with Henry's three children: Marguerite, Elaine, and Henry, Jr. All were quite young when their father died, but they had a version of the manuscript and knew their father's story. Beyond cherishing the memories contained in its pages, they recognized the book's historical significance as a first-person narrative of world-altering events, and gave me their support.

But it is only with the kind permission of Henry's widow, Beatrice Gorrell—to whom this book was dedicated more than sixty-five years ago—that this project could have been completed. To her and to her family I am most grateful.

Kenneth Gorrell
Northfield, New Hampshire

1
PROLOGUE

A CAPTAIN OF THE BRITISH PROVOST MARSHAL STAFF WAS trying his best to make himself understood in conversation with a booted and spurred chief of the Italian police when I entered Tripoli's main square on January 23, 1943.

The Italian was trying to maintain his dignity. He was, after all, a trusted servant of Mussolini charged with preserving law and order in the last colonial city of the Italian Empire. He obviously resented the British officer's tone of voice.

It was an amusing scene, for the red-faced Englishman and the fat, sallow-complexioned Italian were both losing patience and beginning to gesticulate. The Red Caps of the British military police and the tank drivers of the Seventh Armored Division watched the spectacle as they lathered up for an early morning shave alongside their dust-covered Crusaders and Valentines lined up in the square.

"Does anyone around here speak Italian?" the captain asked.

This was my cue to interject myself into the conversation. The Italian officer's face looked familiar, and I was curious.

"I do. How can I help?"

"I'm in a hurry," said the captain, looking relieved. "Ask this fellow the location of police headquarters and City Hall, and tell him to be quick about it. The British army is taking over."

I turned to address the Italian, but before I could open my mouth, he was talking to me.

"Well, if it isn't my old friend the giornalista Gorrell," he said, drawing himself up to full stature with hands on hips, à la Mussolini.

Startled, I acknowledged the greeting, but there was no time for pleasantries. The British captain was nudging me vigorously in the ribs, emphasizing haste.

"The captain here," I said in Italian, "wants to know the location of police headquarters and City Hall. He says he is in a hurry."

It was no use. For the Italian officer this was an auspicious occasion,

6

and when an Italian gets dramatic there's no hurrying him until he has gotten it out of his system. In an imperious gesture of authority, the police chief raised his hand for silence. Then, striking his chest with a clenched fist, he resumed:

"Don't you remember me—Vecchioni?"

I did not. And I had no time to probe my memory because the British captain was clearly losing his temper. Again I demanded to know where Tripoli's police headquarters was, explaining that the British were taking over.

"Oh," he said in a mocking tone, "the giornalista Gorrell does not remember Vecchioni!"

Then, pausing after every phrase, mimicking the voice of doom like a judge passing sentence on a criminal, he exclaimed:

"Rome . . . September, 1936 . . . You were expelled from Italy. I, Vecchioni, had the honor . . . the privilege . . . of carrying out Il Duce's orders!"

Ah, yes, now I remembered. Vecchioni was the fellow in the Ufficio Stranieri (Foreigner's Bureau) in Rome who had read to me Mussolini's expulsion order nearly seven years before. When he saw recognition on my face, Vecchioni clicked his heels, raised his hand in the Fascist salute, and with half a bow placed himself at the disposal of the British conquerors of the Italian army.

"Sono le fortune de la Guerra," he said with a wan smile. Without another word he pointed in the direction of the police station. He then took the lead, with long, military strides, followed closely by the British captain and a dozen burly Red Caps.

A few days later, General Sir Bernard Montgomery formally received the surrender of Tripoli. My "old friend" Vecchioni and I discussed in private the contents of my news story from 1936 that had made Mussolini see red and order me out of Italy. Then, hosting a meal enhanced with Chianti for me and a few American and British correspondents, Vecchioni demonstrated that he personally bore no grudge toward the "giornalista Gorrell." War was war; but for Vecchioni, the war was over.

I left Tripoli shortly thereafter, taking recuperative leave in South Africa from my duties for United Press. The time away from war allowed me to reflect on Vecchioni's overly dramatic reference to the "fortunes of war." Surrounded by British tanks, he had gazed longingly through the majestic pillars of Tripoli Harbor and across the blue Mediterranean Sea toward his native land, now a German satellite. He must have known that for Italy, the worst was yet to come.

• • •

Meeting Vecchioni in Tripoli was an odd coincidence. As the first phase of the Allied counteroffensive against the armies of the Axis came to a close in January of 1943, I was brought face to face with the man who, in 1936, had carried out the expulsion order that started me on my career as a war correspondent. I guess that fate, as well as the fortunes of war, had played a hand. Through no calculation of mine I had seen the creation of the Italian Empire and then its complete collapse on the battlefields of North Africa.

A sad spectacle it has been. Nothing but bloodshed and death have I seen since 1936. Untold thousands of men, women, and children have lost their lives to satisfy the lust for power of the fathers of fascism. In Spain, Albania, Greece, Syria, and the Libyan desert, endless rows of graves mark the path of destruction forged by Europe's most deadly dictators. Now one of them—Il Duce—cringes with fear, imploring aid from the other, his former pupil Adolf Hitler. Nations they sought to enslave now prepare to advance on Rome and the whole of continental Europe. Both aspired to become second Caesars. Mussolini has been taken out of the running. It is now Hitler's turn.

• • •

My first assignment as a war correspondent had been in Spain. Hitler and Mussolini were using this civil war as a testing ground for the "blitzkrieg" methods they would later apply to the broader world war. In Spain I saw many brave men fall on both sides, completely disillusioned. In their dying agony—be they "Red" or "White"—they turned their tortured eyes to the heavens, beseeching remission of their sins. They were mere guinea pigs, human sacrifices to the schemes and propaganda of the dictators who posed as defenders of the faith, sent to rid the world of the "scourge of Bolshevism."

The Spanish Civil War might have ended within a few months with a victory for the people had not Mussolini and Hitler backed the Fascist General Francisco Franco and the wealthy landowners. Franco used the guns, tanks, and aircraft of the Axis against his own people. The Axis would later use these weapons against Warsaw, Paris, and London. Spain today lies prostrate through loss of blood: Nearly one million Spaniards became casualties in three years of war on the Iberian Peninsula. They fought a war which, in the end, nobody won. General Franco, the willing tool of Italy and Germany in the days of their ascension, now flirts simultaneously with the Axis and the United Nations,[1] seeking to stave

1. Winston Churchill first suggested using the name "United Nations" to refer to the wartime Allies, citing Byron's use of the phrase "united nations" in *Childe Harold's Pilgrimage,* which referred to the Allies at the Battle of Waterloo in 1815. President

off his day of reckoning. The Spanish people will assuredly administer justice when they rise again, helped to their feet by those who fight for world freedom.

• • •

I remained in Spain until late 1937. When I returned to New York, I observed the dilemma of my own people as the dictators' propaganda poisoned world public opinion. Americans were not ready to fight another war in Europe and did not yet understand the unfolding tragedy or the dangers to come. Meanwhile the dictators strangled resistance in Barcelona and Madrid, and calculatingly executed a program of "bloodless penetration" in Austria and Czechoslovakia.

Then in London, in September of 1939, as German panzers were overrunning Poland, I saw the sons of men who had died in Flanders twenty years before cross the Channel again, to be pounded to a pulp by the mechanized armies of Hitler, whom Prime Minister Chamberlain had failed to appease.

Had I followed my own inclination, I would have accompanied the British Expeditionary Force to France, but I was not my own master. My superiors at United Press sent me to the Balkans instead. In Budapest I watched pro-Axis enthusiasts toast with champagne the "Victory of Italian Armies." Mussolini, blinded by greed and forgetting the lessons of Guadalajara (where two of Italy's crack divisions were routed), dragged his people into a prolonged war by stabbing a dying France in the back so that he could demand his share of German loot.

In Romania in July of 1940 I watched Stalin kick over the Axis apple cart with his invasion of Bessarabia, and observed the apprehension on the faces of the Germans in Bucharest as they were forced to revise their timetable. They now had to deal with the Russian menace before they had planned. A rapid series of events followed: the German occupation of Romania; the outbreak of the Italo-Greek campaign in Albania; the historic retreat of the British Expeditionary Force from the shores of Nauplion to Crete. Hitler was hurriedly clearing his right flank for the inevitable conflict between Germany and the Soviet Union.

For several months, in between rows with my Gestapo "girlfriend" in Salonika, I watched the systematic destruction of the bulk of twenty Italian divisions in the mountains of Albania. The brave army of Hellas, inspired by the immortal Ioannis Metaxas, defended sacred soil with the bayonet, true to the traditions of Thermopylae. The Albanian campaign

---

Franklin Delano Roosevelt adopted the name, and the first official use of the term occurred on January 1, 1942.

was the beginning of the end for Mussolini's Empire, for Wavell[2] at the same time was beating up the original Italian army of Libya.

For the better part of two years I shared adversity with the armies of the Democracies. Then, beginning with the campaigns in Syria and Persia, I was privileged to witness the turn of the tide. General Montgomery's brilliant advance over trackless wastes in the Western Desert from Alamein to Tripoli sealed the fate of "Imperio Romano."

• • •

From Spain onward to the beginning of Montgomery's Alamein offensive, I got involved with history and war throughout the Mediterranean area. This was not by design: as a staff correspondent of the United Press, subject to orders that could easily have taken me to Timbuktu overnight, I had no particular control over my movements. Of course, Hitler's unpredictable antics also played a hand.

An example of unpremeditated travel is my chapter on the Simpson case,[3] which is wedged in between accounts of my experiences during the Spanish war. Had General Jose Varela's Nationalist forces not taken me prisoner on the Madrid-Valencia highway in October of 1936, General Franco would not have ordered me out of Fascist Spain as a "Red." Temporarily removed from the war zone, I was assigned to sit on Mrs. Simpson's doorstep in Cumberland Terrace, London. This little diversion was a breather for me during an extremely trying period. I have included a chapter on the Simpson case and the abdication of a king, believing that the reader will welcome an intermission from unending warfare.

What follows is a simple narrative of my wartime experiences; impressions of a correspondent who was wet behind the ears when he was given his first foreign assignment. I learned something of what it was all about the hard way, prodded along by the same series of circumstances which have involved us all in this World War Number II.[4]

2. When Mussolini sent more than one million men to North Africa in 1940, General Archibald Wavell had thirty-six thousand men at his command. The Italians made major advances from Libya toward the Suez but were stopped by the British at Mersa Matruh. In December 1940, Wavell counterattacked, pushing back the Italians. In January 1941, the British captured Tobruk.

3. On December 1, 1936, the "Mrs. Simpson" story broke in Britain. King Edward, on the throne just eleven months, abdicated in order to marry his American lover, Wallace Simpson. Shortly thereafter, his brother, the Duke of York, was crowned King George VI.

4. Henry Gorrell refers to the war as "World War Number II" throughout his memoir. During the war, many Americans called it "The War in Europe," or simply, "The War." President Harry S. Truman officially named the war "World War II" in September 1945.

My capacity for getting into trouble has been just as much a motivating factor as actual journalistic qualifications, which perforce have improved with time. I owe a certain amount of thanks to Mussolini. Had he not kicked me out of Rome in 1936, I doubt that I'd ever have been given the chance to become a war correspondent. After all, the United Press had to send me somewhere after my expulsion since they'd spent a lot of time patiently trying to teach me something about foreign reporting. As well, the company had invested some money in my passage to Rome. I arrived there just as Mussolini's Black Shirt legions were slaughtering wholesale the spear-throwing blacks of Haile Selassie in Ethiopia. There was a story to report, and it was my duty to report it.

I make no pretense at presenting a chronological picture of warfare on the Continent, and parts of this narrative are nearly kaleidoscopic. Faithfully I have recorded all of my escapades from 1936 through 1942 as they occurred, including only those episodes to which I myself was an eyewitness.

Henry Tilton Gorrell
Johannesburg
April, 1943

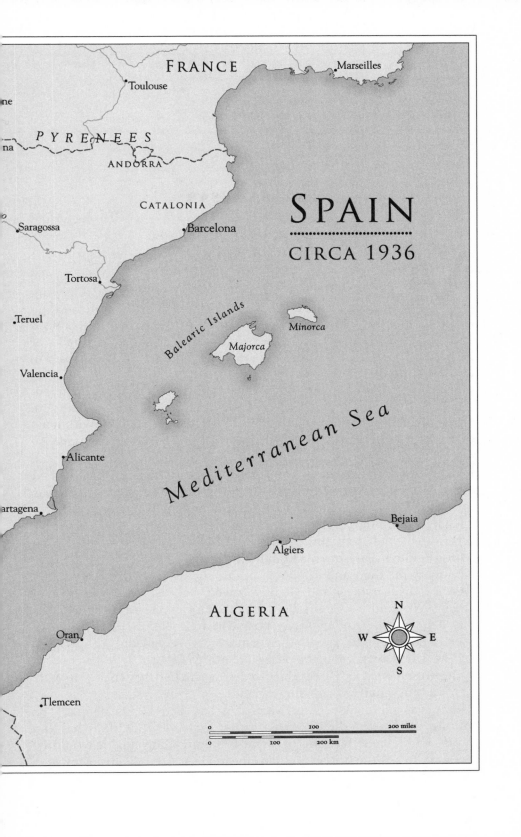

2
LITTLE CAESAR

MUSSOLINI CERTAINLY WAS IN GOOD VOICE ON THAT DAY in 1936 when, from the balcony of the Palazzo Venezzia, he set himself up as Italy's "Little Caesar" with the following dramatic announcement: "Il Maresciallo Badoglio, al capo dei nostri gloriosi soldati stamane a entrato Addis Ababa. Abbiamo il nostro Impero." Literally translated, that means: "Marshal Badoglio, at the head of our glorious troops, this morning entered Addis Ababa. We have our Empire."

There were thousands in attendance, trained cheerleaders included, who had stood longer than was necessary to hear Il Duce proclaim the formation of the new "Impero Romano." Wedged like a sardine within the solid mass of humanity, I watched the swaggering little fellow with the big chest and the square jaw, all dolled up in his plumed Bersaglieri hat, poke his finger in England's eye. I was quite ready to admit that he had turned in a first-class performance. As an orator and actor, Mussolini was tops. His silvery voice couldn't fail to thrill anyone listening, regardless of what he said. And, even for a correspondent whose job it was to sift the facts from the bull, sometimes it was hard to get readjusted after listening to little Benito's dissertations from the balcony.

Many of the thousands gathered in that square wore trousers slightly large for their frames, and slightly frayed, because of the League of Nations' economic sanctions. But when the Duce finished his speech, the folks below bellowed themselves hoarse in approbation. With visions of an extra pork chop to go with their macaroni, they yelled:

"The war is over. Long live peace and our Duce!"

This wasn't what the Fascist cheerleaders wanted, so they chimed in with: "Viva Mussolini! Down with England!"

That was more like it, for Mussolini had lied to his people. The "empire" he presented them was a phony, for never could Italy have an empire without the blessing of Great Britain. Failing this, it would be necessary to lick the British Mediterranean Fleet. An unlikely event.

The war was not over. In reality, it had only just begun. As the people rejoiced throughout Italy in anticipation of nationwide demobilization, more food, and a general reduction of taxes thanks to the "gold and oil" that the Fascist-controlled press had told them would flow from conquered Abyssinia, Mussolini plotted his next move.

In the weeks that followed, the man-in-the-street anxiously scanned the newspapers, searching for evidence of a return to normalcy, only to be confronted with such Mussolini slogans as: "Fighting is in our blood. Only war brings human energy to its highest point and shows the nobility of a race."

Instead of demobilization, more men were called to the colors. The headlines screamed: "Italy must remain strong. She requires eight million bayonets!"

Thus were the masses of Italy led blindfolded into still more slaughter. Mussolini took Hitler into his counsel and plotted a Fascist revolt in Spain as a further step toward control of the Mediterranean.

• • •

Things had been tough enough for the British and American correspondents in Rome before Mussolini declared the existence of the new "Impero Romano." There hung over us the threat of expulsion should the Ministry of Press and Propaganda take exception to anything we wrote. To complicate matters further, anti-British feeling ran high as the Fascists steamed up enthusiasm for their Ethiopian venture by turning it into a grudge match with John Bull on the basis of the League's sanctions. Foreign Secretary Anthony Eden's threat to block the Suez Canal to Italian troop ships bound for Eritrea (which, unfortunately, he never carried out) fueled the fire.

Two English nurses whom I had known during a prolonged illness at the Anglo-American Nursing Home in Rome now came to me, complaining that they had been set upon by young Fascist roughnecks. I myself had been baited on a Rome bus for no greater offense than reading the Paris edition of the *New York World Tribune*. They thought I was an Englishman. I might well have been, for it took several people to separate me from the fellow responsible for the mumbled insult.

The fanatics among the Fascists were victory mad, and the secret police handled us no longer with kid gloves. At periodic intervals each week, I returned to my little apartment, near the Piazza di Spagna, to find my desk in a sad state of confusion. I thought my servant girl, Ada, was guilty and severely reprimanded her, but it was not her fault. Ada told me what had happened on the day I was "invited" to leave Italy. She said that the police had often rummaged through my papers, looking for incriminating documents. They terrified little Ada, who also had her own troubles. For instance, one day I found her crying her eyes out. I asked her what was the matter, and she said there had been a death in the family.

"Oh, I'm awfully sorry, Ada. Who's dead?"

She replied, "The pig. Our pig is dead, and the family will go hungry on the farm in the Veneto this winter because we are so heavily taxed that we don't have the money to buy another."

I shelled out the two hundred lira necessary to buy a new pig, and from that day on I believe little Ada would willingly have followed me anywhere.

• • •

To get away from the Fascist popinjays for a while, I went to Florence, the place where I was born in 1911 to an American father and an English mother. I was hoping to see some of my father's old friends, people who had known me as a boy. I shouldn't have done it. Though I didn't realize it at the time, my visit meant that from the day I looked them up they would be hounded by the secret police as possible sources of information. These men didn't dare to greet me on the street, let alone express an opinion anywhere but in the comparative safety of their homes. The cafés were full of Mussolini's spies and one couldn't refer to the Duce even as Mr. Smith or Mr. Jones, for his stooges knew all the code words. I didn't embarrass my father's old friends by discussing politics with them, for I had already heard much discontent throughout Italy.

Private initiative had been swept away and the Italians no longer were allowed to think for themselves. Il Duce did all their thinking for them, and it was mostly about war. Their little children were becoming parrots of the state. The public schools taught only what Il Duce thought they should know, and to do only what he thought they should do. Mussolini's little children were not to play, except with toy rifles. Educated Italians saw through the Duce's frequent baby kissing expeditions, when he bestowed monetary prizes on the most prolific mothers, telling them that they were producing future farmers. He assured these mothers that their children would, through modern methods, rejuvenate an Italy which had been sorely wounded in the last war. What they actually had been producing for years was cannon fodder.

The "Corporate State," I learned, was only a "teaser" for the gullible Italians who, despite an apparent reduction in unemployment, found their taxes constantly increasing. They found themselves coming more and more under Mussolini's thumb. According to blueprints, the Corporate State, much ballyhooed as the cornerstone for fascism in Italy, would give the masses quite a bit of say about Italy's internal policies and foreign affairs. Personally, I never found any suggestions that this project had developed beyond the blueprint stage. True, the Italian parliament still existed, but one only had to attend a single session of the Chamber of Deputies to get a bellyful. Mussolini, his arms crossed, his jaw set in a pugilistic attitude and looking very ferocious, would sit in a high chair on the rostrum, facing the crowd. The light-headed, black-shirted deputies would rise in unison at a shout from their cheerleaders, shoving out their right arms in salute to the scowling Duce. Then they would render Fascist hymns, sing-song fashion, like elementary school children. The deputies wore splendid uniforms, but their entire demonstration was childlike and ill-suited to the halls of the once great Italian parliament.

• • •

Realizing that I was making my father's friends exceedingly uncomfortable by my continued presence in Florence, I went to the seaside resort of Viareggio where I used to play in the sand as a little fellow. If one speaks the language fluently, as I did, he can better feel the pulse of a foreign country. The people of Viareggio told me how they had become impoverished because of Mussolini's big ideas. For example, there were scores of cafés and restaurants along the main boulevard. They were built according to government specifications, involving financial outlays their owners could ill afford. There were cases of men in Viareggio committing suicide because they couldn't meet construction costs and tax payments on their ornate seaside establishments. They would have been satisfied with a small income from a life as a simple merchant, but their dreams did not fit into Mussolini's grandiose vision.

I wrote a story for *Time* magazine on artillery practice around Viareggio, which shattered the eardrums of visitors trying to get away from war propaganda. The guns certainly were no attraction to tourists. My story never reached the Rome office of United Press. It ended up in the "Gorrell dossier" in the Ministry of Press and Propaganda, later to be produced as part of the evidence against me.

• • •

Shortly after my return to Rome, Stewart Brown, manager of the United Press Rome bureau, was called to Geneva to cover the League's post mortem on sanctions. This marked a crowning success for Mussolini because sanctions were to be repealed in the face of the Fascist fait accompli. The Italians were in Addis Ababa, so what good were sanctions now? They never were very effective, for American oil companies, adhering to their "business as usual" policy, had shipped oil to Italy as before. They had turned the League's attempt at punishment of Italian transgressions into a farce.

In Stew's absence, I was left in command of the Rome bureau. News was breaking fast now, for the Spanish Civil War had begun and there were suggestions that Italian bombers were already being flown in to assist the Spanish insurgent leader, General Franco. During this time, the Forte brothers, Aldo and Ralph, star members of the United Press staff in Rome, turned up a whale of a story. More than three hundred Italian Communists had been apprehended within about ten days in the factory district of Terni, not far from Rome. They had been charged with distributing posters supporting the Spanish Republicans, or "Reds." Under third-degree methods, those arrested had been forced to reveal the location of the printing establishments where the posters where being turned out. With the Forte brothers, I checked and rechecked the story. Satisfied, I took entire responsibility for the consequence of its publication abroad, and over an open line to our London bureau, gave them the whole story. I knew there would be a row over the story, for no Fascist ever liked to admit that such as Communists still existed in Italy. But I never dreamed that I would be given a free ride out of Italy as a result.

About two hours after I had finished dictating the story to London, a police officer appeared at the bureau and said that he had been ordered to accompany me to the Ministry of Press and Propaganda, where Count Emmanuel Grazzi, who later was to serve Italy's ultimatum on Metaxas in Greece, was in command. He had replaced Dino Alfieri, who had become Italian ambassador to Berlin. It seems that I had really started something. As soon as my story appeared under headlines in the newspapers of London, Paris, Madrid, and New York, urgent international telephone calls had been placed to Mussolini himself in Venice Palace.

Unfortunately, the story had not been printed as I had sent it. We had a fellow in the London bureau who was hard of hearing. We used an Ediphone attachment to record dictation on a wax cylinder, and unless the fellow receiving dictation interrupted, we assumed that he had satisfactorily recorded the entire conversation. But the man who was hard of hearing had played the wax cylinder again and again, trying to figure out the actual wording of a sentence which referred to the arrest of certain Fascist officials. In fact I had said that among those arrested in the Communist sweep were some *minor* Fascist officials. By this I meant such people as police officers who had been disgraced for permitting the Communist posters to appear in public. But as the story came out in print, it seemed instead to refer to the arrest of high-level Fascist authorities, and the story was thus ballooned into what appeared to be a plot to overthrow Mussolini.

"You have offended high quarters," said the bumptious, pot-bellied Grazzi, sitting behind his huge desk, trying his best to ape his master.

"How come?" said I. "Isn't it true that you have arrested several hundred agitators in the Terni area?"

"It's a lie. We have no Communists in Italy. You have stirred up London and Paris, just at a time when we were trying to improve relations. I am instructed to notify you that you are to leave the country within twenty-four hours."

I protested, and demanded that Grazzi read my original story.

"That is not necessary," he replied. "The word of our ambassadors in London and Paris is enough for me. You have insulted the Fascist regime. You have printed a report that there is unrest in Italy. Do you not realize that we Italians are as one behind Il Duce? Not another word. You may go. The chief of police will advise you of your future itinerary."

• • •

We stalled them for seventy-two hours, assisted by Mr. Alexander Kirk, then American chargé d'affaires in Rome,[1] who went to Count Galeazzo Ciano[2] personally, and argued on my behalf on the basis of American constitutional principles of "freedom of speech and the press." But Ciano wouldn't listen. He received his orders directly from Mussolini. As I was later told by the police, it had been Il Duce himself who had given the order for my expulsion, or rather, as they more diplomatically put it, my "invitation to leave Italy."

The hours leading to my unceremonious exit from the land of my birth bordered on the comical. I couldn't leave my apartment or office without being shadowed. I got tired of it and several times confronted my shadows, making it understood that I was aware of their presence. To make things easier for them, I occasionally offered to buy them a beer or cup of coffee. They usually accepted, but invariably insisted on buying a second round so that they could not be accused of taking bribes from a fellow about to become a political exile.

• • •

At the end of the seventy-two hours I was hustled around at the double quick by a certain Signor Vecchioni, then an official in the Foreigner's section of the Italian secret police. He read to me Mussolini's expulsion

1. Mr. Kirk would become the first U.S. ambassador to postwar Italy.
2. Italian foreign minister and Mussolini's son-in-law. In 1943 Ciano joined a vote against his father-in-law at the Fascist Grand Council. He was imprisoned and ultimately executed on January 11, 1944.

order and came to the station personally to see me off on the Rome-Paris train. As Vecchioni barked a series of rapid orders to a cordon of his stooges, two burly detectives frisked me for arms and then manhandled me with my one suitcase to the waiting train a split second before it pulled out. Very efficient stuff! The last I saw of the pompous and strutting Signor Vecchioni was as the train was leaving. He was standing on guard by the rest of my luggage which he accommodatingly had promised to forward to me but not, I presume, until he had first searched it thoroughly. What a vast difference there was in the attitude of Signor Vecchioni seven years later when through me, he handed over the keys of the Italian police headquarters in Tripoli to the conquering British army.

On the journey to the frontier I might have been Al Capone, being whisked off to Atlanta Penitentiary, for at every station where we stopped there were at least a couple of dozen secret police on guard. My friends the accompanying detectives used all the tricks in the book to get me to talk. The whole procedure struck me as silly because a day after I'd received my "invitation" to leave, Grazzi had indirectly confirmed the whole story to my colleagues in Rome. But it was Mussolini who had given the order, and he had the reputation of never going back on a decision once made. What those "dicks" wanted was the name of my source for the story. I wasn't talking. Had Mussolini's gangsters got their claws on the Forte brothers, as Italo-Americans, I think they might have suffered. But it does no harm now to reveal that among the sources for that story were a couple or three members of the Italian Senate and Chamber of Deputies. There were no people who amounted to anything in Rome or the Vatican, including Cardinal Pacelli, the present Pope,[3] with whom the Forte brothers were not acquainted.

The horseplay with the security men had been just a bit too one-sided for me, so I plotted my revenge on Mussolini and his crowd. With Turin as our next stop, I expressed the opinion that I should not continue my trip to Paris without first buying a hat. The train was due to wait in Turin station for fifteen minutes. The instructions of those policemen were that I was to be treated as a "guest of the government" until they had washed their hands of me once and for all. Therefore, there being a reasonable amount of time, they could not refuse my request that I be permitted to purchase a head-dress. The hair-raising taxi ride to the hat shop with a detective on each side recalled the days when I used to follow the fire trucks in Kansas City, Missouri, as a cub reporter on the *Journal-Post*.

3. Pope Pius XII, leader of the Catholic Church from March 2, 1939, to October 9, 1958.

The brakes screeched as the driver, having been given instructions to step on it, drew up before the "Borsalino" haberdashery. The "dicks" and I entered the shop together and they stood back at a respectful distance as I proceeded to try on practically every hat in the joint. This was part of my revenge. Therefore, no hat suited or fitted me, no matter how hard the little manager tried to please. Time was flying, and the hats were stacking up. With only about five minutes to go before the train was due to pull out, the two "dicks" held a whispered consultation with the manager, whose face got white as a sheet. But still I insisted that none of the Borsalino hats met with my fastidious requirements. With about two minutes to go one of the detectives jammed a hat about twice too big for me down over my ears and then hustled me out of that shop to the waiting taxi. I resembled a Bowery Jew. The Fascist government paid dearly for that hat, for in their hurry to catch the train, one of the detectives shoved a five-hundred-lira note in the hands of the nearly fainting shop manager, and didn't wait for the change.

The train had pulled out when we got back to the station so I sat in an antechamber, surrounded by scowling uniformed members of the Italian secret police, waiting for the next train. They hesitated to vent their anger because they had been admonished to treat me as a "guest of the government" right up to my entry into France.

We caught the next train after a wait of several hours, and just before we reached the frontier station at Modena, one of the two detectives formally introduced himself. He admitted that I had been one of the toughest propositions they had ever encountered, insofar as getting any useful information out of me was concerned. He volunteered that he thought highly of me, adding that had it not been Mussolini himself who had given the order for my expulsion, the chief of police in Rome might have listened to reason.

"If, within a year, you feel disposed to return to Italy, I think the government will entertain a written request for cancellation of the expulsion order," said the detective.

When I next passed through Italy, Mussolini had already locked arms with the little paper-hanger, Adolf Hitler. Together, their saber-rattling on behalf of the "New Order," which Il Duce had conceived, was leading the innocent masses of Italy to ruin, along with their Fascist masters.

3

CIVIL WAR IN SPAIN

I ONLY STAYED IN PARIS LONG ENOUGH TO BUY A COUPLE OF extra suits of underwear, for no sooner had I arrived from Rome than I received cabled instruction from New York to proceed to Madrid, where brothers and cousins were killing one another in the mad throes of civil war.

It was just as well, for I spoke no French at the time, and it would have been a case of doing office boy stuff for some time before I could be of any real use to the Paris office. On the other hand, except that now and then I had a tendency to mix up Spanish with Italian, I had somewhat of a vocabulary in the former. This business of mixing up the two languages nearly got me shot as a suspected Fascist spy at the outskirts of Toledo a few days after I arrived in Spain.

• • •

The aeroplane trip from Toulouse, France, to Alicante, Spain, was uneventful, though the pilot flew higher than is normal because the few existing Republican anti-aircraft batteries were getting itchy trigger fingers. Alicante and Valencia were teeming with uniformed humanity, including women "Milicianas," many of whom already were in the trenches in the Guadarrama Mountains, helping their menfolk stem the Fascist tide.

The train from Alicante arrived in Madrid central station in the middle of the night, and the passengers, mostly newly recruited troops, groped their way through the blacked-out streets. There were no taxis and no representative from United Press, so I had to walk the distance from the railroad station to the United Press office in the Plaza de las Cortes alone, carrying my own luggage. The boys in the Madrid bureau were working day and night, for Franco's troops—following closely behind Italian tanks—were fast advancing both on Toledo and Madrid.

When I arrived at the press office I was hungry. No one had told me there would be no food available on that long train journey. In token of welcome, Lester Ziffren, then Madrid bureau manager, took me to the rear of the flat we used as an office and waved his hand in the direction of a pile of canned goods stored there.

"Help yourself, Hank," said Ziffren. "What about a couple of sardines? You see, there are no restaurants open."

At about 2 a.m., scarcely having had one word with me because of the fast-breaking developments, Ziffren accompanied me to the Palace Hotel, known prior to the outbreak of the Spanish war as one of the finest in Europe. It now served as headquarters for Russian Ambassador Marcel Rosenberg and his staff. One had to be somebody to get into that hotel now, for the Russians had begun to run things in Madrid. But Ziffren had no flies on his shoes. He had a room there, and would be able get me one, too. Militiamen in blue coveralls carrying sawed-off shotguns stood guard at the main entrance of the hotel, for Rosenberg was "God" in Madrid. The hotel was beautifully appointed, with tiled bathrooms, and fine linen on the soft beds. I slept that night in luxury.

• • •

The next morning, after what they called a "Continental breakfast" consisting of a cup of coffee and a piece of stale bread, I reported for duty. There were several fronts in this war, as General Franco's army was closing in on Madrid from all sides. We drew lots to determine our assignment for the day. The other United Press war correspondents in Madrid at the time were Jan Yindrich, a Yorkshireman who later was to be the only agency man to remain with the Australians in besieged Tobruk, and Irving Pflaum, who became foreign editor of the *Chicago Times*. I drew Toledo on that first day, and was instructed to get there in the rattletrap taxi maintained by the United Press on a twenty-four-hour basis for such purposes.

I had no time to try to figure out what this war was all about, for things were moving pretty damned fast. On that and subsequent days, I watched the pathetic fighting of the rearguard of the "Frente Populare" against the well-trained and excellently equipped legions of General Franco, who had the backing of the German and Italian General Staffs. Together they were driving to throttle the Spanish masses and restore feudalism.

Spanish volunteer troops were dying by the hundreds around Talavera-de-la-Reina, the last important outpost before the walled city of Toledo. They were mowed down by cannon, mortar, and machine-gun fire, and by the aerial bombs Germany was testing in Spain as a preliminary to World War Number II. I watched the fighting in the Guadarrama Mountains as Franco sought to encircle Madrid. The men and women of the Republic had practically no combat training, and often walked into neatly laid traps. Such was the case in the fighting for the little mountain village of El Hoyo ("the Hole"), where the Milicianos were allowed to walk in without a shot being fired. They were then encircled by the Moors, who proceeded to pick them off one by one.

I learned to love the militiamen of the Spanish "Popular Front" who went to their deaths as only Spaniards can, with "gracia." Spaniards had learned how to die in the bull ring.

• • •

I saw a successful Republican counterattack for possession of El Hoyo. The Moors were making a stand in the little cemetery outside the village, commanding the main road. The volunteer company of men and women, some carrying small sacks of French hand grenades, which killed by concussion, charged the cemetery, many of them falling before the machine guns of the Moors who fired from behind the tombstones. The charge was bloody but successful. After the fight, the bodies of the barefooted, pantalooned Moors were intermingled with scores of skeletons unearthed to provide defensive trenches. All but two of the Moorish defenders of El Hoyo were killed.

The militia commandante wished to take those two Moors to Madrid for display, as heretofore no Moors had been captured alive. He summoned a husky Asturian sergeant, and gave him the following instructions:

"You are to see that nothing happens to those two Moors. I hold your head as forfeit."

The Asturiano, who came from that band of fighting miners who gained a worldwide reputation for their use of sticks of dynamite in battle, saluted.

The best way to demoralize his prisoners for the trip to Madrid, the sergeant figured, was to slit the sash holding up their baggy trousers. Thus when he got through with those two, they were a comical sight, marching before him in the direction of the village square, using both hands to keep their trousers up. The "dynamitero" could be reasonably sure that thus occupied, his prisoners would give him no trouble.

There was a crowd in the El Hoyo public square when this strange trio approached. Men and women of the village, many of whom had taken part in the successful counterattack, were gazing in horror at the bodies of an old lady and her daughter, both of whom had been violated and then had their throats cut. This obviously was the work of the Moors.

When the villagers saw the Asturian sergeant approach with his two charges, still tugging at their pantaloons, they set upon the Moors and stabbed them to death on the spot. The sergeant, who had pledged his head for the safety of his prisoners, looked down sadly, but spoke no words. His hand resting on the pistol at his side, he walked slowly back toward the commandancia. Arriving there, without his prisoners, he approached his officer and saluted. He then extracted the gun from its holster, and holding it by the barrel, handed it to the officer, saying:

"Mi Commandante. Acqui tienes mi cabeza," meaning "Commandante, I present you my head."

The officer stood there holding the dynamitero's pistol and brusquely demanded an explanation. The sergeant told him of the incident in the main square.

The commandante drew himself bolt upright, and then to the sergeant, who was expecting to be shot, said simply:

"Sergente, te devuelvo tu cabeza," meaning, "Sergeant, I return your head."

With that the commandante handed the Asturian's pistol back to him with a dramatic sweep and a half bow. The sergeant, without a word, returned it to its holster, saluted, and the incident was closed. To Spaniards, life meant nothing during the war.

• • •

I witnessed the siege of the Alcazar, and retreated with the army of the Popular Front as Franco's legions, preceded by waves of German bombers, rammed their way to the gates of Toledo. I got a box seat to the fighting for Toledo: From a hillock barely a mile distant, I sat watching through field glasses the slaughter of the defending garrison. Tanks had rammed the ancient gates of the citadel, and the Moors were running amok, savagely shooting down and bayoneting the trapped Spanish militia. Then the imprisoned men of the former Moorish garrison broke out of their cells and cut down the people's militia simultaneously from the rear.

"What a story," I thought. I was trembling with excitement as my Filipino chauffeur, Ramon, fidgeted alongside the taxi nearby. Suddenly I felt something jab me in the back, and then I heard the command in Spanish to put up my hands.

"We've been watching you," said an Anarchist captain. "We know you are a spy. Come with us."

In a few hours, I found myself in the dungeons of Madrid's central police station, along with Ramon, both of us under summary sentence of death. The misunderstanding was partly my fault. I had attempted to explain myself to the Anarchist "commandante," and as I proffered my American passport and documents, I mixed up my Spanish with Italian. That settled it: I definitely was a Fascist spy.

• • •

As a young reporter for the United Press in Columbus, Ohio, I'd seen many a man go to his death in the electric chair, but never had I imagined that the tables might turn some day, and that I myself would be among the condemned. As a kid, I thoroughly disliked violence, and the sight of thirty-odd criminals "taking a chair" in Ohio Penitentiary's Death House on the invitation of the tough Warden Preston Thomas had made a lasting impression on me. Now, in that damp, high-vaulted, moss-covered little chamber in Madrid, where five hundred people waited for death before a Spanish firing squad, I recalled the last execution I had witnessed, that of a young fellow sentenced to die for a murder perpetrated while under the influence of liquor. I wondered whether I could face death as calmly as he had.

The condemned killer had been only eighteen, and we had become quite friendly as we spoke daily from opposite sides of the bars, he to ease his mind, and I to obtain material for my hometown newspaper. I didn't print it all, for I learned things about his life that I swore others would never know. He entered the death chamber accompanied by a Catholic priest from whom he had refused the Last Sacrament. Briefly, he faced the audience of witnesses and the warden in that little whitewashed room, whose only furnishings other than the electric chair were pictures of men previously hanged or electrocuted.

"Have you anything to say?" said Thomas.

"I only want to say goodbye," said the boy.

With that he had come straight to me, where I stood in the center of the semi-circle facing the chair, and firmly shook my hand. He did the same with two others and then seated himself, staring straight ahead as the guards adjusted the straps and electrodes. He died without another word.

• • •

Executions in Madrid were far less formal affairs, and by night they used to shoot suspected Fascists in University City by the score. Those were terrible days, recalling the Reign of Terror during the French Revolution when thousands went to the guillotine. A man or woman need only denounce you as a Fascist, and the Anarchists in Madrid— who, at the time, were in control of the prisons—did the rest. It invariably meant a bullet in the back for him who had been denounced.

My request to be allowed to communicate with the American Embassy in Madrid was laughed off, as were my suggestions that as a neutral observer, I should immediately be given my freedom.

They gave me number 62, and Ramon number 63. We were being tagged, just like sheep being marked for the slaughter pens. We were so crowded in that room that we had to take turns sitting down. There were about a dozen women in the cell, including one I saw wearing a fur coat that would have cost at least a thousand dollars in New York City. We huddled by the wall, under the only window in the place, gasping for air. Each evening our guards would call out a series of names or numbers, seldom receiving an answer. We all knew what they wanted, that we would be led out a little side door, never again to see the light of day. They used to lead condemned prisoners in groups of five to waiting automobiles, usually after tying the victims' wrists together. Then, having reached the execution grounds, the doors would be opened, the executioners would bow formally in mockery and invite their passengers to "take a walk." Out they would stumble, perhaps trying to run. They could make it only a few feet until one or more of the group tripped and fell, at which time their executioners would polish them off with bullets in the back. It was a gruesome business. On one occasion I had visited University City early in the morning to count the corpses from the night before, and found that in some instances, men and women were still writhing in their death throes. One fellow, who had been shot through the mouth, bore a tag on him reading: "This is _____ the Fascist traitor. He died like the dog he was!"

• • •

Saturday afternoons, early in the war, they would hold a field day in the Madrid bull ring. There, "Fascists," including some priests, were put up against the wall and shot one after the other. The crowds in attendance munched peanuts, much as we do at a baseball game, and casually looked on. If a man or woman died "con gracia," as a gored matador might in the bull ring, he was jeered by the morbid crowds. Some of the condemned refused the blindfold, and invariably received a sporting round of tumultuous applause. If, however, the slightest sign of cowardice was demonstrated, they would be roundly booed and hissed.

There were similar scenes in Franco territory, as the "Reds" were lined up and shot. And so it went. Approximately one million Spaniards died in one way or another in three years of war, as Berlin and Rome looked on with fiendish glee. Spanish brothers and cousins were encouraged to kill still more, making this testing ground for Axis war machines more realistic.

• • •

Emilio Herrero, veteran Madrid correspondent of the United Press, was one of the first people I spotted in the jail. He had been out Toledo way with me the day before. I had left him holding another box seat to the fighting, on his suggestion that I return in the car to Madrid to file my story and then come back to pick him up. I'd missed Herrero when I returned, but because of the general excitement, hadn't thought much about it. I knew, however, that Ziffren was investigating his disappearance and had already seen half a dozen cabinet ministers on Herrero's behalf, urging them to check the lists of prisoners recently incarcerated in all the Madrid jails.

"Somos perdidos, we are lost," said the ashen-faced, gray-haired Herrero, as the executioners sorted out their struggling victims in the dungeons.

I tried to cheer him up, suggesting that Ziffren would have help on its way, but I wasn't so sure, for how were they to know that Herrero was in jail?

Fate played a hand. They called out Herrero's name, and as he walked a few paces forward to surrender himself for death, he shook my hand solemnly, and whispered "Viva La Republica."

I told him I was certain he wouldn't die, and that I was sure they had come to release him. As a matter of fact, I was rather annoyed with his heroics, and cautioned him not to forget that Ramon and I also were in the jail.

Later that day, after fifty men and women had been hustled to the death wagon outside, my name and Ramon's were called. I felt just about as bad as Herrero, and this time there was nobody to suggest that they had come to let me out. I was glad I hadn't partaken of the bean hash they had dumped in a huge platter in the middle of the dungeon floor, for I rather think I would have coughed it all up then and there. People who were to die within the next few hours grabbed my hand and shook it speechlessly, as I preceded Ramon through that little door. Imagine my instant relief, when instead of the "Black Maria" in front of me, I saw the red-bearded Yorkshireman, Yindrich. He convulsed with laughter as Ramon and I walked into view looking like Death itself. I didn't think it so funny at the time, but I retained sufficient of my sense of humor to joke about it with him later on.

Herrero had done his stuff. No sooner had he been released than he found Yindrich, and together they raced to the headquarters of General Jose Asensio, commander of all Spanish Republican forces. They told him of the predicament we were in and pleaded for our release. Holding the life of Madrid's Anarchist police chief as forfeit should anything happen to us, the general arranged our immediate discharge. Yindrich, bearing a written order from the commander-in-chief, had run to the jail and fished us out.

Safely out of this jam, I walked with Yindrich to the United Press bureau, where we had a sumptuous meal of canned sardines. When Emilio saw me later that evening, he hugged me, and with tears in his eyes kissed me on both cheeks, declaring us "blood brothers." Again, I didn't appreciate the dramatics. I soon put the matter behind me and prepared for the next day's work.·

4

PRISONER OF WAR

THINGS WERE GOING BADLY FOR THE REPUBLICANS IN mid-October, 1936. Franco was closing in rapidly on Madrid, capturing one town after another.

In Spain at the time there were no "conducting officers" such as the British provided for the uniformed war correspondents in this World War Number II. As a matter of fact, we didn't even have uniforms. It was a case of getting as many passes as possible from the Anarchists, Communists, and Syndicalists; barging out to the front and trusting to luck. Not only did we risk walking into serious trouble; there was a good chance of getting one or more bullets in the back, depending on the attitude of the commanders of the outfits we visited in the field. If they didn't like your looks, it meant Taps, no questions asked.

Though I had a few comfortable nights in my fine bed in the Palace Hotel, sleep was limited since I had undertaken not only to work all day covering the fronts, but to handle the night trick at the "Telefonica." It was a backbreaking, twenty-four-hour job covering that war, and with just myself, Yindrich, and Pflaum, we were short-staffed in Madrid.

• • •

I hadn't had much time for extracurricular activities, but a fellow's got to have a bit of diversion, so I asked Lester Ziffren to introduce me to some of his choice girlfriends. There was one young lady, a tall, raven-haired, luscious-eyed queen by the name of Natacha, whom I particularly liked. I met her one evening in one of the few Madrid restaurants where a person could still tear into a steak. Because I had to hustle off to the Telefonica that evening, I jokingly suggested that perhaps she might like to look me up the next day at the Palace Hotel.

Exhausted after an all-night vigil by the telephone, I piled into bed at 9 a.m., leaving instructions to be wakened at noon—I had to go to the front that afternoon as usual. The fronts were getting increasingly close, and it only took an hour or so each way. When my telephone rang its shrill bell

30

at about 10 a.m., I sleepily picked it up, ready to curse the operator for awakening me before the appointed time.

"A lady to see you, sir. Shall we send her up? She says she's your secretary."

I gave the O.K., and donned my lounging robe while gulping down a glass of brandy to help me get my eyes open.

There was a knock at the door. I opened it and there before me stood Natacha. After a moment's confusion, I invited her in. We settled down to a bit of straight drinking, in the midst of which the anti-aircraft batteries of Madrid began a barrage against Franco's German bombers overhead. We had hardly begun to get acquainted when there was a clatter at the door. It was the manager of the hotel, who said the Communist committee of the house would like to have a word with me. I dismissed him curtly, and resumed pleasantries with Natacha. Another five minutes passed and then another clatter and banging at the door. This time it was the Russian Ambassador Rosenberg's personal secretary, flanked by delegations not only from the Communist but the Anarchist and the Syndicalist committees as well, all of which had headquarters in the hotel.

"There is a young lady by the name of Natacha in your room. Mr. Rosenberg would be interested in having a look at her credentials. We require her presence in the lobby immediately."

I had had enough of all this foolishness, so I got dressed, and together with Natacha, proceeded to the lobby. She was trembling and as white as a sheet as she presented her passport on demand. It turned out that she was a White Russian. She had a League of Nations passport which revealed her to be the wife of a certain captain in the Spanish army and the mother of two children. The Madrid police said her husband was not fighting for Franco, but they were going to arrest and jail her then and there as a suspected spy. I insisted that, as my guest, she couldn't be molested, and accompanied her as she was escorted to her apartment down the street. En route, she explained to me that this might be the end for her, because she had made the mistake of representing herself as Rosenberg's secretary to get past the guards at the entrance to the hotel. She didn't tell me more, but it began to appear that Natacha was not the sweet and innocent little girl some people believed.

Before we arrived at her apartment she said to me: "I expect you as a gentleman to come to my assistance when the police arrest me. You must know that while you were answering the door, I took your visiting card from your jacket pocket. I shall present it to the police, and shall tell them that you will vouch for me."

That afternoon I went to the front as usual and the next morning got up at an early hour. I called the office and was told that we had received an urgent cable from the United Press in New York. They were asking us to confirm or deny an Associated Press report that Franco had captured Aranjuez, a station not forty miles distant from Madrid on the Valencia-Madrid railroad.

We drew lots to see who would go to which fronts that day, and I drew Aranjuez. The only way to confirm or deny such a report was to have a personal look-see. My chauffeur, Ramon, had been considerably shaken up by the jail episode weeks earlier, so I saw to it that before we started off for Aranjuez he had a glass of brandy to buck him up. I must admit that I had a few stiff ones myself.

• • •

The old rattletrap taxi, made to run on six cylinders but which now actually functioned on about four, started off with a roar and we were away. I sat in the back and told Ramon nothing of where we were going, merely directing him to the Valencia Road. It didn't look quite right as we approached the village of Sesena, near Aranjuez, for there were hundreds of straggling troops retreating toward Madrid, many of them walking wounded. Ramon began to ask questions, and still I kept my mouth shut, but when we got close enough to Sesena to hear the machine-gun and mortar fire, Ramon put his foot down and refused to go any farther.

I don't know whether it was actually me or the brandy inside of me talking, but I called Ramon a coward and demanded that he continue on his way.

"But they are shooting down there, Señor. I have got a wife and several children."

A big touring car crammed full of militiamen, some of whom stood on the running boards, raced past us at a fantastic speed in the general direction of the fireworks.

"Look, Ramon," said I. "If they can go that way, why can't we? Step on it and follow that car."

We did. Proceeding along at a fast clip for about five miles, straight into the line of fire, we followed the larger car. Suddenly there was a terrific din. Just in front of us we saw that touring car flip over three times without a stop, hit dead center by the concentrated fire of massed machine guns in what turned out to be a rebel ambush. The bullets were buzzing and whining around us like angry bees now, and Ramon stopped our "puddle jumper" smack in the center of the road. There we sat, with Ramon scratching his head in a complete trance. I spoke softly to him, but even as the bullets began smacking our car, Ramon sat there like a statue with a silly grin on his face. I couldn't budge him, but when I saw tanks on the road ahead I opened the side door and hurled myself onto the side of the road. Ramon must have seen the tanks coming, too, for all of a sudden I saw that car of ours leap into action like a frightened colt. Ramon reversed direction by executing a hairpin turn on two wheels, and as I lay on the side of the road with the bullets whizzing about my ears, he gave me a jaunty wave of the hand and raced on without me toward Madrid and his wife and kids.

I heard the rattle of tanks and turned my head. I could see them advancing, their multiple machine guns vomiting a stream of fire. They were Italian Whippet tanks, and the lead machine was making straight for me as I lay there at the side of the road. I rolled over and over toward the field, trying to get out of the tank's way. The tank driver obviously intended to run me down because I was now inside the range of his machine guns. The guns were set to fire at about the height of a man's chest, and the bullets were passing well above me. Out of the corner of my eye I caught a glimpse of Ramon barreling down the road with three tanks giving chase. He must have been going pretty fast, for those Italian Whippets can do forty-five miles per hour at a pinch. I guess the bullets were goosing him along to glory.

Next thing I knew I had fallen into a deep culvert, miraculously located under the road just below the spot where I had lain. Beside me, only a foot from my head, its tractors still churning madly in the air, was the Whippet tank that had tried to run me down. It had become stuck in the culvert. Machine-gun fire was still whistling through the air from all directions. I don't know why I did it, but when I saw the helmeted driver of that tank trying to extricate himself from the turret, I decided to help him get out. He was a little fellow, but he had gotten stuck and was right in the line of fire. I stood up, ran around the tank, and pulled him bodily through the turret hatch and onto the ground. When the shooting stopped we both stood up and the little tank driver clicked his heels and gave me the Fascist salute. I had been used to the clenched-fist Communist salute in Madrid, so without thinking, that was how I replied. When he saw me stick my fist in the air, he stooped down like lightning to pick up his revolver that had fallen on the ground. He jabbed it in my belly and ordered "Mani in alto," or "Hands up."

With my hands reaching for the sky, he marched me to the road and handed me over to a crowd of pretty tough customers in the form of baggy pantalooned, barefooted, and bloodthirsty-looking Moors. They proceeded to deprive me of everything essential, including my wrist watch, my fountain pen and pencil, and the "lucky dice" I had won years ago in a game in Columbus, Ohio. They even demanded the silver-buckled belt off my trousers. I figured that since they had taken my belt I wouldn't be needing the pants very much longer: The bodies of scores of

Spanish Militia lying thereabout told me the rest. They got the cuff links off my right sleeve and were removing those on the left one when I began jabbering a mixture of Spanish and Italian, the essence of which was that I was an American newspaperman and as such a neutral in the war.

I saw a glint in the eyes of the nearest two Moors who were looking down the barrels of some very ugly pistols pointed at my chest. I figured it would soon all be over for Gorrell. But my luck was still with me, for the little Italian tank driver sprang into action. He kicked the nearest Moor in the seat of the pants and knocked the gun out of the hand of the other, announcing that I was his prisoner. An Italian officer on horseback, who turned out to be the commander of the Italian tank unit leading the advance on Madrid, then questioned me. Satisfied that I was an American and an unarmed newspaperman, took me back to the Spanish commander of his regiment.

The Spanish colonel looked me up and down and then said, "Are you the fellow we just picked up down the road?"

When I answered in the affirmative, he said: "You are a very lucky man, indeed." He continued in perfect English as he offered me his hand: "We take no prisoners. This morning we have killed over 350 Reds on this road. You are the only one so far who has escaped with his life."

It seemed that if the machine guns or the tanks couldn't do the job, the mop-up squad of Moors finished it. As I later learned, they were permitted to loot, but not from dead bodies. They could take a man's belongings before they shot him, but not afterwards. In the course of my journey in custody through the Franco lines, I saw any number of Moors carrying dead men's underwear, shoes, and other valuables in their knapsacks.

• • •

I spent about a week in Franco-controlled Spain, mostly in and out of jails. But what made me even more uncomfortable than being a prisoner again was the fact that I had been interviewed as a P.O.W. by an Associated Press correspondent in Talavera-de-la Reina. I had thus been "scooped" on my own story, for the United Press correspondents covering the Franco side of Spain were in Bilbao at the time, unaware of my capture.

I made my forced exit to France in company with Denis Weaver, of the *London News Chronicle,* and James M. Minifie, of the *New York Herald Tribune.* Both had been captured in the vicinity of Sesena about one hour after I was. I got drunk on brandy in Sesena with the Italian tank driver, who at one point put his arms around me and explained that had he known I was an American "and not a Red," he would never have tried to kill me.

Finally Weaver, Minifie, and I were escorted to the frontier at Irun. Franco had ordered us expelled as Communists from rebel Spain. Not so long before I had nearly been shot in Madrid as a suspected Fascist spy. Funny world.

On our way to the border I realized that I had a big problem: I had no passport. I had had to leave it in Madrid with the police in order to receive a visa permitting me to stay in Republican Spain for another month. Minifie and Weaver both had British passports in hand. I had seen them through Franco Spain, interpreting for them all the way, but because I know no French, I solicited their assistance to get me through the border crossing.

It was pouring rain as we stood there on the Spanish side of the International Bridge between Irun and Hendaye, France. A Spanish police chief gave us his instructions.

"When you get to the middle of that bridge, don't stop, for you're not wanted in Franco Spain."

"But I have no passport," I remonstrated in Spanish. "Suppose the French don't let me in?"

"In that case," he said ominously, "we shall take you down the river, and you will have to swim across into France. We have only bullets for you on this side."

We were met by the French border guard at the end of the bridge. Minifie and Weaver got through all right, but the guard, on demanding my passport and finding I had none, merely yawned and waved me back to the Spanish side of the bridge. I didn't know what to do and certainly had no desire to take a swim in a crossfire of French and Spanish bullets down the river. So I yelled to Minifie and Weaver to hurry up and get help for me, and strolled through the rain to the middle of the bridge. I sat down right on the line, with one foot in France and the other foot in Spain, awaiting the arrival of the American ambassador to Madrid, Claude Bowers, formerly editorial writer on the *New York World*. He had his residence just across the border at St. Jean de Luz.

The rain was trickling down my back and I was miserable. I hadn't changed my socks since I last was in Madrid, and hadn't had an opportunity to wash, shave, or brush my teeth. The Spaniards glowered at me from one side and the French customs guards looked me up and down stupidly from the other. I racked my brain for a way to get out of this mess, and seeing a new French customs officer stroll down to the bridge, I hailed him and asked him if he could spare a cigarette. He only had one cigarette left in his case, so I told him that I couldn't accept it, but asked him if he would be so kind as to accompany me to one of the frontier shops so I could buy myself a pack.

"Mais oui, Monsieur," said he. "And what are you doing sitting there in the middle of the bridge anyway?"

I explained that I was an American newspaperman who had been captured recently by Franco and had been expelled from Spain, but had no passport.

He burst into hysterics as I described my treatment on the bridge. He extracted a Hendaye newspaper from his pocket, pointing to an article with regard to three journalists having been captured, and asked me if I was not one of the trio. I was. That settled it.

The officer was treating me to my first decent meal in days when Ambassador Bowers showed up in his limousine. There was a lot of bowing and scraping by the French, and although I looked like a bum, I rode in the ambassador's limousine to his residence at St. Jean. He put his wardrobe, whiskey, and typewriter at my disposal, and I wrote the story of my second escape from death.

5

THE SIMPSON CASE

MY LONDON OFFICE SENT ME THREE THOUSAND FRANCS, and I spent the lot in a few days re-outfitting myself and celebrating my rebirth in the border hot spots.

It seems that for eighteen hours I had been believed dead. My chauffeur, Ramon, had reported on arrival in Madrid, sans Gorrell, that the last he had seen of me through his rearview mirror had been my legs sticking out from under an Italian Whippet tank. So when I demanded dictation on being connected by long-distance telephone with my London office, the boys there figured somebody was pulling their leg.

"Gorrell? He's either dead or a prisoner in Spain," an earnest young voice informed me.

"But this is Gorrell, you damn fool. I'm not dead. I'm not in Spain. I'm sitting here in St. Jean de Luz—in France. Now give me dictation, please."

In my story I revealed that it had been an Italian regular army tank unit that had run me down on the road to Madrid. There had been many rumors concerning Italian and German intervention in Spain's Civil War, but this was the first eyewitness account of an Italian tank action in connection with Franco's drive on Madrid. Franco's lieutenant, General Varela, had told me that Italian assistance would be terminated with the surrender of Spain's capital "within eight days." Varela had even showed me a sheaf of envelopes on his desk, each bearing the mark "Ministerio de Guerra, Madrid." He had laughed when I asked where he got those envelopes, and offered to let me read their contents—military orders, he had said, issued daily to the Spanish Republican defense forces by General Asensio, then commander-in-chief in Madrid.

"We have the orders of General Asensio just about as fast as his commanders receive them in the field," Varela chuckled.

It certainly looked bad for the defenders of Madrid. The ring of steel was fast closing in, and Republican secrets were known to Franco's forces. But at that stage, we knew nothing of the International Brigade which was being organized for a last-ditch stand in the University City and Casa del Campo.

• • •

I eventually received orders to report to London. United Press had not yet figured out what next to do with me. Barely a month had passed since I had been kicked out of Italy, and now General Franco had thrown me out of Spain. I needed a breather anyway, so I made no protest when Harry Flory, then UP's assistant general European news manager, instructed me to come to London via Paris for consultation.

I had a sticky time of it in Paris since I had no passport. All they would give me at the American Embassy was an affidavit in which I stated that I was an American who had got into a bit of trouble in Spain and now desired to proceed to Britain. In an emergency I have always found that diplomatic red tape smacks you full in the face. I took my signed and sworn statement regarding my situation to the British Embassy, where they refused to stamp a visa on it. They unhelpfully pointed out that they did not know whether I was who I said I was. After hours of rigmarole (during which I almost missed dodging those machine-gun bullets back in Spain) the British Embassy man fixed me up with a temporary document permitting me to proceed to London. I was warned, however, that I was not to try to look for a job while in the United Kingdom. I assured them that I already had a job with United Press, but frankly I wasn't entirely sure that was the case. I did not know the attitude of my masters at UP. By this point, they might well have been fed up with my shenanigans.

• • •

They were working like madmen in London when I got there because a juicy story was boiling up. It was the story of the king versus Parliament. A certain American, Mrs. Simpson, was in the middle of the controversy. I didn't know much about it, and cared even less, frankly. This business of being suddenly transplanted from war to a place where nobody gave a damn about the war had slightly upset my thinking.

I told Flory that I needed a rest, and preferred not to come to the office for a few days. His compromise was to fix me up at his home where I was to "monitor" radio speeches by such as General Quiepo do Llano, Franco's drunken radio spokesman. This was far worse than dodging bullets in Spain. I sat for hours by Flory's radio, with static numbing my brain. I became morose and bitter, since all I was doing was providing content to amuse those who would read their morning newspapers over a cup of coffee. They could read about death and the destruction of a nation, satisfying their lust for excitement, while ignoring the realities of the war. Despite increasing evidence that the Germans and Italians were getting away with murder at the expense of the poor Spaniards, most people outside of Spain did not want to know the deeper truths. They were too busy making themselves comfortable.

The public's collective consciousness seemed to be saying, "Let the saber-rattling dictators rave on. They're lunatics. Spain is a country of no real interest. All this is a side show, anyway. Let Franco win—at least he is a gentleman. We can deal with him. We can't deal with the Communists— the dirty Reds—or those fools the Anarchists."

No, England at this point didn't want war. France certainly did not, either. Appeasement was the thing. Appease the dictators. Business and pleasure as usual. Meanwhile, refugees were streaming in from all over Europe as Hitler prepared for the big show by waging preliminary war against the Jews. In London, the attitude seemed to be, "Let them find work, if they can. Let the agitators rave on in Hyde Park. We've had enough of war. Too many were killed in the last one. We must not jeopardize the lives of our youth."

Quiepo do Llano's ranting over the radio from morning to night didn't help my attitude. I was sick of all this, and was already debating a request to be allowed to return immediately to Madrid, when I received instructions to report to the office for a big story.

"Forget the war, Hank. This is big stuff," I was told. "The Simpson case is reaching a crisis; King Edward may abdicate. Baldwin and company are putting pressure on him. We are staffing the biggest story in the world right now. We've got men at the law courts. We've got men at Buckingham Palace. We need a man at Cumberland Terrace, the home of Mrs. Simpson. Go there and see what's what. She is expected to arrive by plane soon from Paris. Grab a taxi and give it the works."

I was pathetically ignorant of the facts of the Simpson case. In those first few days in London I had not bothered to read the newspapers. My mind was still in El Hoyo and on the road to Madrid. My mind was with the ragged army of the Spanish Popular Front, fighting for its life.

Arriving at the designated address in Cumberland Terrace, I found a crowd of about thirty news hawks and photographers sitting on a stone wall in a body, their eyes fixed on the front door of the Simpson residence across the street. Two London bobbies were pacing back and forth in front of the house, seeing to it that these newspaper roughnecks didn't disturb the peace in their eagerness to get a story or a picture. The boys must have thought I was goofy when I asked them what they must have considered to be the most elementary of questions about this, the "biggest story in the world." But I needed to get up to speed quickly and was not about to read back editions of the newspapers.

The butcher, the baker, the candlestick maker came and went. We kept our eyes on the front door. But the door seldom opened except to admit solicitors in striped pants and frock coats. Whenever such a personage put in an appearance, the cameramen would get busy at once. But their pictures were usually only of a rear view, for these men would rush up the steps, present their card, and be ushered into the house by a watchful butler.

By about 1 p.m. on that first day I telephoned the office from a call box at a grocers down the street and asked if I could go home for the afternoon. The butcher, baker, and candlestick maker knew nothing about the goings-on in the Simpson residence, the solicitors weren't talking, and the bobbies were keeping us at a respectful distance. There was no news to report.

"What's the matter with you, Hank? Have you forgotten that you're a reporter? You Spanish war vets give me a pain. Not every story has to be about the war. Go back there and see what goes on, and call me back at about 6 p.m."

And so I sat. And so did the other news men. We sat there together for three days more, with not even a whiff of a story. Finally I mutinied. I returned to the office without instruction. The late Webb Miller, then European manager for UP, called me into his office. He recently had been brought to London from Spain to handle the now fast-breaking Simpson case in Parliament, and understood my feelings. We had a good, long talk. I told him that I was fed up with all this foolishness and resented being made to warm my fanny on a stone wall in Cumberland Terrace. Webb agreed that there wasn't too much to be gained from this, and suggested that I try to get an interview with Mrs. Simpson's aunt, Bessie Merriman, who lived with her.

"Try it out, Hank, and if it doesn't work, come on back to the office. You won't have to sit there anymore."

I'd have done almost anything for Webb. And the fact that he had dropped the war for a while and had swung into the Simpson case made me realize that, after all, perhaps I was losing my sense of proportion regarding the importance of news stories.

• • •

I went to my hotel and there plotted a method for obtaining entry to Mrs. Simpson's home. I selected my most formal bib and tucker, including a starched white collar, and after gulping a quick drink in the Savoy Bar, hailed a taxi.

"I'm an American, and I want you to help me to do a job," said I to the taxi driver.

He turned halfway round, grinning, and said, "You didn't have to tell me that, sir. What's up?"

I explained that I wanted him to drive me to the Simpson residence in Cumberland Terrace, and to keep his motor running while I sought entry. I promised him a five-bob tip and he was game. I wanted him to keep the motor running just in case that very efficient butler booted me down the steps. After all, if I failed I didn't want to be left standing there so that the news-hungry photographers could make a fool out of me with their cameras. And for lack of other pictures, a news hawk being booted out of the Simpson home wouldn't have been bad.

Arriving at Cumberland Terrace, I ran up the steps and pressed the door bell. From the corner of my eye, I was relieved to note that neither of the two bobbies had made a move in my direction. There was no answer for a second or two, but then a cellar window opened, and what looked like the family cook, a white peaked cap stuck on her head, looked out, craning her neck in my direction. She was part of Aunt Bessie's permanent domestic bodyguard.

Apparently I passed muster, for shortly the front door was opened about six inches, and a hand holding a silver tray such as English butlers use for calling cards was thrust out. I was prepared for that also, and the card I dropped into the tray made no reference to the United Press of America, but only to one Henry T. Gorrell, Esq.

There was another brief pause. The butler must have been satisfied that I was a "gentleman" for he opened the door and bowed me in.

The hall was reeking with the smell of all types of flowers, for the king usually sent about five pounds' worth a day to his future wife. It made me dizzy, and the butler who looked me up and down in a snooty fashion made me more than slightly nervous.

"Whom do you wish to see, sir?"

"I came here to pay my respects to Mrs. Merriman," said I.

He cleared his throat and answered with a "Thank you, sir." With that he walked to the end of the flower-bedecked hall, holding my calling card between thumb and forefinger as though it were something dirty, and presented the card to a maid at the other end. She in turn disappeared up the staircase, also holding the card between thumb and forefinger. I remained standing uncomfortably in the hall as the skinny and very snooty English butler fingered his black tie.

It looked as though I might be successful. After waiting a few more minutes, Mrs. Merriman herself suddenly appeared. A plump lady with a rosy complexion and a full bosom, she was garbed in a black silk dress, set off tastefully by a great strand of pearls. She bounced out of a door opening into the hall, and without further ado confronted me with:

"And who, may I ask, are you, sir?"

It was do or die now, and I hurriedly advised her that I represented the United Press of America and would like a few words with her.

She blushed a beet red as she stammered: "Young man, I never interview anybody. You may go."

With that she retreated backwards, and in her haste missed the door and bumped her plump backside against the wall. Her face was even more red now, and so was that of the butler, who had stopped fingering his black tie and wore a very ugly look on his face. His jaw thrust out, he approached me slowly (for an English butler never hurries regardless of the circumstances), and I just a bit more hurriedly retreated backwards in the direction of the front door. I managed to get my hand on the door knob and open it. I was edging myself out backwards, so that the boys waiting outside with the cameras wouldn't recognize me, but the butler jammed the door shut and caught my foot in it just in time to have the last word.

"You Americans!" he said. "One never knows what you will do next. Good day, sir."

With that he gave me a mild shove. I managed to keep my balance and made it to that taxi, which thank the Lord, still had its motor running. Together we beat a hasty retreat. After paying off the amused taxi driver, I changed clothes in my hotel, then returned to the office. I sat gloomily by my typewriter, hands cupped in my chin.

Webb Miller came and asked me whether I had got the interview with Mrs. Simpson's Aunt Bessie. I explained sadly that I had not, and told him about how I had managed to break through the Merriman bodyguard, including the bobbies, the cook, the maid, and the butler, but had drawn a goose egg in the form of the plump Aunt Bessie, "who never interviewed anybody."

This tickled Webb's funny bone, and he said that I should write the story just as it happened, namely, of the interview that I did not get. I did so, and it was cabled back to New York and was run the next day.

The Simpson case continued to its climax: the abdication of King Edward and his succession by the present King George VI. I pitched in on that story until it was cleaned up. Then one morning I received a telephone call at my hotel. It was Ed Keen, vice president of United Press for Europe. He told me he needed a new manager in Madrid, and asked if I was willing to take the job. I jumped at it. Inside of twenty-four hours I was back in Paris arranging air passage to Barcelona and Madrid.

That was where I belonged.

6

THE SIEGE OF MADRID

I USED TO DUCK INSTINCTIVELY IN LONDON WHEN I HEARD the sound of aeroplanes overhead, and I suffered from a severe case of cold feet as we approached besieged Madrid by motor-car.

There was no other means of entry. Franco's army had cut the Madrid-Valencia railroad, and his guns were ranged in a wide semi-circle on three sides of the city. One could only enter Madrid from the east. The crash of shells and the machine-gun fire unnerved me. Mine was something like the case of the pilot who has cracked up in an aeroplane and wonders whether he can face the music again. But an even worse case of jitters seized my companions at the sound of the firing. They were new to all this, for they had never been in Spain before. Strangely, seeing them jump calmed me.

Later during my stay in Madrid I would force myself to walk along the Gran Via at a snail's pace during heavy shelling. I realized that if I once broke into a run, my nerves would let me down and I'd have to pull out.

If we had been short-staffed during the early days of the war, we were far worse off in Madrid now. One of our Spanish staffers had beat it to join Franco's publicity staff, Emilio Herrero was now in Paris, and Ziffren was gone. There were only Yindrich and Pflaum left to hold the crumbling fort. When we arrived, Pflaum was in bed at the American Embassy with a severe case of flu, and Yindrich was struggling on alone in the emergency.

The bureau was deserted, not even an office boy being around, so I went out to try to find Yindrich on the front line in the University City, only a streetcar ride distant. I got my baptism by fire almost immediately. Promptly at 10 a.m., Franco's artillery began shelling. It was demoralizing. At the time, angered at Madrid's resistance, the enemy was even using anti-aircraft guns against us. There was a mad scramble as the early morning crowds in the market square, consisting largely of women and children waiting for their daily rations of bread and vegetables, dived for cover. I saw more than a score laid out that day. Some of them appeared to have been untouched and were lying virtually naked on the pavements, stripped of clothes by concussion. Ambulances were scarce, so garbage carts were pressed into service when the "all clear" was given.

I found Yindrich, much thinner that he ever had been but with his red beard flourishing. They used to call him "Barba Roja," and it was good to see his trademark was intact. I couldn't do much work after what I had seen, so with Yindrich I joined Pflaum at the embassy and we toasted the reunion of the "Three Musketeers" with the whiskey I'd bought in Paris to fortify myself against future ordeals.

Madrid stood firm, and despite violent onslaughts, General Franco was unable to breach defenses manned by the famous International Brigade. But the bombardment of Madrid became so intensive that I saw troops on brief leave from the trenches voluntarily return after a day or two, for they would "rather be in the line, where at least you have an even chance."

They used to shell Madrid regularly at 10 a.m. and 4 p.m. You could set your watch by it, the methodic German influence obvious. Franco meant to paralyze activity in central Madrid and force closure of the shops so that he could starve the town. But he couldn't break the spirit of the women of Madrid, who would stand in line patiently for hours, scattering only when shells burst nearby. I saw people in a queue laid out by shell fire and then watched the line re-form even as the dead and wounded were being taken away. One had to eat, and the women of Madrid willingly risked their lives to feed their young ones.

In between fixed shelling, there were intermittent bombardments, designed to catch the people off-guard. One such occurred as I sat in a Gran Via restaurant with a Swedish correspondent who had come to Madrid "on leave to have a look at the war." I had just bought a morning newspaper from a newsboy when it started. A shell crashed into the pavement outside and broken glass, china, tables, and chairs flew all over the place. The Swede was trembling violently under the table. It wouldn't do to stick around, for one shell meant that there would be another and another in a few seconds, and I prevailed upon him to clear out. Leaving, we saw the body of the newsboy from whom I had just purchased the newspaper, torn and bleeding outside. A woman also had been hit. All that was left of her were bits of flesh and remnants of her dress, shoes, and stockings. The Swede had seen enough of the war, and sprinted back to the Hotel Florida, where he checked out immediately. He left for Valencia that afternoon.

The Telefonica was the place where all war correspondents shared a huge room as a common office. It was very near the censorship office, and since office boys could no longer be prevailed upon to run the gauntlet of shell fire, most of us prepared our dispatches there. One morning while at my typewriter, two burly figures walked in. There was no need to look up immediately, for I could smell a "flat foot" a mile off. They were cops all right and demanded to see me in private at once.

The only place where one had any privacy was the lavatory, so the policemen and I held our conference there. They got to the point immediately.

"You are the periodista, Gorrell?"

I was.

"Do you remember Natacha?"

Natacha, Natacha, Natacha, I thought with some foreboding. I hadn't had much time to reflect on former escapades from my previous time in Madrid.

Then, shoving my own visiting card under my nose, one of the policemen said he was prepared to refresh my memory.

"Oh, Natacha! Why of course. She's an old friend," I said, recalling the little Russian girl's fears that she would be shot as a spy after our tête-à-tête at Rosenberg's headquarters, the Palace Hotel.

"Oh, so you do know her? That's fine. She'll be glad to see you, for she has been in prison since you left Madrid so hurriedly."

I explained that my departure had been unavoidable, since I had been taken prisoner on the Madrid road.

"We came to advise you that she is under death sentence, but the chief of police thought he would delay the execution as a matter of courtesy to the foreign press, since when we arrested her she presented your card, and said you would vouch for her."

I broke out in a sweat. The thought of the beautiful Natacha being under sentence of death while I sat on Mrs. Simpson's front doorstep in Cumberland Terrace, London, made cold shivers run up and down my spine. And the chief of police had awaited my return so that I could vouch for her. Suppose I hadn't returned, for I certainly hadn't planned to.

I displayed extreme anger and demanded to know why a friend of mine, a lady who had done no one any harm and had two little children, should be thus humiliated by being kept in jail. I gave them a cock-and-bull story to the effect that I had known Natacha for years and that she never had harmed anyone. As for her husband being a captain with Franco's army, how could she help it?

"What's a woman got to do with her husband's business anyway?"

The police were dumbfounded at my anger and began apologizing, assuring me that Miss Natacha would be treated with all consideration and would be released in short order. She never was released, but neither was she shot. Repeatedly, I tried to get her out of jail, but several months later, when I left Madrid for the last time, she was still in prison. Perhaps Franco supplied the story with a happy ending, for I must believe she was given her liberty when the Fascists emptied the Madrid jails.

There were thousands of casualties on both sides as the battle for Madrid raged. All the big hotels, including the Palace, had become hospitals; their dining halls turned into huge operating theaters. There were not sufficient anesthetics, and many a man and woman died in agony. Fever broke out in Madrid but there were not sufficient doctors or medicines to go round. They even used to eat stray cats in Madrid and one couldn't help noticing that there were increasingly fewer dogs about. The people were starving. Retiro Park was a favorite hunting ground for stray cats. Crowds of women gathered there every morning armed with nets and hampers. The "beaters" among the women would comb the park in a body, gradually closing in on the unfortunate cats, while the "net and basket brigade" waited to pounce on them when they made their appearance. The police tried to put a stop to it but they couldn't compete with determination born of hunger.

A piece of sausage fetched a handsome price in Madrid. I kept one in my clothes closet in the Hotel Florida for several weeks, nibbling at it occasionally. I also managed to obtain a few fresh eggs, which I would cook in secret on a little electric stove. Others in the Florida had the same idea, and drain on the current was such that frequently fuses blew and the hotel manager would go from door to door, angrily demanding to know who was using an electric stove. When this occurred there was a mad scramble to hide cooking utensils and victuals under beds since the manager never took you at your word, personally inspecting each room.

The Hotel Florida was only a stone's throw from the front. Frequently it was struck by shells, and one of the boys went home once to find that his bed and bathroom were in full view of the street below. He had been on what the manager called "the safe side" of the hotel. For this journalist on that day it turned out to be safer at the front.

I was sleeping soundly one morning when Ernest Hemingway, the famous novelist, wearing a nightgown, hat, and overcoat, stormed into my room. He made more clatter than the firing down the street, which was pretty heavy. General Miaja was counterattacking in the Casa del Campo and the barrage of his massed guns had just started.

"Hear that?" said Hemingway, as he shook me violently. "Snap out of it, kid, it's a big story. Let's go."

I turned over in my bed, yawning, whereupon Hemingway dragged me bodily out of the bed, practically choking me as he thrust the neck of a brandy flask down my throat to wake me up. He was so excited that he was prepared to go to the front with his nightgown on. But I ribbed him sufficiently to provoke a quick change into something more appropriate.

As Hemingway and I walked out the front door of the hotel, bullets were ricocheting in all directions and a couple had already smashed the window at the main entrance. There wasn't far to go as the trenches were less than a mile away. The earth trembled to the crash of Miaja's artillery. As the firing reached a crescendo, an entire squadron of bomber and fighter planes—Russian—roared overhead as a surprise for the rebels. As they dived and dropped their bombs, they resembled glittering silver pendants hanging in midair against the early morning sun. There were tremendous explosions as the bombs found their targets.

The Fascists in the trenches in the Casa del Campo fought like wildcats as the International Brigade went over the top with bayonets. In that storm of bullets little children were running around along the Gran Via shrilling excitedly as their fathers and mothers in pajamas yelled at them from balconies. In besieged Madrid, little tots often played soldier as shells whistled overhead and crashed all around them. Unexploded grenades were among their playthings as they rummaged in the debris of shell- and bomb-torn houses.

It was getting pretty hot now, so hot in fact that the sentry in a concrete pillbox barring access to a bridge across the Manzanares River didn't even stick his nose out as Hemingway and I walked past. The artillery were firing from behind us, and shells were landing in the Fascist trenches only a few hundred yards distant. Russian fighter planes strafed the hell out of the hard-pressed Fascists, and the place was a general bedlam. It had been very one-sided for the first half hour, but soon German and Italian artillery opened up, and Hemingway and I were in the middle. One shell lopped off a tree, clean as a whistle at its base just a few feet in front of us. Hemingway grinned and was having the time of his life, but it hadn't been long since that I had been taken prisoner under heavy fire, and I was in no grinning mood. I was gun-shy, and with bullets crackling on all sides, I executed what must have been a world-record standing broad jump when a courier's motorcycle started off with a roar behind me. That really fetched a laugh!

Hemingway and I spent the rest of that morning in a ruined house overlooking the battleground, watching the infantry and tanks in action. We drew the odd sniper's bullet as the rays of the sun caught our field glasses, and once or twice the Fascists even sent a couple of shells our way. The firing was so intense that it sounded like the drone of thousands of bees, and one tank after another erupted in flames. Again and again, the Republicans attacked and were driven back. I left Hemingway in the look-out and returned to the Telefonica with the story. I had to pull a censor out of the cellar to have it okayed for transmission to London because Franco, venting his spite on the populace of Madrid, had retaliated with one of the most vicious shellings experienced thus far. Six- and eight-inch shells crashed with clocklike regularity against the reinforced-concrete-and-steel walls of the modern, American-built Telefonica. The building trembled as though in the grip of an earthquake. The Republican attack failed and we settled down again to siege.

During what turned out to be nineteen consecutive days of bombardment, Yindrich and I sat one afternoon in Chicote's bar on the Gran Via. It was about 3:55 p.m. that I spied two very pretty young ladies in yellow dresses walking hand in hand on the opposite side of the street. They were beautiful little creatures and a treat to sore eyes, for nice girls seldom went out of doors in Madrid. I told Yindrich that I intended to invite them to our table. He looked at his watch and said:

"O.K. Hank, but better hurry—the music is about to start," meaning the four o'clock shelling.

I left the table and had reached the exit when there was a rush overhead as of a freight train coming to an emergency stop, followed by an ear-splitting explosion. An eight-inch shell had crashed into the Gran Via not a hundred yards away. Broken glass was all over the pavement and the smoke was such that one couldn't see across the street. When it finally cleared, there were the two little girls in yellow dresses, now a bleeding and torn mass of flesh. One of them was headless, the other was without any arms or legs. It had been a close call for Yindrich and me, but instant death for those girls. Speechless, we proceeded to get drunk on cheap Barcelona cognac.

• • •

On the sixth day of that shelling I had been waiting for several hours by the telephone booths on the main floor of the Telefonica, trying urgently to get either Paris or London. The wires between Madrid, Barcelona, and Paris remained intact, and we normally used this method for filing our dispatches from Madrid. When the Paris call came through, there were no censors around because another heavy bombardment had just begun. Big babies were socking the Telefonica and the only protection I had on the main floor were stacks of sandbags reaching about halfway up the two-story windows looking out on the Gran Via. The censor normally stood close by with his finger on the control key, ready to cut off the conversation if the dictating correspondent strayed from his text. But there was no censor now, and I was free to dictate to my heart's content, provided the artillery didn't interfere.

The office boy in our Paris bureau was recording the conversation. He gave me the "go ahead" after setting the Ediphone recording device at the other end. I dictated for twenty minutes, interrupting only once to go outside for a quick look-see as a shell hit a streetcar full of people just outside the Telefonica. The fellow in Paris kept asking what the noise was all about as shell after shell struck the building. Somehow, the idea that I was reporting from a war zone hadn't fully registered. By now the place was reeking with fumes, but I was practically through. Then the kid in Paris interrupted with a yelp:

"Oh, I'm awfully sorry, Gorrell. Now don't get sore, but you see I've forgotten to put in the wax cylinder and I'm afraid you'll have to start all over again."

The strain had been too much for me, and I used all the dark adjectives in my vocabulary to tell that fellow what I thought of him. He interjected in a plaintive tone:

"You shouldn't really be sore, Gorrell. I'll remember something of what you told me, and truthfully there wasn't any need for you to waste your time dictating this stuff. We have a message from New York saying that there's a big divorce case in Hollywood, and they only want fifty-word bulletins from European bureaus today!"

I nearly smashed the telephone against the desk. The shelling hadn't stopped, so I joined the censor and hundreds of trembling refugees in the sub-sotano (cellar) where I watched stretcher bearers bringing in the mutilated remains of the women and children of Madrid. Reference to that "big divorce case in Hollywood," which was so important as to have overshadowed even this horrible picture of slaughter, embittered me. I didn't telephone a line to either Paris or London for three days. In fact, I nearly resigned then and there, but I couldn't abandon my friends in Madrid.

• • •

Franco temporarily diverted his entire attention to the north. In the battles in Guernica, the Germans razed the town to the ground as Hermann Goering's bombers carried out a realistic test of blitzkrieg in preparation for Warsaw, Amsterdam, and London. I recognized then that this was no longer just a civil war in Spain, but a rehearsal for World War.

The political issues of the war became hopelessly mixed up. I found on questioning people at random in the Republican stronghold of Madrid that many of them didn't know the true meaning of communism, the ideology many of them were supposedly fighting for. They replied simply:

"Russia is Communist. The Russians are our friends. We also are Communists."

I have seen some of these "dirty Reds" mortally wounded and kissing the Cross that they had kept hidden under their tunics.

To take but one example, my servant girl was a fervent Catholic and a Republican who welcomed Russian support against Franco. Some say she had once been a nun in the Guadarrama Mountains. All I know is that she always was dressed in spotless white, and acted the part. Her name was Aurora. She used to wait up for me until three or four in the morning, and then if they were shelling Madrid, and I hadn't appeared, she would call in the police. When I would finally show up, she would automatically bring me a bottle of brandy and then sit there silently, with her arms folded, as I gulped two or three quick shots. She never allowed me to have the fourth. Regardless how much I complained, she would lock up the bottle and stare me down as I raved on. She was no Red, and she loved her people. Later, according to Harold Peters who replaced me in Madrid, she married his Anarchist chauffeur.

I knew many of the boys of the International Brigade, including Englishmen, Americans, Germans, Jews, and Italians. Some of them were soldiers of fortune, but the majority were Communists. There were also soldiers of fortune on Franco's side. I have met some of them since leaving Spain, in Greece and in the Western Desert: sons of English aristocrats who as sportsmen backed Franco, the "Gentleman of Spain," against the Reds. Who are the gentlemen now?

Russian aid to Republican Spain was largely in the air, though they did send technicians to Spain and trained the officer corps. But they sent no infantry. There were Russian tanks in Spain, but few Spaniards or members of the International Brigade were allowed to go near them. I was told that the Russian tank proved superior to the German and Italian designs. The Russian tanks at the time had far greater firepower than those of the Axis. Spain, in tank design alone, provided a valuable lesson to the German and Italian General Staffs.

Russian aeroplanes in Spain were also excellent. Most of them were copies of American military aircraft, but the Russians had improved substantially on fuselage design as testified by the men who flew them, including American volunteer pilots. There were many Russian regular army pilots in Spain, but they were not allowed to mingle with either Spaniards or members of the International Brigade. Russian bomber and fighter aerodromes were well guarded, and as a general rule no matter how trusted were the volunteer American pilots, they seldom were allowed to fly aircraft other than those the Russians considered out of date. Although outclassed in numbers, Russian aircraft competed very satisfactorily in Spain against the Luftwaffe and Reggia Aeronotica. But there came a time when, disheartened because France and England showed no sign of giving the Loyalists material support, the Russians themselves began to pull out. Soon, because of lack of replacements, Franco attained air superiority, which ultimately had much to do with forcing the Republicans to their knees.

I knew the American aviators who flew for the Republican Air Force, including Whitey Dahl, who later was to be taken prisoner by General Franco, and Frank G. Tinker,[1] former navy pilot and graduate of the U.S. Naval Academy. Tinker became an ace, shooting down more than a dozen German and Italian planes in Spain. The aviators commanded high salaries and were promised a premium of a thousand dollars for every plane shot down.

Tinker once told me of a dogfight he had with a Messerschmitt:

> It was one of the toughest fights I've ever had. Eventually I got him and followed the plane down until it crash-landed behind our lines. I was curious as to the identity of the pilot—he had put up quite a fight. Imagine my surprise when on inspecting the wreckage of the cockpit I found a dead German wearing shorts and jersey, with rouge on his lips, mascara on his eyebrows and red polish on his finger nails! I guess looks aren't everything! What ever else he may have been, the fellow was a tough customer in the air.

On June 8, 1937, my twenty-sixth birthday, I had a party for the volunteer aviators at my apartment in the outskirts of Madrid. The boys had a good time—that is, most of them.

But there was one fellow whom we used to call "El Japones" who wasn't enjoying himself. I tried my best to make him feel at home, but to no avail. Something was bothering that fellow. A few weeks later, in Valencia, I learned what it was.

My friend Tinker was returning to America, his contract having expired. I met him in Valencia by accident, and in the course of our conversation he asked me if I'd heard the latest. I hadn't.

"Haven't you heard about El Japones? He was executed by firing squad in Valencia this morning. The Russians claim he had been spying for Franco."

I went to the jail where El Japones had been shot, and asked to see the sergeant of the guard. The fellow confirmed that he had supervised the

---

1. Frank Glasgow Tinker, America's only ace of the Spanish Civil War. Tinker was credited with eight downed enemy aircraft. He and fellow pilot Whitey Dahl would later figure in their friend Ernest Hemingway's story "Night before Battle." Tinker wrote the book *Some Still Live*, published by Funk and Wagnalls Company in New York, 1938.

execution of El Japones and even offered to give me one of the bullets that had killed him.

"How did he die?" I asked.

"He was a man. I've never seen a Spaniard die more bravely. He refused the blindfold and just before I gave the order to fire, he shoved out his right arm in the Fascist salute and shouted:

"Arriba Espana, e viva El Japon!"

All this time this fellow had been shooting down German and Italian planes, he had been providing information to Franco through the Japanese Legation in Madrid.

• • •

Madrid was well defended. There was no getting into the city by direct assault through the University City area or the Casa del Campo, so Franco had another try from the direction of Guadalajara. It was to be entirely an Italian attack, involving two motorized divisions. Using the same tactics as Badoglio had employed in his grand march on Addis Ababa, the Italians roared along the paved highway, with Madrid as their goal, looking neither to right nor left. The Russians had anticipated such a move and the International Brigade was ready for them. It had been raining hard for days and the fields on both sides of the road had become quagmires. At a crossroads the defenders of Madrid lay in ambush for the Italians with a handful of field pieces, mortars, and machine guns. Supporting them was practically the entire Republican Air Force, including bombers and fighters.

The Italian armored column, preceded by fast scout cars and motorcycles mounted with machine guns, ran headlong into a torrent of fire. Approximately 350 men, mostly Czechoslovak Jews, confronted the spearhead of the Italian attack, but to see the Italians turn tail and run, you'd have thought they were a division strong. The column, being well over two miles long, could not simply reverse gear and turn back the way they had come. The tanks, armored cars, and trucks took to the fields to try to escape and got hopelessly stuck in the thickening mud. What followed was mass slaughter. In the midst of the panic Russian bombers and fighters bore down on the army that was the pride of Italy. In the end there were burning vehicles by the score and Italian prisoners by the hundreds. The entire column might have been rounded up had not the inclement weather interfered. Thousands of Italians took to their heels along that road, leaving their vehicles stranded behind them. Sufficient equipment and ammunition were captured on that day to last the defenders of Madrid for months.

I interviewed several Italian prisoners, one of whom, a father of six children, told me that he had believed he was going to Ethiopia to take over a tract of land and establish a household. Instead, he found himself on a troop transport bound for Seville.

"I didn't come here to fight, but they told us it would be all over pretty soon and, anyway, we were doing to the world and the Church a service by defeating the 'Bolsheviki.' They said it would be easy, but when we ran into the ambush on this road I thought of my wife and children, and I ran. Wouldn't you have done the same?"

• • •

I remained in Madrid until late August 1937, then took sick leave, for I had lost about twenty pounds in weight and was exhausted. Just prior to my departure I gave a farewell party at the Hotel Florida. Espionage had been rampant in Madrid, for Franco had a powerful ally in his famous "Fifth Column." A friend of yours might be a nice fellow, and still a dangerous spy. It was all right provided you kept your mouth shut, and after all, we American newspapermen in Madrid were neutrals.

There were two spies at that party, one a Fascist, and the other a Loyalist.

Among my guests was an ex-boxer by the name of Carlos Quintana, a nice little guy at whose recent wedding I'd acted as best man. I'd even swiped chickens under the noses of the Russians to provide food for his fiesta. All I knew was that Quintana was of the Republican Militia, and one didn't ask too many questions in Madrid. Another guest that evening was a Spanish captain who had participated in the defense of Malega. He was a thorough gentleman.

At the height of festivities I was called outside to settle an argument between two of my guests. It was a sham, cooked up by Quintana, who had been looking for an opportunity to do his stuff. Until that day I hadn't known that he was of the secret police in Madrid, and that he had taken advantage of his friendship with me to do his sleuthing more effectively. In the press corps, we had many and varied acquaintances, not all of whom were on the up-and-up.

Quintana had come to my little party with two of his lieutenants, both armed to the teeth. The argument outside settled, I heard a commotion in my room and reentered to find my friend the captain from Malega with his hands in the air, his face white as a sheet, looking down at a .45 automatic that Quintana was pressing against his wishbone. The little ex-boxer was loudly denouncing the captain as a Fascist traitor.

"What's the trouble?" I demanded.

"This man is a spy," said Quintana. "I have been trailing him for weeks. His documents are false and he is under arrest."

So far as I was concerned there would be no arrests that night, and I told Quintana so, stressing that those in my room were guests and that there mustn't be any gun play. The Spaniard, be he "Red" or "White," is a born gentleman. Quintana and his two lieutenants surrendered their artillery to me. So did the captain. With their pistols locked up in my closet, the Flamenco singers and guitarists started up the music again and the party continued as though nothing had happened.

At 2 a.m. the captain asked leave to be excused, whereupon Quintana demanded that I return his gun.

"Listen, Carlos, you have chosen the wrong place for trouble. If you must, arrest the captain tomorrow, but not here, not now. What do you say that I give El Capitan a five-minute head start, after which you can follow him?"

For the captain, this was like a reprieve from a death sentence. Both parties agreed and, having given me their word, I returned their pistols. The captain was off like a flash of lightning. Quintana looked at his watch, and on the stroke of the fifth minute he too was tearing down the stairs. I heard a lot of shouting, but no shooting.

They didn't get the captain that night, but they did so on the next day. Just before I left Madrid I read in the official gazette that my friend the captain from Malega had been executed on charges of high treason.

7

INTERLUDE:
REFLECTING ON EVENTS, 1936-1939

I HAD BEEN LOOKING FOR PEACE AND QUIET ON MY RETURN to America in late August 1937, but was sorely disappointed. The backwash from Europe was beginning to have its effect in my own country; Capital and Labor were already at one another's throats.

Mass production, when world demand was drying up as were our fields in the Middle West from drought, was partly responsible. But newspaper headlines featuring the "Jewish problem" and the "Bolshevist menace" were having their effect on a restless people. The activities of paid propagandists who did their work unmolested were provoking rioting in our great automobile manufacturing centers, in line with the plans of European dictators to sow unrest in the Democracies. Hitler and Mussolini were systematically wearing down the morale of the Democracies in preparation for World War. Why should the Axis fight us, when it would be easier if our brothers and cousins fought amongst themselves as the people of Spain were doing?

The Spanish war was approaching its climax. So much blood had been shed already that the country was on its last legs. The will to resist was dying in Spain. When the war was over, Spain would lie prostrate, to become the prize of the strongest European power. So far as Spaniards were concerned, no one had won the war. They fought to the point of exhaustion, with the result that the masses were trodden underfoot by Franco and his clan—puppets of Berlin and Rome. That Franco is a Fascist through and through cannot be doubted. Is it not sufficient proof that his Tribunals are still passing death sentences on those accused of being party to the assassination of Spain's Fascist martyr, José Clavo Sotelo, in 1936? His assassination triggered a civil war in which so many countries played a part, increasing the misery of the Spanish people beyond anything they could have imagined.

We in America, as early as 1937, were unwittingly aiding and abetting Hitler's schemes. If the man in the street in New York, Chicago, or San

Francisco did not realize it, Roosevelt did. He was well aware of the significance of the Spanish Civil War; he knew that Franco's victory meant a triumph for the Axis powers and another step toward the dictators' bid for world domination. Control of the western Mediterranean, even if only partly achieved through Italian and German intervention in Spain, was essential to the programs of Messrs. Mussolini and Hitler.

Equally essential was that in the great Democracies, Capital and Labor should be crossing swords. Germany had plotted, before even firing a shot on the field of battle, to break up the world coalition by systematically disarming and encircling the Democracies so that she could attack them at leisure when ready.

"While the Democracies taught their people to think of passive defense, the Germans got themselves thoroughly ready for the offensive," wrote Walter Lippmann in *Life* magazine ("America's Greatest Mistake," July 21, 1941). "[I]t was this ruthless political strategy which set the stage for the military victories of the German army. It has been our wooden-headed conception of foreign policy which had brought us to the pass where Germany, recently encircled and isolated, is now threatening to isolate and encircle us."

• • •

When I reached New York toward the end of the Spanish war, I was astounded to hear people talk openly of prospects for serious trouble "if Roosevelt doesn't let up on Capital." No longer thinking for themselves, and partly hypnotized by foreign propaganda, it struck me that some of our moneyed people were beginning to think along Fascist lines. Violating the fundamental doctrines of the Constitution, they seemed to consider anyone who used his hands to make his living as in the opposite camp—or a "Dirty Red." We have a great middle class in America, but blinded by the concerted efforts of our enemies we were beginning to ignore it. The middle man was being shoved out of the picture, and it was getting so that, even in America in 1937, a fellow was either a "White" or a "Red." There was no in-between. But was this fair? Would you consider the poor people described by John Steinbeck in *The Grapes of Wrath* as "Reds"? In the main, they were no more Reds than were the majority of the poor of Spain who fought so bravely against the Axis-equipped Fascist legions of Franco.

My nerves were shot as a consequence of the pounding of Franco's guns ranged around Madrid, and I tried to close my ears to political bickering and to the insults hurled publicly at Roosevelt and his advisers. It seemed ridiculous to me that we in America should begin fighting amongst ourselves. We had practically all that anyone needed in our country, despite the worldwide economic upheaval.

Because of my state of mind, I found it hard to settle down in New

York. There was too much noise, too much traffic; and unless one had good friends, a big town can be very cold toward a stranger. I felt myself a stranger now, for it seemed that I no longer spoke the language of my own people. To hear some of them talk, they knew all there was to know about the situation in Europe. If one suggested that perhaps they were talking through their hats and, like the ostrich, were burying their heads in the sand—if one suggested that they were being led blindfolded into war—he got the cold shoulder. So I kept my mouth shut. After all, what was the use of trying to tell anyone that the Russians were not nearly so bloodthirsty as German and Italian propaganda depicted them, when few were inclined to listen? What was the use of suggesting that Russia was the only country with real farsightedness and was doing the world in general a service by resisting the Fascist avalanche in Spain? Why, the red herring of Bolshevism need only be dragged across the front pages of our newspapers, and everyone was either up in arms or hiding under the table. This, the anti-Bolshevist hue and cry, proved a very effective weapon in the hands of the dictators as they prepared world public opinion for the war to come.

When I crossed the Franco-Spanish frontier in 1937, I believed myself so hungry that I could eat a meal fit for three. I ordered such a meal, on the train en route for Le Havre. I was kidding myself, though. In my mind only was I hungry. My stomach, used to staples such as garlic soup, augmented with blood sausage every couple of weeks and buffalo meat from the Madrid Zoo on feast days, had shrunk. I couldn't take a real meal. The fellows in Madrid were starving while the world went merrily on its way and Geneva toyed with nonintervention control.

• • •

I arrived in New York on the S.S. *Britannic*. There, in those first days, I would stand for ten or fifteen minutes at a time in front of the display windows of delicatessen shops, feasting my eyes on the eggs, bacon, cheeses, and hams that had existed only in my mind's eye in Madrid.

To escape the noise and confusion of the city, I took two months' vacation on the old family farm in Northfield, New Hampshire. I had the jumps, for it's a shock to be suddenly transferred from a country torn by civil war to the luxury of carefree living. I asked my Aunt Edith, my dead father's sister, to give me some hard work to relieve my mind. I chopped wood for several hours every day.

One morning I was out in the woods clearing a path through scrub pine when buckshot began whistling around my ears. For a moment I figured the war had started all over again. But it was only a couple of city fellows, appropriately dressed from top to toe, firing at everything that moved. As I later learned, this was the opening of partridge season. My father's twelve-gauge shotgun, which he hadn't fired since he was a kid but which my aunt kept oiled and ready, served me well. I stalked those two city fellows and let fly with buckshot over their heads. I reckon maybe they're still running. I laid aside the shotgun, and continued chopping wood.

After two months on the farm I reported for duty at the offices of the United Press in New York. One of the big shots figured that I was still "muscle-bound" inside; he put me on the cables desk so that I should "see how the wheels go round." It was partly my fault, for I didn't want to return immediately to the horrors of Spain. To tell the truth, I wasn't in the mood to do anything at all at the time, but how was he to understand? Being young, why wasn't I capable of doing a job after two months of fresh air? Anyway, in the long run it didn't do me any harm.

I got myself an apartment above the "Elevated" on Second Avenue. I shut the windows, but I couldn't keep the noise out of my ears. What I wanted was a desert island with no one around. Instead, I bought myself a houseful of furniture, foolishly figuring on settling down as a tired war veteran. I was only twenty-six, but felt all of fifty. The Second Avenue joint was ill-advised, for they were blasting a tunnel under the East River. The dynamite sounded like bombs and shells crashing, and more than once did I wake up to find myself under my bed, shoving like mad against the springs, which in my dreams had become the riveted sides of the Italian tank that had run me down on the Madrid-Valencia road on October 25, 1936.

A little blonde helped to pull me out of it and to a certain extent I regained my poise and sense of humor, though I drank more than was good for me.

• • •

Throughout late 1937 and the whole of 1938, tremendous stories flowed over the United Press cables desk. Hitler and Mussolini were on the march.

I had only been on the job in New York for a few months before Austria was overrun, and then Czechoslovakia. There were bulletins at brief intervals and extras appeared with regularity on the streets of New York. Roosevelt fought hard against Fascist penetration in Spain, and I don't believe he wanted to recognize Franco but found himself hog-tied by propaganda concerning the "Bolshevist menace" and Franco's "Holy Crusade." In America itself, unrest grew by leaps and bounds. There were strikes and riots. We in America were swinging on a trapeze over an abyss but didn't know it. Roosevelt saw extreme danger in this home-front turmoil, which paid propagandists were fostering in the Land of the Free. He saw a coming war and struggled against odds to hold things down. First and foremost for Roosevelt were the masses, for after all, are they not the foundation of American life? That's why he developed the Public Works Administration. He was seeking to pacify the bewildered masses even as he took measures to reduce the power of the rich. There had to be some measure of control, for Wall Street seemed to be going mad. American oil moguls had made a farce out of the League of Nations sanctions during the Ethiopian War, allowing Italy to overrun still another country and proceed unhindered toward control of the Mediterranean. Fascist theory in America was gaining increasing support, especially among the rich, as all sorts of shirts—green shirts, silver shirts—sprouted up and people such as Father Coughlin defended the "True Faith" and in camouflaged terms championed the "New Order."

Roosevelt alone remained clearheaded in this tangle. He set his democratic jaw and steered a true course. He realized that the Democracies would soon be fighting for their lives. There can be no doubt that when the fight is over and peace has been restored, the name of Roosevelt will live as that of one of the greatest statesmen of modern times. Similarly will the names of Churchill, Stalin, and South Africa's Smuts live on.

• • •

I saw few of my friends of the Spanish Civil War during this interlude from armed conflict. But among others there was a captain, whom I shall call "Captain Smith," from my own state of New Hampshire. He had volunteered to fight in Spain merely for the excitement of the thing, and had fought brilliantly with the International Brigade at Madrid and Teruel. In two years he had become a seasoned soldier, aware that the war in Spain was only the beginning of wars to come. One time in Madrid, I had given him my last two packs of American cigarettes as he left for the front. He came back a month later, shell-shocked. All he could remember of that battle—in which he had lost a majority of his company and from which he had barely escaped with his life—was that he had had to leave those two packs of cigarettes in a trench, where they had fallen into the hands of the Moors. In New York I offered him hospitality, but he was even more affected by the blasting on the East River than I. Leaving him alone in my apartment, he once wrote himself out a check in my name for more than I had in the bank. They caught him red-handed, but I prevented the police from preferring charges and imprisoning him. He was no criminal. But he no longer understood or was understood by his wealthy family, and felt himself strangled in the highly civilized rush and bustle that was America. Captain Smith couldn't understand why people should have money and be enjoying themselves when he could not, because of his state of mind. He never meant to steal from me or anyone else. This fellow figured that the world owed him something. Perhaps it did.

And then there was the case of my friend Tinker, who had flown for the Republican Air Force in Madrid. One day as I struggled with cables from Europe, a two-line item came over the domestic wires of the United Press datelined, as I recall, "Little Rock, Ark." It read as follows:

> Tinker, aviator, recently returned from Spain, where he flew for the Red Air Force, was found dead today in a hotel room, a .22 caliber automatic at his side. Suicide was the verdict of the coroner.

Tinker's home was in De Witt, Arkansas, and when last I saw him in Valencia he had been looking forward to going home. I learned later that his mind had become so confused in the Middle West that on more than one occasion he had hired an aeroplane and "shot up" the main street of his village, flying barely above the telephone wires. I guess he must have been trying to kill himself even then, but he was too good a flyer for that. Here was a man who somehow hadn't been able to regain his step in the country of his birth, to which he had wished to return seeking tranquility and peace. It was a tragedy, but who was to blame? His own people, who didn't realize what he had done for them in Spain? Tinker told me that he found himself no longer able to talk to anyone.

"The Spanish war? What's that to us? Aw, forget it, fellow, and get down to earth again. You're back in America now." That was the attitude he probably encountered. Tinker was a good American and should be considered a national hero.

• • •

Later on, I would occasionally open my mouth and try to explain the significance of the Spanish war as I saw it. I like my comfort and my white collar and good food as much as anyone else. But because I publicly supported the underdog and not the rich who wished to maintain feudalism in Spain and were playing along with the Fascist dictators, I was openly called a "dirty Red" in New York. Let it be understood that I thoroughly dislike extremes. I believe, insofar as possible, in following the middle of the road and am ready to take suggestions from one and all. Frankly, before I was through in Spain, I was fed up with both sides. There was no rhyme or reason to it all, and the middle of the road no longer existed. People were tearing at one another's throats in the mad frenzy of a killing spree. It was disgusting and at the same time a sad spectacle. Spaniards, like the tortured and deliberately goaded bull in the ring, were being cheered on to still more bloodshed by the Fascist warmongers. It was no longer possible to strike a happy medium in Spain, but did that mean that we in America, with our inherent rights of "freedom of speech and the press," were also to be led up the same garden path by the Germans and Italians?

Perhaps the newspapers were partly to blame for the general mix-up, for in their search for flashy headlines they had not devoted sufficient space to an explanation of what the Spanish war was all about. Suffice it to say that even today I find people very much confused as to who was fighting who in Spain. Terms such as "rebels," "insurgents," "Nationalists," and "Fascists" with reference to Franco's side, and "Republican," "Loyalist," and "Red" with reference to the Madrid faction, were so liberally used as to make readers of the newspapers dizzy. Had we had the guts to say so at the time, we could have made it far more simple by boiling it all down to a fight between the minority of people, namely the aristocrats and landowners, against the masses, who invariably were poor, for in Spain one had to use a magnifying glass in an effort to find a middle class.

Not only did many of us not know the difference between rebels and the so-called Reds in Spain, but whatever propagandists had to say about Bolshevism, the people agreed. It was a crazy muddle. Were not we lambasting the Russians, the hated Bolshevists, who were to become our allies in future years, while Fascists and Nazi propagandists who pretended to be our friends benevolently looked on? Now, the masks have been removed and Russia is applauded as "our noble ally." But wasn't she also our ally in Spain? Who would have admitted it then?

In one of my last letters to my father before he died, I remember complaining that I appeared to suffer from claustrophobia in New York and felt myself suffocating in the big city. It seemed I was struggling for air, and couldn't breathe. I saw it again in Tel Aviv, Palestine, the modern city built in the desert during the past two decades by wealthy Jews, refugees from Hitler's tortured Europe. There in an open-air café one night, I met two Australians who had been several months in besieged Tobruk. They were the "rats of Tobruk." To them, the moon was a "bombers' moon" and their enemy. Said one of them to me: "Why don't the bombers appear, Yank? They always did. These people around here drive me mad. They seem to be dreaming and making money out of it. And, Yank, I wonder what I'd do now even if one of our planes appeared overhead. I think I'd run like Hell. Wouldn't you? But I guess it wouldn't do to run, because these people would think I was scared. Tell me, Yank, why don't they let us go back to Tobruk? That's our home. The bombs and shells were music to us; and it was like food and drink to us to hear the Dagoes scream when we stuck them with the bayonet. But here, if you got drunk and stuck somebody with a knife, they'd make a helluva fuss about it. It's all crazy, isn't it? But you can't explain it to these people."

I told them I'd felt somewhat the same after Spain while in Paris, London, and New York. Maybe my friends "Captain Smith" and Tinker had felt that way, too. My father replied from Ecuador, where he had retired, urging that I refrain from "getting cynical" and plant my feet on the floor. So I tried to shake myself out of it.

• • •

My father's death in mid 1939 was a shock to me. I tossed aside the cables on my desk, borrowed several hundred dollars, and flew to South America to pay homage at his grave. I returned to New York two thousand dollars in debt. I'd seen "how the wheels went round" all right, but to get way away from the rush and bustle of New York proper, I had taken an apartment in Great Neck, Long Island, bought a Buick, and lived nearly a thousand dollars per year over my income. I was seeking the peace and quiet that somehow didn't exist, and had managed to compound my problems in the process.

Webb Miller, the greatest war correspondent of them all, who had been my mentor abroad as European manager of the United Press, visited with me and then left New York a disillusioned and disappointed man. He too, had been in Spain, and he perhaps more than others of our clan was conscious of terrible times ahead. Webb spoke of them to anyone willing to listen.

"We're going to war," said Webb. "But Hank, nobody wants to hear me, they don't believe it. I'm tired of talking myself hoarse and I'm going back. I guess I'll be seeing you soon." It was August 1939.

The day the foreign editor of the United Press in New York telephoned me with urgency asking if I was prepared to take ship for London within eight hours, I felt myself reborn. I didn't bother to sell my car; didn't leave any instructions as to the disposal of my furniture and other belongings in Great Neck. I was going back to where Webb Miller had gone—to London, a place where people would understand.

8

LONDON: SEPTEMBER 1939

THE SS *MANHATTAN* WAS BEING STRIPPED DOWN TO accommodate hundreds of American refugees from Europe when I boarded her for Plymouth. Partitions were being erected in her great saloons and those of us who were going overseas had the ship pretty much to ourselves because the flood of news bulletins heralding the war around the corner had caused hundreds to cancel their reservations.

The voyage was a hectic one with alarming reports coming in by radio. Double watches were set on deck against the possibility of a surprise submarine attack. Sailors were painting the American colors prominently on the ship's sides, balancing themselves on platforms as the *Manhattan* plowed through stormy seas.

The Germans were well on their way to overrunning Poland when I reached England on September 1, 1939. They were preparing for air raids in Plymouth and barrage balloons swung lazily at their moorings in the harbor as British customs officials checked the passenger lists. I entrained immediately for London, and on arrival didn't even stop to check in at a hotel, reporting directly to the United Press bureau in the "News of the World" building.

Parliament had been in almost constant session, and the boys were working hard on the crisis debates. It seemed that Chamberlain was still sitting on the fence, hoping to the last to prevent world catastrophe through his dying policy of appeasement. Londoners were up in arms. England and France had pledged their word to Poland. It must be kept.

There were pathetic efforts by a public wholly unprepared for war to fortify London against aerial attack. Children were being evacuated by the thousands, and hospitals were being cleared for action. Doctors were mobilized as the debate in Parliament continued.

The minds of the British public were made up now, and as the man in the street snapped up "extras," one could see anger on his face as the headlines revealed that no decision had yet been taken. The Londoner was tired of efforts at appeasement. He was weary of the German war of nerves and now was convinced of the inevitability of world conflict. He realized that Hitler could be dealt with only in his own language: with force.

The debate came to a climax as the British ambassador in Berlin handed to Hitler the ultimatum of His Majesty's government to get out of Poland or take the consequences. Chamberlain, an aging and disappointed man, shelved his umbrella, which had been a symbol of Democracy's desire for continued peace, and took up the musket.

• • •

Sirens screaming throughout London on that Sunday morning, September 3, 1939, punctuated the melancholy words of the prime minister as, his voice trembling, he announced to his people that "now we are at war." There was an instant feeling of relief. "Now," said the people, "we know where we are." There were no demonstrations, for the Englishman knew only too well what modern warfare might bring, but I saw no hesitation as English youth responded to the colors.

At Victoria Station I watched the Tommies, 1939 edition, preparing to entrain for Channel ports en route to France where their fathers had fought and died twenty years before. In the eerie glow of the shaded lamps, their faces were grim. Victoria Station resembled a huge tomb. Off they went by the thousands to be flung, when Hitler chose, against the phalanx of advancing steel. They were an ill-equipped army compared to the German panzer divisions.

The women of Britain responded just as quickly as had their menfolk, presenting themselves as ambulance drivers, fire wardens, and nurses. Men in khaki, belonging to the handful of regular divisions then available in England for immediate service overseas, filed through the blackout to the waiting troop trains. There were no weeping wives, mothers, or children to say goodbye. There was no time for that, for Hitler might strike anywhere, at any time.

"We must have war correspondents," said Hugh Baillie, president of the United Press, after a morning conference with Webb Miller. I looked up in anticipation, but my lack of French put me in the discard and I remained in London while others donned the British uniform and crossed the Channel to France.

• • •

There were feverish preparations to make London ready for ordeal by fire. In Hyde Park they were digging trenches, and on the Strand shopkeepers were trying to protect their display windows with sandbags.

London was teeming with excitement, but there was no panic. The Bulldog had set his jaw. He was to be severely pummeled and mauled, but still he was to stand his ground.

At any other time one could not have been blamed for laughing at the sight of plump women in their unmentionables rushing headlong down carpeted stairs, unmindful of their appearance, seeking protection in the so-called shelters of the luxurious hotels of London as the scream of sirens ordered an air-raid drill. Below, women and children were fainting from lack of air, and inexperienced air-raid wardens were reluctant to let anyone out. I nearly suffocated along with them. The congestion in those makeshift London shelters reminded me somewhat of the hellhole of the Madrid jail, when I was up for execution by Anarchists in 1936.

The Londoners' sense of humor never wavered, and people who were later to be bombed out of house and home settled down to grim days ahead. No one ever doubted that the Englishman could take it, and yet those who realized how unprepared Britain was for war couldn't help but feel sorry for her.

Because I had seen heavy bombing during the Spanish war, someone asked me to pass judgment on a Fleet Street shelter. I looked it over and laughed.

"Well, what would you do about it?"

"I'd start in all over again and make the place safe for bombing beyond your imagination."

They called the first few months of the war the period of the "phony war." It was phony only because the British were not in any position to take the initiative, except possibly at sea, and the Germans were not yet ready to invade France, where the Tommies were waiting in the underground vaults of the Maginot Line to fight a defensive battle. Disaster after disaster lay ahead, though, for Germany was prepared and the Allies were not.

Meanwhile, the Irish Republican Army was raising Hell in London. It did not help the situation any, especially since infernal machines were going off all over the place, shattering the already jumpy nerves of the man in the street. One night, as I emerged from the underground in Piccadilly Circus, there was a series of deafening explosions. They were time bombs planted outside shop windows by Irish saboteurs. The damage was slight, the bombs being homemade, but several innocent passersby ended up in hospital. To cope with this new emergency, the finest police force in the world, the London bobbies, moved in and the I.R.A. soon found themselves unequal to their sworn program of inciting panic behind the lines.

Gas masks were being issued to all. The day I went to get mine I heard a choice argument between an Air Raid Precaution warden and an elderly lady with her little Pekingese dog in leash, who insisted that the cur, too, should be fitted with a "Mickey Mouse" mask. She said the dog was her best friend.

Still, Germany did not strike. Possessing the most formidable land army in the world, she could bide her time. Meanwhile, long-planned steps to strike down Britain's might on the seas were being placed into active operation. The German surprise weapon of the early days of this war, the magnetic mine, had been sown throughout the Channel. I was covering the Ministry of Information at the time. Whenever the Naval Intelligence four-striper appeared before the journalists and cleared his throat for an announcement, we knew that another ship had gone down. There usually was no explanation.

I recall an eighteen-hour shift on the London cables desk when first blood was drawn by a German magnetic mine. A Dutch passenger ship was sunk within sight of the English coast and more than 250 refugees, mostly women and children, were drowned. Other disasters followed, for German U-boats were out in packs and raiders such as the *Graf Spee* were roaming the seas. I remember the day in November when the British armored merchant cruiser HMS *Rawalpindi* went down after an unequal exchange with two of Germany's battle cruisers. Riddled by cannon shells and with the Union Jack still flying at the mast, she took more than 200 men to their graves. Her loss was not in vain: she managed to signal the position of the German warships. Rather than chance a confrontation with the British Home Fleet, the Germans returned to port, failing in their mission to break out into the Atlantic. The fighting spirit that had built up the British Empire was very much in evidence as England waited for Hitler to strike.

My great-aunt, nearly ninety years old, whom I went to visit at Lyme Regis, Dorset, just before entraining for Budapest late in 1939, greeted me with a wizened old smile and a mischievous glint in her fading eyes:

"Dear great nephew. I have been waiting to die, but I am going to live until this blighter Hitler had been beaten to his knees. The British Empire will send him to Hell."

My uncle, Bob Barry, who had helped build up the Empire in twenty years of trading in the China seas as a captain of the famous P&O Line, cursed the gray-beards in Downing Street "who were holding us back with their small talk and inactivity. Feed the Hun shells and lead," he said. "That's all he knows." His son Dennis, my first cousin whom I had never seen, but with whom I had frequently argued by mail across the Atlantic concerning American versus English football, was away before I was, serving with the British Fleet.

• • •

The German-Soviet Non-Aggression Pact signed at Moscow on August 23, 1939, was a bombshell. The world was confused, for had not Russia fought against the Germans and Italians in Spain? And the "I-told-you-so" men in Parliament, including the venerable David Lloyd George, were so gloomy about the prospects when confronted with what looked like a Russian sell-out to the Nazis that you'd have thought the war couldn't last six months and that Hitler and Stalin soon would be carving up the cake. The fact that Germany and Russia shortly divided Poland between them didn't improve the outlook.

As events have since proved, Russia even then was on the defensive against Germany and was stalling for time. Russia knew full well that Britain and France could not implement their pledge of assistance to Poland. Since Warsaw's capitulation was unavoidable, why shouldn't Russia move into Poland herself, thus creating a buffer in the form of a great expanse of territory in eastern Poland against the day when Hitler would have his hands free to attack the Soviet Union?

With the Allies cooling their heels in the Maginot Line, the press of the world was hard up for headlines. The Russian invasion of Finland on November 30, 1939, was just what they needed. Nobody bothered much then to figure out what it was all about. The attitude seemed to be, "There's a war on and here is a good fight. Let's go to town with it." Little Finland put up a very brave exhibition. It was a good story, for she was a small nation being invaded by the "Russian bully." The issues were clouded in the public mind to such an extent that we had the strange spectacle of the Germans and Italians on the one side, and Britain and France on the other, both sympathizing with the Finns as the underdog. Have you ever seen a group of boxers, blindfolded in the ring, flaying the air looking for their opponent? Somewhat similar was world confusion over the Finnish show. Even in Finland, Russia was acting to save her skin by creating a buffer against Germany in the north. She was acting defensively and at the same time cleverly bluffing, thereby deliberately seeking to confuse the German General Staff concerning her real strength. Meanwhile, Russia was insulted right and left by the Democratic press, which still accepted Fascist propaganda concerning the Bolshevist bogey. Is it any wonder, therefore, that the people of the Democratic world and those of the Soviet Union since then have found it difficult to understand one another?

Later, in the Balkans, I was to see further evidence of the imminent struggle between Germany and the Soviet Union. When the order to proceed to Budapest to take over Balkan coverage for United Press arrived late in December 1939, I thought I was being side-tracked. As it turned out, I was walking into trouble aplenty.

I flew from London to Le Bourget, Paris, and again saw my old friends of the Spanish war. The feeling among my colleagues in Paris at the time was one of extreme pessimism. France, politically, was rotten to the core. In many respects she was even less prepared than was Britain for war. Since the 1918 Armistice, seldom had the Quai d'Orsay taken any important steps on its own, playing second fiddle to Downing Street. Red tape between Paris and London was of such proportions that it took days to make decisions concerning the conduct of the war which, with reasonable prior preparation, could have been taken in a matter of hours.

The white-haired marshals of France were thinking of war in terms of 1914-1918: "We have the Maginot Line, why worry?" To the observer, the methods that had been adopted to safeguard the populace of Paris against aerial attack or gas seemed grossly inadequate. The anti-aircraft defenses of Paris were pathetic. It also appeared that the French army of 1939 lacked not only modern equipment but also discipline, and that the sons of the men who had died at Verdun were going into battle grudgingly.

The people of Paris were eating, drinking, and behaving pretty much as they had done in the days of the Spanish war. On the surface, their attitude suggested nonchalance, but few Frenchmen reveal their inner thoughts. It was considered bad taste, for example, to refer to such things as the German reconnaissance planes that appeared regularly overhead, out of range of the anti-aircraft batteries.

France was breathing her last as a free nation. These man-made birds were harbingers of doom.

SLOVAKIA

POLAND

U.S.S.R.

Dniester

UKRAINIAN
S.S.R.

⊙ Budapest

HUNGARY

•Cluj

TRANSYLVANIA

B E S S A R A B I A

•Chisinau

•Odessa

•Timisoara

•Brasov

ROMANIA

•Galatz

Danube

⊙Belgrade

•Bucharest

Danube

Black
Sea

•Sarajevo

YUGOSLAVIA

•Pleven

•Kotor

⊙Sofia

BULGARIA

Burgas•

N

•Skoplje

W E

Tirana ⊙

RUPEL
PASS

Istanbul

S

ALBANIA

•Salonika

TEPELENI
GORGE
○ •Premeti
•Saranda

Corfu

GREECE

TURKEY

Ionian Sea

•Thermopylae

Aegean Sea

•Izmir

•Patras

Athens•

•Nauplion

•Kalamata

THE
BALKAN
PENINSULA
• • • • • • • • • • • • •
CIRCA 1940

Rhodes

•Heraklion
Crete

0   100 miles
0   100 km

9

BALKAN POWDER KEG

JUNE 22, 1941, WHEN HITLER ORDERED HIS PANZERS TO ATTACK the Soviet Union along a two-thousand-mile front, appears to be universally accepted as the day that the Russo-German war began. I don't agree.

I believe that history will bear me out when I say that the first shot in the Russo-German war was fired not by Germany, but by Russia in the Balkans on July 8, 1940, when the Soviet Union invaded Bessarabia. I saw the invasion. It threw the German timetable completely out of gear. Joe socked Adolf on the nose in Bessarabia and got away with it, for Hitler could do nothing about it at the time, although his stooges in Romania were pretty sore.

Technically, Russia's first shot against Germany was fired in Finland in November of 1939, three months after the signing of the Non-Aggression Pact. Yes, Russia also double-crossed Germany in Finland, but the shots she fired there were only duds. They were meant to fizzle slightly, so that the German General Staff, which sooner or later was bound to tackle Russia, would underestimate her real strength.

Russia, and then little Greece, did us a pretty good turn in 1940. There was no saving the Balkans, for eventually they would have been flattened out anyway by the German steamroller, but I maintain that in striking first, Russia, in Bessarabia, and then Greece, in Albania, possibly saved us from destruction. German attention had to be split between England and the Balkans.

• • •

Things were going fine for the Germans when I arrived in Budapest in January 1940. They weren't in any hurry, and at the time they were using the Balkans as a sounding board for the "nerve warfare" wherewith it was hoped to lull the Allies into a false sense of security as the Reichswehr plotted the invasion of Denmark, Norway, and the Low Countries. When France had been dealt with and England brought to her knees, there would be plenty of time to put the squeeze on each little country in the Balkans, thus clearing the right flank for the inevitable attack against Russia.

Here was the German timetable as I saw it then:

1. Crush France;
2. Neutralize English influence on the Continent;
3. Flatten out the Balkans even as the Italians batter their way to Suez and mop up North Africa;
4. Take over the key countries of the Near East, namely, Syria, Palestine, Iraq, and Persia, without firing a shot, thus isolating the Soviet Union;
5. Attack Russia; occupy Moscow and link hands with the Japanese in India and the Persian Gulf, thereby paving the way for a two-ocean attack on the North American continent.

The German formula for flattening the Balkans looked simple enough on paper. The operation involved bribing Hungary by promising to carve a chunk out of Romania in the form of the rich estates of Transylvania; Germany then could throw Romania to the wolves by simultaneously sicking the Bulgarians on her. This wouldn't require much prompting: Bulgaria had had a bone to pick with Romania since the last Balkan war when the Treaty of Bucharest (1913) gave Romania the formerly Bulgarian region of Southern Dobruja. After that, Yugoslavia would be surrounded and Germany would be free to blackmail and strong-arm the Greeks into submission.

While Goebbel's boys were expertly beating the drum in Hungary, Yugoslavia, and Romania, deliberately manufacturing rumors of an immediate German invasion to lull the Allied General Staffs to sleep, Joe Stalin watched them closely. Not yet prepared to muscle into the game, he shrewdly remained in the background as Germany, seemingly possessing all the cards, made fools out of her future victims.

• • •

Budapest, Axis playground and center of German-Italian espionage, was indeed a lively city when I arrived in midwinter. The Hungarians, tipped not to worry, were genuinely amusing themselves while the world in general danced rather uncomfortably to the tune of Goebbel's "jitter orchestra." Hungary's counts and countesses, who ran the only remaining feudal state in the world, were going to have their revenge, for Germany had promised to restore to them their ancestral estates in Transylvania. "Let the English and the French worry now. They left us to fend for ourselves following the last war. It's their turn to suffer. Austria-Hungary will rise again," one Count told me. He expressed a sentiment shared universally amongst his social peers.

Budapest was a brilliantly lighted jewel with the snow and ice-bound Danube as a background. There was no thought of a wartime blackout. Cabarets were doing a booming business, patronized by people who seemed to have money to burn. Goebbels was kind to his servants.

It was strange to see British people nonchalantly rubbing shoulders with Germans and Italians in Budapest. They were on their way out, while the Germans and Italians were only looking over the ground preparatory to taking it over. Meanwhile, this artificial paradise suited them as a playground for the Gestapo. Why not allow the British and French to remain for a while? Also, why interfere with the foreign journalists? They all could be kicked out in due course. In the meantime they might be made to serve a purpose. Newspapermen in Hungary had their own paid informants, but never could it be taken for granted that an item of news was reliable. It had to be carefully sifted and weighed, especially since confirmation or denial by the Hungarian Foreign Office meant nothing, it being under the thumb of the Germans, at whose beckoning everyone from the foreign minister down to the Hungarian chief of Press and Propaganda would jump about like marionettes.

A favorite haunt for journalists in Budapest was the "Café Angly" overlooking the Danube. There in the winter of 1940 German and Italian newspapermen would sit over their coffee only a few yards distant from Allied and neutral correspondents. They seldom spoke, and perhaps it was only coincidence that frequently a waiter would deposit a German news bulletin on the Allied journalists' tables, walking off without a word. The flames of war had not yet been sufficiently fanned to arouse hatred in the minds of the journalists of the warring nations, and the English journalists used to send their news bulletins to the Germans by the same method.

For a few months life in Hungary was rather agreeable, but it wasn't to last for long. The ever-mounting number of German "tourists," garbed in golf knickers, pullovers, and golfing caps, carrying Leica cameras and handbags of uniform design, were the writing on the wall. These were the vanguard of the German army which in its own time was to invade Romania, Yugoslavia, and Greece, using Hungary and Bulgaria as stepping-stones.

Jitter warfare in the Balkans reached its peak following the German invasion of Denmark and Norway in May 1940. All the Balkan capitals were jumpy. Goebbels was really beating the drum now, and there appeared strong evidence that the Germans planned to move south.

German divisions were massing on the Austro-Hungarian frontier and in occupied Czechoslovakia. In Budapest and Belgrade, the German terror film *Drang nach Osten (Drive toward the East)* was dusted off and exhibited. Depicting the methods used in crushing Warsaw, this film also had been shown in Oslo just prior to the German occupation of Norway. Thus did Goebbels focus world attention on the Balkans.

Reports of German troops massing on the Hungarian frontier were true enough, but the whole thing was a clever bluff. At the Hungarian Foreign Office everyone appeared unduly calm. Why not? They were in the know, and to help out their German masters they even appointed air-raid wardens in Budapest and made pretense of arming the huge suspension bridges across the Danube with anti-aircraft guns.

One morning at about 4 a.m. I returned to my room at the "Duna Palota" hotel in Budapest after a spot of nightclubbing. The bed appeared to weave as I disrobed, and sleep was an attractive proposition. I couldn't have been asleep more than a few minutes before the telephone rang. I lifted the receiver, and when the operator said that "New York was on the line," I slammed it down again, angry that anyone should pull a gag at such an hour. It rang again and I was about to fire off a couple of adjectives when I found myself talking to a fellow whose voice I seemed to recognize.

"Hello, Hank, this is Peg Vaughn in New York. How are you doing?"

"Oh, fine, fine. And how are things with you?" I inquired, trying to wake up and sober up at the same time.

"Any trouble your way?"

"Only my head," I said, but I don't think he caught my meaning.

Vaughn, a veteran at this sort of thing, was being cagey over the transatlantic telephone, feeling that perhaps he might otherwise be cut off by a censor. The Associated Press had carried a scarehead story suggesting that the Germans were going to enter Hungary overnight, and my New York office had adopted what they considered the quickest method for obtaining confirmation or denial.

"They say the squareheads are moving your way," shouted Vaughn from New York.

I was holding the receiver in one hand and my head with the other, and still I didn't quite get the idea.

"No, no, there aren't any squareheads around here."

"You mean that we can deny the story?"

"Sure."

Whereupon Vaughn shouted "bulletin" and "boy" at the same time as he swung into action. I heard the clatter of a typewriter in New York as he dashed off my formal denial of the AP story from Budapest.

Peg's sudden flurry of excitement pulled me together and I began to think and talk coherently. I pointed out, as Vaughn fired questions at me over the telephone, that there was no immediate indication of a German move southwards, despite the deliberately spread German rumors and the dummy precautions taken by the authorities in Budapest. In fact, I suggested to New York that they had better look elsewhere.

"You mean that the squareheads are going to move in somewhere else?" shouted Peg.

"Well, I don't think they'll show up around here for some time."

"Thanks for the interview, Hank. It's a daisy. And by the way, where are you now? At the office?"

"No, I'm in bed."

"What? In bed? With the hottest stuff breaking," he shouted as he virtually tore the wires apart. "What time is it there, anyway?"

"It's five o'clock in the morning," I groaned.

"Oh, I'm sorry, Hank. Hate to bother you, but I guess that fixes things up. And by the way, how's the liquor thereabouts?"

I guess that I hadn't covered myself as well as I thought. The conversation, which must have cost United Press a lot of money, ended with a few trivialities and I returned to sleep.

My head and I got up later that morning, and the first thing we saw in the paper was that the Germans had invaded the Netherlands. It was May 10, 1940. I drew a cable of congratulations from New York for "accurate reporting."

The jitter warfare eased up a bit as the Allies unsuccessfully sought to hold the German panzers along the Belgian frontier. The Balkans were forgotten now, for the Netherlands folded up on May 14 and the Belgian army capitulated on May 28. The British Expeditionary Force (BEF) was retreating through Dunkirk and England had a new prime minister. A month later Paris was occupied and France surrendered to Germany. The only news of any interest in Budapest was the arrival of German "trade experts."

• • •

I had a permanent shadow in Budapest all this time, in the form of a Gestapo artist by the name of Kornhuber. He used to follow me everywhere, except to the toilet, and then usually he was hanging around the door when I came out.

He must have resented me because I was a permanent assignment for him, and I used to sit for long hours in the stalls of the famous cabarets *Arizona* and *Moulin Rouge,* guzzling champagne to the accompaniment of giggles from my blonde girlfriend, Zizi. The goings-on in France were a headache for me and I was straining at the leash, figuring that I had been hopelessly sidetracked. The champagne helped temporarily but in the morning it usually bounced and made me feel worse. Sometimes I would look out the corner of my eye to see whether my shadow was still there. He invariably was. I'd had about enough of Kornhuber, so one morning I had a showdown with him in the "Hungarian" bar.

The barman, being a Yugoslav and not at all particular to Hitler's boys, was at least moral support. The Gestapo agent, a pasty-faced, square-jawed yeg with cauliflower ears, was sprawling in a leather chair at the other end of the bar, directly opposite me. You'd have thought that he and I were married. I gulped three or four stiff ones and then ambled across to have words with him. My German, which Zizi had so painstakingly taught me, wasn't bad that morning.

"I'd like to introduce myself, Herr ____," said I, standing before my shadow.

He grunted and stood up, grudgingly shoving out his paw. "Kornhuber, es freut mich," he snarled.

We both sat down and I proceeded to give him the works.

"Now listen here, Kornhuber, I know you are Gestapo. We might just as well talk things over."

Whereupon I began to outline exactly how Germany was going to lose the war. Herr Kornhuber, primed by the whiskies readily dished out by my friend the Yugoslav bartender, became increasingly oratorical as he offered keen counterarguments in a high-pitched voice. Soon we were arguing so vehemently that our hands were flicking one another's noses. He fetched me a neat slap with his right and hurriedly excused himself. I handed it back in good measure and the bartender had to separate us. Before he cleared out, Kornhuber managed a snappy "Heil Hitler" salute.

The next afternoon there was a loud knocking at the door of my hotel room. I opened it and there before me stood Herr Kornhuber, grinning sheepishly. He must have been there before, for he walked straight to my desk, extracted a folded map of the world from my file of papers and, with his finger, proceeded to outline exactly what he and his pals proposed to do with Europe, Africa, and the Far East, as well as North and South America. He was having the last word before leaving town.

"I presume you feel the same way as you did downstairs this morning," he snapped. "I can see that you 'democraten' have thick skulls. I came here to say farewell, for I am returning to Germany. But I warn you that another will take my place."

With that, and another "Heil Hitler," he stalked out. I was to see more of Kornhuber's breed later in Romania and Bulgaria.

Once, in the Hotel Athenee Palace in Bucharest, just prior to the German occupation of Romania, I saw a crowd of "German golfers" trying their best to look the part, sitting upright in easy chairs in the lobby. When another "golfer" with close-cropped hair stomped in, these sportsmen bounced up in unison and gave the visiting golfer a snappy, heel-clicking "Heil." He turned out to be the general. Later, when I saw him in his dress uniform, he was indeed an imposing sight.

• • •

Italy entered the war on June 10, 1940, and shortly thereafter I was called hurriedly to Bucharest. The Russians had just invaded Bessarabia. Upwards of forty Russian divisions had broken through the Carol Line and were moving westwards to the banks of the Prut River. The Russian move then appeared to have the approval of the Wilhelmstrasse, for the German-Soviet pact was still in existence, but as I later learned from an official of the Hungarian Foreign Office, Moscow gave Berlin exactly twenty-four hours' notice. It was another Russian countermove of the first order.

Just as Stalin had hoodwinked Hitler by invading Finland, so had he now punched him in the gut in Bessarabia. It looked for a while as though the Russians would not stop at the Prut, and in Bucharest I heard the radio blare instructions to the public to be prepared for Russian parachute landings. By her invasion of Bessarabia, Soviet Russia had eliminated all hope of a Germano-Russian understanding and had upset German plans in the Balkans. Stalin, spurred into action by the sudden collapse of France and anticipating further German moves, had deliberately challenged the panzers of the Wehrmacht.

The Germans moved fast. They had to, and sooner than they had wished. Immediately they threw Romania to the wolves, keeping its promise to the aristocracy of Hungary. I witnessed the uprooting of entire Romanian communities in Transylvania. It was a tragic spectacle, with women and children riding in ox-carts astride their hastily collected belongings, jamming King Carol's highways in the trek to Bucharest. Aided by the "German minority" in Transylvania, the Gestapo deliberately provoked rioting. Their work was so effective that the stampede westward couldn't have been more effective had Goering's Messerschmitts been pumping bullets into the backs of the withdrawing civilians as they had done in France.

Simultaneously, Hitler gave the signal for a coup d'état by Antonescu's green-shirted Iron Guard in Bucharest. To prevent undue bloodshed, King Carol abdicated, and with the beautiful Lupescu, fled for his life. The Green Shirts unsuccessfully attempted to blow up the royal train at Timisoara. A Fascist government was now in power in Bucharest, but there still remained the Romanian army. To render it impotent and without defense works, Hitler gave Bulgaria the go-ahead and King Boris's German-trained troops advanced northward into the Dobruja.

If I had been bored in Budapest, I certainly got into hot water in Romania. I was in the thick of the rioting in Cluj, Transylvania, as the Hungarian army of occupation, accompanied by their German boyfriends, advanced westward. Had it not been for my French bulldog, "Captain Jinks of the Horse Marines," I might no longer have been of service to the U.P. Whenever a crowd got out of hand and the shooting started, I'd make my getaway by unfastening "Captain Jinks's" leash and running after him through the crowds as fast as my legs could carry me. At night after curfew, when the snipers were busy, I used to follow "Captain Jinks" at the end of a leash to the post office to telephone my dispatches. After all, who was going to shoot a guy out walking his dog?

• • •

Shortly after the Russian fait accompli in Bessarabia, when the excitement had subsided somewhat, I had occasion to speak to a German press attaché at a function in the Romanian Foreign Office.

"The Russians say they have massed forty armored divisions along the Prut River," said I. "What's Germany's attitude?"

The fellow's tongue, possibly loosened by drink, replied angrily and without hesitation:

"Yes, we know all about their forty divisions, and if they make another move, the Reichswehr and the Luftwaffe have the means to stop them."

I wrote a story thereafter suggesting that Russo-German relations were not of the best, and remember receiving a mild rebuke from London cautioning me against "undue speculation."

The Germans were in a real hurry now, for Russia was no longer to be trusted. Stalin's surprise move provoked urgent consultation at Berchtesgaden. The German army must move south to take up defensive positions along the Prut River and to prevent sabotage of the Allied-owned oil fields of Romania, which Germany so badly needed for operation of her war machine.

One day a German of military bearing came to my hotel and presented the visiting card of the United Press manager in Berlin, Frederick Oechsner, who had written that this fellow was a friend of his and that he would appreciate it if I "showed him around" in Bucharest.

I took the German out to lunch, and over wine and good food we became fairly friendly. He was not of the Nazi type. In exchange for news from Germany, I gave him a fill-in on what had been going on in the Balkans. It was only repetition of what I'd written day by day for the United Press, but to him it was entirely new, and shed a light on developments. He had been ordered to Bessarabia, he said, to help supervise the exchange of German nationals. When lunch was over, however, he stood up, bowed, and revealed his true identity.

"I am an officer of the German army, at your service," said he. "We don't get much news in Germany. I am deeply indebted to you for what you have so kindly told me."

I had not pulled any punches. German or no German, as a neutral I had given him to understand that I sincerely believed Germany would lose the war. But even then this officer was grateful. He was hungry for news.

The German occupation of Romania was not carried out overnight. They used the Hungarian reoccupation of that part of Transylvania that Hitler had ceded to her as a blind. Thousands of Germans moved into Transylvania along with the Hungarians, while King Carol struggled to hold his throne. During the week prior to the actual entry into Bucharest, however, German intentions began to come into the open. I got a tip from a friend, then Hungarian chargé d'affaires in Bucharest, that two trainloads of German troops had crossed into Romania through Timisoara. He said the Germans would be in Bucharest within three days.

Carefully checking the story, assisted by Frank Stevens, then local United Press correspondent in Bucharest, I held my fire. Stevens was an old-timer in Bucharest, with twenty years' residence. He knew everybody from King Carol himself and his Jewish paramour, Lupescu, down to the lowest clerk in the Foreign Office. Stevens knew that to break such a story might bring serious consequences, especially since he had land and property in Romania. But when through his own sources he was able to obtain confirmation that advance troops of the German army had actually entered Romania, we broke the yarn, scooping the world by twelve hours. I phoned the story to Zurich at four o'clock of a Sunday morning, bluffing the telephone supervisor at the International Telephone and Telegraph into believing that I was going to phone a personal message.

The next day there was hell to pay at the Bureau of Press and Propaganda, since all the other correspondents in Bucharest had received queries. In Berlin, Dana Schmidt, of the United Press, had telephoned the Romanian legation.

"Our Bucharest office reports that German troops have entered Romania," said Schmidt over the telephone to the Romanian chargé d'affaires in Berlin.

"That is true."

Schmidt at once wrote a bulletin confirming my story from Berlin. The Romanian chargé d'affaires in Berlin must have been severely rebuked by the Berlin Foreign Office for his indiscretion, because there were all manner of attempts thereafter at camouflage, with denials issued even in Bucharest. So well had the occupation been prepared that repeated efforts by correspondents to locate the German troops were unsuccessful. They had been strategically scattered throughout the country.

I had expected to be expelled from Romania for that story, and in fact so had Stevens, but since the actual occupation of Bucharest was imminent, the Germans didn't bother. The next day when I showed up at the Foreign Office I was told that I had made a mistake.

"You have said that German troops have entered Romania. That is wrong. General Antonescu has agreed with the German General Staff that a German military mission is required in Romania. The men who have arrived in Romania, are 'missionaries.'"

I went back to the hotel and wrote:

"Additional thousands of 'missionaries' have arrived from Germany. More are expected tomorrow, accompanied by large numbers of Gestapo 'missionaries.'"

This met with the approval of the Romanian press bureau.

The Iron Guard ran riot in Bucharest preparing the ground for entry of the German army. German-trained torturers, including a cripple who used to give the signal for such as the extraction of toenails and fingernails from his wheel chair, behind a screen, had a field day. British oilmen were kidnapped and Jews were hanged and shot by the score. Antonescu's Green Shirts felt themselves strong now, hence it was not surprising that one of them unceremoniously entered the office of the American manager of the International Telephone and Telegraph Company in Bucharest and, pounding on the desk, told him that he would have to nominate a new board of directors acceptable to the Iron Guard, within a few hours. He didn't even give the fellow time to consult his firm in New York.

In the midst of all this I returned to the Athenee Palace one afternoon to find an urgent call awaiting me from my Zurich office. When I finally contacted them by telephone I was advised that an Englishman had been kidnapped from my own hotel according to Reuters Agency.

"Fine reporter you are, Hank. Let's hope the day you're kidnapped we'll have the story first."

The story proved correct, and Reuters had obtained the scoop through the oil man's secretary, who managed to escape the Green Shirts and immediately rushed to the British Legation.

I gained the impression during the week prior to the German occupation that the Germans were genuinely afraid of the Russians. They were tight-rope walking; leaning over backward trying not to antagonize the Soviet Union. In this connection, the Germans used all manner of subterfuges to get their army to the new frontier with Russia. One method was the repatriation of German residents from Bessarabia. Their pact with the Soviets still holding good on paper, the Germans prevailed upon the Russians to allow them to withdraw their nationals from Bessarabia. The exchange would not have required any great organization to carry out, but the Germans sent hundreds of men to border towns such as Galatz on the grounds that they were needed to supervise the evacuation. Actually, these men were German troops in plain clothes.

Three days after I had reported their crossing of the frontier into Romania, the German army appeared in central Bucharest in full bloom, complete with staff cars.

So far, so good, as far as Germany was concerned. Romania was now under the Nazi heel, and Germany had a railroad right-of-way through Hungary and Romania direct to the new borders with Russia. In a pinch she could deal with her. But the picture was not complete. The Balkans must be completely dominated to eliminate a threat from the flank. Failing to achieve this, Hitler was in no position to reply to the shots Russia had fired in Bessarabia. So he gave Mussolini the signal in Greece. But again Axis plans misfired, for when Count Grazzi, the fellow who had ordered me out of Rome in 1936, and now Italian minister to Athens, served Italy's ultimatum on Greece on October 28, 1940, Metaxas gave his immortal reply:

"Come and take us, if you can."

Italy was supposed to throttle Greece within a few weeks. Thus, Yugoslavia would be isolated and the Germans would have time to bring the masses of Bulgaria, which were 50 percent pro-Russian, around to their way of thinking. It wouldn't be hard, especially if Germany offered to return Thrace to Bulgaria.

My work in Romania was done. The Germans were running the place now and little news other than that which they had personally okayed could leave the country.

Shortly after the outbreak of war between Italy and Greece, I was ordered to Bulgaria, where I was to see German "golfers" come in by the thousands. Then I joined the brave men of the army of Hellas in the mountains of Albania.

10

NADIA OF THE GESTAPO

I HAVEN'T BEEN ABLE TO MAKE UP MY MIND WHICH WAS THE toughest job for me during the Greco-Italian war: trying to keep up with the wiry little Evzons as they chased the Dagos over snow-capped Albanian mountain peaks in subzero temperatures, or matching wits with the Gestapo in Salonika.

I did both, the former in the line of duty as a war correspondent, and the latter out of no choice of my own. A woman was behind it all.

In mountain climbing, I did the best I could. It wasn't easy, what with the snow and ice, and sometimes ankle-deep mud, not to mention the opposition Mussolini's Alpini put up with their artillery, mortars, and machine guns. But I can truthfully say that I came out on top in my private war with the Gestapo in Greece.

Here's how it all happened:

While taking a "breather" in Sofia, Bulgaria, after the German occupation of Romania, I met a hostess in a nightclub whom, for the sake of convenience, we'll call Nadia. That is not her real name, but what's the use of telling you that, as maybe she's going to try to reform some day.

Nadia was clever, but too sentimental to be a good spy. She was what in the States you might call a cabaret stool pigeon. As an actress, she knew all the tricks, although when I first spied her she looked innocent enough. I saw in Nadia a little girl in the wrong joint—something like the victims of the White Slave traffic I'd known in Buenos Aires. She was a beautiful, homesick girl sitting with chin cupped in small tapered hands of white marble, alone at the bar, with lovely black tresses tucked behind dainty ears and full red lips puckered in faraway thought.

"Dance?" said I.

"Merci, monsieur," and she was off the bar stool in a jiffy, with a graceful flip of her shapely hips, showing herself off at her best. It wasn't any ordinary sort of evening frock she was wearing. It was velvet, but not the tight-fitting, flowing kind. It had a delicately embroidered, heart-shaped white lace collar with frills, such as our young ladies wear at finishing school.

As we danced a slow fox-trot, Nadia's deep blue eyes and winning smile made me forget the Germans in plain clothes who guzzled beer and exchanged crude jokes in the stalls around us. This girl's voice was throaty but musical, like Garbo's. She had the cutest little Adam's apple I have ever seen, and it enchanted me as it popped up and down. We talked of everything but the war, in French and in English. I returned the next night and the next.

We had a pretty good time together in those few weeks in Sofia preliminary to my transfer to Salonika, mingling with Hitler's "golfers" in cafés and cabarets. I got to know Nadia pretty well, but not well enough. A woman of moods, she could look and play the part of a sweet girl in her teens. Just as effectively could she change her role to that of a mature, God-fearing, and highly respectable woman of the upper middle class, on which occasions she looked angelic and sometimes even nunlike. But her most exciting and natural attitude was that of an exotic woman of the East, from the serpentine quiver of her hips to the mystic and devilish glint in her eyes, which now contracted and became a greenish blue, and cruel.

Nadia had worked hard for a living as an "artiste" since running away from her home in Budapest as a kid. She knew six languages other than her native Hungarian, including Arabic, Greek, and Persian. With her poise, beauty, build, and ability to dress, she'd have been a knock-out at anybody's party. The inner secrets of Baghdad, Teheran, Bombay, and Shanghai were an open book for her, for Nadia had traveled.

That she had become fond of me there was no doubt, for that night in the cabaret when I told her that I had been ordered to proceed to Salonika, her face went white. Then came a rush of tears as she staged an exhibition such as I have never seen in a nightclub. Smashing one champagne glass after another until her hands were bleeding, she then threw the contents of a couple of glasses in the faces of some potbellied Germans sitting in a booth nearby. They thought she was drunk, and brought the police in to throw the two of us out. But it was only an extremely strong-headed girl's reaction to my laughter when I rejected Nadia's plea that she be allowed to accompany me to Greece.

• • •

I started off the next day by automobile, with two English journalists, Cedric Salter of the London *Daily Mail* and Derick Patmore of the *News Chronicle*. Nadia, beautiful despite a sleepless night and wearing the black velvet gown with the school-girl collar in which I had first seen her, saw us off in tears. She proffered sandwiches she had prepared herself, and coffee in a Thermos. Last of all, she pressed into my hand a medallion she said she had bought at the church of St. Sofia after burning a candle at the altar on my behalf.

Things happened too fast thereafter for me to give much thought to the beautiful Nadia. Salonika was a shambles when I arrived on November 14, 1940. Italian bombers, guided to their targets by German agents, had wreaked havoc. The Germans enjoyed the status of diplomats, for they were all registered as attachés to the German Consulate General in Salonika. They were deadly but untouchable, and this was only the beginning.

Annoyed by the deliberate obstructionism of a Germanophile censor in Salonika by name of Cantoupoulos who sabotaged every item of news we tried to send from Macedonia, even refusing us the right to use the international telephone and cables, I made arrangements to proceed immediately to the front and file all of my dispatches via Athens. It was about the time that the Greeks, having hurled back the Italian motorized columns in the mountains of the Pindos, were counterattacking all along the line.

Advancing through snowdrifts that only pack mules and donkeys could negotiate, the bearded little Greeks stampeded the Roman Legions out of Koritsa and pressed on to Pogradetz, on the shores of Lake Okhrida. At about the same time, in the central front, they occupied the important town of Premeti, while on the shores of the Adriatic they took over the ancient town of Haghioi Saranda, or "Porto Edda," as Mussolini had renamed it after his daughter. Thus, the Greeks deprived the Italians of important lateral lines of communication on which they relied for their advance. The boomerang had turned on the Italians. It was the Greeks who now were on the offensive, and their slogan was "Into the sea with the Macaronades." I honestly believe that had the Germans not interfered, the Greeks would have carried out their threat. But sooner or later the Germans would act, for the Balkans were to become the right flank of their attack against the Soviet Union.

Fighting conditions in Albania were deplorable. Yellow mud, which had lain inches deep on the roads, oozing through the boots and cotton socks of the men of the army of Hellas, had frozen solid. The suffering was indescribable, but the Greeks continued their winter offensive.

Twice, I followed the Evzons into attack through slippery, snow- and ice-covered mountain trails in the region of Pogradetz. Each Greek soldier had only one blanket for protection against the alternating snow, rain, and sleet. They had been virtually foodless for several days, but still they pressed on, vaulting over the frozen corpses of men and mules, through an inferno of mortar and machine-gun fire, shouting their ancient war cry "Aria-Aria"—"Make way"—as the silvery notes of their bugles echoed through hills and valleys ordering "Prohorite"—"Attack."

The fighting was mostly hand-to-hand and four Italians fell for every Greek. It was bitter cold and even as the attack progressed, hundreds of Greek troops, their rugged faces distorted with the pain of frostbite, were stumbling afoot to hospitals far behind the line. There was no transport, for mules and donkeys were needed for hauling ammunition and food and none could be spared. Many were those who reached hospital unconscious, carried on the backs of comrades, whose own horribly swollen and bandaged feet left scarlet-red marks on the fresh fallen snow. They never walked again.

• • •

Returning to Salonika for provisions just before Christmas, I found several letters from Nadia, who had tried to follow me but had only got so far as Istanbul. She pleaded that I obtain permission for her to cross the frontier and join me in Greece.

Considering conditions at the front, I should have dismissed her pleas. Just prior to my departure for Salonika I'd barely escaped with my life from a five-hour artillery bombardment during which shells burst so close to us that my interpreter and I were covered with clods of mud. Yet I was then very susceptible to womanly charms. Therefore, pledging myself as security for Nadia's behavior, I prevailed upon the Greek minister for Public Security in Athens, Konstantinos Maniadakis, to wire the Greek Legation at Istanbul authority to issue a visa to Nadia. She arrived within a week, disheveled and high-strung. Four days without a break in a second-class train compartment is enough to get anybody down, so I attributed her peculiar behavior on arrival to exhaustion. I lavished attention on her, striving to please, but there was no getting away from it: she was not the Nadia I had known in Sofia. Everything I did was wrong, and the little love nest I'd built up in my mind's eye became a bed of thorns.

We spent Christmas together in a Salonika hotel, but it was only heated a couple of hours during the day because of a shortage of coal, and we were miserable. I thought perhaps a change of environment might improve Nadia's disposition, so I wore out my shoes looking for a cottage in which to install my little firebrand. I found the place I wanted, near the sea front. I furnished it, hired a cook and a maid, and tried to settle down.

I had planned to make a home of this little cottage by the sea, but as soon as Nadia and I moved in, so did the Gestapo. No, they didn't eat and sleep in the place, but their agents came and went with such regularity that you'd have thought it was their headquarters in Salonika. Vegetable vendors and hawkers of all descriptions came in droves to the back door, always demanding to see the lady of the house. I didn't catch on at first, but soon Nadia herself was to give me the lowdown.

The first element of mystery in connection with Nadia's arrival was a telegram from Hamburg delivered by a very tough-looking gent to our hotel. He refused to leave it with the manager, who didn't have our forwarding address, saying that he had been instructed to deliver it personally.

"The man said the telegram was from Miss Nadia's brother in Hamburg, and that it required personal reply," said the manager, reporting the incident to me. I smelled a rat, but didn't press the point with Nadia, who refused to comment on her "relations in Hamburg."

If the constant stream of vegetable salesmen pounding on the back door had annoyed me, so did Nadia's comings and goings in a taxi. She never seemed to be home, hence the cook and maid got out of hand and I found myself more often in the kitchen preparing the three times daily diet of bacon and eggs than at the office of Le Progress where I used to do my work. Nadia became jumpier than ever. She fired one cook and maid after the other and even got me to beat the carpets and empty the garbage cans. Sometimes I thought I had her in hand, but then Mussolini's bombers would put in an appearance and muck up the works again.

We got along like a couple of fighting cocks in opposite pens and one argument followed another. She'd just fired the third cook and was in an ugly mood, so when she disappeared again by taxi I hopped out and bought a couple of chickens, figuring that a little expertly cooked grub might do the trick. Had they been eaten at the proper time, when they were nice and brown and hot, the chickens might have been pretty good. As it was, trying to keep them warm I kept them in the oven far too long and they burned to a crisp.

The house was full of smoke when Nadia returned late that evening. "What are you trying to do, set the place on fire?"

I'll admit I'm no cook, but I'm just as temperamental as any cook could be, and there was a showdown then and there.

Even the most beautiful girls can look ugly when they're in a bad mood and Nadia certainly had a long nose that night. We had a terrific fight, during which she volunteered that while she had been very fond of me in Sofia, now she hated me. Point blank she announced that she was a German spy and that now that she was in Greece she intended to continue her work without interference. The matter of the telegram from Hamburg was suddenly cleared up, for Nadia told me it contained coded instructions from the Gestapo.

"I came here for a vacation, and I intended to do no work," said Nadia. "Are you a fool, or have you not noticed these people who come to the house every day asking for me? They also are of the Gestapo. So long as there was a chance of living happily with you, I refused to listen to their demands that I resume my work for Germany. But now I detest you and all your friends, and should you try to interfere with me, I shall denounce you as an accomplice in espionage!"

There was no question of returning to the front under these circumstances, with a stick of dynamite in my lap in Salonika, so I stuck around, sitting up nights trying to figure things out. Then started a game of wits between myself and the Gestapo. First of all, I warned Nadia that if she moved out of that house, other than to go to the corner grocery store, or attempted to do any work for her German friends, she would suffer the consequences.

She laughed, and charged off in a taxi, to return within an hour freshly primed by the German consul and his Gestapo pals.

"Go your way, you young fool, and I shall go mine. I am no longer going to sit in Salonika but intend to travel henceforth. Do you think you have the brains to outwit the German Secret Service? If so, try it!"

The next morning I fired my opening round. I had pledged myself to the Greek police as security for Nadia's behavior. Were I now to tell the police that I felt myself no longer responsible for her actions, she would be summarily deported. So I went to consult my friends of the Greek police.

To be fair to Nadia, I sincerely believe that she came to Greece seeking refuge from those for whom she had been working as a cabaret informant in Beirut, Baghdad, and Teheran. But there was no getting away from it now: she had become decidedly dangerous. The Gestapo had haunted and tormented her until her mind no longer was her own, and like one under a hypnotic spell, she responded to the beckoning of her former masters. Had she carried out her threat to denounce me as an accomplice in espionage, my career as a journalist would certainly have suffered.

It was in consideration of all this that I decided to coop up little Nadia in her bird cage overlooking Salonika Bay. In this I was aided by my friend the police chief of Salonika, a certain Major X. Had she been heart and soul a spy, I would not have hesitated to expose her as such. But since she was being victimized by Himmler's machine, I determined to give her a chance to think things over.

I gave the police chief a song and dance to the effect that Nadia was suffering mentally, and had on more than one occasion threatened suicide. The latter, by the way, was a fact. She had once swallowed a bottle full of some very suspicious-looking pills, saying that she meant to end it all as I no longer cared for her, and the German consul and his crowd of roughnecks were driving her crazy.

The police chief was most accommodating and put my mind at ease by posting a permanent police guard around our little cottage, presumably to prevent Nadia from carrying out her suicide threat. Now as I look back at the whole thing, I recall a wry smile on the face of my friend, Major X. I guess the Greeks also were aware that all was not right with my Nadia. They were no fools and must have noticed the comings and goings around that place, otherwise I doubt whether they would ever have posted a day-and-night shift of police around the Gorrell establishment in Salonika.

With Nadia where I wanted her, I hopped into the rattletrap Model "T" Ford that I was hiring by the month from an Albanian in Koritsa, and in company with my interpreter, Koutsakous, who had given me up as a man gone completely domestic since he had several times seen me beating rugs, headed for the central front at Premeti. King Zog's roads soon shook the cobwebs out of my brain as we bounced along to war in a flivver. Having shaken myself loose from my modern Matahari, I was in my element again, and the bitter cold of the Albanian mountains was a tonic to my domestically frayed nerves. There would be no more rug beating, and there was no need to worry now that Major X's policemen were keeping an eagle eye on Nadia.

• • •

The Greeks had destroyed one Italian division after another (they accounted for approximately twenty divisions out of Italy's total of seventy-five in the course of the Albanian campaign). When I rejoined them at Premeti in the central front, they were beginning their drive to bottle up the Italians at Kleisura, which would open the road to the famous Tepeleni Gorge. The region between the Greek frontier and Premeti was a series of mountain peaks overlooking great valleys. Italian defenses atop these snowbound mountains appeared impregnable, and yet the Greeks, carrying out sickle-shaped drives, somehow always managed to sneak up on the Italians from the rear. The situation was so bad for Mussolini's army in Albania that there were cases of Italian soldiers being tied to their machine guns to prevent retreat. The Italians were hard-pressed, fearful of defeat, and the Duce was flying reserves to Albania to hold the ground still left to his new "Impero Romano" in King Zog's old domain.

The Greeks, too, were suffering; nevertheless their will to win spurred them on. There was not enough food to go around and the fare consisted mainly of black bread, captured Italian macaroni, and Albanian cheese. The general and the colonel ate no better than the private, each considering himself lucky to have a wild rabbit to roast over open fires. But there was no holding back the Greeks, who were confident of victory. Between attacks they amused themselves by hurling captured Italian grenades and mortar shells back at the enemy, with such remarks as:

"Here's one for Benito—and two more for his little boys."

During the battle of Kleisura the Greeks took five thousand prisoners, and killed and wounded as many more. We were bombed to
blazes as we crouched in an abandoned Italian trench atop a high hill,
together with officers of the Greek General Staff. Italian planes came
over unmolested in formations of twenty, thirty, and even sixty at a
time, seeking to blast the Greeks out of the mountains. They failed.
When the battle was over there were hundreds of dead Italians in those
hills. I feel certain that if the Greeks had had proper aerial support they
would have rounded up not five thousand but twenty-five thousand
Italian prisoners that day.

• • •

I visited the front line at Argyrokastro and Himars, along the coast, and
after about three weeks returned to Salonika, to resume my argument
with Nadia and the Gestapo.

By this time she was behaving like a caged tigress.

"It's about time you came back, you idiot," was her greeting. "Why
did you stay away so long with the Greeks? Don't you realize that you
are wasting your time and that this war will end as soon as Hitler gives
the word?"

I didn't answer, and that made her furious.

"And as for these fools outside—these policemen—they will pay for
keeping me shut up in my own house. Haven't you seen them pacing the
pavement?"

No, I hadn't noticed them, and waved my hands in reply.

"They think they have me, but I'm too clever for them," said Nadia.
"Yes, it's about time you returned, because I want you to take me to
Athens. You will take me to Athens, won't you?" she added coyly.

OK, I'd take her to Athens, but only if she behaved herself. It was
necessary for me to go there anyway and I thought perhaps a change of
air might do her good.

On the trip down she was almost the Nadia I had known in Sofia.
She even promised that she would give up her friends of the Gestapo.
Arriving in Athens, however, I took no chances, and seldom let her out of
my sight. I bought her clothes and perfume and entertained her royally.
But one afternoon she managed to give me the slip.

I was working in my room in the King George Hotel when there was
a telephone call. It was the manager, who said the police wanted to
see me in the lobby. I rushed downstairs. Nadia was in the center of a
crowd, screaming and kicking and talking incoherently in a mixture of
Hungarian and Greek. The gist of her rant was that if the police didn't

let her alone, she would gouge their eyes out. Nadia had not forgotten the policemen who had maintained a constant watch on our cottage in Salonika, so when two policemen approached her in the lobby of the King George, she thought the game was up. They had her passport, which she had told me had been illegally issued in Hungary. The mass of visa stamps on it—a consequence of her far-flung traveling—were sufficient to arouse anyone's suspicions. I noted that only one page for visa stamps remained in the passport; the others having been filled.

I vouched for Nadia to the Athens police and apologized to them for her threats to gouge out their eyes. We had a drink in the bar and the incident was closed. But this affair in the lobby ruined the trip to Athens. We took the next military train back to Salonika.

I was really fed up now, and told Nadia she would have to clear out of Greece, for henceforth I would refuse to be guarantee for her conduct. Predictably, she flew into a rage and threatened to kill herself. In reply I think I invited her to go to Hell and stay there.

Next thing I knew she'd made an effort to throw herself out of the train while it was traveling, at high speed, and was barely prevented from doing so by a group of highly excitable Greek soldiers who nearly laid me out in anger, for she knew sufficient Greek to complain that I had been ill-treating her.

We all but threw pots and pans at one another on returning to our little domestic flea bite in Salonika. Things certainly were getting hot. The following afternoon she flew into another tantrum and said that first she would do away with me and then with herself. To make good this threat she produced a sharp butcher knife and tried to stab me. I took the knife away from her and she countered by swallowing another whole bottle of pills.

My Albanian chauffeur was sitting outside in the flivver, awaiting instructions, for I had been planning to return to the front. I sent him out for a doctor and he returned in about half an hour with two fellows. The elder of these said he was the doctor and introduced the other man as his son. To me these gents looked like undertakers, but since one of them carried a small satchel, I didn't dispute his claim to be of the medical profession.

"Just sit here with my son," said the phony doc in his broken English, "while I go in and have a look at your wife. You see, she mustn't be further excited."

I agreed, and sat it out for half an hour with the doctor's "son" who stared the whole time at the floor, exchanging not a word.

Ultimately the fellow with the satchel came out and said he had administered a hypodermic "which will keep her quiet." He assured me that his services would no longer be required and the two of them walked out, bowing stiffly as I opened the front door.

Nadia slept the whole night. The next morning she revealed the true identity of the "doctor" and his "son."

"You can't get away from them, Henry. Those men also were of the Gestapo. You might as well let me continue my work here. In fact, they told me that if you further interfered, there might easily be a murder in Salonika."

I pretended that I'd reached the end of my rope and that I was now resigned to allowing her freedom of action. I was so nice to her in fact that she agreed to let me go to Athens, on my promise that she could join me there within a few days. This time, I was determined to see the thing through. When it came to threats of murder, the situation was coming to a pretty pass. It was now a matter of self-preservation, and I went in for a bit of dirty work myself.

Nadia became mildly suspicious prior to my departure for Athens when I asked her to give me her passport and then went to the Turkish authorities and got them to put their visa on it. She flew into another rage.

"Don't you know that I have only got one page left for visas in my passport, and that this means I shall either have to marry a German to get another passport, or return to Budapest, where they will put me in jail for traveling under falsified documents? And who said anything about going to Turkey?"

My plan was to get her to leave Greece voluntarily and follow me to Istanbul on a ruse. I sent a letter addressed to Nadia in Salonika within a covering envelope to a friend in Istanbul with instructions that he post the enclosure to my little Matahari. The idea was that in this letter I would advise her that I had been suddenly transferred to Turkey, and request that she join me.

I went to Athens, and awaited results for several days. One evening I got a telephone call from Salonika. It was Nadia. She had been tipped off by the Gestapo that I was in Athens and not Istanbul, and had caught me red-handed. She wasn't budging from Greece.

So I played my trump card. I went to Metaxas's right-hand man, Konstantinos Maniadakis, then chief of police in Athens. It was Maniadakis who had signed the papers whereby Nadia had been allowed to enter Greece from Turkey. He liked my work at the front and despite his outward callousness, was an understanding fellow. He listened attentively to my little speech, which was more or less a repetition of the line I'd adopted with the police chief in Salonika concerning Nadia: namely, she was mentally ill and that her repeated threats to do away with herself were making life miserable for me and preventing me from doing my best work in Greece. I left the Gestapo out of it.

Between us (and the Greeks love a bit of intrigue here and there) Maniadakis and I cooked up a scheme whereby Nadia would be advised that I had been expelled from Greece as a result of a cabaret row and deported to Turkey. This information having been conveyed to her through police channels to avoid the scrutiny of the Gestapo in Athens, I checked out of the King George Hotel and installed myself incognito in a second-rate hotel, again awaiting results. To let the Gestapo know that I was in Athens would not do, for then they would again tip off Nadia in Salonika, and she would merely laugh at suggestions that I had been kicked out of Greece. After all, the Gestapo men might still have a few tricks up their sleeves.

Nadia hung on for nearly a week in Salonika, as her friends of the Gestapo combed Athens unsuccessfully looking for me. So long as they could establish that I was still in Greece, Nadia might not be kicked out. That is, unless I withdrew my guarantee for her behavior, which might easily have meant a bullet in the back in a dark alley some night.

I have never been so relieved as on that day when Maniadakes informed me that Nadia had crossed the Turkish frontier and that simultaneously he had issued an order to all Greek frontier posts preventing her reentry.

I sent money to Istanbul so that Nadia would have the wherewithal to start anew. Perhaps somehow she has since managed to escape the clutches of the Gestapo, but I doubt it.

Nadia's soul belongs to the Gestapo. She sold it to them on the day that she accepted their first payment for services rendered, in a Baghdad cabaret.

Despite the mental tortures to which she subjected me, I sincerely hope that one day after the war when the Gestapo is no more, this beautiful girl—and others like her—will be allowed to live a life free of plots and intrigue.

11

LIEUTENANT BILL BELLE

I MADE AMENDS FOR BRINGING NADIA OF THE GESTAPO INTO Greece. During the evacuation of the BEF from Nauplion, four months after escaping Nadia's web, I facilitated the escape of a woman agent of the British Intelligence Service.

For purposes of camouflage we'll call her Diana. She was Greek, golden-haired, and even more beautiful than Nadia had been.

Garbed in battle dress, with two pips on each shoulder and what remained of her golden tresses tucked under a steel helmet, Diana— or "Lieutenant Bill Belle" as we named her for the occasion—was the only woman to be evacuated with the Press Corps from the shores of Nauplion.

Her story:

As I carried my private war with the Gestapo to a successful conclusion, a crisis was rapidly developing in the Balkans.

The battle in Albania had reached a deadlock as the Greeks failed in a determined effort to take the mountain stronghold of Tepeleni. Casualties on both sides had been heavy, and Greek hospitals were filled to capacity.

Italy had a much greater reserve of manpower than little Hellas, and Mussolini, the honor of his country at stake, flew heavy reinforcements into Albania preparatory to General Ugo Cavallero's "grand offensive" in early February to crush Greek resistance once and for all.

Metaxas was dead now,[1] but his spirit lived in the hearts of the rugged Greek troops who made mincemeat out of such crack Italian divisions as the "Wolves of Tuscany" as they attacked en masse, wave after wave, only to fall in heaps before the Greek defenses.

Cavallero's offensive failed after ten days, with thousands of casualties the only measurable result. But it had weakened the Greek army at a most dangerous time, for now it was clear that Germany would intervene.

---

1. Ioannis Metaxas died in Athens on January 29, 1941. He was succeeded by Alexandros Korizis.

Although only half that number were required to do the job, Hitler sent upwards of twenty German divisions into Bulgaria. Yugoslav statesmen were summoned to Hitler's presence at Berchtesgaden, as the British Imperial General Staff in Athens sought to convince the Greeks that they should now accept substantial assistance. During this period of extreme tension, I was ordered back to Salonika with instructions to "sit on the coffee pot" until it boiled over.

When I got there, the curtain had already gone up on the first act of the German invasion of Greece, for Bulgarian and German aeroplanes were constantly flying over Thrace, never to be fired at by the Greek ack-ack. The Greeks, to the very end, clung to their theory that so long as they fought the Italians fair and square in Albania, Hitler would not stab them in the back.

Not being permitted to leave Salonika by the Greek military authorities, who argued that the mere presence of a foreign journalist in border communities was sufficient to provoke the Germans, I placed my own spies in the important Macedonian tobacco centers of Xanthi and Cavala. Each day they reported to me deliberate violations of neutrality by the Bulgarians and Germans, whose warplanes flew so low over Macedonian towns that one could easily discern the Swastika. This was deliberate terrorism, calculated to stampede the civilian population of Thrace and Macedonia, thereby clogging roads and centers of communication preparatory to the German invasion. It was the old formula that had been successfully used in France, Norway, Belgium, and Romania. Refugees were streaming into Salonika and south to Athens by the thousands, using everything from trains and trucks to horse- and donkey-drawn wagons. Such was the congestion in Salonika when British General Archibald Wavell and the Greek General Staff were plotting the defense of the country that hundreds of refugees had to be forcibly ejected.

We in Salonika knew that Macedonia and Thrace were to be sacrificed, as were the brave Greek garrisons that undertook to defend to the last the famous Rupel Fortress and Gap leading from the hills of Bulgaria. It was suicide to try to hold the Macedonian Plains against twenty-odd German divisions, hence the Allied line was formed from Mount Olympus overlooking the plains of Thessaly and Larissa, stretching northwestward through Serbia and Veria Passes to the shores of Lake Okhrida on the Yugoslav frontier. New Zealanders had been given the coastal pass sector defending the Valley of Tempe, while Serbia and Veria were covered by an Australian division and two Greek divisions under command of General Henry Maitland "Jumbo" Wilson. West of Serbia other Greek divisions took up the line to Lakes Okhrida and Prespa where the Italian line in Albania began.

In Salonika I made a pact with the assistant British naval attaché, somewhat to this effect:

There were substantial supplies of petrol, arms, and ammunition in Salonika. Someone had to dispose of them, for why should they be left to the Germans? The officer in question had sealed orders which he was to carry out in the event of a German occupation. He knew not their contents, but one could easily guess. In fact, he faced a highly dangerous assignment: blowing up the petrol storage tanks in Salonika right under the noses of the German army. The naval officer and I bought ourselves .45 caliber automatic pistols on the black market, and I hired a dinghy at the outrageous rate of one thousand drachmas a day with instructions that it stand by against an emergency. In addition, there was my tumble-down Model T Ford with a Koritsa license, which had taken me hundreds of miles over the Albanian front. My friend the lieutenant and I agreed that we might have to shoot our way out after blowing up the works, pushing that puddle-jumper for all it was worth in an attempt to make a getaway. For him, it was duty; for me, a major story.

But the last-minute arrival of approximately 150 Royal Engineers in a very trim yacht relieved the naval officer of his responsibility, and soon I received urgent orders from General Headquarters in Athens to return immediately. I guess they wanted no nosy newspapermen around as witnesses to an unavoidable catastrophe.

The game was up, and it was now only a question of days before German panzers would take over, but Greek military authorities, leaning over backwards not to offend the Germans, still denied the British the right to have any uniformed troops in Macedonia.

Thus, they refused the Royal Engineers in Salonika Bay permission to come ashore unless they were agreeable to wearing such as golf knickers and ill-fitting tweed coats that had been purchased hurriedly for them in the stores of Salonika.

In a way, the Engineers looked even funnier to me than had the German "golfers" in Bulgaria and Romania, for at least the Germans' costumes fitted them, whereas those loaned to the indignant and tough R.E.s did not. The pained expressions on their faces as they sat in the cafés of Salonika, trying their best not to split their pants, were quite sufficient to give away their identity.

Complying with orders from G.H.Q., I took one of the last trains out of Salonika. It was on this train that I saw the futility of a British attempt to try to save Greece in the form of several burly Germans, comfortably seated in a compartment marked "Reserved," who, notebooks in hand, were checking off British military equipment as it rolled northward to Volos, Larissa, Serbia, and Veria along the Athens-Salonika railroad line.

These German pigs had been riding up and down that line for days, even facilitated by the apologetic Greeks, who were so sure that Germany would not hit a little fellow as long as he behaved.

In Athens at Piraeus Harbor I saw more evidence of German cock-sureness. British Imperial forces were arriving from the desert, and as equipment of war, including artillery, light tanks, and Bren carriers were unloaded, Germans in plain clothes checked them off in notebooks, unmolested by the Greek police. To the Germans it was a matter of simple arithmetic: "They have so many tanks, so many guns. We need only double or treble that number, and we have them."

The Australians and New Zealanders sent to Greece from the Western Desert were seasoned fighting men, and willing, but as one man put it to me, "You can't bark against thunder." They faced insurmountable odds, in numbers and equipment. In the air, the Royal Air Force was hopelessly outclassed by the Luftwaffe.

The German minister, whose wife had even made pretense at solidarity with the Greeks by knitting socks for their troops in Albania, daily informed Berlin of all that occurred in Athens. As an example of German audacity, the German military attaché in Athens, dressed in plain clothes, made so bold one day as to motor to an Australian transit camp on the outskirts of Athens and, casually passing cigarettes around, engage a substantial group of Diggers in conversation. He got away with it, for his identity was revealed only after he had gone by a Greek passerby, who asked the astonished Aussies if they had known to whom they were talking.

• • •

Germany attacked the Rupel forts on April 6, 1941, and the brave Greek defenders held their ground for days under vicious dive-bombing and parachute attacks. In so doing, they gave their comrades in the Passes to the southwest time to hurriedly organize the defense of Greece proper. It would soon be over, for the Germans had rapidly overpowered Yugoslavia and were pouring through Skopje down Monastir Gap to strike at the center of the Allied line, while other panzer units joined the Italians on the shores of Lake Okhrida.

Firing point-blank with their 25-pounders and mediums into columns of Germans advancing four abreast, the British mowed down hundreds of the enemy, but still the Germans advanced, the living walking over the bodies of the dead. An Australian brigadier told me later that he had never dreamed such slaughter could be inflicted and that still the Germans would press on.

"True to the traditions of Waterloo," said the brigadier, "we gave them rapid fire at three thousand yards. I saw German infantry regiments completely disintegrated, but still they came on. Our boys were tired of killing and the sight of blood. They fired until their ammunition ran out, or their overheated guns jammed, but there was no stopping the Hun, who knew he had us because of our lack of adequate aerial support."

Most of the British casualties during the retreat to the final Allied line at Thermopylae were from Stuka raids.

An artillery sergeant told me:

"We were supporting the Australians at Serbia and fired our 25s until they were red hot, mowing down Germans by the score as they attempted to throw pontoons across the river. But then we were outflanked and ordered to withdraw to Thermopylae. We retreated in leap-frog order, fighting a rearguard action as we retired. We had only ten casualties in our company, all of them from dive bombing, and it broke our hearts when we received orders to blow up the guns. Would you believe it, I saw our sergeant kiss the No. 1 gun before he wrecked it!"

The tired Greeks, who were holding the left flank, began to give way and it became necessary for the BEF to withdraw simultaneously or be hopelessly cut off. Fifth Columnists holding key posts in the Greek General Staff now showed their colors by deliberately distorting orders to the commanders in the field, with the result that entire regiments of Greeks began streaming back, in some cases even without rifles. The Germans had their agents scattered throughout the battle area and used all manner of devices to provoke panic in the line. An Australian officer told me that a man dressed in Greek uniform approached him with information that the Germans were just over the opposite hill. "I drove for miles in the direction along which he had pointed, and found no sign of the enemy," said the officer. "Sheep herders" were arrested by the score. Invariably they were equipped with mirrors for heliograph signaling.

Athens in the meantime was seething with rumors as the German-organized infiltrators did their work. With a carefully prepared program, involving liberal use of the telephone to spread scare stories, these Fifth Columnists systematically whittled down morale in the rearguard, precipitating a Cabinet crisis. After one stormy Cabinet meeting, at which the king himself appeared to demand an explanation regarding Fifth Column activity, Prime Minister Alexandros Korizis returned to his home and shot himself through the head while sitting in the bathtub. Thus, at a period of extreme crisis, with the Germans only a few miles north of Athens, the Greeks were once more without a leader.

• • •

Several days before Larissa fell, the rumors spread throughout Athens that German troops were on the outskirts of the city. Entire military hospitals were suddenly emptied on the basis of such fabricated reports. I saw many Greek amputees, still wearing pajamas, desperately hobbling on crutches through the streets of Athens. Many wore the Greek War Cross on their lapels.

I saw one man who had been prematurely released from hospital throw his crutches at the gates of Greek G.H.Q., and then fall prostrate on the sidewalk to be picked up and carried away by two other wounded comrades.

• • •

One day King Peter of Yugoslavia and his staff suddenly appeared in Athens, checking in at the King George Hotel. Yugoslavia had collapsed and they had fled for their lives. Such was the efficiency of the German agents in Greece, however, that not five minutes after the royal plane had landed at an emergency aerodrome near Athens, the place was bombed by the Luftwaffe and the plane destroyed.

An RAF pilot told me that with his squadron of Gladiators he had flown several hours from one aerodrome to another, only to be bombed shortly after landing at each one.

"There was no getting away from them," he said. "There were German agents all around and they made free use of mirrors and bonfires to convey their messages to the German army and air force."

When the Greek Army of the Epyrus broke before determined German attacks, the debacle was complete. The Allied left flank had collapsed, and King George and the government fled to Crete. The panic was on.

Richard McMillan of the United Press, who had been with the BEF in the field, returned from Thermopylae and told me that the retreat to the sea was a matter of hours.

German planes were then diving only a few hundred feet over the tops of Athens buildings, in disdain of ack-ack batteries and of the RAF, which, with the exception of a few Hurricanes and Gladiators that had survived the Blitz, no longer existed. Piraeus Harbor was a shambles, having been largely demolished when a German bomb hit a munitions ship. German planes were soaring lazily over the harbor, laying mines to bottle up the BEF. They no longer bothered to bomb the city itself, for Athens would be theirs shortly and further destruction was unnecessary.

• • •

I had known Diana only casually. She used to hang out at Maxim's café in central Athens, and there was much competition for her favors. McMillan knew her better than I.

"I'm going to try to get her out of Greece, Hank," said Mac, "for if she remains here she will be shot by the Germans as a spy. You see, she has been working for us."

It was only a passing remark, and I had too much work on my hands at the moment to think any more about it, for I was virtually alone in the United Press office. Our Greek tipsters had long ago panicked and abandoned the fort.

On that last morning in Athens, my portable typewriter on my knees, I banged out one bulletin after another in the lobby of the King George. Diana and Mac made their appearance.

"It's the old red-tape again, Hank," said Mac. "I've seen all the big shots in the army but they say they can do nothing for Diana. Perhaps between the two of us we can swing something. In the meantime, how about Diana sitting in the lobby with you until the order comes for us to leave Athens? Couldn't you use her as your messenger boy?"

I could, because my legs were just about worn out. Diana rushed to her home, changed into blue silk coveralls, and returned to the King George prepared for duty. I worked all that afternoon and she ran as fast as her dainty little legs could carry her back and forth to the post office with my dispatches to the United Press, chronicling the dying hours of Greece. Frequently, she brought me sandwiches and coffee to keep me going, for I had been without sleep for two nights. Filing my last dispatch, with reference to the flight of the royal family and members of the Greek Cabinet, Diana and I made our way to the Anglo-American club where the war correspondents were awaiting transportation south with the British army.

Diana had never once spoken a word on her behalf, but the look in her violet eyes was sufficient. They resembled those of a little puppy, trusting in and at the same time pleading with its master. With her wan smile and crumpled golden curls, she looked truly angelic. I was determined that Diana should not be left behind.

The British public relations major, a military man of the old school with a black patch over a blinded eye, who had once been police chief in Baghdad, didn't think he could do much for Diana, but agreed to accompany us to the office of British Military Intelligence in Athens where it might be possible to obtain authority from higher up. This failed, for the intelligence records had been burned, and there was no one to testify as to Diana's identity.

I wasn't altogether dependent on the British army. I had a Ford Coupe with red plush leather seats and whitewall tires that I had bought a few days previously from an American tobacco man in Thrace, so I decided to make it to the Peloponnesus with Diana, there to try to obtain transport by fishing boat to one of the Greek Islands. Diana and I were unloading my kit from one of the P.R. trucks that was being held in readiness for the retreat when McMillan held a hurried consultation with one of the conducting officers who had fought for the International Brigade during the Spanish Civil War.

"Listen, Hank, don't be a damned fool. The old major isn't such a bad sort, and it's possible he'll close his other eye at the last minute and help us to get Diana out of this. Hang with the convoy in your Ford and follow us to Nauplion. The conducting officer and I will do the rest."

As the advance column of the British army left Athens, Greek men and women rushed to the trucks. With tears streaming down their cheeks, they kissed the battle-worn troops.

"Long live Britain and Greece," they shouted. "We'll be waiting for you when you come back."

• • •

In my deluxe Ford (which would later become the property of a German general), Diana and I drove all that night, following the miles-long column of British army lorries laden with troops heading to the shores of the Peloponnesus. We were not permitted to use lights, for that might attract the Luftwaffe, and frequently vehicles ahead of us plunged headlong into twenty-foot bomb craters. Once the unlucky vehicle had been freed, the crater had to be filled up by groups of men with picks and shovels in order for the rest of the column to pass. As we crawled along at three and five miles per hour, Greek soldiers in pajamas hobbled south on crutches, trying to escape the advancing Germans. Sometimes, the column stopped to allow trainloads of British wounded to pass. Most of these men would in the end be left behind.

It was a race to get across the Corinth Canal before German parachutists were able to blow up the bridge. We made it, arriving in Nauplion at dawn the next day, although the road was strewn with time bombs that were going off almost faster than the sappers could deal with them.

At one point our section of the column was diverted to a wheat field, alongside an olive grove. We dispersed our vehicles and waited for the Luftwaffe to attack. No soldier could have behaved better than Diana, as we lay in that field under a scorching sun with practically no protection while formations of nine and twelve Messerschmitts at a time swooped down and machine-gunned us checkerboard fashion. There was no guarantee that we would ever get out of the place, and we wore ourselves out, digging slit trenches in between raids. Diana also pitched in, working until her little hands were raw and blistered. Occasionally, we took turns sleeping while our comrades stood by as lookouts. As I stretched out on my valise under an olive tree, Diana suddenly shook me roughly. Her warning had been just in time, for in what seemed like a split second, explosive bullets were crackling about us like hailstones. A Greek peasant was nearby, hugging his knees and writhing on the ground screaming bloody murder. We joined two New Zealanders in a shallow ditch and repeatedly switched from one side to the other as the Germans criss-crossed over us, spitting death. Diana never complained, and her smile was never lacking through this ordeal. The last raid had been so bad that a New Zealander shook me by the hand as we emerged from the ditch, saying, "I guess we'll make it all right. It can't again be much worse than this."

As the order came to demolish our vehicles, Diana among others reported to the major for duty. Apparently, he had closed his good eye, for he pretended not to see her. By now she had cut off her golden hair with fingernail scissors and donned a steel helmet and battle dress, loaned to me by a corporal in exchange for the .45 automatic pistol I'd bought in Salonika. On each epaulet she had two pips that I had scrounged from officers in nearby units so that I could pass her off as a first lieutenant of the British army. So effectively did she aid in demolishing the P.R. trucks, even volunteering to take pot shots at the tires with a rifle, that we dubbed her "Lieutenant Bill Belle" then and there.

• • •

We were told that the navy was on the job and would take us off at nightfall. We made a big meal of our remaining provisions, sitting under the olive trees. The major then lined us up for final instructions:

"Gentlemen—and, er," spotting Diana in the line, firmly gripping a typewriter, "—er, ladies. I am instructed to advise you that in the event of an air raid we are not halting. You will walk three abreast. Anyone who steps from the ranks to seek cover from aircraft will be left behind. If any of you are wounded, we shall do our best to see you aboard the transport. The dead, naturally, will be left behind."

We started off singing "Tipperary" and "Keep the Home Fires Burning," and one of the boys struck up the "Star Spangled Banner" as we joined ten thousand British troops marching in endless file through a lane of bomb-torn sycamores, flanked by fields of scarlet poppies. The column reached Nauplion Bay without incident. Miraculously, the Luftwaffe did not interfere, even though Fifth Columnists were reported lighting bonfires in the surrounding hills seeking to attract the enemy, and a munitions ship was burning in the harbor. The ship cast a red glow over the beaches, silhouetting the faces of thousands of troops. Watching the fleet and the transports that were to take us off the beach exchanging

Morse signals in the night was an unsettling sensation, for had Goering's bombers swooped in, there would have been wholesale slaughter on shore, and the ships would have been sunk in the bay.

Three transports, *Glenearn, Glengyle,* and *Ulster Prince,* were waiting offshore. For hours we remained on the quay, for the *Ulster Prince* had grounded herself on a sand bank and there were frantic efforts to get her unstuck. She remained there and was bombed and destroyed the next day.

More than eleven thousand men were evacuated that night by the fleet. Some of the evacuees were crammed aboard the cruisers and destroyers, which were full to overflowing, making up the space lost when the *Ulster Prince* was abandoned. The seas were rough and several lighters capsized as the troops boarded the waiting transports, drowning many within mere yards of safety. But little "Lieutenant Belle" set her pretty jaw and put up perhaps the bravest show of all.

It was now our turn to board the *Glenearn,* and the war correspondents, with Diana in the middle, moved up to take their places in the waiting lighter. She had followed my instructions to the letter, keeping her mouth shut throughout the march to the beach; her soprano voice might have led to questions. They loaded about fifty of us into a lighter, including about a score of Australians. I watched Diana closely, and when the order was given to "straddle the benches"—we were to sit front-to-back to make more room—she became confused. I grabbed one of her legs and tossed it over the bench.

Bucking a rough sea, we made it to the side of the *Glenearn.* This was the most difficult period of all, for I felt that in the scramble for the transport's rope ladder, little Diana might be shouldered overboard. But the corporal who had loaned me his extra battle dress for Diana was there. We waited until all the Australians had cleared out of the lighter (in fact, every time Diana had made a move to get up, I'd shoved her down again), and then the corporal and I saw her safely aboard.

On such desperate occasions the British navy has never been found wanting. Although we were packed in the transport like sardines, no sooner had we arrived on board than tea and ship's biscuits with cheese were ready for one and all.

Diana now became a proper "Madame X." She was wearing dark glasses and looked like a little drummer boy in her oversized khaki rig. She dared not enter the officers' saloon for tea, and instead huddled on a pile of kit in the passageway as troops and sailors passed back and forth. McMillan and I remained on guard and on several occasions we were asked, "What's the matter with the kid?" No need to answer. But when the ship's Third Officer came up and asked me "if the kid is sick," I decided to spill the beans.

"This is no kid, sir. This is a lady. She is of the British Intelligence Service in Athens and favorably known to military authorities. Could you help her?"

He gallantly gave her his cabin for the night while the rest of us slept on the floor under tables in the mess. Next day one of the ship's officers, Lieutenant Commander Best, R.N.V.R., took Lieutenant Belle out of hiding and she became the toast of the transport.

After enduring hours of dive-bombing we reached Crete, where I parted with Diana. She marched ashore very much in step, with her steel helmet cocked over one ear and still smiling, although now very pale.

The one-eyed major with the patch approached me as we were being billeted in Crete.

"Everything in order, Gorrell?"

I saluted in the best guard's manner and reported in the affirmative.

"And Lieutenant Belle?"

"She's safely ashore, sir."

Mopping his brow with relief, the old major told me that he could no longer keep his remaining eye closed. I understood the risk he had taken: he might easily have been court-martialed for permitting a woman without sufficient documentation to board a British transport.

Perhaps had he known that Crete was to be invaded during the next few days it might have been different, but we both felt that Diana was quite safe now. And, as it turned out, she was safe. I saw her in Cairo on my return from Syria a few months later. Her golden curls had been restored and she gave me the biggest kiss of my life when we met by accident in the Hotel Continental.

For Diana, life especially in the past two years had been cruel. Recently widowed, she had lost her RAF fiancé in Greece, killed in action. Her father, mother, and baby boy were presumably wiped out during the German blitz of London. But "Lieutenant Bill Belle" was, as of this writing, still working for the Allied cause somewhere in the Middle East.

12

HITLER: "CARRY OUT PLAN NUMBER FOUR!"

W E WENT THROUGH HELL AT NAUPLION, WHICH WILL rank as a second Dunkirk, but it was even worse between Crete and the North African coast.

On the shores of the Peloponnesus, we had been mercilessly machine-gunned by German fighters while huddling in olive groves, awaiting evacuation by the British Fleet. But from Crete to Alexandria, we were dive-bombed by Stukas day and night, and repeatedly attacked by torpedo bombers while the German and Italian submarines played hide-and-seek with our zig-zagging escort of cruisers and destroyers.

As the enemy hurled bombs and torpedoes at our convoy, I lay helpless in a bunk on H.M. Transport *Corynthia*, constantly attended by an Australian army nurse who was wearing a life belt. The ordeals of the retreat had been too much for me, and I now had a temperature of 103 degrees and was unable to move without extreme pain. An officer of the Australian Army Medical Corps cleared out several cabins on each side of mine because he thought the symptoms indicated spinal meningitis. Imagine his surprise the next morning when I asked for an aspirin and then bounced up, dressed, and without permission went up on deck for a stroll. I had merely suffered a severe attack of the chronic malaria that I had picked up in Macedonia.

I shall never forget those splendid Australian nurses who, at the last minute, had to be forced to board the waiting troop transports at Nauplion because they refused to leave their wounded. They yielded only on assurance that a majority of the surgeons, whom I had seen operating on urgent cases with razor blades by the light of shielded flashlights, would remain behind to await the Germans.

At the height of the dive bombing, and as the *Corynthia* trembled from the concussion of depth charges dropped by British destroyers to ward off submarine attack, I remember suggesting to my nurse that if we were badly hit, she should forget about me and make her way to the lifeboats. Her answer was sharp:

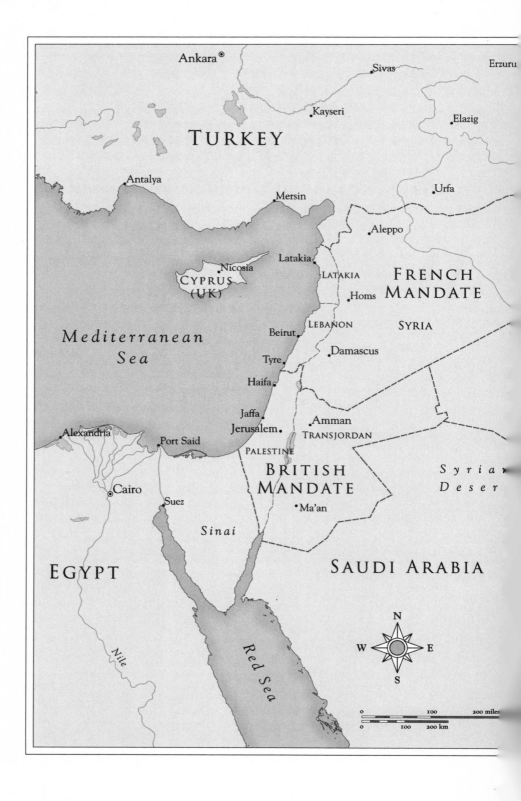

Ankara ⊙

Sivas •

Erzuru

• Kayseri

• Elazig

TURKEY

Antalya •

• Urfa

Mersin •

• Aleppo

Latakia •

LATAKIA

FRENCH
MANDATE

Nicosia •

CYPRUS
(UK)

• Homs

LEBANON

SYRIA

Mediterranean
Sea

Beirut •

Tyre •

• Damascus

Haifa •

Jaffa •

Jerusalem •

• Amman

TRANSJORDAN

Alexandria •

Port Said •

PALESTINE

S y r i a
D e s e r

Cairo ⊙

Suez •

BRITISH
MANDATE

Ma'an •

Sinai

EGYPT

SAUDI ARABIA

Nile

Red Sea

N
W   E
S

0   100   200 miles
0   100   200 km

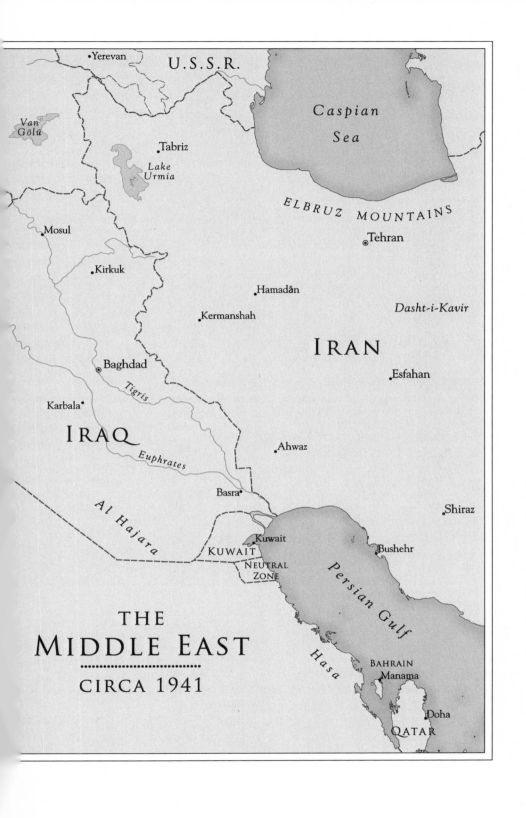

Yerevan

U.S.S.R.

Caspian
Sea

Van
Gölü

Tabriz

Lake
Urmia

ELBRUZ MOUNTAINS

Tehran

Mosul

Kirkuk

Hamadān

Kermanshah

Dasht-i-Kavir

IRAN

Baghdad

Tigris

Esfahan

Karbala

IRAQ

Euphrates

Ahwaz

Basra

Shiraz

Al Hajara

Kuwait

KUWAIT

Bushehr

NEUTRAL
ZONE

Persian Gulf

THE
MIDDLE EAST
• • • • • • • • • • • • • • • • • • •
CIRCA 1941

Hasa

BAHRAIN
Manama

Doha

QATAR

"Not on your life! If they get us, I'll carry you on deck, and if the lifeboats are full I'll toss you over the side and jump in after you. Think I can't swim?"

We made it to Alexandria all right, and no sooner had the transports unloaded than they went out to sea again, Crete-bound, to evacuate the next contingent of the British army of retreat. Things looked extremely bad for the British in the Middle East.

To send two divisions to Greece, complete with equipment (all of which, with the exception of small arms, had been sacrificed), General Wavell had been forced to dangerously weaken British defenses in the Western Desert. Tobruk was now under siege, and the Allied line had been pushed back from Benghazi to Halfaya Pass. The mere holding of Rommel's Afrika Corps was a tremendous undertaking. Scores of British fighter planes had been destroyed on the ground in Greece, and the RAF in the desert struggled for survival as it awaited badly needed reinforcements.

British forces in the Middle East at the time numbered something over a half million men, including English, Australians, New Zealanders, South Africans, and Indians, together with a sprinkling of Free French, Poles, Czechs, and Greeks. Theirs was a seemingly hopeless job, for not only did they face Rommel's panzers in the Western Desert, but they also had an area of about two million square miles to protect, extending from the Russo-Iranian border in the north to the Anglo-Egyptian Sudan in the south. British tanks were Matildas, Valentines, and Honeys, all inadequately armed for the task of taking on the powerful German Mark IIIs and Mark IVs. German anti-tank guns had long range and terrific muzzle velocity. But as my friend Ed Kennedy of the Associated Press (my chief competitor since the days of the Spanish War) put it to me at the time:

"God is an Englishman, Hank, so I guess they'll pull through."

I smiled, but only half-shared Kennedy's sentiments, for the way trouble was brewing from Persia to Crete, it looked as though my "Cook's Tour" with the armies of the world would soon come to an end.

• • •

I didn't have much time to nurse my malaria, for a few days after my arrival in Egypt, the Iraq revolt broke out and I was ordered to Palestine post-haste. Hitler had dusted off what we might call "Plan Number Four" concerning the conquest of the Near East and ordered it placed into immediate operation. This fit with the timetable I had laid out in my head while in Budapest back in January of 1940.

With the then punch-drunk BEF standing guard at Halfaya Pass, the Germans would take over Iraq, Syria, Palestine, and Persia without firing a shot, thus delivering a mortal blow to the Allies and ending the war before it had lasted two years. Turkey would be cut off as Yugoslavia had been, and Britain's lifeline to the Indies would be severed. Russia, hopelessly isolated, could be dealt with at leisure. To Germany would fall the immense Mosul-Kirkuk oil fields and the rich deposits of the Anglo-Iranian Oil Company in southwestern Iran, as well as the refinery at Abadan, Iran, largest in the world, and all the oil deposits of Iran's Bahrain Island in the Persian Gulf. With this great store of oil, coupled with what Germany already had stolen in Romania and what she could later exploit in Russia, Hitler would have the wherewithal to strike with Japan against the North American continent, a victory nearly assured. But before doing this, Germany would attempt to tie America's hands by occupying Palestine and imprisoning the world citadel of Jewry. By keeping all its occupants as hostages for the good behavior of the Jewish masses in America, Hitler could effectively immobilize American belligerency.

For Hitler, Rashid Ali's revolt in Iraq was the key to opening the door to the Near East.

• • •

Just as in Spain the Axis threw Catholicism into the propaganda cauldron and beat the drum about the "Holy War" against Bolshevism, so now in the Near East did they try to incite the Muslim masses to revolt against the Jews and Christians. They could not very well use the "German minority" formula, for the Germans were comparatively few in the region, although there were many paid agents in such places as Beirut, Damascus, Baghdad, and Teheran. Instead, they would start the Arabs on a killing spree against Jews and Christians, and would then intervene as "liberators" of the Arab world. This plan would place Turkey in an awkward position, because were Germany to intervene openly in the Near East on the pretense of aiding Muslims, and were the Turks to side against Germany, they might easily be accused of fighting against their coreligionists. This was all very minutely planned.

That the propaganda they put out at the time consisted mostly of obvious lies didn't matter to the Germans, who were willing to act both ruthlessly and shamelessly. For example, while Berlin radio was broadcasting reports concerning alleged rioting by Arabs at Nablus in Palestine, claiming heavy British casualties, I was witnessing an Arab recruiting march through Nablus, the birthplace of the biblical Jacob, with scores of turbaned desert horsemen demonstrating and making speeches pledging their intentions to take up arms in support of the British Empire.

The German Quisling in Iraq was Rashid Ali, who, at a word from Berlin, declared himself prime minister of Iraq, formed a rebel government, and led his army against the British after stirring up as much anti-British feeling amongst the Arabs as possible. Rashid Ali fired the shot that would signal the doom of the British Empire. If successful, there would be a revolt on a grand scale in the desert. Christians and Jews would fall to the disciples of Mohammed.

• • •

The invasion of Crete was timed to begin approximately three weeks after the inception of the Iraqi revolt. But things didn't go quite as the Germans had planned, and although systematic and thorough, the Hun has never taken any prizes for improvising. That's why the cat sneaked out of Hitler's bag in the Near East in the summer of 1941.

If the plan had gone according to schedule, by the time Goering's parachutists were descending like locusts over Crete, Rashid Ali would have kicked the British out of Iraq. As it was, Ali's revolt was petering out as the result of quick action by a British Expeditionary column and the stubborn resistance of the RAF garrison at Habbaniya aerodrome on the Euphrates River near Baghdad. At the time, restrictions of censorship did not permit publication of the full story of the siege of Habbaniya. But the story, which will take its place as an epic chapter in British air force history, can now be told.

Flying old Oxfords, Gordons, Audaxes, and Gladiators, most of which had seen their heyday and were now being used mostly for trainers, nearly four hundred officers and men in the Habbaniya training school challenged and whipped an army of five thousand Iraqi troops. These troops were equipped with thirty cannon and 150 machine guns, and for several days they besieged the aerodrome.

The RAF couldn't spare many planes for the defense of Iraq, for it had suffered heavily in Greece and most of their available aircraft were necessary to hold the Luftwaffe at bay in the Western Desert. The Iraqis had at their disposal an air force of about seventy planes of all types, of which about fifty were first-line aircraft, superior in performance to anything available to the British at Habbaniya. They had American Northrop and Italian Savoia twin-engined bombers as well as British fighters. The machines available to oppose the Iraqi force were the training planes of the Service Flying Training School consisting of about eighty aircraft, of which only fifty-six could be used for operations. To augment these, nine time-expired Gladiators from the Western Desert were pressed into service. But there were insufficient pilots to fly all of these aircraft, as only about thirty-five men, none of them experienced operational pilots, were available. Most were instructors who had done nothing but circuits and landings since their original training some years previously. Two or three were pilots who, having done an excessive amount of operational flying, had been sent to Habbaniya for a rest.

In the words of Wing Commander Dudgeon, whom I later interviewed concerning the siege of Habbaniya:

> On hearing that Iraqi troops were congregating in Fallujah and Ramadi, a demonstration was staged using every available pilot, including some of the more experienced pupils and some Greek instructors. Thus, four squadrons in diamond formation, with the Oxfords doing "S" turns above and three Gladiators with a freelance commission below, sailed majestically back and forth over the two villages and Habbaniya, thereby demonstrating British air might.
>
> During the night of April 29, 1941, considerable forces of the Iraqi army moved out from Rashid Camp toward Habbaniya. They were observed by watchers in the British Embassy at Baghdad and a warning signal was sent to the base. The alarm was sounded at once. When dawn came, the plateau overlooking the aerodrome was occupied by Iraqi forces in considerable strength. The Iraqi forces had arrived during the night, and with their guns and pom-poms on the plateau, they covered the whole of the main aerodrome and camp at point-blank range.
>
> Iraqi troops were visible marching about digging trenches, installing machine guns, and generally settling themselves in. The Iraqi commander sent a polite note to the effect that the camp was surrounded, all flying activity was to cease and that any aircraft taking off would be fired on. The A.O.C. stated in reply that on no account would he cease training flying and that if any aircraft was fired on, it would be an act of war and immediate reprisals would be taken.
>
> Repeated protests and demands by the British ambassador that the Iraqis should leave the vicinity of Habbaniya produced no result. At 8 p.m. on May 1, a conference was called at H.Q., it being decided that if the Iraqis had not retired by morning, they would be bombed. The plan was to keep up a continuous bombardment and orders were to have as many aircraft as possible in the air before light.
>
> Before dawn on May 2, everyone was at the hangars and the aircraft took off in the half-light. Soon there was an astonishing number of planes flying around over the small target area. Planes would approach unseen and with inexperienced pilots at the controls, flash past, causing some of us nearly to die of heart failure. Camouflaged and uncamouflaged Audaxes went past at every angle, and Wellingtons would sail overhead leaving the training planes buffeting about in their slipstream. Dead on five o'clock the first bombs were dropped and within five minutes the Iraqis were fiercely shelling the camp. The flashes of the guns gave away their positions

and they received a most excellent pasting. The pom-poms firing tracer rounds into the sky could be clearly seen and were avoided at all costs. Even so, some of our planes were hit and holes could be seen in the wings. Several aircraft had bullets through the cockpits and one Oxford was shot down, with the loss of an instructor and two pupils.

The siege continued by day and night, and little sleep was possible as hundreds of shells fell on the camp.

They even stripped down, cleaned, and overhauled two field guns that had been ornaments in front of headquarters officers' mess since the last war. They were used against the Iraqis after the removal of seventeen coats of paint.

"The morale effect was greater than the material," said Dudgeon, "as the Iraqis thought the guns had been flown up from Basra."

On the third day,

Four Blenheim fighters arrived at Habbaniya and, owing to the lack of prior information, came in to land doing normal approaches. One of them actually flew through the dust of a 250-pound bomb burst dropped by an Audax who was flying around attempting to keep the Iraqis' heads down.

After five days, reconnaissance aircraft reported large enemy reinforcements of guns, men, and armored cars approaching from Baghdad, but at the same time the Iraqis on the plateau decided that they had had enough. The advancing and retreating forces met about five miles east of Habbaniya at about the time that every available Oxford, Audax, Gordon, and Gladiator with bombs on improvised racks was let loose on them.

After two hours, and 139 aircraft sorties, the road was a solid sheet of flame for about two hundred yards, with ammunition bowsers exploding and cars burning by the dozen. All that with the loss of one Audax shot down.

The Iraqis were licked, for the British relieving column from Palestine consisting of about two thousand troops had arrived. Four days after the defeat of the Iraqis on the plateau, two German Heinkel IIIs arrived at Mosul, and on May 12 another dozen Heinkels and Messerschmitt 110s arrived. But it was too late. The Germans had missed the boat.

• • •

During a British raid on Rashid aerodrome in which two Messerschmitt 110s were shot down, the head of the German Mission in the Near East, Field Marshal von Blomberg's son, was killed. This helped considerably as German personnel and machines who were waiting at Palmyra in Syria did not receive the instruction they were expecting, and by the time the Germans had the ensuing confusion sorted out, it was past the point where the German air reinforcements could be of any real assistance.

Dudgeon told me later that "the Iraqis were absolutely paralyzed by the effort of our instructors and pupils, some of whom at the start of the siege did not even know how to aim a bomb. They never realized how weak we were. Had they picked up their feet, they could have just walked into Habbaniya and grabbed the lot of us. There wasn't much to stop them."

There were 25 to 30 killed at the flying school and from 100 to 120 killed in the Habbaniya military camp, but resistance of these men proved too much for Hitler and Rashid Ali.

• • •

Twenty-six-year-old Wing Commander Dudgeon composed this poem during the Iraqi siege of Habbaniya:

> "Battle of Habbaniya"
>   What did you do in the war, Daddie?
> I was hustled and ordered about,
> Then everything canceled and changed, laddie,
> I thought I was turned inside out.
>   Bombed up and started then stopped, laddie,
> Headquarters was certainly crazy.
> Stood by and stood down and stood up, laddie,
> With never a chance to be lazy.
>   Obsolete trainers to fly, laddie,
> And enemy guns on the hill,
> That covered the whole of the 'drome, laddie,
> And worked like a permanent pill.
>   Real guns with no gunners to shoot, laddie,
> Bomb sights and no aimers to fly,
> Night flying without any flares, laddie,
> And seldom a moon in the sky.
>   Soldiers that wouldn't advance, laddie,
> We thought they were made out of wood.
> Once dug in and watered like plants, laddie,
> They must have grown roots where they stood.
>   I fear that you think me a bore, laddie,
> I know that you think me a fool.
> If you take on a country at war laddie,
> Please—don't take it on with a school.

The Iraqi revolt collapsed on June 1, simultaneous with the evacuation of Crete.

The Luftwaffe and Germany's parachute regiments suffered heavily at Crete. The heroic resistance of the Australians and New Zealanders also did much to save the Empire, for Germany was not soon to recover from her losses in the air, which again threw her out of step, since these gliders and troop carriers that had been used in Crete were later to be used for the invasion of Cyprus, Syria, and Palestine.

I wasn't in Crete during the historic battle for possession of the island, but some of the boys who participated in the defense afterward gave me graphic word pictures of the destruction they inflicted on the Luftwaffe before fighting their way out to the sea.

Regimental Sergeant Major William Burgess, of Reddish, Manchester, was an artillery man who fought the rearguard action at Thermopylae, mowing down hundreds of Germans at point-blank range with a troop of four guns. He told me that when the remnants of his outfit arrived in Crete, they were split up and given certain areas to defend as infantry, since they had been forced to abandon their artillery equipment in Greece.

"One afternoon we were subjected to three-and-a-half hours of high- and low-level bombing and extremely low-level strafing preparatory to the arrival of transport planes with parachutists. Out of every thirty paratroops that dropped, only about ten hit the ground alive. We even used 55mm anti-tank shells on them as they came down. Then the Bren gun came into its own for our boys had perfect targets when the parachutists who landed alive rushed to join their leaders."

Captain Ronald Vine, a Regular from Sussex, who with the Seventh Medium Artillery Regiment had been fourteen years with the army in India, Palestine, and Egypt, said:

> We were turned into infantry after the retreat from Greece and took over from the elements of the Black Watch at Heraklion Aerodrome, which we were to defend. The fun started on the evening of May 19. All we had were small arms but when the parachutists started dropping, there were soon bodies of Germans all over the place, even hanging from the telegraph wires. It was an amazing sight. They used different-colored parachutes, and varied the procedure from time to time. All the parachutists that dropped at Heraklion were killed and I myself saw seven Ju-52 transport planes shot down in flames. It was a horrible sight to see the troops in those planes trying to save themselves. The planes were shot down at about three hundred feet as they came in from the sea like great gulls. The majority of the men dropped to the ground like stones and died instantly, while the open parachutes of others were burning as they came down.

It was the Aussie ack-ack that got most of the Ju-52s. They were huge flying crates made of corrugated iron and each carried about eighty men. At my post, I buried twenty-one Germans, and another lad, a sergeant, buried about twenty. They were all very young and looked it. I inspected their identity cards and found that most of them had the birth date 1920 or 1922.

After the first do, there was nothing left of the German air infantry. Of course there was the odd fellow in the corn field, but he didn't matter much. One German landed in a buttercup field. The first thing you know, he had taken off all his clothes, discarded his kit, and was coming toward us naked, with his hands in the air. Obviously he had seen the planes on fire all around, and hearing our small-arms fire thought it was all over. After the first day, the Black Watch had taken about four hundred German prisoners and lodged them in Heraklion barracks. I got a pally with an M.P. officer in charge of them, who told me that the Black Watch had examined some of the containers of equipment that crashed with the transports. There was an incredible array of material, including binoculars, rifles, and land mines. They also found motorcycles and heavy machine guns, all in containers with shock absorbers. The Germans had no food and no water, but otherwise they were equipped to the very smallest detail. . . .

After knocking off his parachutists, we thought Jerry would crash-land infantry, but he didn't around Heraklion. And it certainly was a strain waiting, as obviously he was going to throw in all he had and we knew that soon we would be outflanked, outnumbered, and possibly wiped out. For the nine days that followed, we used to stand-to, and the drones kept coming in. We could see his troops dropping at a rate of more than five hundred men a day with supplies, several miles away, and couldn't do anything about it. All we could do was to watch them, in the meantime counting them and trying to figure out his total. Toward the end, he was even dropping anti-tank guns.

On May 28, I was called to a conference of officers and was told that we were evacuating. But I didn't tell the men. That evening we marched out to the beach and at midnight saw two cruisers, *Dido* and *Orion*, coming into Heraklion Bay. With them were three destroyers. We didn't get started boarding until daylight, and eventually three hundred of our regiment was safely aboard *Orion*. Then at 6 a.m. we were dive bombed, and I shall never forget it. It continued unabated until 2 p.m. for we had no air protection, and we got three direct bomb hits, two of them on the gun turrets. Then, they hit Sick Bay. By this time the chaps were throwing themselves out of port holes because something had happened in the magazines and an emergency flooding of the lower hatches was necessary to save the warship.

At one time the list got so bad on *Orion* that a whole lot of us were ordered to get on one side of the ship. Then another hit killed the Skipper. The lights went out and the water poured in. It was a floating Hell and besides the direct hits we received a great many near misses.

I must say the navy boys were grand. We shared the pay master's cabin and he spent the whole time trying to cheer us up. I remember one very jolly Able Seaman who was constantly handing out drinks. He was full of wise-cracks and would make remarks such as, "Don't worry chaps; we get this sort of thing every day." Most of the officers were like ourselves, though, far from cheerful, for there were many casualties and the billiard tables in the Officers' Ward Room were being used for operations. A lot of the casualties were from blasts. My batman was killed, and I saw him buried at sea. I took thirty-one of my men on board the ship but only twelve of us walked off at Alexandria. The rest were either badly wounded or killed. Some of the latter were buried at sea, but most were simply blown to bits.

• • •

With Crete occupied, the Jews of Palestine were in a panic, for there was evidence of a German plan to invade Palestine through Syria. If Hitler's Quisling in Iraq, Rashid Ali, had failed his master, perhaps his Syrian Quisling, the Vichyite General Dentz, might be depended upon to carry out his instructions. There was no doubt that the Germans intended to take direct action sooner or later to throw the Near East into pandemonium and close Britain's lifeline to the Indies.

On the Syrian-Palestine border, frontier police were on the alert, for upwards of eighty German planes were reported to have arrived at Damascus and Aleppo, and refugees from Syria and Turkey were streaming into Palestine, further fraying the nerves of the terror-stricken Jews, many of whom hurriedly threw their entire savings into diamonds that they carried in vest pockets preparatory to a hurried getaway.

Upwards of a hundred reconditioned French tanks had been reported massed under German command in the region of Tyre, Syria, a few miles from the Palestine border.

Refugees especially flocked to Jerusalem feeling that they would not be bombed in the Sacred City. It was a motley crowd, including Muslims, Christians, Jews, Druzes, Bahais, and Hindus. Because of the terrific influx, rents were hiked 200 percent and hotels were so jammed that after hours of search I could only find lodging in a shabby room in a third-rate pension.

With the war drawing closer to the Holy Land, my landlady, a German Jewess, upon learning that I was American said:

"Can't you please telephone Roosevelt and tell him to hurry up?"

Of the approximately six thousand Jews in Palestine claiming American citizenship, a large proportion was clamoring at the consulate in

Jerusalem for visas to the United States. Hundreds were demanding visas for India, and throughout the Holy Land they were building air-raid shelters and sand-bagging churches and other buildings dating from biblical days. Bethlehem, where Jesus was born, teemed with Christians who believed that "they certainly will not bomb the scene of the birth of Christ the Savior."

There were German-instigated demonstrations throughout the Near East including Beirut and Baghdad, with paid agitators seeking to stir up the Muslims. Arrivals from Syria revealed that a Berlin radio station was broadcasting nightly in numerical code to German agents in Syria. The Germans got about 150 Iraqi students at the American University in Beirut to appear before the Iraqi and Egyptian consulates shouting Nazi-inspired slogans supporting Muslim revolt. One young man told me that this "was not a war between Muslim and Christian, or Muslim and Jew, but between civilization and barbarism." But that sentiment was drowned out by the loud, organized demonstrators.

The leading Bedouin tribes were not taking the Nazi bait. They remembered the lessons of the four-year desert war and, anyway, to them people such as Rashid Ali were trashy townsmen, with whom they desired no traffic whatsoever. So the Bedouins decided to let the British deal, if necessary, with the Reichswehr and Luftwaffe on ground surveyed years before by such men as Lawrence of Arabia. In fact, the Muslim leader Nuri Sahib Pasha, who fought alongside Lawrence and was four times premier of Iraq, a man of tremendous influence with the desert tribes, was in constant consultation with the British High Command in Jerusalem. The Trans-Jordan frontier police, consisting mostly of Arabs and pride of the British Empire, had contributed effectively to liquidating matters in Iraq. Their continued loyalty impressed the Arabs, for every Arab tribesman with any background had at least one or more brothers or cousins in this unit. Therefore it was a matter of pride for him to remain loyal to the British with whom their relations have broken bread and shared salt.

• • •

It was fifty-fifty whether the Germans or the British would attack first along the Syrian-Palestine border. And it was a welcome sight to see Australian veterans of the Western Desert and Greece streaming into Palestine early in June 1941, even as Cabalist mystics drew lines with chicken's blood along the biblical frontiers. According to their beliefs, this would strengthen Palestinian defenses. Their ceremony was preceded by incantations invoking divine powers to safeguard the Holy Land. I watched them do their stuff. It required twenty-four hours and involved the slaughter of seven black cocks in a subterranean synagogue.

Were I to have the choice between holy chicken blood and Australian guts I'd most certainly back the latter against the Hun. And it wasn't long before I was to march into Syria with the "Men from Down Under."

13

VICHY TREACHERY

THE ALLIES HAD TO TAKE A LOT OF VICHY INSOLENCE prior to their decision to kick over the apple cart and occupy North Africa, but the boys who swallowed the most were the Australians during the Syrian Campaign of June-July 1941.

Imagine a tough bunch of troops being told to go to war "with an olive branch in one hand and a grenade in the other." And how'd you like to have been in their shoes when, proffering the olive branch under a white flag, they were mowed down by murderous machine-gun and mortar fire?

We learned in Syria that it doesn't do to mix politics with war; that it doesn't pay to act the part of gentlemen with guys who just don't want to play. That sort of business cost the Diggers a lot of casualties, especially since a French Fascist by the name of General Henri Dentz was in command in Beirut.

Now that some of the men of Vichy have been unmasked, perhaps the censor will have no objection to the truth being told concerning the Syrian Campaign. After all, many of the boys who fought Dentz's crowd of madmen are back home now, and all Australia knows about it. So why shouldn't the world?

Many times were we war correspondents cursed, and with reason, by the Aussies in Syria whose buddies had become casualties in the fighting for Beirut. They'd heard the BBC tell the world the night before that everything was lovely, although perhaps our former allies, the French, were being just a bit trying.

"Why don't you guys tell the truth? Why don't you tell 'em there are Diggers being killed around here by French soldiers? Why, my pal was killed yesterday . . . ?" And so it went. We had to gulp, apologize, and swallow it, because we knew the boys were right. In their eyes we were a pack of liars. But what was the use of telling them it was the censor's fault, not ours? How to explain that Downing Street was using kid gloves, hoping to appease their former allies, now enemies, the men of Vichy?

The straw that broke the camel's back so far as I was concerned, though, was the half-hour pounding we got from the guns of the French Fleet. A French cruiser and destroyer shelled the hell out of the Aussies as they fought a bloody hand-to-hand battle with the French foreign legion at the Litani River, north of Tyre. This was a definite act of war against the British Empire. But the world heard nothing about it, for there was still a chance "the misguided elements of Vichy" could be brought around and made to see the light. After dodging shrapnel from French naval guns on the rocky Syrian coast, Harold Laycock of the *Christian Science Monitor* and I rushed our dispatches to the censorship in Jerusalem only to find that there wasn't a hope of the story being approved for publication. It's all past history now. Nevertheless it is well worth mentioning, if only to ensure that history accurately records what the British were up against after the Germans took over France and installed their Quislings in the Vichy cabinet.

General Dentz and company were a cold-blooded bunch of Fascist cutthroats. Because these French officials were working hand-in-glove with Berlin, they gave orders whereby Allied soldiers were killed and wounded ruthlessly. Although short-lived, the Syrian Campaign was at times most intense.

Ten days before they were to move into Syria, the Australian "desert rats" who were to form the spearhead of the surprise attack moved up to the frontier, dispersing themselves so efficiently and under such effective camouflage that war correspondents who had been tipped that something was afoot and had scoured the countryside for days looking for their positions had little success. This maneuver was done with such stealth that Arab, Jew, and peasant townsmen of Palestine were still discussing the possibility of a German invasion even as the Aussies were advancing on Beirut.

Twice, orders to attack were countermanded because of London's hesitation to take drastic action against Vichy if an alternative could be found. But the extent of German activity in Syria forced Britain's hand, resulting in a council of war at Haifa attended by General de Gaulle where final preparations were made.

I marched into Syria with the Australians at 3 a.m. on June 8, 1941— my thirtieth birthday. The Australians, backed by mixed British units, including cavalry, were to advance on Beirut along the coast, while several thousand Free French troops under General Le Gentilhomme penetrated the lava-covered, oven-hot plains of the Djebel Druze. Damascus was their objective.

"It's going to be a delightfully mixed show," an Australian brigadier told me, "for we don't know whether we're going to war or not." He spoke even as he picked his squad of huskies, equipped with everything from knuckle-busters to tommy guns to pick-axes. These men were to sneak up on French outposts to prevent them from blowing up the cliffs along the coast road, blocking that point of entry. "We've got to do everything from frontier patrol to policing captured villages and towns, while avoiding land mines and other traps. And, they say we have to be nice about it." He chuckled, then continued, "We're even instructed to leave some of our men behind to act as a reception committee for Frenchmen expected to desert into Palestine come morning. My boys are tough, and they're scratching their heads a bit, but we'll do the best we can. As for the olive branch and the hand grenade," he added with a wink, "I've told my Diggers to throw the heaviest one first, should they run into trouble."

For twelve hours there was practically no resistance, and even the Arabs joined in chasing groups of mounted French and Colonial troops as they scattered over the hilly Syrian countryside. But as the column pressed on to the Litani River, Dentz's forces opened up on them with all they had. The Aussies, still not sure how to strike the delicate balance implicit in their orders, hauled out the olive branch and sent it forward with a group of "Parliamentarians" under a white flag. The whole lot of them were mowed down by machine-gun fire. The Aussies then decided to toss a few grenades and hold their line.

That night as the Australian field commander prepared for "fun and games," I talked with a French pilot held in the Tyre jail. He had been captured after inadvertently landing his aeroplane after the British occupation of the formerly French airstrip. I referred to British gratification that the French had not committed all their forces to battle against the Allies, but he shook his head grimly and warned us that it was only a strategic move.

"We are soldiers," he said, "and General Dentz has ordered us to resist. Every man will fight."

The battle began along the Litani River at dawn the next morning. French troops, backed by long-range German mortars and Spandau machine guns, fought to remind the world of the age-old reputation of L'Armées française. They were matched against stubborn Australians, slashing away at close quarters so that the French should not forget the "Diggers" of the last great war.

My report of the battle, contained in a dispatch submitted that day, was stopped by the censor. I think it is fitting that I quote it now:

Date: June 9th, 1941. With British Imperial Forces advancing on Beirut: French warships, throwing in their lot with the men of Vichy in the battle for Syria, dueled with British light artillery on the Syrian coast this morning, as Australian shock troops attacked at the Litani River, six miles north of Tyre.

It was the first time since the French collapse and the establishment of the Vichy government that French warships had been in action in the Mediterranean. But this time, the warships—a cruiser and a destroyer—were fighting for the Axis, rather than alongside the British Imperial Fleet. Flying the "Tricouleur," these two ships, once part of one of the most formidable fleets in the world, suddenly struck France's former allies from behind and then ran, hotly pursued by a strong unit of His Majesty's forces. The Royal Navy is playing an important role in the operations in Syria.

As I write this dispatch, British warships are chasing the French raiders aided by American-built Tomahawk fighter planes. Through my field glasses I can see vivid red dots on the horizon as naval guns fire from more than half a dozen British cruisers and destroyers. I can see black smoke preceded by blinding flashes as British and French warships fight it out.

The torrid ground trembles with the burst of six inch shells, fired in salvos by British warships a few miles off shore. In fact, this entire morning the rocky Syrian countryside has reverberated to the crash of bombs and shells fired from land and sea as the troops of Vichy battle at the Litani River to bar British access to Beirut.

As I moved up with the Australian striking force shortly after sun-up and watched them go into the attack using pontoon boats to ford the river, I soon found myself in one of the hottest spots of a lifetime. I was intensely watching a duel between British 25-pounders and French 105s, 75s, and German long-range trench mortars when suddenly a French destroyer and cruiser, weaving drunkenly, opened rapid fire against Australian reserve troops and vehicles. Dust and shrapnel flew in all directions as the French warships, about five hundred yards off shore, gave us the works. British batteries reacted quickly and as their shells plowed the sea on all sides, the French warships threw out a dense smoke screen under cover of which they continued shelling us for half an hour. I curled myself around a rock and every time I ducked to avoid the flying shrapnel, thistles punctured my pants. There were no casualties, although an Australian major laughingly told me that a piece of shrapnel had whizzed harmlessly between his legs.

At the time of the incident a number of British warships were patrolling in the vicinity of Haifa, hence the French ships were practically out of range when help arrived. It appears that the object of the French shelling from the sea was to divert British gunners as well as to demoralize British reserves preparatory to a counter-attack across the Litani River, for after the naval shelling had subsided I could see figures on the north bank of the river seeking to ford it at its lowest depth where it joins the sea, in the face of terrific Australian machine-gun fire. British artillery spied the situation and banged away. Panic resulted on the north beaches of the river as the French infantry, some of them waist high in the water, scrambled for cover. Some fell and picked themselves up again, while others lay inert on the beaches as water and sand erupted from bursting shells. Behind them a wheat field was blazing furiously from an hours-long British barrage, resembling a prairie fire. The Aussies persisted in their attack, but were repeatedly driven back by French machine-guns.

Later, when the Australians breeched the French defenses, I talked to survivors of a small band of Commandos, mostly Scotsmen, who had landed slightly north of the Litani River before the main battle began, seeking to take the French defenders from the rear. Again the British High Command was trying to prevent undue bloodshed. It was preferable that the French should be rounded up from behind and taken prisoner, but it hadn't worked out that way.

The French were manning the beaches and set a trap for the Commandos as they were landed in invasion barges. Many Commandos in this unit were killed by snipers, invariably shot at the back of the skull, while others were taken prisoner and held as hostages by the French, only to be freed by the Australians twenty-four hours later.

"It was hell," said Private Ian Peet of Buckhurst Hill, near London. "French machine guns and snipers were there by the score. Deliberately, they permitted us to advance, and then when we went down on our knees or otherwise sought cover from their machine guns, the snipers perched in trees behind us had a go. But we had a job to do and carried it out to the best of our ability."

Sergeant Tommy Worral from London, whose tommy gun was put out of action by salt water, grabbed an empty French revolver with which he pounced on a French officer commanding a battery of four 75s.

"We were one officer, a bombardier and a lance corporal, who was badly wounded in the arm," said Worral. "We seized one of the 75s in the battery, and with it blew two of the three remaining cannon from the face of creation at a distance of twenty yards."

Sergeant Major Lewis Tevendale, from Stonehaven, for three years police heavyweight champion in his district, said that he and several of his men were taken prisoner and held as hostages in a cave after their commanding officer was killed.

"The major was being fired upon by four or five machine guns, when a bullet grazed his tin helmet. He turned around to joke with us regarding his good luck, after which he got another bullet in the head and a third in the back."

The Australians took several hundred French prisoners in that first engagement, including an Australian volunteer in the French foreign legion, who expressed surprise that he should be captured by his own countrymen.

"Dentz told us that we should fight to the end against the Italians," said the confused Digger.

It struck me that in resisting at the Litani the bulk of the French prisoners had been acting merely as automatons, under orders. The French foreign legion, which bore the brunt of the Aussie attack, is noted for its blind obedience. A French noncommissioned officer said to me:

"We gave our superiors our word as soldiers of France that we would fight. They told us we must fight to preserve French honor."

That was one soldier's attitude, but there were many Frenchmen among those taken prisoner who were open in their hatred of the British. And no wonder, since Beirut had been repeatedly bombed by what they thought were British planes. As it later developed, most of the raids on Beirut during the Syrian Campaign were carried out by German bombers from the Island of Rhodes. I was able to confirm this later through Harold Peters, of the United Press, who was with the Vichy French in Beirut throughout the siege, and who compared his record of actual raids with RAF logs placed at his disposal. As further proof, British bomb disposal squads later dug up unexploded German bombs that had buried themselves in the hilly countryside surrounding Beirut. Yes, the Germans had bombed the town night after night, to stir the French populace.

Resistance along the coast continued as General Dentz massed his available tanks in the plains of Sidon against the Australian infantry. There was hammer-and-tong fighting, in which the Diggers crawled on their bellies to throw "sticky bombs" at the heavily armored French tanks. Adhering to the sides, they would explode, leaving a gaping hole, through which the Aussies could draw a bead on the crews with rifles and tommy guns. Several French tanks were captured by this method, then quickly repaired and used by the Diggers against the French, for the Aussies were equipped only with light Bren carriers.

With the coastal campaign dragging on, we war correspondents used to spend some of our time in Haifa, which was repeatedly bombed by the Germans who now were trying to destroy the petrol refineries there. I've never seen a heavier barrage than that put up by cruisers and destroyers of the British Fleet in Haifa harbor during these night attacks. There was more noise than damage from the German bombs, for the British naval ack-ack was too much for the German pilots.

But French artillery work was magnificent, and they had many cannon, for Syria had been used as an artillery training ground. They also were well-equipped in the air. Like the British, the French had Glen Martin bombers, and generally one didn't realize an attack was in progress until the French bombs screamed into the ground just before one's nose.

Dentz was being steadily pushed back all along the line now by the determined Australians, who had dropped their olive branches for good. In response, the Axis air force came in to try to save the day. On several occasions as the British Fleet shelled French entrenchments along the coast, I saw German dive bombers attack British warships, which defended themselves with everything from pom-poms to six-inch guns, usually emerging without a scratch as big stuff exploded in the water all around. But still the British pulled their punches. Had the guns of the Mediterranean Fleet really been used with effect, Beirut would have fallen long before. As it was, never did they shell a town; only French gun emplacements and other military targets that had been spotted by Australian patrols.

In the central front, where Tommy infantry and Cheshire cavalry cooperated with the Australians, it was always the policy of the British High Command to take villages by encirclement, thus avoiding bloodshed. But the French used all manner of treachery. Once, they allowed a unit of about 150 Aussie Pioneers to enter a village in the region of Merjayoum, then suddenly opened fire on them from prepared machine-gun positions and mowed down the lot. While the British had orders not to shell or bomb Syrian towns or villages, as soon as they themselves entered a town, French artillery and Franco-German aircraft would bomb and shell them to a pulp.

The toll of prisoners mounted as the Allied advance progressed. I saw a group of about 150 French prisoners strafed from the air by Vichy fighters as they were being marched to the rear, with fifteen killed and twenty-five wounded.

To enter the village of Jezzine, in the central front, I had to negotiate two stretches of highway that the Aussies had nicknamed "Hell's Hundred Meters" and the "Mad Mile." There, Dentz had massed the bulk of his artillery, stalling for time to enable fortification of the Damour River as Beirut's last-ditch defense. These sections of road were under point-blank fire of the French batteries. Four times, Jezzine had changed hands in furious hand-to-hand fighting. With Captain Hugh Laming (who had helped me in connection with my lady friend's escape from Greece) as our conducting officer, Harold Laycock and I decided to have a look at the village.

"The road ahead is not so good and has lots of curves, but you'll easily make it if you travel at sixty miles an hour," a sentry had said. "You'd better not slow down because you'll be in full view of the French 75s."

We stopped just before entering "Hell's Hundred," at the terminus of which one generally was greeted by "hurrahs" from grinning Aussies who in their idle periods laid bets as to whether the Vichy artillery would get you or not. While forcing a couple of sandwiches down my throat, amid gloomy suggestions from Laycock that this might be our last meal, we heard the roar of Vichy guns ahead. At one time there were thirteen bursts in a row, following which careening British trucks flashed past us at full speed after having run the gauntlet of shell fire.

For luck we picked up a timid little Arab girl with bare feet who said she wanted to go to Jezzine, and then resumed our trip feeling somewhat like little kids about to have their first ride on the "Big Dipper" at a summer fair. The speedometer registered forty miles an hour, then fifty, then sixty, and we soon recognized "Hell's Hundred" from the gaping shell holes on both sides of the road. Subconsciously we held our breaths as the guns opened up only a few hundred yards to the left of us, and the Arab girl became excited and grabbed my knee. After a few anxious moments we were in the clear.

Jezzine, once a pretty little village nestling between peaks resembling sharks' teeth, was now a pitiful conglomeration of wrecked houses. Such had been the tempo of the fighting that there had not even been time to bury all the dead civilians and domestic pets, so we held our breath as we bypassed long-dead donkeys, cows, and mules on the roadside. The little Arab girl made her exit, and still blushing scarlet red from the excitement of the ride, groped her way through the debris of the central thoroughfare. After a short rest, we negotiated the "Mad Mile" in reverse, without a scratch, receiving the thumbs-up salute at the end of the run from enthusiastic Arab children who offered us a tribute of eggs and bananas.

• • •

The Free French under General Paul Louis Le Gentilhomme, who himself was wounded in the fighting, had by this time systematically undermined the last defenses of Damascus, capital of the Arab world.

Things were going fast now, and I decided to make a quick trip to the Damascus front prior to rejoining the Australians on the coast road. The trip through the lava-covered desert of the Djebel Druze took three days, and once as we slept on newly threshed wheat under the stars, we were nearly ambushed by a patrol of Vichy French, for several pockets of resistance remained behind the furthermost Allied lines.

At Cheikh Meski the British commander told us how only the day before the field yonder had suddenly swarmed with French infantry.

"The Free French heard what they thought were comrades shouting

'Avant mes amis.' They approached them, only to be attacked with the bayonet. But despite the element of surprise, they quickly drove the Vichyites back, killing and wounding many. It was the first time that the Free French had fought their countrymen in Syria hand-to-hand."

Frequently piling out of our automobile to escape road strafing by Vichy and German planes, we pressed forward to the Free French defense line just outside Damascus and struggled to keep our balance as we stumbled uphill through brittle lava rock resembling clinkers from a furnace. The siege guns in the Damascus forts were firing their last salvos and the huge shells were bursting harmlessly in the desert.

I saw Indian and Australian troops join with the Free French in the final assault, as General Dentz hurled his available bombers and fighters against them to prevent the collapse of the "Pearl of the East." It was a dramatic battle in which hill after hill was stormed and captured at bayonet point by Allied troops, including huge barefooted Senegalese with their murderous knives. The fighting at Mezze in the outskirts of Damascus, which had been penetrated by Indian infantry, was as vicious as I have ever seen. The Indians, entering Mezze, blew up the railroad tracks, whereupon Vichy tanks hurled themselves at the mud huts the Indians were using as barricades, systematically demolishing one after another. From an observation post I saw Vichy shells explode in Mezze aerodrome with the double purpose of holding the advancing Indians and Free French and destroying abandoned aircraft there. From six to twelve Vichy bombers at a time flew over the Artouz-Mezze road and dropped sticks of heavy bombs on the aerodrome runways, even as British 25-pounders exploded on a hill just ahead, wiping out Vichy machine-gun nests. Damascus proper, with its famous mosques and princely mansions containing priceless specimens of Arabic art, was not touched. However, I saw a blinding flash and heard a tremendous explosion as a lucky British shell struck a huge munitions dump on the outskirts of the city just below the famous Ommayad Mosque.

An American volunteer with the Free French, Jack Hasey, age twenty-four, of Bridgewater, Massachusetts, was seriously wounded in the fighting for Damascus. Hasey only recently had been decorated as a sublieutenant in the foreign legion for capturing formidable Fort Victor Emmanuel outside Massawa in Eritrea. With his platoon of forty Legionnaires, he broke Massawa's defenses, facilitating the opening of the Red Sea to American shipping. Now, at the gates of Damascus, slim, sandy-haired, blue-eyed Hasey fell while leading his troops against strongly fortified Vichy positions.

Norman Jeffreys from Williston Park, Long Island, a volunteer worker of the American Field Ambulance unit who attended to Hasey in an advanced casualty clearing station outside Damascus, told me later that Hasey, although his jaw had been largely shot away by machine-gun bullets, wrote a note while lying on a stretcher, asking what progress had been made in the attack on Damascus. Although in extreme pain, he didn't mention his own wounds. He also had been hit in the stomach and the left hand, but insisted on holding the instruments to help the surgeon insert a tube down his throat enabling him to breathe.[1]

• • •

Through the ages, Damascus had been the prize of hundreds of battles, falling to generals such as David, Darius, and Alexander the Great. During his battle with the Philistines, David stormed and captured Damascus, killing twenty-two thousand of its inhabitants. Now again the city found besieged forces within its gates. Allenby and Lawrence of Arabia had been the last to enter. Now Australia's Blamey, England's Wilson, and fighting France's Le Gentilhomme were the conquerors.

To file my dispatch I motored all the way to Jerusalem, only to find that Germany had declared war against Russia. What news items could compete with that? The Germano-Russian war overshadowed subsequent heavy fighting for possession of Syria, including the battle of Damour along the coast where massed British 25-pounders and naval guns supported by the RAF crushed Beirut's final defense line.

More than thirty thousand shells were fired into Damour village and the olive and banana groves surrounding it, which had been honeycombed with barbed-wire entanglements and concrete-reinforced machine-gun nests. The Australians were giving no quarter now, for it was plain that unless General Dentz were beaten in the field he would not yield. Just before the battle of Damour, the Germans, in a frantic attempt to hold Syria, even released French prisoners of war from concentration camps in Germany and flew them to Syria via Italy and Greece.

British cruisers and destroyers coordinated with more than sixty field guns and howitzers to batter Dentz's last line of defense. British warships hurled tons of explosives per minute in ear-splitting salvos at six thousand yards range while the RAF and AAF carried out massed bombing. The Vichy command ordered two vital bridges blown up. Nevertheless, under protection of the Allied barrage, the Diggers, carrying automatic

1. Jack Hasey survived his wounds. This American became a captain in the French foreign legion and later a senior operations officer with the CIA. He was one of four Americans (including Dwight D. Eisenhower) decorated with France's highest World War II honor, the Companion of the Order of the Liberation. Hasey died of a stroke in Arlington, Virginia, on May 9, 2005, at age eighty-eight.

guns, waded the Damour River and in hand-to-hand fighting steadily
pushed back the Vichyites in the direction of Beirut.

His line broken, Dentz's emissaries emerged from Beirut under white
flags in compliance with the ultimatum of General "Jumbo" Wilson. An
Armistice Convention was signed shortly after at Acre, Palestine. Dentz,[2]
surly to the last, was not there, sending as his representative the Vichy
French General Joseph de Verdillac.

The hostile attitude of the men of Vichy who had sworn to save Syria for
the Axis became apparent during that conference when open suggestions
were made that it was folly to continue the war against Germany.
Remarks bordering on insults were dropped by a representative of the
French Foreign Office, but General Wilson tolerated no nonsense, making
it plain that if Dentz's delegates insisted on wasting his time he was quite
willing that hostilities should be resumed.

With the signing of the Acre Armistice Convention on July 14, 1941,
the Syrian campaign came to a formal end and took its place in history
as another episode in World War Number II. Relief was the sentiment
throughout the Middle East. Perfectly timed to put fresh heart into Turkey,
where the menacing examples of Greece and Crete had given rise to
despondency, this annexation of Syria, politically as well as strategically,
was a major Allied victory.

It was not a popular campaign. The crazy course of the gigantic struggle
between Hitlerism and Democracy decreed that blood spilled in Syria
should be that of former friends and allies. Many good men were killed
and wounded on both sides. Contrasting with Hitler's armistices, there
was no fanfare, pomp, or ceremony to mark termination of hostilities.

The entry of the Australians in Beirut a few days later marked the
forced abandonment of Hitler's "Drang nach Osten" dreams. Iraq and
Syria now had been snatched from Hitler's reach. Soon the combined
armies of Russia and Great Britain were to remove the Axis threat to
Persia.

2. After the war, Henri Dentz was sentenced to death for collaborating with Nazi
Germany. The sentence was later commuted to life imprisonment, and he died in
Fresnes prison in December 1945.

14

TAXI TO TEHERAN

EXCEPT FOR THE TROUBLE I HAD TRYING TO CATCH UP WITH the Indian army in the taxicab I hired in Baghdad, I think I'd unhesitatingly bestow the prize for soft assignments on the Persian campaign, where I didn't even hear a shot fired.

No, I wasn't at all sore, for I'd had enough shooting in Albania, Greece, and Syria to last me for a long time.

To crush what a Russian general later described to me as a "German subversive movement in the Near East of greater scope than any uncovered in the first World War," British Imperial and Russian troops invaded Persia simultaneously, on August 25, 1941, the Russians entering from the north and the Indian army from the south and west.

I was in Cairo when the campaign started, and got off on the wrong foot, because the chief of the British army public relations, without any nomination from us, had selected a group of British and American war correspondents, including my rival, Ed Kennedy of the Associated Press, and flown them to the starting point of the British drive at Basrah, on the previous afternoon.

The big shots of the United Press in New York on hearing of this were tearing their hair and firing all sorts of cables across the Atlantic. Here are a few examples:

"Gorrell make every effort to join British forces Iran first possible moment"

"Has Gorrell left for Persia? If not keep pressure on getting him started"

"Gorrell depending you overtake and out-pitch opposition Persia"

With the heat on to this extent it was "get the story or else," so I just about split my galluses trying to catch up with Kennedy somewhere in Persia. Luck was with me and I obtained a seat on an Imperial Airways plane to Basrah, arriving there the day after "hostilities" had begun.

The first British officer I contacted at Basrah, a Rip Van Winkle type of community at the mouth of the Tigris River, told me that "the war around here has just about packed up. And if you want to see any action, you'd better hurry north."

While pondering future strategy, I noticed a nattily uniformed little fellow with coal-black hair in the lobby of Basrah's main hotel, arguing with a group of white-clad porters. On questioning one of the porters, I was told that he was a Persian frontier officer who contended that if the British "hadn't come in from the wrong direction," the Iranians at Abadan would still be holding out. It seems this little guy put up a one-man battle on the other side of the Tigris River on the morning of the British attack, blazing away with his rifle as his soldiers legged it; finally to surrender himself to overwhelming numbers of grinning Gurkhas and Sikhs.

People in Basrah were still in a daze, and it was only by a tooth-pulling process that I was able to reconstruct what had happened. It seems that the roads from Baghdad to Basrah had been jammed with military traffic for days before General Wavell began his Persian blitz. Then at the "go ahead" signal the Indian army had thrown pontoons over the Tigris and crossed into Iran as tugs, sloops, and troop-carrying aircraft landed soldiers on the Abadan waterfront. Shooting, by those who heard it at all, was described as exceedingly mild.

Had it not been for several-score Iranian prisoners being marched into concentration camps by turbaned Indians, I'd have sworn I was in the wrong place and that nothing ever had or would happen here, in what once might have been the "Garden of Eden," but now struck me full in the face as the "Orifice of Creation," with its stifling heat and the monotonous drone of flies worrying the noses of the yawning brown-skinned, nightgowned townsmen.

Ascertaining that my friend Kennedy and his pals were hopelessly stuck in the desert in the vicinity of Abadan, I immediately booked a seat in the air-conditioned sleeper to Baghdad, from where I planned to catch up with the British column now moving northward into the interior of Persia.

On the train I met an Englishman who was planning to join his family in Teheran "in two or three days." He told me the Shah might have been able to put up a far better fight in the air if nine out of ten Tomahawk fighters he got from America a few weeks before ever had been removed from their packing crates. "I saw them myself on a Persian aerodrome," said the Englishman, "and talked with the Curtiss representative who delivered them to the Shah and was supposed to assemble them. Then, mysteriously, after he had put one Tomahawk in condition to fly, the Curtiss fellow went sick and nine out of ten fighters are still in the packing crates."

On arrival in Baghdad, which, incidentally, contains more flies and smells even worse than Basrah despite what you might have read in the

"Arabian Nights," I arranged to hire a taxi at a fantastic rate in which I would attempt to catch up with the Indian army.

I demanded speed from my Persian driver, so with nuts and bolts rattling on the pavement behind us, we drove like mad to Kermanshah along the famous "Golden Road to Samarkand," a prehistoric caravan route trod for centuries by the bandit legions of Genghis Khan. But the forty-mile-long British Imperial motorized column already had passed through and was pressing on to Hamadan, 180 miles northeast, and the Russians simultaneously pushed rapidly south with indications that there would be a juncture of the Russo-British armies in the vicinity of Kazvin, 90 miles northwest of Teheran. The only signs of opposition I saw in a 300-mile trek over the baking desert and into formidable Paytak Pass from the Persian border was a short, stubby, fat-faced German engineer who had been nabbed at Karind and swore he had been a resident there for several years, planning the construction of a huge hotel on the main route from Baghdad to Teheran. This little gent claimed he had no connection whatever with the Axis schemes.

We caught up with the British column in the vicinity of Paytak Pass. The only signs of life we saw in the desert as we drove behind Ford scout cars and camouflaged Chevrolet and Dodge transport trucks, chauffeured by troopers holding handkerchiefs over their noses to prevent inhaling too much suffocating dust, were sheep and goats tended by sleepy Arabs. There were also Arabs, Sikhs, and Gurkhas stark naked and sitting neck-high in irrigation ditches and mud holes seeking refuge from heat of such intensity that I hurriedly withdrew my hand as I touched a chrome-plated handle in my hired Buick taxi.

In comparison with Greece, Syria, and the Western Desert where the tide of the war could easily be traced by wrecked and burned-out trucks and cars, and carcasses of mules and donkeys, there were no such scars in the Mesopotamia that had seen so much bloodshed in the World War. I noticed only one overturned truck and two flimsy stone barricades. The landmarks of the last war when the Turks were ousted from this district by the British were much more discernible, for there were still huge piles of tin cans, marking the old camping grounds.

To escape boredom during this wild goose chase over hundreds of miles of nothing at all, I occasionally engaged in arguments with my taxi driver concerning the rate I should pay per kilometer, for we had only struck a tentative agreement in Baghdad, and I was now beginning to wonder whether the United Press would be willing to pay the bill. But equally bored was an English major of the Indian army whom I questioned at Paytak Pass.

"The Persians," said he, "have been on the run from the beginning. We were prepared to fight a man-sized war but we can't find it here. Even in this pass, which I will wager could have been stoutly defended by fifteen determined men with machine guns, eight thousand Persians broke and ran when our artillery started pounding them. They are reported sixty-five kilometers ahead, and still running. We believe the officers are well ahead of the troops, for our advanced outpost saw them take to waiting automobiles as soon as things got hot, leaving the soldiers to find their own way to safety over the mountain peaks."

Passing through Persian villages, the only human beings we saw other than blind beggars were a few Persian policemen in robin blue uniforms with similarly colored French-style helmets studded with huge silver multipronged stars. They stood awkwardly at attention as our taxi passed, grinning with all their teeth. The Persian countryside is extremely barren until one reaches the plateau in the north. The Shah never paid much attention to irrigation except for his own huge estates. There was evidence of dire poverty all around as we continued toward Kazvin. I had never known what real rags were until I saw the tattered excuses for clothing draping the scrawny underfed bodies of the Persian peasants. All this appeared unjust to me, for Iran's oil revenues are fantastic. The trouble is that the Shah is the only one who controls the resources and benefits from the revenues.

With the meeting of the Russo-British forces imminent, I pushed the taxi driver another several hundred kilometers through alternately oven-hot valleys and chilly mountain ranges to the Shah's estate at Siadhoun, where I contacted the first group of Russian soldiers. My trip into northern Persia had not yielded any real signs of war until this point, where there were numerous bomb craters in the road—the work of Russian aviation—making it necessary for the taxi to swerve sharply.

Approaching the Tabriz-Kazvin road I noticed a Ford truck packed with troops undergoing emergency repairs. We passed, thinking they were Iranians, but after a second look we backed up for further inspection. As the Buick came alongside the truck, its occupants grabbed their rifles and were on the alert, but my shout of "Rouski?" put them at ease. They answered "Da," and seeing the British uniform, eagerly leaned from the truck, extending rough peasants' hands in greeting. They were wearing khaki coveralls and ammunition belts, with khaki slouched hats similar to those used by tennis players. A red felt star with a hammer and sickle in brass stood out prominently on their hats.

Through my Persian chauffeur, who spoke a few words of Russian, I told them I was an "Americansky" journalist. Thinking that I was an American officer, one of them who was wearing a Polish steel helmet, on which he rapped sharply with his knuckles to demonstrate its strength, asked if the American army were approaching Teheran. I laughed that one off and asked them where they were going, to which they replied "Teheran," at the same time offering Russian cigarettes in exchange for British ones. Occasionally they leaned from the truck to pat me on the back and squeezed their hands together to emphasize solidarity with the English and Americans.

We pushed on to Kazvin, arriving just too late to see the British brigadier and the commanding Russian general in northern Persia toast the Allied cause over vodka. I wished I could have been there.

Eyewitnesses say it was a comical sight. The Russian general and the brigadier were seated opposite one another at a small, linen-covered table in the restaurant of the only hotel in town. There were two bottles of vodka on that table, one containing a stronger brew than the other. There were also two glasses, one larger than the other; the Russian officer had the small one, the British officer the other. The boys say that every time the Russian lifted his glass to toast Stalin, Churchill, or Roosevelt (and there were many others) he filled his smaller glass with the weak vodka while pouring the stronger vodka to the brim of the brigadier's man-sized mug. It was bottoms-up time and again. Finally, the Russian stood up, bowed, and through his interpreter suggested that the red-faced brigadier and his staff stay the night, for it was a bit late to return to British lines. In the morning, the brigadier was somewhat the worse for wear. While investigating the prospects for breakfast, he bumped into his Russian counterpart who immediately produced a bottle of vodka. There was nothing else but for the extremely polite brigadier to resume the round of toasts before beating his retreat.

• • •

In Kazvin I was impressed with Russian military efficiency. The Russian army had taken over completely, and at every street corner one saw black-booted, helmeted Russian troopers directing traffic in stiff, semaphore fashion. At the entrance to the Kazvin hotel, which had become Russian headquarters, two short slouched-hatted sentries, shouldering rifles equipped with short stubby bayonets, stood guard. A few feet distant three more Russian troopers armed with automatic rifles paced stiffly back and forth. The hotel bustled with activity as Russian motorcycle couriers garbed in dusty blue-gray coveralls with helmets to match stomped up and down the creaking wooden stairs to deliver their messages.

Before continuing in the taxi to Teheran, I was surprised to see several buxom Russian women of the peasant type, wearing field gray uniforms with Sam Browne belts and huge revolvers strapped to their wide hips, come down the stairs of the hotel from the direction of the general's headquarters. One such woman passed a Russian officer of high rank, whereupon both saluted smartly. I asked a commissar nearby who these women were and he answered:

"They are doctors, nurses, and typists."

"But why do they carry pistols?" I asked.

"To defend themselves," he replied.

"Against whom?" I asked jokingly. "English and American newspapermen?"

With that, the commissar clamped his jaws together, bowed stiffly, turned on his heels and stomped off. Apparently he didn't see the joke.

I needed to file my story as quickly as possible in Teheran, so I went to the nearest filling station for petrol and found it guarded by two Russians with automatic rifles who stared suspiciously at my khaki war correspondent's uniform while holding their weapons in a most discouraging manner. They were making their rounds with weapons at the ready, resembling hunters stalking big game. A Russian officer, wearing an old-style visored cap and an unpolished double Sam Browne offsetting his blue-gray uniform, appeared just in time and advised me through my chauffeur to look for another filling station since the Persian attendants at this one had scrammed, and the keys of the pump were not available.

Obtaining gasoline at another station, we continued in the direction of Teheran but were shortly waved down by three Russians, one of them armed with a machine gun and the others with rifles, all pointed in our direction. It was a bit sticky because we couldn't make them understand who we were. Then a young officer appeared and, grinning from ear to ear, motioned his soldiers aside. With a "good morning" he briefly studied my passport and waved us on.

There was no further opposition to Teheran, a spotlessly clean city with buildings of stone and cement, and wide boulevards. Immediately on arrival, I proceeded to the post office and filed a long cable dispatch to London concerning the meeting of the Russo-British armies at Kazvin, with which I scooped the world by a good twelve hours. I'd done it "the hard way" and the following day received cabled cheers from the United Press in New York.

Prior to returning to Baghdad, I made a trip along the Shah's private highway to the Caspian Sea through sprawling ranges of mountains and jungle constituting the Shah's private domain. On the shores of the Caspian I found the Red Fleet in complete control. Efficiently and without any show of occupation, Russian marines and troops had been landed at strategic points along the southern coast of this vast inland ocean.

Russian naval officers, wearing faded blue smocks resembling those of French dock hands, were exceedingly accommodating and furnished me with a pass permitting me to circulate east and west at will in my taxi. There was no formality and although Russian marines were frequently in evidence along the coast road, they did not interfere with the Persian police who remained at their posts.

I continued westward where I saw Russian destroyers and gunboats on patrol a considerable distance offshore. Finally I reached Ramsar, where I found the dapper little Swiss manager of the Shah's model tourist motel—the most sumptuous and elaborate hostelry I have ever seen— still at his post. We were greeted like royalty by the Persian chief of police, who had been advised that we were en route, and much to my surprise I found that the Shah's chef had already prepared a menu with caviar leading the bill. It was a mild shock because I'd expected to find Red officers and marines treading the expensive Persian rugs in this resort hotel built by the Shah as a major attraction for the tourist trade in Iran.

The only other guests in the hotel, which was beautifully landscaped and gardened, with statues and fountains all around, were a Swiss couple from Teheran who had been vacationing at Ramsar when the Russians took over.

The Swiss manager said he was still functioning as he had "not received any counter order from His Majesty, although I am still in contact with the Court over the Shah's private telephone."

We slept in the hotel that night and in the morning asked for luggage stickers as souvenirs, but the manager told us that such things were not permitted by the Shah. As we prepared to return to Kazvin, where I had been promised an interview with the Russian General Max Sinenko, the chief of police insisted that I remain to hunt tigers on a vast preserve as the Shah's guest. It might have made for a good story, but the general was waiting.

• • •

After considerable palaver I was ushered into the general's headquarters. Sinenko, a man of about forty-five with graying, close-cropped hair, faced me across a small desk as orderlies and uniformed commissars walked in and out without ceremony, delivering messages. He was wearing a soiled uniform on which the only sign of high rank was four small oblong insignias in red stone on both collar points, and one large and two small gold chevrons on his cuffs. At the general's left was a Russian in civilian clothes, wearing a shabby felt hat pulled low over his ears. He introduced himself as the general's interpreter, but he certainly was a much bigger shot than that, for often he didn't even refer my questions to the general but answered them directly. Once, the fellow with the felt hat shoved his right arm across the general's nose to pick up a pack of cigarettes on the other side of the table and offer them to me. Seeing that I didn't have a match, he did it again without even a blink of an eye from Sinenko. I determined later that this fellow was a big bug at the Russian Embassy in Teheran.

Two other high-ranking officers sat speechless on an old-fashioned iron single bed with a red comforter as the general told me that "Germany's aggressive plans in the Near East have been paralyzed." The Russian army, he added, had "attained bloodlessly all its objectives in north Iran and with the cooperation of British Imperial Forces was now in a position to checkmate any German move." A staggering blow has been delivered to Germany, he added.

Following my interview I talked with a Russian commissar who showed me a German "Walther" pistol in a neat package, explaining that the Russians had seized hundreds of these in Persian police stations in Russian-occupied territory. The commissar showed me twenty-five bullets in the package, including three poisoned bullets. He said that each package was similarly equipped, with elaborate instruction for use, in Persian. He expressed the opinion that these were to have been distributed among Persian Fifth Columnists when Germany gave the word for a revolt.

With me, on the return trip to Baghdad, was an English army captain, acting as His Majesty's courier. The road south was barred to us by several Russian troopers who kept us waiting under guard for some time. This considerably irritated the captain, who suggested that a protest was in order, so we returned to Sinenko's headquarters. Speaking a combination of French and German, I delivered the captain's informal protest.

In reply, the general said:

"I must apologize to His Majesty's courier for the delay he suffered, which can largely be explained by the fact that a good many of my men are illiterate, hence could not understand the documents in his possession." And there was a glint of pride in the general's steel-gray eyes as he concluded, "Yes, many of my men are illiterate. They are simple peasants, but tell the honorable captain that they know how to fight as he shall see."

On the return trip through Kurdistan we picked up a Persian officer leading his little boy by the hand. He had just been demobilized and was returning to his village. There were not many refugees, although we saw numerous Persian men in civilian clothes carrying their discarded uniforms in bundles under their arms. The ragged Persian peasants appeared completely uninterested in events of the past several days. They presented a picturesque sight as they rounded curves on the broad,

well-graded highway with their legs flopping Don Quixote fashion from
the flanks of tiny donkeys. Persians go in for colors, mostly vivid blue,
although their rags emphasized their extreme poverty. The huge expanses
of Persia are not convenient tourist country because distances are too great
over the desert; however, I felt it was exceedingly worthwhile to see the
Persian mountain ranges, a cross between the Badlands of the Dakotas
and the gorges of Arizona. I'd never seen anything like the rugged
formations of rock shooting straight up, or the monstrous mounds of rich
reddish-brown loam in fantastic shapes suitable for a Dracula film.

No sooner did I reach Baghdad than I was urgently tipped to return
to Teheran, for it had now been decided that the British and the Russians
would proceed right up to the outskirts of the capital. The taxi was now
in a state of collapse, so I returned to Teheran in an Indian army vehicle,
traveling the same route over which the Shah had fled from Teheran to
Sultanabad. The new move was largely predicated by continuous activities
of Axis agents in the Iranian capital who, among other things, made so
bold as to continue sabotaging British and American correspondents'
dispatches in the face of the Russo-British occupation.

The Persians have been terrified of the Russians since the last war,
and now as the two armies converged on Teheran, we met numerous
limousines containing rich Iranians fleeing in terror.

The Russians did the job in fine style, even landing troops by parachute
on the outskirts of Teheran. Also, to guard against possible German
intervention, they landed scores of Russian bombers and fighters on
Persian aerodromes. The hands of the Axis were now tied.

As I entered the city again I saw several hundred gray-clad Russian
troopers marching four abreast toward their campsite ten minutes from
the city center. They were well equipped with grenades in their belts and
dragged machine guns on trolleys behind them.

As the new Shah, the former leader's son, was enthroned under Anglo-
Russian pressure, the Germans and Italians in Teheran took the tip and
evacuated the city in large bodies. The German legation in Teheran was
closed, and instead of the Swastika, the Swedish flag now flew at its mast.

It seemed to me that as the Persian campaign thus came to an end,
the Axis never would have obtained a foothold in the country had the
Allies properly ministered to the needs of the people after the last war.
It was the Allies who had installed the old Shah in office. He ruled the
country as a despot, in the manner of his ancestors, and while he became
fabulously wealthy from the oil lands which the British were exploiting,
his people were in rags and starving. I left Persia with the impression that
it must not be allowed to happen again; that England and America must
do something to help the countries of the Near East regain their feet after

this war. After all, here was Persia, a county rich in natural resources, a country three times the size of France, which since 1918 had been rotting away because of negligence. The piles of rubbish and rusty tin cans left behind by earlier armies, together with a crude monument to the Punjabi dead in Paytak Pass, were emblematical of all this. So far as I could see these were the only heritages left behind by the conquering armies of the last war. Otherwise, Persia had been largely forgotten.

As the Iraqi minister to Persia explained it to me during my brief stay in Teheran:

"We are poor countries. The Democracies must do something to help us."

Referring to the methods used by the Axis powers to establish a foothold in the Near East, the minister pointed out that in a recent year, Iraq had had a very good cotton crop, and had offered it to Britain, which demonstrated no interest.

"As a result," he said, "the Japanese bought our cotton at virtually double its normal price. By mutual agreement, for every million pounds of cotton purchased by Japan, Iraq would buy one and a half million pounds worth of Japanese goods. In reality, therefore, Japan bought our cotton for far less than was apparent, and at the same time achieved her aim of weaning the people away from the capitalistic democracies." Similar methods, he said, "were used in Iran by the Germans who flooded the market with their goods in exchange for Persian crops."

Such situations must be corrected. Otherwise there will be no end to world strife. When, after the defeat of the Axis, the time comes for the Democracies of the world to seriously discuss reconstruction, I sincerely hope that they will not forget such poor countries as Persia. I certainly shall not, for before my eyes remains the specter of women and children and blind beggars in rags, stretching out their emaciated arms, beseeching alms.

"Baksheesh!" they implore. It is the cry of the East.

138

Henry T. Gorrell.

COURTESY OF THE KEVIN
MANNIX COLLECTION.

Gorrell as a child in Italy. He is in the third row, fourth from the right.

COURTESY OF THE KEVIN MANNIX COLLECTION.

Gorrell with Greek troops in Albania.

COURTESY OF THE KEVIN MANNIX COLLECTION.

Gorrell in Syria.

COURTESY OF THE KEVIN MANNIX COLLECTION.

Gorrell at the souk.

COURTESY OF THE KEVIN MANNIX COLLECTION.

Gorrell trading cigarettes with Iraqis.

COURTESY OF THE KEVIN MANNIX COLLECTION

Gorrell inspecting entrenchment, Middle East.

COURTESY OF THE KEVIN MANNIX COLLECTION.

Gorrell with a British truck.

COURTESY OF THE KEVIN MANNIX COLLECTION.

Gorrell with Indian soldier.

COURTESY OF THE KEVIN MANNIX COLLECTION.

Gorrell at grave site.

COURTESY OF THE KEVIN MANNIX COLLECTION.

A United Press ad featuring war correspondent Henry Gorrell.

COURTESY OF UNITED PRESS INTERNATIONAL.

144

Gorrell receiving the U.S. Army Air Medal from Major General Lewis H. Brereton, Commander, U.S. Army Forces in the Middle East. COURTESY OF THE KEVIN MANNIX COLLECTION

Gorrell with his wife, Beatrice, and daughter, Marguerite, visiting Laconia, New Hampshire, shortly after the war ended.

COURTESY OF THE KEVIN MANNIX COLLECTION

A United Press ad featuring Gorrell and the Air Medal. COURTESY OF UNITED PRESS INTERNATIONAL.

Gorrell working at home.

COURTESY OF THE KEVIN MANNIX COLLECTION

15

INTERLUDE
OCTOBER 1941–MAY 1942

THE "DOC" JUST ABOUT WROTE ME OFF IN CAIRO IN OCTOBER 1941. Malaria, again. I'd had a walking case of it in Syria and Persia and subsequently in the Western Desert, and the whiskey I drank to keep me on my feet hadn't helped any.

"You're washed up for a while, young fellow," said the doctor as he ordered me into the Anglo-American Nursing Home. And then, in consultation with Walter Collins, Cairo manager of United Press, he'd added something about high blood pressure and a dilated heart. Rest, that was the prescription. "The fellow needs rest."

But for a month thereafter it was atebrin and plasmoquin and hospital diet for me. The bed was luxurious and the nurses were nice girls. I'd known a couple of them in 1936 in the Anglo-American at Rome. But I couldn't rest, for things were moving again. With the Near East now at least temporarily put out of danger, increased quantities of equipment, including Grant and Lee tanks, and American 105mm cannon mounted on Caterpillar tractors, were arriving in the Middle East. General Sir Claude Auchinleck was planning his November offensive in the desert that would liberate Tobruk and take the Eighth Army to Benghazi again.

"I've got to go back to the desert, doc," I insisted. "I can't miss the big show." But he wouldn't tolerate any nonsense.

When the November offensive began I was convalescing in the mountains of Syria, and the United Press, now in league with my doctor, sent in an alternate, refusing to permit my return to the desert. By mid-December 1941, as the Eighth Army slugged it out with Rommel's Afrika Corps, I was on my way by air on forced convalescent leave to the Union of South Africa.

• • •

America was now in the war. Singapore had fallen, and there was evidence that the Germans in conjunction with the Japanese in the Indian Ocean were plotting a move whereby they would cut the vital Cape route. By pure coincidence, therefore, I was going to South Africa at a most interesting period.

The first part of the trip south, over hundreds of miles of desert, was dull. There was only the endless serpentlike Nile to relieve the monotony as we traversed the Anglo-Egyptian Sudan. Thereafter, as we floated at two hundred miles an hour over the dense jungles of Uganda and Kenya, the trip grew exceedingly interesting.

I'd been mixed up with wars so long that it was hard for me to realize that here in Central Africa they'd never even heard about the First World War, let alone the second. Here, the natives still run around virtually naked as their medicine men indulge in acts of barbarism to drive off evil spirits. The doctor was right. A change of air was what I needed, and this sudden contact with a carefree and only half-civilized world bolstered and invigorated me. At Malakal, Sudan, I listened with deep interest to an American Presbyterian missionary, the Reverend Donald McClure from Pittsburgh, tell of his battle of wits with the black medicine men. They still fight with spears in these parts, and many sorely wounded natives are treated by McClure and other missionaries. On occasion these fine fellows even do a bit of dentistry, although they make no pretense at a painless job.

Especially interested was I in the methods used by McClure, who incidentally is reputed to be one of the best big-game hunters in his district, to win the superstitious blacks of the southern Sudan away from the medicine men.

"One day as I walked along one of the jungle paths," said McClure, "I heard a girl screaming. Investigating, I found a little native girl struggling flat on her tummy as two medicine men slashed her back, arms, and legs with a crude knife to the accompaniment of tom-toms. I pushed the medicine men aside and they nearly came at me with their knives, for this to them was an exceedingly solemn occasion. The little girl had complained of tummy ache and they were carving her up, as they said, to draw out the pain. I cured her in my own house. Salts soon eliminated the tummy ache, but it was some weeks before the gashes in her body had been healed."

McClure, who with his wife and two children lives in a district abounding in lion and other wild beasts, far away from any other white settlement, told me that he deliberately makes fools out of the medicine men to shame them before their black disciples. Once, pointing to a pigeon perched in a tree a good hundred yards distant, he asked a witch doctor whether he had the power to bring the pigeon down with his witchcraft.

"The fellow shook his head, whereupon I made a wager with him that I could kill that pigeon from where I stood. I added that I would do so only on condition that once having done this, he would acknowledge me as his superior and hand over his charms, which consisted mainly of beads and pieces of bone. I shot that pigeon down with my rifle and then took away the witch doctor's tools, throwing them to a group of native children nearby as playthings.

Although the world is going crazy all around them, the blacks of Central Africa are oblivious of any change. The women of the Dinkha tribes I saw at Juba still use the prehistoric type of rouge—red mud—which they daub in profusion over their gracefully slim naked bodies as a mark of beauty. The mud also protects against ticks and the swarms of jungle mosquitoes. Along with elephants, buffalo, zebra, and gazelle, I saw groups of naked black villagers scatter with terror as our Lockheed Lodestar of the South African Air Force roared just above tree level over districts few white men have ever trodden. This is one part of the world that has not yet been completely spoiled by the schemes of modern man.

At Nairobi, capital of Kenya, they have no wartime blackout rules. Once, just after Italy entered the war, Kenya was seriously threatened by the Italian armies. But the menace was effectively dealt with by the Sudan Frontier Police Force, which bluffed an enemy much superior in numbers until Expeditionary Forces could be organized in South Africa and Egypt to drive the Dagos out of Eritrea and Abyssinia.

Unless one wants to listen to the BBC over the radio at Nairobi, one need know nothing about the trend of the war to live quite nicely in Kenya. They are slightly behind the times down there in East Africa, for although it had been months before that the BEF retreated from Greece, one still saw posters in Nairobi beseeching financial help for the Greek army. As for me, I temporarily put the war behind me. My only challenge in Kenya came when a monkey, chained in a tree in the yard of a Nairobi hotel, swooped down suddenly and grabbed my pipe out of my mouth. I threw my hat at the monkey, whereupon the critter flew into a screaming rage and angrily hurled my pipe to the ground, breaking it in half.

• • •

In South Africa it was different. Whereas up to the time of Pearl Harbor they had felt themselves very far away from the war, just as had we in the United States, recent developments in the Pacific, including the fall of Singapore, appeared to have opened the Union's back door to the Japanese.

When I arrived at Durban, a modern city on the shores of the Indian Ocean reminding one of certain parts of Florida and California, the newspapers were embarked on an all-out campaign for "adequate defense of Union ports." At the same time, the South African and Allied

Supreme Commands were consulting on measures necessary to defend the vital sea lanes around the Cape to the Middle East and India.

While newspapers stressed the vulnerability of Durban and Cape Town in the event the Japanese Fleet penetrated the Indian Ocean, plans were under way for the partial evacuation of coastal cities should serious emergency arise. But comparative calm prevailed as it was generally felt that in Jannie Smuts, South Africa had a man who knew all the answers.

The Union's predicament following Japan's entry into the war was understandable, since its entire war effort up to that point had been directed at driving the Italians out of Abyssinia and strengthening the defenses of Suez. The bulk of South Africa's fighting forces and equipment were at the time in Libya.

I was impressed with South Africa's war effort, for in December of 1941 approximately 6 percent of the Union's entire European population— men and women alike—were already in khaki. More were volunteering daily, and their industrial plants were working overtime turning out everything from army boots to gun carriages and shells as the country underwent a rapid transformation from a peacetime to a full war footing. If we in America at the time had had 6 percent of our entire population in khaki, it would have meant something like 7,860,000 people under arms.

In eighteen months, upwards of half a million British and Imperial troops had passed through Durban, known as the "Halfway House to the East," en route to Suez and Singapore.

Although Japanese submarines had been reported operating a hundred miles from the Cape, South Africa's greatest concern early in 1942 was the great island of Madagascar, the largest in the world, and ranking with Malta and Cyprus strategically. Because there were fewer than three thousand white troops in Madagascar, which then was still under Vichy French control, it was doubted in the Union whether the island would be capable of protecting itself against a Japanese blitz. Additionally, considering the experience with the men of Vichy in Syria and the Vichy sell-out in Indochina, the Allies were keeping an eye peeled for signs of treachery.

Home defense was the major topic on the agenda of Parliament as it convened in Cape Town in January 1942. Meanwhile, business in South Africa was booming, partly because of the expansion of industry to meet war needs, but also because of the tremendous sea traffic and the presence of thousands of evacuees from the North in the Union. Taxes were not excessive, food and money were plentiful, and unemployment at a minimum. Working shifts were being extended by vote of the laboring man himself.

I enjoyed myself in South Africa, whose hospitality is unrivaled. In this, I am sure, thousands of troops whose convoys have touched at Durban and Cape Town will bear me out. The men in khaki have always been royally feted in the Union and there have been cases of a single South African family taking in as many as fifteen Tommies at a time, not allowing them to pay a penny for food, lodging, and entertainment during their stay. The fine boulevards of Durban and Johannesburg reminded me of the more prosperous cities of America, with their scores of sleek automobiles imported from the USA.

The Japanese menace had sobered the people of South Africa, and united them in the realization that the Union was directly in danger. True, there were political differences, for South Africans thrive on politics and for some, it has been difficult to forget the Boer War, but compared to the early days of the war, dissension was at a minimum and Field Marshal Smuts, with a comfortable majority in Parliament, ruled the country justly and with a firm hand. It hadn't been easy to wear khaki in the Union in late 1939 when "Jannie" Smuts shoved his War Resolution through a semi-hostile Parliament in Cape Town and asked for volunteers to kick the Italians out of Abyssinia and fight in the Western Desert. Nevertheless, volunteers came up by the thousands. There were troublemakers aplenty, some of whom on principle didn't see the point of South Africa going to war against anybody, and there were disturbances in some towns, with volunteers severely handled by antiwar demonstrators. Additionally, as had occurred recently in Mexico, a so-called Fifth Column in the Union (largely organized and paid by foreign elements) threw a lot of muck around—I.R.A. fashion—in the form of crude, homemade bombs.

But Smuts was farsighted. He knew his people—knew that they would respond wholeheartedly in the long run—and quietly but steadfastly went about the task of isolating and pinning down the troublemakers, preparing his country for a long, hard war.

The aged premier was right. The public's response was spontaneous as events proved the soundness of his policy and the need for a nationwide effort to keep the enemies of Democracy at bay: events such as the collapse of France; evacuation of the BEF from Greece; the German occupation of Crete; and the increased activity of submarines on the high seas. This last threat, punctuated by the treacherous Japanese attack on Pearl Harbor and the reverses in the East, endangered vital shipping traffic around the Cape to India, the Persian Gulf, and Suez.

Prior to my return to the Middle East, I was privileged to see Smuts in action in Parliament. The opposition, not having much of a leg to stand on following the series of alarming developments in the Pacific, was indulging in what Smuts, in his reply, termed "an academic debate on the merits of a Free Republic." I watched the silvery-haired, white-bearded prime minister, clad in dark gray suit, blue shirt, and tie, with handkerchief to match, yawn and stretch as he sat out the opposition's harangue. He then plugged their case full of holes with quips that reduced the government supporters to helpless laughter. Smuts knew that he stood on firm ground now, for it was clear that even the most hardened neutral might jib at surrender to the Yellow menace. Smuts minced no words as he pointed out that he had never known the opposition to adopt a weaker attitude.

"I am pleasantly surprised," said he, "that nothing more is heard of that old plea for neutrality or for a separate peace. These issues are stone dead now."

Smuts added that he thought the opposition's present attitude was "due to the surprising change that has come about in the war situation," emphasizing that they repeatedly had stated America would never enter the war; also that Russia would only last a few weeks. "But," he added, "there possibly is another reason for the opposition's change of attitude— Japan is now an ally of Germany, and a German victory would mean a Japanese victory. Recent events have given the answer to the argument that South Africa should stay out of the war. Many countries that used the same argument have been destroyed. South Africa today stands in line with the strongest countries of the world."

Smuts received thunderous applause from the government benches.

• • •

I stayed long enough in South Africa to get married, and then early in May 1942 returned to the Middle East by convoy through the Red Sea. As our transport, full of South African volunteers, slowly progressed northward with battleships and cruisers of the British Fleet protecting us against attack from the Japanese, we listened to radio reports on the British campaign in Madagascar. In a short time this campaign eliminated the Axis threat to the Cape sea route. The Madagascar expedition was timely, for things had come to a showdown in the Far East, as Rangoon and Mandalay fell to the Japs and the U.S. Fleet fought it out with the Japanese Armada in the battle of the Solomons.

I never again want to go through the tortures of that trip in convoy to Suez. The humidity was such that we experienced the equivalent of two or three Turkish baths a day. There were amusing touches, however, such as my conversation with a South African volunteer who had left eleven children behind. I asked him how he had found it possible to leave such a big family. "Oh," said he, "that's easy. I left the kids with the old woman. She's the one who made me join up."

• • •

Arriving in Cairo on May 23 I found an entirely different atmosphere from that prevailing five months before, despite the only partial success of Auchinleck's November offensive. The Eighth Army was on the defense along the Gazala line, but public optimism was at a peak, largely due to the spectacular success of General Semyon Timoshenko's armies in Russia, and the man in the street in Cairo for the first time was openly discussing when he thought "the war would end."

Prices were skyrocketing due to the shipping situation and Egyptian profiteering. Whiskey was practically unobtainable, unless you were ready to pay a small fortune for a bottle. A pack of American cigarettes cost fifty cents and an average English pipe twenty dollars. A live chicken fetched a dollar and a half and an old automobile one had purchased two years before for a few hundred dollars was now worth well over a thousand. Tires were a hundred dollars apiece.

• • •

On May 27, Rommel attacked along the Gazala line in the region of Bir Hacheim, with Tobruk as his immediate objective. It was the start of an all-out Axis offensive aimed at the Delta. For days the Fighting French held on grimly to their Bir Hacheim positions at the southern extremity of the Gazala line as bombers and fighters of the RAF, including newly arrived Spitfires and Kittyhawks, inflicted heavy casualties on the enemy. Soon, however, the situation became serious, for Germans within a few days had succeeded in creating two gaps about fifteen miles wide in the Gazala–Bir Hacheim Line, thereby relieving their supply situation and managing to get tanks through for purposes of reconcentration.

A tremendous tank battle raged for days in the region of Knightsbridge. The losses were heavy on both sides, with hundreds of tanks knocked out, but Rommel recovered more quickly than did the less-experienced armored units of the Eighth Army. He resumed his offensive, backed by strong reserves of Mark IIIs and Mark IVs which he now threw into the line against our "General Grants" and "General Lees," which in limited numbers were in action in the desert for the first time.

The British were fighting hard to maintain a foothold in the Knightsbridge box, west of El Adem, and the situation was becoming critical, for there was danger of the First South African Division and the Fiftieth Division being cut off in the region of Gazala. But still, the people of Cairo and Alexandria, lulled into a sense of false optimism, amused themselves. There were cricket matches at Cairo's Gazira Club, and hundreds flocked to Alexandria for bathing and weekend horse racing.

There was no prospect of my going to the desert, for the British army then only allowed one man to represent any one agency at a time in the field, and the veteran correspondent Richard McMillan was in the line for our agency. The United Press therefore arranged to have me accredited to the British Mediterranean Fleet to fill a sudden vacancy. The assignment was timely, for while Rommel tried for a knockout in the desert, the Luftwaffe was making a determined effort to smash Malta, and Axis submarines were massing for a showdown with remnants of the once-powerful British Mediterranean Fleet. The "Battle of the Mediterranean" now had begun in earnest.

16

MALTA CONVOY

I F EVER I'VE BEEN AFRAID OF DISPLAYING FEAR UNDER FIRE IT was on June 13, 1942, when I boarded a British cruiser at the start of a convoy to Malta.

Odds were heavily against the British Mediterranean Fleet and a number of warships were certain to be sunk, for the entire Italian battle fleet was waiting for us, supported by strong forces of shore-based bombers, submarines, and motor-torpedo boats. An effort had been made at maintaining secrecy, but to no avail. German stratosphere reconnaissance planes, penetrating as far south as Port Sudan, had recorded every move of the convoy as it approached Suez. RAF fighters could give us protection for only about a hundred miles, after which the fleet would have to shoot it out—alone.

It was a dramatic showdown because Malta was running short of supplies and might not be able to hold out much longer. The beleaguered island was the key to control of the Mediterranean. "Malta must be held at all costs," ordered the Admiralty.

The Allies could not afford heavy losses at sea, for the fleet had suffered mightily at Crete; there were now no capital ships or aircraft carriers in commission in the Mediterranean, and none could be spared from the Atlantic, Pacific, and Indian oceans. Therefore, as reserve cruisers and destroyers were ordered into this inland sea in mid-June in an epic attempt to save Malta, Goering's high-level torpedo and dive bombers prepared for the kill. What could the British Fleet do, with only cruisers and destroyers in line, against the Luftwaffe and Italian battleships? Mussolini had carefully nursed his fleet, and now had released them from their ports of refuge in Sardinia, Sicily, and southern Italy for a showdown in *Mare Nostrum*.

But there was one little item upon which the Germans and Italians had not counted: heavy bombers of the U.S. Army Air Force.

Arrival of the huge four-engine B-24Ds capable, says tradition, "of dropping a bomb into a pickle barrel from twenty thousand feet," had been a well-kept secret—so well kept in fact that days into the mission when the British gunners spied them as mere specks in the sky over our convoy, they let the Americans have it, mistaking them for German bombers. The Yanks then proceeded to dust the decks of two Italian battleships and several cruisers and destroyers with bouquets of 500-pound bombs, sending them scurrying home to Benito in panic. Later, at their base in Palestine, "Dusty" Rhodes, good-natured Texan pilot of one of the bombers, told me:

"Those limeys sure did some fancy shooting—too fancy to suit me. I wouldn't want to be Fritz for long over a British convoy."

I can verify that statement because, in the course of a three-day nightmare, I saw the better part of twenty-seven enemy planes shot down by British four-inch guns and pom-poms as the Luftwaffe tried its damnedest to sink the fleet. But I also was to witness the loss of the cruiser *Hermione,* the destroyers *Airdale* and *Hasty,* and two merchant ships under dive-bomb and torpedo attacks.

Newcastle was one of several cruisers loaned to the Mediterranean Fleet especially for this job. The merchants, carrying badly needed supplies for Malta, were to be protected by an escorting squadron, including substantial destroyer reserves, under the command of Admiral Sir Philip Vian. His flagship was to be the cruiser *Cleopatra,* with Admiral Tennant, who commanded *Repulse* at Singapore, second in command. British naval discipline does not permit of asking many questions, hence when with David Prosser, British News Reels photographer, I entered the wardroom, the officers spoke of everything else but what obviously lay ahead. The admiral would advise us of the nature of the assignment only when the convoy was well out to sea.

It was thrilling to see the Greyhounds of the Sea dart off at the starting signal, zigzagging at full speed through the water like graceful silver fish, with their sailors standing at rigid attention as they passed the flagship. The boys on our cruiser crowded to starboard to watch the sleek destroyers dart past.

"There go the real sailors," they said. "Those are the boys who run the sea."

"See those beauties? That's one good thing about being on a flagship. They never lose you."

Acting the part of a battleship, for we had none in the line, was an ancient hulk. Riding high, with cork and air-filled drums in her insides to prevent her sinking, she might have been funny to those of us who watched her, but it was no laughing matter for the men who sailed her, for their job was to deliberately draw enemy fire. She certainly did her job on that convoy for we saw her hit dead-center by bombs at least a couple of times and sprayed with tons of sea water from innumerable near misses as her gallant crew, determined to fight back, fired Oerlikon guns at low-flying aircraft. They sounded like popguns compared to the pom-poms and four-inchers of the other warships.

At nightfall, Admiral Tennant addressed personnel through the ship's radio loudspeakers.

"Well," said he, "here we are about to play a major match. It will probably be a tough one. The eyes of the world may shortly be turned our way and in any case, the eyes of all who know are watching us and wishing that they were in our places.

"We have a chance to do a great bit of work for the Old Country, for we shall only win the war by inflicting damage on the enemy's armed forces. We may face a great number of enemy warships, aircraft, and undersea craft, in which case we'll hit them hard. I wish you all a glorious success."

The admiral's reference to "winning the war by inflicting damage on the enemy's armed forces" was the first tip-off that the Admiralty also had a few aces up its sleeve. Through the grapevine, we soon learned that not only was the RAF also in this show, but heavy bombers of the U.S. Army Air Force had arrived in the Middle East under General Lewis Brereton and were standing by with loaded bomb bays prepared to give the enemy a taste of its own medicine. We were therefore not only a safeguard to a vital convoy, but ourselves a decoy for the Italian battle fleet, which it was hoped would now come out in chase of "easy game" and receive a thorough hiding.

Now the captain was speaking over the radio amplifier:

"Officers and men," he said,

> we are out to help Malta which has been bombed steadily and has been a splendid example of sticking in. We are seven cruisers including four of the Dido class, and can do a lot of damage.
>
> We are the forces of the Eastern end. The convoy is just ahead and we are going to join up with them at 6 a.m. and take them through. When we do, we'll have a lot more destroyers with us. We have fine anti-aircraft defenses, better than any city or even Malta itself can throw at aircraft. We must expect to be attacked, for the enemy is out to get Malta. There will be submarines and we are close to enemy aircraft from Crete and Libya. They'll probably attack day and night. There is also a chance of meeting the Italian battle fleet. As you see, we must be prepared for anything. But the convoy from the Gibraltar end is on its way now and it will stretch the Italians to get at us both.
>
> There is a chance that we may have to turn back, for there is a battle going on in Libya, but we can rely on considerable air support. There are some Beau fighters with us and tomorrow we shall have

more. Should the entire Italian fleet come down on us we might
have to turn back; otherwise we shall try to drive the enemy off and
push the convoy around the corner to Malta. The operation has been
carefully prepared and splendidly organized under the leadership of
Admiral Sir Philip Vian of *Cleopatra*. It will be a wonderful and big
achievement if it is really seen through. So be on your toes to slip to
action stations and snatch sleep whenever you can.

Prosser had been on numerous convoys and had seen much action
with the fleet in the Mediterranean, but he confided to me after the
addresses of the admiral and the captain that he didn't feel too perky over
this assignment. He added that he thought I was "dotty" to take this trip
when I didn't have to. We spoke frankly. One does when death is lurking
around the corner, and the enemy already was dropping blinding white
magnesium flares, mapping the course of the convoy for the submarines
and Italian motor-torpedo boats known as E-boats. I told David as we sat
on a pile of rope in the look-out locker on the starboard lower bridge deck
that I had come not only because I felt it would be a big story but also
because I wanted to prove to myself that I could face fire again, especially
after what the doctor had told me in Cairo last November about being
"washed up."

At 10:30 p.m. the captain broadcast his opinion that it was almost certain
we would not be attacked that night. The flares were still illuminating the
convoy and warships, but we were still in range of our protective screen
of fighters from Africa, and the enemy most likely would await a more
favorable opportunity to attack.

Starting on the Sunday morning of June 14, things really began to
get hot. The yellow air-raid alert flag was hoisted repeatedly as enemy
aircraft were reported in the vicinity, but the RAF was on the job and
only once did a formation of high-level bombers manage to break
through our protective screen and attack the convoy. They dropped their
bombs in salvos and chalked up their first victim—a merchant vessel
which I saw hit amidships and burst into flames. She was settling down
slowly as screening destroyers closed on her and picked up survivors.
That morning the RAF intercepted and drove off repeated waves of
bombers, one wave consisting of forty Ju-87s and 88s escorted by twenty
Messerschmitts.

By midafternoon we were out of range of our fighters and the bombing
began in earnest. From then on the men on the signals bridge were kept
busy hoisting yellow and red flags, warning of impending air attacks.
Stukas screamed out of the sun by the dozens, but the fire of the fleet's
guns was so accurate that they were forced to pull out of their dives

prematurely and all of their bombs exploded harmlessly in the ocean, sending up huge geysers of white foam.

I was below decks when the gunnery officer, nicknamed "Guns," opened his running commentary on the "start of the away match" over the radio amplifiers. One couldn't help but be inspired by these men below decks who couldn't distinguish between our own gunfire and the exploding bombs, and yet never looked up as they stood at their posts, wearing life belts. These men who kept our ship running on what seemed the brink of Hell appeared superhuman, yet they proved themselves very human indeed. During attacks that seemed to offer little hope of surviving, they hummed familiar ditties such as the British favor: "She was poor but she was honest, victim of a rich man's whim." "Guns's" commentary amused the boys, who poked fun at the Luftwaffe as he told them that so far only one ship (the merchant vessel bombed in the morning) had been hit.

They came at us with a vengeance for the duration of the afternoon and I saw at least five planes shot down in flames, one of them hit squarely by a four-inch shell as it leveled out for its bomb run over us. Every man gave every ounce of his strength, with action stations constantly maintained and meals served to the men at the guns by the ship's cooks. The fleet was fighting for its life, and the loaders, operating in relays, were feeding the hungry red-hot four-inch guns and pom-poms with the precision of automatons. The cheerful attitude of the men throughout the action was a tonic. There were some amusing moments, such as watching a searchlight crew playing with a pet turtle which drew in its head hurriedly as the "Alarm Red" flag was hoisted and hundreds of guns began firing with an ear-shattering rumble. After near misses shook the cruiser from stem to stern one could hear the boys say: "Very rude of them, wasn't it?" and "Try it again, Jerry, your eyesight's bad."

That evening, torpedo bombers appeared for the first time. Flying almost level with the water, they were hard to spot in the yellowish light, so the cruisers and destroyers maintained a barrage with four- and six-inch guns. The din was terrific, and such was the intensity of our bombardment that a pall of smoke swathed the convoy. The barrage was too much for the enemy and the torpedo bombers veered off, firing their tin fish haphazardly. We could see many torpedo tracks amongst our zigzagging warships. Destroyers seemed to be literally spinning around on their sterns as they took avoiding action. There were no hits and the red flag was lowered, marking the end of the attack.

I would be kidding myself if I said that I wasn't scared, but I found myself joining the gunners in their songs between alerts as I stood alongside David Prosser, who kept loading and snapping his camera throughout the action. Our "battle station" was on the flag deck of the cruiser and we both wore an antiflash hood—a fireproof covering to protect us against flames from explosion or incendiaries—along with fireproof gauntlets, steel helmets, and the cumbersome but comforting life preservers known as "Mae Wests."

The battle was now approaching peak intensity. At 8 p.m. we were attacked by Dorniers, three of which flew directly over us and dropped their bombs so close that we were showered with sea water. Five minutes after they had been driven off, an emergency green signal was hoisted, and as Prosser nudged me I looked over the port side just in time to see a torpedo approach. One of our spotters had seen its tracks in time for the cruiser to maneuver out of its way. There were to be many more tin fish in the days to come: The U-boats had joined the melee. Ominously, I heard an officer remark to one of his mates that "we'll see many more by this time tomorrow." There was to be no more sleep for the crew, who already had been subjected to terrific strain keeping their eyes glued to the horizon for low-flying planes, submarine periscopes, and the wake of torpedoes. Throughout Sunday night the sky was brilliantly lit with flares through which German and Italian planes showered tons of bombs. It was unnerving to see those flares float slowly down and then to hear the whistle of bombs followed by muffled thuds as they struck the water. Within a few hours, hundreds of shells had been fired by our gunners, and they were watching the ammunition closely now. We still had a long way to go and the decks of the cruisers were already piled high with empty shell casings.

At midnight, long-range RAF reconnaissance planes reported having sighted E-boats about twenty miles ahead of the convoy. Normally, with sufficient air support, destroyers would have been dispatched forthwith to deal with them, but this time it was inadvisable. We had no air protection, and individual destroyers would most likely be attacked as "easy targets" by enemy aircraft. In his next commentary, "Guns" warned of grave danger henceforth from the E-boats. I walked to the bridge and noticed the admiral, captain, and other officers straining their eyes, trying to spot the deadly little ships in the darkness. The flares were turning night into day, but the fleet did not fire, for it would only give away the position of the convoy.

Suddenly, a flare dropped just ahead of us and I heard Admiral Tennant say, "Ah, that's just what I wanted." With that he took up his glasses and scanned the water. He didn't care about the bombs that inevitably would follow. Instead of cursing the blinding light of the flares, he was thankful, for they would help him find any E-boats that might be lurking nearby. "Guns" told me that he hoped they'd come on, as he was certain we'd "get the little bastards."

We were now eighty-five miles south of Crete and about eighty miles north of Derna, the principal Italian E-boat base of North Africa. Everyone aboard set his jaw against new ordeals ahead, while the ship's padre circulated below decks encouraging the men.

At about 1 a.m. Monday I fell asleep atop a pile of hammocks on the lower flag deck. I knew nothing more until about 4 a.m. when I awakened to a clatter of running feet as buglers sounded the "Alarm to Arms." I picked myself up in a daze and poked my nose over the starboard side just in time to see an E-boat silhouetted in the glare of our searchlights about eight hundred yards distant.

"Open fire!—open fire!—open fire!" "Guns" shouted from the bridge. But nothing happened. Then I heard him shout, "Look out below, torpedoes approaching to starboard."

He meant me, because I was still gawking like a country bumpkin over the side. Within a matter of seconds, I was knocked flat on my back by a terrific explosion followed by a blinding flash. A torpedo had struck us with a metallic crash much louder than the explosion of a six-inch gun. I was extremely lucky, because by all laws that blast should have blown me overboard. I went to the bridge and found it absolutely calm, with fellows still scanning the water with their night glasses. The captain silently came up to "Guns" and very quietly asked, "What has happened?"

"The pom-pom to starboard jammed, sir. They say the safety was on."

The captain asked no more questions and returned to his position on the bridge.

There was no excitement evident as they awaited the engineer's report; though for all we knew it might soon be necessary to give the order to abandon ship. The explosion had jarred the ship considerably and water was now pouring into the men's mess forward. Below decks, there was not a murmur and not a man left his post. Shortly, a young Irish midshipman appeared on the bridge. He had been below decks and heard a consultation between the Engineer officers.

"There's not a chance of her sinking, sir," he shrilled, his enthusiasm provoking a general laugh.

The flag lieutenant on the bridge had saved the day, spotting the E-boat in time. The boat had fired two torpedoes at us but only one of them had hit us, and the impact had been in the chain locker as the cruiser had heeled sharply over by order from the captain.

The only casualty from the torpedo hit was a pet parrot living in the men's quarters that had had most of his feathers blown off. As seamen raced through the fumes to his rescue, trying to extricate the parrot from under a mass of kit, the critter was heard squawking and cursing. With water rising around him, the bird, between oaths, would scream: "Jolly good show! Jolly good show!"

We lost speed as shipwrights repaired the damage. But remarkably soon the section of the ship that had been flooded was shored up and the cruiser managed twenty knots as she rejoined the rest of the squadron. The fellows below were placed at ease by the verdict of "Guns." One of them puffed his cigarette casually as he remarked:

"Bit of a thrill, eh?"

Another rubbed his eye sleepily and said, "Gave us a bit of a shock, that one."

At 5:30 a.m. the destroyer *Hasty* just ahead of us caught a torpedo in the forward magazine. There was a tremendous flash and a great fork of smoke as *Hasty*'s bridge telescoped under the impact.

She was finished, and as we passed her, her forward guns were pointing into the water, which was filled with bright flakes of burning oil resembling fireflies. It was sad to see the mortally wounded destroyer drifting by helplessly as hooded figures groped along her shattered, burning decks, preparing to abandon ship. The torpedo that got her had been one of two fired at us by a U-boat. We had taken evasive action and *Hasty* had maneuvered straight into its path.

About an hour later, as destroyers reported having recovered all but fourteen of *Hasty*'s crew, the cruiser *Hermione* was struck by two torpedoes and sank within three minutes. There was a gigantic sheet of flame on the horizon from the explosion, and as destroyers hurled depth charges against the unseen submarines, there was a patchwork of red tracers resembling neon lights gone mad as nearby warships fired their guns along the beams of their searchlights at E-boats. I saw one E-boat rammed by a destroyer and then polished off with pom-poms. A naval photographer who was aboard *Hermione* when she was hit told me later, "It seemed every bone of my body was being crushed, such was the concussion of the destroyers' depth charges as they fought off the submarines while we struggled in the water." Surprisingly, *Hermione*'s casualties were not heavy. I heard not a word of comment on the bridge as Sparks reported the *Hermione* had gone down. None of us slept the rest of that night, for there were frequent submarine and E-boat alerts before dawn.

At first light we were attacked by a strong formation of dive bombers. Despite the fleet's furious barrage of ack-ack they stuck to us for a good half hour. Then came a report that the Italian Fleet was bearing down on us.

"Do you blame me for being pessimistic?" said Prosser.

The Italian force consisted of two Littorio battleships, two eight-inch gun cruisers, and several six-inch gun cruisers, along with ten or more escorting destroyers. They were only about a hundred miles distant, but our cruisers never altered their course. Just before 9 a.m., the yellow alert flag was hoisted, soon to give way to the "Alarm Red" when a formation of heavy bombers had been sighted. These turned out to be the Americans who, in an attempt to identify us, had made the mistake of flying directly over the convoy and escort. The British gunners had itchy trigger fingers and they let them have it, but fortunately none of the friendly bombers were hit.

During the next hour, we were not molested. The Italian Fleet was on the defensive, catching hell from the American B-24s and torpedo bombers of the Royal Air Force. Both battleships were reported hit, and two cruisers and at least one destroyer were struck by bombs and torpedoed. One Trento-class cruiser was later reported sunk by torpedoes from British submarines that had lain in wait for the Italians.

Now was the time to push the convoy through, but our warships had fired so much ack-ack that the ammunition supply was virtually exhausted. As the Italian battle fleet scurried for cover, we were forced to turn back. We made it to Alexandria on the evening of June 16, but not without further losses, for enemy air attacks were incessant and E-boats and submarines hammered away without respite in a determined effort to cripple the fleet. During one frenzied attack in which several German planes were brought down and others vomited black streams of smoke as they retreated to their bases in Crete, I saw the destroyer *Airedale* struck by two 1,000-pound bombs. After her survivors were rescued, she was subsequently sunk by our own destroyers as Admiral Tennant signaled: "Shells on the water line, and quickly."

When we reached Alexandria Harbor there was an alert, for we had brought the Luftwaffe with us. In Alexandria we heard that the Gibraltar end of the convoy managed to punch several ships through to Malta. The convoy had not been completely successful. Several ships loaded with badly needed supplies, including an oil tanker in our unit that had miraculously weathered the deluge of bombs, had been forced to turn back with us.

Admiral Harwood, of *Graf Spee* renown, who commanded the British Mediterranean Fleet at the time, congratulated the warships under Admiral Vian for their exceedingly accurate anti-aircraft fire. "At least we have pushed some ships through to Malta and we have achieved one success—drawing enemy forces from their area of safety and inflicting heavy damage on them."

• • •

Later I interviewed Lieutenant Commander Lynch Maydon, A.S.O., whose submarine torpedoed an Italian Trento-class cruiser after it had been bombed by American heavies. Maydon, who was born in South Africa and lived in Dorset, England, said the Italian Fleet was thrown into "wild confusion difficult to describe" by aircraft of the RAF and USAAF.

We were shadowing the Italian battle fleet and had picked out two battleships and two cruisers in the line ahead as targets to our torpedoes. But when we were about to attack, we found to our astonishment and mortification that they had turned ninety degrees away from us. We soon learned the reason: They were being heavily bombed, and our own submarine was in the unenviable position of being in the center of a fantastic circus of wildly careening capital ships, cruisers, and destroyers, none of which maintained course sufficiently long to justify firing torpedoes.

At times we were tempted to fire Browning salvos[1] but we submerged amidst the bomb splashes, none of which, fortunately, were very close to us. At one time there was no point of the compass which was not occupied by Italian warships weaving crazily to and fro. In fact, there was a tendency to stand and gape through the telescope in utter amazement at the extent of their panic.

The battleships disappeared behind a haze of smoke from what turned out to be an Italian cruiser already on fire from bombing. We waited in what we believed would be the subsequent path of the enemy warships and turned out to be correct. They came back. We fired a salvo and got a hit on one of the Italian battleships of the Littorio class. She was then doing twenty-five knots and later was reported doing only ten, indicating serious damage. As we fired our torpedoes the situation was further complicated by a second bombing attack which in fact was nice for us because the Italians could have come back looking for us.

An Italian cruiser was now belching fire from its funnels and another cruiser and two destroyers were circling it, laying an ineffective white smoke screen. Meantime, we were working madly to reload our torpedo tubes, and once had to dive deep because the Italian destroyers were getting suspicious and menacing us. One of them passed directly over our submarine.

We completed our loading and fired two torpedoes; then we went deep and got the hell out of the way. Seven depth charges

---

1. The term "Browning salvos" refers to salvos of torpedoes aimed at a convoy or group of ships as a whole without singling out any particular ship.

dropped pretty close to us after which we surfaced and found all the destroyers were busy picking up survivors from the cruiser which had gone to the bottom in less than three minutes. All that was left was a tremendous cloud of smoke.

As of this writing, the Italian battle fleet has not again left the security of its naval bases.

17

THE RETREAT TO ALAMEIN

H AVE YOU EVER CELEBRATED BEING ALIVE? IT'S A marvelous experience; far better than a birthday. The world can be tumbling down around your ears, but you're blissfully unaware of it.

I was in such a mood on June 17, immediately following my return to Alexandria with the fleet from the Malta convoy. I had two reasons for celebrating. First, I congratulated myself that I had not been forced to swim for it when that torpedo struck the *Newcastle;* second, I had just received word from my wife in Johannesburg that our first child was on the way. Nothing mattered except that I was alive on that stool in the Windsor Hotel bar and that soon I would be a Papa. I couldn't even get really sore at the RN naval commander who had slashed to pieces the yarn I had written on the sea battle, on the grounds that maybe the Hun didn't know he had sunk a few of our ships. I was knocking off one Scotch whiskey after another, unaware of the presence of anybody else, when an English officer in a tattered, dusty uniform, his face looking as though he'd just come out of a flour mill, pulled me out of my trance with:

"Won't you have one with me?"

"Sure, thanks!"

It developed that both of us were there for the same reason, for this fellow also felt that he was living on borrowed time.

"My company was cut to pieces at Gazala," said the officer, a blond giant from Kent. "Originally, thirty-two of us were taken prisoner. We made a break for it under heavy fire and sixteen of us got out. I have just hitchhiked back to Alexandria, for I have lost my unit. Tonight I am supposed to be dead, but tomorrow I'll fool them!"

There were many such instances, for as the laconic communiqués put it, the fighting in the Western Desert had become "fluid."

Rommel's panzers were making headway fast, as General Neil Ritchie completed new dispositions of his forces, successfully withdrawing the First South African Division and the old Fiftieth from their positions

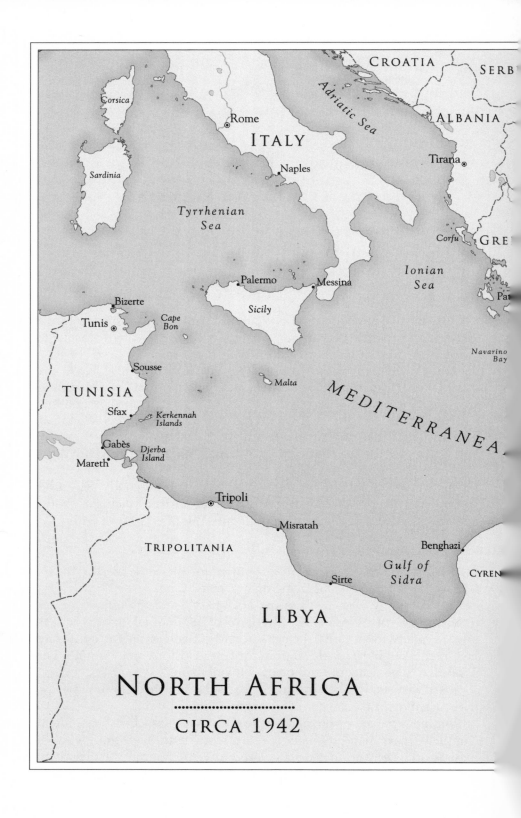

CROATIA

SERB

Adriatic Sea

ALBANIA

Corsica

Rome

ITALY

Tirana

Naples

GRE

Sardinia

Tyrrhenian Sea

Corfu

Ionian Sea

Palermo

Messina

Pa

Bizerte

Cape Bon

Sicily

Tunis

Navarino Bay

Sousse

Malta

MEDITERRANEA

TUNISIA

Sfax

Kerkennah Islands

Gabès

Djerba Island

Mareth

Tripoli

Misratah

Benghazi

TRIPOLITANIA

CYREN

Sirte

Gulf of Sidra

LIBYA

NORTH AFRICA

CIRCA 1942

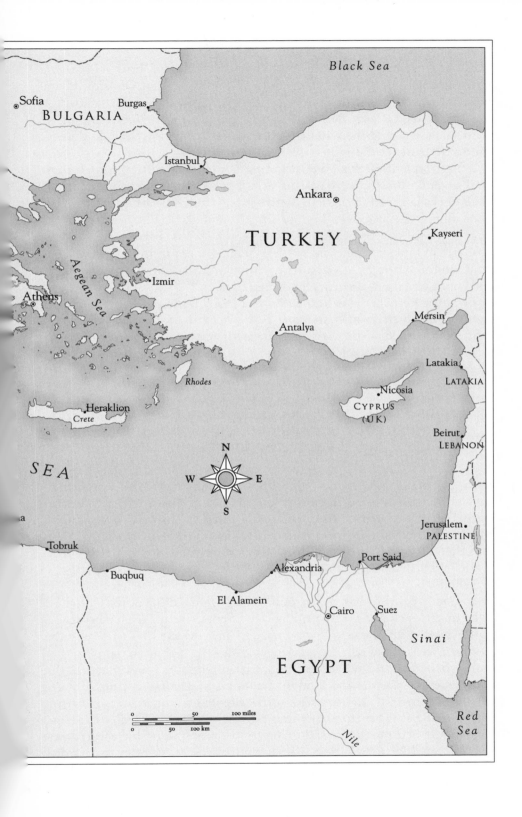

south of Gazala. Shortly we were to be advised that Tobruk had fallen, with thousands of troops of the Second South African Division taken prisoner. With the Germans steering their panzers straight at the heart of the Nile Delta, General Bernard "Tiny" Freyburg's Kiwis were coming to the rescue, crossing the Sinai Desert from rest camps in Syria to defend Mersa Matruh and Egypt.

American motor-torpedo boats, in service in the Mediterranean for the past several months, were roaring at full speed into Alexandria Harbor, their decks jammed to capacity with serious stretcher cases, for they had been among the last vessels out of Tobruk, and had facilitated the escape of other naval vessels by laying down a smoke screen between the booms as German tanks and mobile artillery shelled them from the jetties. One boat, commanded by a Canadian lieutenant, reached Alexandria with forty-two survivors aboard, all hospital cases.

Over the Reuters ticker at the Windsor Hotel I saw a bulletin datelined London, in which it was stated that "Rome's claims of surrender of Tobruk may be assumed to be correct." I immediately made arrangements to proceed to Mersa Matruh with Lieutenant Commander William J. Russell, an Australian who was worried about the fate of his "A" lighters, some of which had been reported sunk or captured at Tobruk.

The drive along the coast road to Matruh took hours. Everything not essential to a last-ditch stand was moving east in a miles-long column, throwing up tremendous quantities of dust which, mixed with sweat from the broiling desert sun, turned the tired faces of the men of the British army of retreat into yellowish masks. Trucks and trailers hauling damaged tanks, RAF cranes, petrol bowzers, staff cars, and water purifiers all rolled eastward three and four abreast, inches apart, at a funeral pace. Had it not been for the watchful air force, the historic "Battle of the Mediterranean" might have ended in a shambles of twisted steel then and there. It was "Stuka paradise" and a depressing sight, but the Luftwaffe had been badly mauled by the RAF and was licking its wounds.

When we reached Bagush, one of the main RAF desert aerodromes, it was already being evacuated. Ground crews were pulling down tents, and even the ack-ack guns were pulling out. Obviously, this was to become a battle area within the next few hours, and since Mersa Matruh was some distance west of Bagush, I experienced a sinking feeling in the pit of my stomach. There was no getting back that night, and I wondered at the time whether Russell and I might not soon find ourselves unwillingly paying our respects to Jerry. The scene that greeted us at Mersa Matruh that evening was far from encouraging. The advance guard of the New Zealanders had moved in and taken up positions along the escarpment overlooking Matruh, a little coastal town well inside the Egyptian border.

But fatigue units were already dismantling equipment and loading all valuable army supplies onto waiting lighters.

Matruh was a shambles. It had been bombed and shelled repeatedly in two years of desert warfare, and scarcely one house in this little town had a roof. Contributing to the bleak atmosphere were the bombs dropped by the Luftwaffe scarcely half an hour after Russell and I arrived. At "Navy House" overlooking the harbor, I met again my old friend Lieutenant Commander Best, R.N.V.R., who had treated Diana so well on the *Glenearn* en route to Crete. Best, the naval officer in command at Matruh, was trying to answer three field telephones at one time as the British High Command prepared for siege. He took one look at me and said:

"My God, is it you again? I thought I'd got you out of trouble once already!"

There was no talking to Best at the time, so, wandering around in the rubble, which now was being fortified to withstand the shock of Rommel's next attack, I attempted to piece together what had happened at Tobruk. On entering the dugouts of the Matruh field hospital as Stukas dropped their bombs, I had a pleasant surprise. I met an American, David Potter of Greenwich, Connecticut, a member of the American Field Service. Through him I met several soldiers and sailors who had escaped from Tobruk.

One was V. V. Gird, lance corporal and former insurance clerk at Cape Town who, with several other South African troops, had played hide-and-seek with the German panzers and armored cars for hours in a camouflaged Dodge truck and finally reached the British wire. Gird had a broken right leg and a bruised thigh sustained when a British mine in the Tobruk perimeter blew up his truck. Grinning cheerfully as he spoke to me, Gird said he reckoned he was pretty lucky, and explained the operation whereby the Germans penetrated Tobruk, carefully illustrating his comments with rough sketches on notepaper.

> The Germans attacked from the southeast, systematically wiping out our ack-ack guns by dive-bombing. Jerry used dive bombers as a cover, and then with tanks managed to force a gap in the perimeter. First to go through the gap were about five German tanks plus infantry. Next thing we heard, Jerry had shoved about forty tanks through and they were going straight for South African G.H.Q. and Tobruk Harbor. We heard machine-gun fire all day and as the Germans progressed they shoved in more and more tanks, at the same time laying down a heavy artillery barrage. Much to my disgust, I saw one German bomb blow up the NAFFI,[1] and I thought to myself, "That's bad. There goes

1. A NAAFI is a Navy Army and Air Force Institute, a British term for a service member store.

our gin and beer." We waited at our posts throughout the night under German fire, and at about 4:30 a.m. Sunday got into our trucks and made a break for it. In all we did 130 miles to get to the British wire, although the actual distance is about 70 miles from Tobruk.

Then I interviewed Lieutenant R. P. Bethan-Green from Hull and H. F. Briggs of London. They told me how, in a British staff car, they joined a German convoy moving eastward, and even experienced being saluted by German troops who thought they were part of Rommel's staff.

"We were an anti-aircraft unit largely recruited from Nottingham and Sherwood Forest," said Briggs. "We turned our ack-ack guns on the German tanks as they came at us thirty at a time, and fired until there was only one gun left. Rather than let this one fall into the hands of the Germans we blew it up. Then our unit retreated to the sea and re-formed with small arms to resist the enemy. When, the next morning, we were informed that Tobruk had surrendered, the boys started fashioning a raft from old tires and bits of board to make a break by sea, but then a German armored car approached us and we had to put up our hands. Some of the boys were in tears as they marched off with other columns of prisoners, while we, as officers, were loaded into a German lorry."

In the subsequent confusion, Briggs and Bethan-Green appropriated a car and made their getaway.

> At one point our car stalled and we had to pull up on the side of the road next to a minefield. We kept a whole column of German artillery waiting, their horns tooting impatiently, and in broad daylight worked so frantically to get the car started. We made it and continued in the direction of the British wire, passing one German vehicle after another. All we had to do was blow our klaxon and wave them aside. There were so many captured British vehicles in the column that no one bothered to investigate ours, and the Germans are so well disciplined that when they saw our staff car, invariably they'd pull out and let us pass.

After three hours under their own mortar fire, Briggs and Bethan-Green managed to reach the British line. To get through, they shouted "Kamarade" and, with their hands up, walked toward a lad with a broad Lancashire accent. The soldier nearly fainted with surprise when his "prisoners" turned out to be British officers.

• • •

Where there is drama, there usually also is humor. The funniest story out of Tobruk was that told me by Captain Patrick D. Cook, from

Johannesburg, of the Second Transvaal Scottish, who made his escape with a Coldstream Guards unit.

"Sitting bolt upright and statuelike in their vehicles, much the same as they might on parade, with the visors of their caps low over their noses, the Guards made a leisurely exit under a hellish barrage of Jerry cannon, mortar, and machine-gun fire," said Cook. He said they had been more concerned regarding the axles and springs of their vehicles than with their safety.

> I suggested to my driver that I didn't mind if he went a bit faster, but he didn't blink an eye and kept up his funereal pace, remarking, "No sir, I'll have to go careful like over these bumps. Must look after the vehicle. I can't risk busting the springs, sir." The fellow sat straight as a die with heavy stuff exploding all around the truck and I thought I'd better sit the same way, although I can tell you I certainly felt like ducking at times. My driver, while negotiating the German barrage, steered with one hand and picked the skin from his sun-burned nose with the other, the whole time looking straight ahead, solemn as a judge. The Guards rarely exceeded twenty-five miles an hour over the desert and you'd have thought it was a routine desert march.
>
> Once, a single truck passed us at about thirty-five miles an hour and my driver remarked, "That fellow's panicking, sir." We made it to the wire all right, and do you know what those guards did when they got there? They shaved!

• • •

I met a fellow who swam for ten hours east of Tobruk Harbor before he was picked up and taken to the hospital at Matruh. I also talked to a British seaman who swam two miles after his vessel was sunk by gunfire, and had rescued a petty officer whose leg had been blown off. On hearing that the petty officer was dying in the hospital, the sailor, who himself had been wounded by shrapnel, crawled to the man's bedside and prayed for his recovery. Several men who had swum for it said they were machine-gunned by Italian E-boats while helpless in the water, and that a German plane had machine-gunned the Italian E-boats to get them to stop.

From a naval point of view the most dramatic episode at Tobruk was when the South African minesweeper *Parktown*, which went down with the White Ensign and the Union flag still waving at the mast, fought an unequal half-hour duel with four Italian E-boats. Among the seriously wounded men at Mersa hospital was Sidney Watts, from Cape Town, steward of the *Parktown*, who had been left for dead when the enemy warships abandoned her as she burned. Breathing with difficulty as he lay in his cot in the underground hospital (which a few hours later was to be occupied by the Germans), Watts, who had been wounded in the chest and back by shrapnel, told me that when the order came to abandon the *Parktown*, he was left semi-conscious among the debris of the sinking vessel:

"I tried to rise to my feet to ask for orders," said Watts, "but when no one replied I knew I was lying amongst dead men. The ship was still smoldering from fire which had miraculously stopped just before reaching me. A torpedo boat was approaching to finish us off. I came out of my stupor, realizing they were going to sink my ship. I struggled to my feet and they took me off, and then sank her with depth charges."

At Mersa pier I was able to pick up the full story of the battle of *Parktown* from her chief engineer, Harold Heineman, of Rondebosch, Cape Town, as he reported again for duty. He had barely escaped death but was determined to have another whack at the enemy.

"We were just going to pull away from the jetty, at Tobruk," said Heineman, "but stayed behind to help a burning tug. Survivors of the demolition squad were clamoring aboard. We must have picked up thirty-five of them. Just before we shoved off, a couple of lorries came along. The men in them were in khaki, and we were going to give them a lift, but we soon changed our minds when we noticed these fellows mounting machine guns on the jetty, and especially when they opened fire. They were Germans.

"Stoker Cook, being pretty sore about it, immediately manned the Oerlikon gun and mowed down twelve or eighteen of them," said Heineman.

> We got about four shells into us as we were pulling out; two of them in the casing, one in the funnel, and the other low down which killed one of the survivors we had just picked up. We got through the boom OK, what with the smoke screen the American motor-torpedo boats were laying. And we had no trouble until the next day, when we were given instructions to take a tug in tow. The tug was capable of making only four knots, and we had an awful time trying to tow it, because the hawser kept getting mixed up with the screw. One time the chief and a stoker jumped over the side to fix the thing and all this time we were only a few miles outside of Tobruk.
>
> At about 6:30 a.m. Sunday we sighted four E-boats through the slight haze. We parleyed with them for awhile, trying to identify them, and then the skipper called Mersa Matruh by radio for help. As they came in close, to about 150 yards, they opened fire on the tug, which we still had in tow. The rope parted again, and then we opened up. We gave them all we had, including the Oerlikon, the four-barrel 50-caliber machine gun; two Lewises and an American Merlin. The skipper fired the first rounds from the bridge with a Lewis gun.

I was firing a Hotchkiss, but it soon jammed. I tried others, but they too were jammed, so I handled the Merlin. They were replying with two- and three-pounders. Three of the E-boats were shelling us, but the fourth pulled out of range, apparently on the look-out for our ships.

We were pretty hard hit in the first exchanges, and the ship was soon alight. A burst of shrapnel on the bridge got the skipper, the coxswain, and a pay officer from Tobruk. The number one, Mr. Francis, was on the Hotchkiss forward. It jammed, so he went to assist on the multiple point five. Then Mr. Francis was badly hit.

I went below to look after the engines just as a shell hit the boiler and knocked the valve off. I called the bridge on the voice tube, but got no reply. The engine room was getting full of steam, so I sent my men up, and then followed myself after shutting off a couple of valves.

There were dead and wounded all over the decks. The situation was desperate and, using the last drum of ammunition on the Oerlikon, we nailed the gun crew of the nearest E-boat. I saw four of them go down like bowling pins, but now we were out of ammo. The skipper was dead and the number one was badly wounded. *Parktown* was afire, and sinking. There was nothing for it but to abandon ship, so I told the boys to get the floats over the side. At that, the crowd of survivors up forward came out.

In all, we had about twelve badly wounded out of a crew of twenty-four. The rest had been killed. As we were abandoning ship, a fellow next to me who had been firing a rifle at the E-boats asked me a question. I turned to answer him and saw him standing there with no head. There was so much noise about; I don't know what got him. We lowered Mr. Francis into the raft, on which only three could sit at a time. There were sixteen of us on the raft, and two of them died before we were picked up.

While we were struggling in the water, the Italian E-boats were still firing. A Jerry plane came over and put in a burst in front of them, to make them stop shooting at us. The plane circled for some time and then made off. Ammunition aboard the *Parktown* was exploding and the plane appeared satisfied she would sink.

When we had been about two hours on the raft, I could see that Mr. Francis was in terrible pain. His leg was gone, but even then he apologized for not having mailed a letter for me in Tobruk. After we had been on the raft about six hours, Mr. Francis guessed we didn't have much of a chance, and pleaded with us to toss him off the raft to make room for the others who were in the water, holding on. We finally were picked up after we had been ten hours in the water. We had a young crew, and it was the first time any of them had been in action but no one dodged anything. They took all that was coming, and gave the enemy all they had, in return.

With the New Zealanders in battle formation along the escarpment, and South African engineers and naval officers supervising demolition on the jetties, laying depth charges with seven- and fourteen-day time fuses in the black water to catch unsuspecting enemy naval craft when the town fell, Commander Russell and I left Mersa Matruh the next morning for Alexandria. It was practically deserted. Italian prisoners, who had been used as dock hands, were being marched out, and the only Britishers besides Lieutenant Commander Best and his small group of officers were Red Caps. They stood at the crossroads amidst debris from the night bombing, directing the now almost nonexistent traffic in stiff, semaphore fashion. I've always admired these fellows, for their job is a thankless one, and in a retreat their chances of escape are none too good.

• • •

Alexandria was now teeming with excitement as units of the fleet prepared to pull out as a precaution against aerial bombing, and British nurses who had been recently evacuated from Tobruk by the American Field Service applied unsuccessfully for accommodation in the over-crowded hotels. The American boys had done yeoman service during the withdrawal, and several had been reported missing at Bir Hacheim.

Since Bagush aerodrome already had been evacuated and the navy was blowing up the jetties at Matruh, the situation had become critical. The name Alamein meant nothing much to anybody then, for if any sort of a line had been under construction there it was a well-kept secret of the High Command. I can honestly say now that after the loss of Tobruk and the Eighth Army's retreat to Mersa Matruh, I envisioned the possible loss of Egypt, Palestine, Syria, Iraq, and Persia, with the Germans linking arms with the Japanese over the Persian Gulf, isolating Russia and China. This would leave only the British Isles and the then unprepared Union of South Africa as united nations against the combined armies, air forces, and fleets of Germany, Japan, and Italy. It was a gloomy prospect indeed, for it would have meant thirty, fifty, and perhaps a hundred years of war, with the North and South American continents bearing the brunt of the burden in a wearying struggle of economic strangulation.

The night following my return from Mersa Matruh, cold shivers crawled along my spine as I watched British ack-ack and red tracer firing horizontally over Alexandria Harbor, trying to wing German aircraft soaring lazily a few feet over the water, laying mines to block the harbor as they had done at Piraeus during the evacuation of the BEF from Greece. They weren't bothering to bomb Alexandria; the Germans were getting greedy and didn't want to destroy by bombing what they felt would be theirs anyway within a few days.

Freyburg's New Zealanders put up a magnificent stand at Matruh. He issued a dramatic order: "Here you are and here you stay until all your ammunition is gone. Then you'll stick them with the bayonet."

German panzers were knocked out right and left as they tried to rush the Kiwis' lines amidst a torrent of fire from British 25-pounders and anti-tank guns. At night the Maoris (native New Zealand troopers) went out barefooted and attacked German infantry riding hand-wagon style in caterpillar troop carriers. When the Germans panicked, the Maoris stabbed them with the bayonet.

On one occasion a New Zealand unit was cut off. The commander messaged Freyburg:

"We are surrounded. Casualties are heavy. What next?"

Freyburg, who himself was wounded in the fighting, signaled in return: "Get out your cooks and batmen and fight on."

As the fighting withdrawal was carried out and the battle drew ever closer to the Delta, there was near panic in the rearguard, where no one had dreamed that the Germans ever would penetrate into Egypt. In Alexandria there were even street brawls as the Fighting French, recently returned from Bir Hacheim, bloodied noses of Vichy French sailors belonging to units of the French Fleet that had been interned in Egypt since the collapse of France. The atmosphere was tense, for the Eighth Army had their backs to the wall. The melancholy communiqués reporting still further progress by the enemy east of Mersa Matruh did not help. Alexandria was now directly menaced, but while rich Egyptians pulled out, bound for Palestine and the Sudan, the poor, who only live from day to day, didn't blink an eye.

An Indian army officer who had fought for seventeen consecutive days and had rushed to Alexandria with urgent dispatches told me good-naturedly that no sooner had he dismounted from his motorcycle in front of the Hotel Cecil, his suede desert shoes and uniform covered with dust, than a little Egyptian tugged at his tunic and said:

"Shine, Captain?"

Red-fezzed hawkers still roamed the streets in their flowing robes trying to sell dirty postcards and horse-hair fly swishes, and organ grinders continued to drive late sleepers crazy with their never-ending renditions of such as "Roll Out the Barrel" and "Tipperary." A naval officer who had the room next to mine in the Windsor couldn't stand it any longer. One morning at the height of the crisis, after barely escaping with his life from dive bombing as he brought equipment in a lighter out of Mersa Matruh, he had had enough. He just about drowned the unsuspecting Italian organ grinder and his monkey in a bowl-full of dirty water.

There was no real reason for the "flap" in Alexandria and Cairo, for the Alamein line had been well chosen by General Auchinleck as a final defense for the Delta. Barely forty miles long, and located between the northern edge of the famous Qattara depression and the sea, it forced the Afrika Corps into a bottleneck of Auchinleck's own choosing, easily defended, and a splendid springboard for attack, affording speedy communication with British supply bases. On the other hand, the farther the enemy advanced, the weaker he got, for he now had extremely lengthy lines of communication. The British had lost heavily in tanks and aircraft, but so had the enemy, and British repair and supply bases were immediately at hand, whereas Rommel had to supply his army largely from Benghazi. Meanwhile, American and British bombers were harassing his convoys.

The RAF never let up, and, with New Zealanders fighting the rearguard from Matruh, was a main factor in halting Rommel at Alamein. Under orders from the fleet press liaison officer, who, despite our protests, claimed that we were "nonessential," the fleet correspondents were evacuated to Port Said at the peak of the crisis, June 29, even as final units of the fleet left Alexandria harbor for ports farther east.

The Greeks in Alexandria were frantic, for they took these precautions as indicative of the inevitable defeat of the British. The Greek manager at the Windsor Hotel, whose eyes resembled a couple of carpet-bags from loss of sleep thinking what would happen to him and his business if the Hun came in, and whose fifteen-year-old-son already had taken French leave because of the talk around Alexandria, bade me farewell with tears in his eyes.

"What are we poor Greeks going to do? The Italians certainly will want to have their revenge on us after Albania. And where are we to go?"

On the other hand, Italian residents of Alexandria were elated. I saw one fellow walking down the street singing Italian patriotic songs at the top of his lungs. You'd have thought Mussolini was going to enter Alexandria the following day.

The high spirits of the Italians were fostered by a story then going the rounds in Alexandria to the effect that women of the Italian colony had bought out the chocolate shops, in anticipation of entry of the Italian army of occupation.

• • •

I'll never forget the trip to Port Said. The train was jam-packed with humanity, and Egyptians were even sitting on the roofs. Behind us as we pulled out of Alexandria under a full moon we could see tracers streaking the skies and occasionally we heard the crash of a land mine, for German reconnaissance planes had seen the fleet pulling out, and the Luftwaffe was trying to provoke further panic among the population.

At one of the many stops along the line, with frantic crowds trying to board the train, a fellow suddenly poked his head into the window of our compartment and said:

"Is there a seat for a lady?"

He was an army officer. When we replied in the affirmative, he hoisted his plump wife bodily through the window and then without further ado, tossed about ten bags, big and small, after her into the carriage. Finally in came a wooden box weighing a couple of hundred pounds which one of the fleet photographers and I were to hold on our knees for the next three or four stops. The grand climax came when the dog and the baby were heaved onto our laps. We were nearly suffocated while the good housewife nursed the baby in the aisle.

Larry Allen, of the Associated Press, who now is a prisoner of war in Italy, had two girls under his wing, one of them his girlfriend whom he called "Honey Chile," and the other her partner in an American dancing troupe that had performed nightly before capacity crowds of naval officers at an Alexandria cabaret. Both girls were from Los Angeles. "Honey Chile" was complaining bitterly because in her haste to join Larry on the Port Said train, she had left her beloved fiddle behind.

We were not long in Port Said, which was overflowing with naval personnel. It was distinctly uncomfortable there, for the few hotels were crowded, and one had to wait at least an hour for a cup of coffee in the restaurants. Among refugees in Port Said were several-score "Wrens" who had been torpedoed in one of the last naval vessels to leave Alexandria. They were walking about in trousers and shirts borrowed from British naval officers. One "Wren" officer, an exceedingly strong swimmer, had swum a mile to a destroyer, and then found too much of a crowd trying to get aboard, so had turned around and leisurely covered a further half mile to another destroyer, laughingly refusing assistance from a sailor who had offered to save her. She later referred to the incident as though it were nothing at all.

Reporting to the admiral in command at Port Said for information after our first night there, during which the harbor had been thoroughly pasted by German bombers, we were told that the situation at the front was now "well in hand." Thereupon, as a body, we naval correspondents demanded to know why we had been so hurriedly evacuated from Alexandria. The admiral answered:

"Damned if I know, fellows. So far as I'm concerned you can return to Alexandria tomorrow."

We took the tip and the next day we were back at our hotels in

Alexandria. The sight of us was like a reprieve from imprisonment for the wretched Greek hotel managers and employees who had felt that they'd have to start polishing up their German.

18

ROMMEL HITS A STONE WALL

I RETURNED TO ALEXANDRIA FROM PORT SAID TO FIND THE town a mere shell of its former self. The usual rush and bustle was gone and hotels practically empty. The main railroad station, where twenty Egyptian porters could be expected to compete to carry your typewriter, was empty. It appeared I had returned to a city of the dead. This impression was heightened as I stepped into the blackout and found Alexandria's searchlights groping the skies with their ghostly tentacles, searching for what was not there but probably soon would be.

In pitch darkness over cobblestones that echoed the horse's hooves a hundred fold, I rode in a rickety taxi to the Windsor Hotel and received a royal greeting from the manager and porters. They took my return and that of the other naval correspondents to mean that everything would be all right. To them, this was a sign that the Germans, who now were scarcely a couple of hours' automobile ride from Alexandria, would get no farther.

If a pin had dropped in the lobby of the Windsor after I walked in, it would have made a helluva clatter, for the place was virtually deserted. I found the manager bent double over the Reuters ticker, anxiously scanning the last-minute news bulletins from the battlefront. He treated me like a warden arriving to let him out of prison rather than a client extremely tired after a tedious train ride and looking for a bed. I went into the bar and found the Greek barman, spotlessly clean in his white tunic, staring blankly at the wall opposite, supporting his chin on his elbow. When I hoisted myself onto the stool in front of him he might have been Rip Van Winkle awakening from a long sleep, except that this guy was clean-shaven.

"Whiskey and soda, please," and the barman nearly broke half a dozen glasses and the whiskey bottle in his haste to serve one of the first customers in several days.

A couple of quick ones put me in the mood for a meal, so I strolled into the restaurant, only to be confronted with an imposing array of neatly set tables, but no guests. I felt like shouting to see if anyone would answer, for this place seemed exceedingly spooky, when suddenly I spied what looked like human beings in one corner of the great saloon. Was it a mirage? No, it was not. Advancing stealthily, I spotted none other than my pal Lieutenant Commander Russell, who, with his Good Man Friday, Lieutenant Commander C. S. Pottinger of Bath, England, were feting the manager's daughter as though she were the Queen of the May.

"My God, 'Misery,' is it you?" demanded Russell, using a nickname I had picked up somewhere in North Africa. Pottinger simply gaped at me with wide-open mouth.

"Blow me down but I'm glad you've returned, Hank. I need protection around here," continued Russell.

"What's the trouble, are the Huns in town?"

"No, no, it's that little French doctor who looks after the girls in the Carlton cabaret. You see, I walked into the hotel tonight for the first time since the 'flap,' and the first person I met was the doc who suddenly grabbed me and kissed me on both cheeks. He chattered something about 'Ah, se fleet, she is returned, yes?' and was going to kiss me again, but I beat a hasty retreat and then asked the manager if I could have the loan of his daughter as a bodyguard. So here we are. Have a drink with us, Hank."

Russell and Pottinger had stuck by their "A" lighters in Alexandria Harbor and it was by pure coincidence that they had chosen this night for a fling on the town. I needed the company.

The next morning I made the rounds in Alexandria and contacted several army officers who popped in from the front line for a quick shower, shave, and whiskey-soda. It reminded me of Madrid, when I used to take a streetcar to the front, for the Hun was now only seventy miles distant. Due to the eight o'clock curfew and a strong body of military police, there had been no disturbances. Otherwise, Egyptians and sailors of the interned Vichy French Fleet, who still were granted shore leave, had the town pretty much to themselves. Most of the British naval personnel had left by sea and the army was busy in the desert. Hawkers who in past months had made small fortunes selling worthless trinkets to soldiers and sailors now had plenty of time to meditate on their sinful profiteering.

In line with precautions adopted by the British Fleet, thousands of tons of valuable navy stores had been safely removed and the inner harbor was practically deserted. Outside the booms, British warships patrolled the coastline, keeping the Italian Fleet at bay, as sweepers dragged their paravans searching for mines dropped by German aircraft.

At the Cecil Hotel, I met McMillan of the United Press and members of the P.R. staff who had come to town for the first time in six weeks, having witnessed the retreat of the Eighth Army all the way from Gazala. They were in their element: the hotel and restaurant owners were so relieved to have clients that anything they wanted was theirs for the asking.

With McMillan was Major General Charles L. Scott, former commander of the First Armored Corps in the United States and now senior American military observer in the Middle East, who, with Major Henry Cabot Lodge, ex-senator from Massachusetts, had been in the thick of the desert fighting. Both had endeared themselves to the men of the British armored divisions, for they were often to be seen walking alone in the midst of the smoke and shell-fire of battle. On several occasions Scott and Lodge had rapped apologetically with their revolvers on the steel doors of Grant and Lee tanks, hitchhiker style, seeking momentary refuge and a ride back to the base.

Scott, a wizened, gray-haired little man from Alabama of the type who thrives on war, was preparing for his first bath in weeks when I knocked at the door of his suite in the Cecil seeking an interview. Sitting in his underwear on the bed, luxuriously rubbing his feet, Scott dictated the following exclusive statement to the United Press:

> I think that now at Alalmein the splendid cooperation between infantry, artillery, armor, and air has Rommel definitely stopped.
>
> In other words, the enemy will now have to reorganize for a new offensive. How long it will take him I do not know. But now is the crucial time to hit him particularly with air reinforcements. This, in my opinion, should be the time for a counteroffensive which might prove decisive provided we have strong air reinforcements, especially in bombers.
>
> As an old cavalryman I believe this is a signal opportunity for us.

The General signed the statement so that I would have no trouble getting it through the censorship, and I rushed to the cable office to dispatch to the world the first pleasant bit of news in a month. It was July 4, American Independence Day. Scott's statement heralded a turn of the tide for the Allies.

Rommel had been brought to a halt by the valiant rearguard action of the New Zealanders under General Freyburg, V.C., by the RAF, which had fought an engagement second in importance only to the Battle of Britain, and by the massed weight of British artillery. He was in a bad jam, for he had stuck his neck out too far. The Germans had suffered in tank losses almost equally with the Eighth Army, so much so that in a frantic effort to break through the Alamein line they had used captured and reconditioned British tanks, marked with the black-and-white cross, to supplement their remaining Mark IIIs and Mark IVs. The farther east the enemy advanced, the more difficult it had become for Rommel to place his plans into execution. Rommel now had an acute supply problem: his petrol was getting low, and so was his water.

Tor Torland, of Seattle, Washington, onetime ski instructor to the U.S. army and for the past several months an ambulance driver for the American Field Service, told me of the enemy's extreme shortage of supplies:

"We have handled several wounded Jerries. They told me the Afrika Corps is so short of medical supplies that they are amputating without anesthetics. The Germans said they were giving their prisoners only half a cup of water daily because of the extreme shortage."

The American boys, operating sixty-six ambulances in the desert battle area, had suffered numerous casualties including one killed, others wounded, and several missing and believed captured. The latter at the time included Alan Stuyvesant of New York, whose whole section had not been heard of since they left besieged Bir Hacheim with the Fighting French. Ambulance man George Tischener had been killed in the retreat from Bir Hacheim when his ambulance was machine-gunned and set on fire by aircraft, with all patients on board burned to death. Arthur Stretton, recipient of the Croix de Guerre in France, who was a co-driver in the ambulance with Tischner, was wounded by a burst of aerial machine-gun fire. Tischner got down from the ambulance and was trying to help Stretton when he was struck in the head by a bullet.

According to John Nettleton, from Cheshire, Connecticut, who with Torland and Bill Carter, champion swimmer from New York, had evacuated the English nursing sisters from Tobruk, there was heavy fire during the Fighting French withdrawal from Bir Hacheim. The enemy tried its utmost to prevent anyone from getting through to safety. Our fellows repeatedly exposed themselves to danger, stopping to pick up wounded and crawling on their bellies toward the British lines as Bren carriers and tanks fought it out.

It was largely through the work of the American ambulance boys, who now were attached to the New Zealanders, that I obtained a description of the epic rearguard action the Kiwis had fought from Matruh. Red-faced, jovial, husky John S. Carter of St. Louis, who was wearing the ribbons of the last war, told me how the Kiwis had lain in wait for the German panzers in slit trenches resembling graves in the sand, let them pass by (or in some cases even run over them as they lay prone in their coffin-shaped holes), and then hurled deadly "sticky bombs" and bottles of flaming petrol to knock the tanks out.

"They even climbed atop German tank turrets and tossed in grenades, making mincemeat out of the German crews," said Carter. "I have about twenty-five American boys with me," he continued, "including the son of my buddy of the last war in France, Joseph des Loge, Jr., seventeen years old. There was also Edward Sullivan and Tom Depew of St. Louis, and Jerry Harding of Boston, of the well-known Bigelow clan. We lost one of our boys the other night—a fellow by the name of Foster. They were bombing the New Zealanders by the light of magnesium flares which made it look like broad daylight. The magnesium would break up into little pieces and run along the ground like quicksilver. The last time anyone saw Foster, a bomb had dropped just in front of his ambulance. He is reported missing."

A New Zealand captain by the name of Jack Tolbert interrupted:

> These American fellows are tops with our boys. I reckon the Americans saved from 30 to 38 percent of the serious cases by getting them to rear dressing stations first, and then to the hospital in Alexandria. And their dressings are first-class. To give you an idea how they operate, one of our workshop lorries went up in flames during a night bombing attack. Luckily, your fellows were beetling over the ridge under fire. As the ambulance came lurching over to us someone leaned out and asked if any of our guys was hurt. Yes, you'll find them arriving seemingly from nowhere. Where they come from, we don't know, but they're there all the same.

Carter said he spoke to a German prisoner and asked him who the Germans feared the most. "He promptly answered, 'the New Zealanders.'"

During the retreat to Alamein the New Zealanders nearly always counterattacked at night. In a recent attack a Maori officer estimated that ten Jerries had been killed for every New Zealander lost. They caught the Germans napping as they attacked on the run with the bayonet and grenades, shouting their blood-curdling war cry.

I mingled with the New Zealanders at the southern extremity of the Alamein line following a brilliant counterattack resulting in the capture of forty German and Italian guns and several hundred prisoners. The Kiwis had taken heavy losses but put up a heroic fight. Officers and men took little credit for themselves, enthusiastically paying tribute to Freyburg and his picked lieutenants, Brigadiers George Clifton and Howard Kippenberger.

They told me that when Freyburg was wounded in the withdrawal to Alamein, colonels, majors, corporals, and privates went about white-faced, whispering, "Is it right the Old Man's taken a hit? Poor old-timer."

The following incident illustrates why the New Zealand fighting man looks upon "Tiny" Freyburg with reverence:

It seems the "Old Man" was watching a dogfight over the desert. Alongside him was a lance corporal. Both got pretty excited and Freyburg said:

"They've got him, Alan."

Lance Corporal Alan, looking up excitedly and shielding his eyes from the sun, answered:

"Don't talk such silly rot, they haven't got him yet."

"You're right, Alan, they haven't got him yet."

And then there was the case of the Maori sergeant whom the boys had nicknamed Tai, meaning in Maori "slow-going." Freyburg once had recommended this man for a commission. Tai was a damned good soldier. For example, when in Greece with the Germans fighting behind him, Tai reached the beach with twenty men and then went back with a lance corporal who had a tommy gun and brought back about a hundred more. Another time he had stalked a German around a square water tank for twenty minutes and finally got him by poking his rifle suddenly around a corner and pulling the trigger with the forefinger of his left hand. Tai was pretty disappointed about the commission, which hadn't come when he'd expected it. One day, as Freyburg was inspecting Tai's unit, he came upon the sergeant and said:

"What's the matter, Tai? Why are you still in the ranks? Didn't I recommend you for a commission?"

"Yes sir," answered Tai, "but they thought I wouldn't make a good officer because I talk kinda slow, so they drummed me out."

"Oh, is that so?" said Freyburg. "You come up to Division H.Q. for your commission tomorrow!"

Tai paid off his debt to the "Old Man" at Mersa Matruh. He was killed there, leading a bayonet charge against the Hun.

As the New Zealanders retired over their own minefields from Matruh to Alamein, one sapper had both his legs blown off by a mine. He was badly shocked, and as they were applying tourniquets he opened his eyes and asked what happened:

"What is it, skipper?"

"You've lost 'em both, chappie."

"OK, you bastard, but no lousy German is going to make a bum out of me. I'll meet you on the docks at the Wellington with a bottle of beer in my hand when you come back."

The fellow died four hours later.

From their commander on down the ranks, the spirit and drive of the New Zealanders was unparalleled in the Western Desert. With Freyburg

it was, "You fight, men, and I'll fight with you." His motto was "Smash
the enemy on land, sea, and air. Attack!" That's why the boys worship the
ground he walks on and that's the reason the Hun had the wind knocked
out of his sails before he ever reached the Alamein line.

New Zealanders, South Africans, Indians, and famous British artillery,
cavalry, and infantry units, including the Rifle Brigade of Waterloo fame,
presented a barrier of steel at Alamein, upon which Rommel eventually
broke his back. It had now become a battle, not of tank-versus-tank as
had been the case at Knightsbridge, but of British and Imperial guns and
guts versus German panzers.

• • •

The South Africans held the center of the line at Alamein and opposed
the enemy with small, hard-hitting mobile detachments.

"We stopped Rommel on July second," said a South African major.

> The fighting was of intensity equal to Sidi Rezegh where the Germans
> hurled scores of tanks against us hoping for a breakthrough. The
> panzers never got more than 1,500 yards from their starting points
> even though enemy artillery, including captured British 25-pounders,
> were shelling hell out of us. One of our brigade's gun columns armed
> with 25-pounders was all by itself in a perimeter 800 by 1,000 yards in
> diameter, and although ten thousand German shells landed around
> our gun emplacements, he didn't manage to force a gap.
>
> We couldn't see our own gunners for dust, but the boys banged
> away, breaking off action only when one of the brigade cooks, who
> had prepared his meal under fire, shouted at sundown, "Come and
> get it or I'll chuck it away."

It was the Australians, the "desert rats of Tobruk," rushed into the
breach from their Syrian rest camps late in July, who put Jerry on the
defensive at Alamein. In the first thirty-six hours of fighting the Diggers
broke out of the Alamein box to Tel el Eisa along the coast, taking fourteen
hundred prisoners. Within ten days the total prisoners had soared to six
thousand.

I visited Tel el Eisa during the battle and saw upward of forty German
tanks that had been knocked out by Australian artillery and anti-tank
guns. I walked to front-line positions with Lieutenant Colonel Hammer
of "Hammer's Hill" fame, and talked to Australians who the night before
had charged German posts at Tel el Eisa station.

"It was bloody hell yesterday," said a corporal. "He attacked our
positions with twenty and thirty tanks at a time, but we knocked them
out fast. One man got three out of four Mark IVs with a 2-pounder anti-

tank gun. Jerry was so mad he hopped out with his bayonet at the ready, but he never got more than a few yards. We aren't afraid of his tanks, let alone his bayonets."

"We are gradually wearing the Germans down," Colonel Hammer told me.

> We've had lots of casualties, but we've killed a lot of Germans. He's had much heavier infantry casualties than we. Jerry has attacked these ridges lots of times and frequently pounds us with his artillery, including a big gun that we have nicknamed "Alamein Annie." We buried seven of his men last night. They hadn't the guts themselves to go out under fire and fetch them. At the same time we got two of our own men back after they'd been out two days and nights. One of them, who was very badly wounded and had lost far too much blood, greeted me with a grin and said, "We're certainly glad to be back home, Colonel."

Corporal Gordon Ranford, from Western Australia, colorfully described how his mate and neighbor back home, Corporal J. S. Hogan, had himself—although wounded—captured nine Fritzes.

"The Germans are scared yellow of their own shrapnel," said Ranford.

> Hogan got nine of them and started walking back to our lines, covering them with a Bren. They were all armed, for there had been no opportunity to grab their weapons. Suddenly Jerry began shelling his own evacuated positions. Hogan pushed his prisoners into a shell hole and made them face him on their knees with their hands up. He told me he nearly died laughing when German shells busted around that hole in the ground, for the Jerry prisoners invariably flopped down, looking for all the world like praying Arabs. Eventually I showed up and Hogan handed them over to me so that he could go back and have his wounds dressed.

The Diggers who had fought almost incessantly since their return to the line were philosophical about their losses. One fellow who was naked to the waist and clean-shaven, although for days he had not moved from his slit trench except when ordered to attack, told me of a recent night engagement in which he had participated.

"It was sad, sir, three men fell on my right and two on my left. It was them Spandaus, sir. They're nasty things. I had to go on without my boys as there was no stopping them. We took our objective all right, sir, but the shrapnel was pretty bad for Jerry was using air bursts on us and the shells exploded fifteen feet in the air. Also, they were using the hopping shell which hits the ground and then jumps another hundred yards or so before it bursts."

I walked with Colonel Hammer along the famous "Hill of Jesus," which really wasn't a hill at all but a sort of mound sticking up like a temple in the desert, and full of shell holes. At every other step, I kicked a jagged fragment of shrapnel. Aussies, at the ready in slit trenches, grinned at us as we passed. I wondered why they didn't walk around like the colonel and soon found out, for all of a sudden there was a series of shattering explosions and mortar shells were peppering the hillside.

Between shellings the Aussies refreshed themselves by plunging into a swimming hole in a cove along the beach at Tel el Eisa. Colonel Hammer's boys now faced the bulk of the Fiftieth Light Division and a whole regiment of crack German infantrymen from Crete, who had been flown in to reinforce the line along the coast.

The Germans were facing a deadlock; hence they resorted to treachery to achieve a breakthrough to the Delta. On one occasion about six hundred German infantrymen started walking toward the British lines with their hands up. Suddenly they flopped to the ground in a body as mobile guns behind them opened up on the British. Lord Lloyd's son was killed by the first burst. So incensed were his men that, unmindful of the continued pounding to which they were being subjected by the German guns, they cut loose with their Brens and mowed down virtually the entire six hundred Germans. And in the south, the New Zealanders and Indians got their own back. In the early days at Alamein the Germans had cut down with machine-gun fire an entire unit of Indians that had put their hands up in token of surrender. Now the Indians captured more than fifteen hundred German and Italian prisoners and killed at least an equal number.

On July 13 Alamein was pronounced momentarily "safe." A few days later Auchinleck was preparing a counteroffensive. The second Battle of Alamein was about to start, with the initiative now in the hands of the Eighth Army.

19

"THE LULL CONTINUES IN THE WESTERN DESERT" —BBC

O N JUNE 20, 1942, WHEN TOBRUK FELL, PRESIDENT ROOSEVELT, following a conference with Prime Minister Churchill in Washington, made a decision that was to turn the tide for the Allies in the Western Desert.

"On that dark day," Churchill later told the British Parliament,

> I was with President Roosevelt in his room at the White House. Nothing could have exceeded the delicacy and kindness of our American friends and Allies. They had no thought but to help. The president took a large number of their very best tanks, the Sherman tanks, back from the troops to whom they had just been given. They were placed on board ship in the early days of July and sailed direct to the Suez under American escort. The president also sent us a large number of self-propelled 105-mm guns which are most useful contending with the 88-mm high-velocity guns of which the Germans have made so much use. . . .
>
> At the same time, we re-created and revived our war-battered army. We placed a new army at its side, and rearmed it on a gigantic scale. By these means, we repaired the disaster which fell upon us and converted the defense of Egypt into a successful attack.

But a lot happened in Egypt of which the world has heard little. Convoys don't traverse the oceans overnight, and hundreds of men fell as unsung heroes at Alamein in July 1942 while the urgently needed reinforcements of troops and equipment wended their way to Suez.

Although the "new army" of which the prime minister spoke—in the form of the famous Highland Division and the British Forty-fourth Division, well equipped with British-manufactured 6-pounder anti-tank guns, 25-pounder field pieces, and Crusader tanks—was already en route, they had twelve thousand miles to cover. Even on arrival it would be necessary to train the troops in use of their new weapons.

It was up to General Auchinleck to hold the Alamein line against Rommel's Afrika Corps during the dramatic midsummer race of supply and reinforcements. The odds appeared to favor Rommel, for he then had superior forces of tanks and had reached a point in Egypt only a morning's automobile ride from Cairo. In the supply race, the Axis also had the edge on us because the route across the Mediterranean was short, and despite the combined efforts of the British navy, RAF, and heavy bombers of the USAAF, large quantities of Axis war materiel were getting through to North Africa.

Attack was the best form of defense for the Allies. It would not do to let Rommel rest his forces for a new assault at Alamein. By constantly engaging the enemy, a heavy drain would be imposed upon their already strained and extremely long supply lines overland from Benghazi. So Auchinleck resumed the offensive with his veteran New Zealanders, South Africans, Australians, and Indians, supported by home county regiments and what remained of the British armor after the retreat from Matruh. Reserves of tanks were few and largely confined to those repaired by hard-working crews in the Alexandria recovery shops, mostly staffed by South Africans.

Many a man spilled his blood and gave up his life on the desert sands of Alamein to give the reinforcements from England and America time to reach the Nile Valley. I saw much of the fighting, having been relieved as fleet correspondent by George Palmer, of the United Press, who had recently arrived from New York. The correspondents could tell their agencies little of this moving story of human sacrifice. All of Auchinleck's attacks were repulsed, and there also had been costly counterattacks by an equally determined enemy. It would not do at this critical time, said the censors, to tell the world much about the fighting. Otherwise, they explained, the enemy might take advantage of British losses.

Crack New Zealand battalions were the spearhead of Auchinleck's first attempt to dislodge the Germans and Italians at Alamein. Advancing with the bayonet on the night of July 14-15, through complicated German minefields with the famous Ruweisat Ridge as their objective, the Kiwis, including New Zealand's V.C. from Crete, Captain Charles H. Upham, immediately encountered strong opposition. However, in bitter fighting they reached the summit of the highly strategic ridge, taking sixteen hundred prisoners and holding their positions for two days. On July 16 they were forced to withdraw, after repulsing repeated assaults by many as fifty-seven panzers at a time. They knocked out several tanks by climbing on top of them and hurling grenades into their turrets.

The loss of Ruweisat Ridge was a great disappointment because there had been heavy losses, including Captain Upham, who was taken prisoner after having twice been wounded as he led his company against machine-gun nests on the rocky, undulating slopes of Ruweisat.

Said Brigadier H. K. Kipperberger, D.S.O., to me after the attack:

"If Upham had not been captured, I think sooner or later he would have been killed. He was a grand lad. Why, one night during heavy fighting he went out alone in a jeep looking for a lost company. He ran into a large number of the enemy and shot up the lot, single-handed."

An officer who had known Upham since he left his sheep in New Zealand to join up, described him to me as "an indifferent sort of fellow, high-strung, and a madman in battle. That's why he killed so many German parachutists in Crete. I remember the day of grenade-throwing practice back home when the instructor had to tell him to take it slow and easy, because his hand was shaking so. I guess the Germans wish Upham had followed the fellow's advice!"[1]

A second attack by the New Zealanders occurred on the night of July 21-22. I drove for hours over a desert track to reach the New Zealand positions. It was a harrowing ride, for armor reserves were on the move, creating a storm of smothering, powdery red dust that billowed into our utility through windows, floorboards, and hood, creating a mask on our faces thicker than any clown ever wore in a circus.

When we reached the southern terminus of the Alamein line the attack was all over. Like the first, it also had been still-born. The artillery was laying down a barrage, covering efforts to retrieve British tanks that had been abandoned in enemy minefields during the withdrawal.

One of the first men I met was Brigadier George H. Clifton, D.S.O. and Bar, M.C., who had been taken prisoner by the Germans in the mêlée yet had managed to escape and return to the New Zealand lines after helping to collect seriously wounded on both sides. Clifton, a man in his early forties, large of build and of pleasant countenance, himself had buried one of his battalion commanders before he made his getaway, digging the grave under fire from artillery and tanks.

The brigadier was regarded as one of the toughest regular army soldiers in the Western Desert. At Sidi Rezegh, where a New Zealand unit was completely surrounded, he had saved the day by personally pushing a convoy of ammunition, food, and water through the enemy lines. As the artillery pounded away, I reached the brigadier's H.Q. truck on the shell-scarred escarpment that had been the starting point for the battle. Speaking as though it was all part of a day's work, he described to me what had happened:

1. Captain Upham survived incarceration in the German prison at Colditz Castle and returned to his prewar life as a New Zealand sheep farmer. He died in 1994.

We had heavy casualties as a consequence of repeated infantry charges against tanks and enemy strong points, but our boys carried out their orders and cleared one or more gaps through the enemy mine fields.

Myself satisfied that the pre-designated objectives had been reached, I went forward with Brigade H. Q. and three liaison officers from the armored brigades, only to run immediately into five German tanks. These we fought off with our anti-tank guns and stood by as our various infantry battalions settled down awaiting armored support. But it failed to arrive and in the early morning hours, in pitch darkness, we were attacked by at least twenty tanks, mostly Mark IIIs, which were hull down along the northern rim of the depression. They were shooting blind for the moon had gone down, but unfortunately an early burst set fire to an ammunition limber and another vehicle quickly followed. The resulting fire made shooting much more accurate. They quickly knocked out the Crusader and Honey tanks of our armored liaison officers and then concentrated on our anti-tank guns, particularly those in action.[2]

The area was congested with trucks and vehicles which had not had an opportunity to disperse, and the concentrated enemy fire did a lot of damage. Most of our wireless vehicles were hit early in the attack and by 6 a.m. our anti-tank guns had either been knocked out or dispersed. The panzers then rolled over this area. A few of my men escaped in vehicles and ran the gauntlet of fire not only from the pursuing tanks, but also from flank positions which had not yet been mopped up. Some two hundred tried to withdraw, but the distance to the next ridge was over one mile, and with no cover in daylight retreat was hopeless. They were shot or rounded up.

When the panzers closed in to three hundred yards, Brigadier Clifton decided to run for it under cover of smoke. Accompanied by Captain Pemberton, M.C., and his driver, Clifton negotiated eight hundred yards in the jeep before it was hit and knocked out.

"The place was a bloody mess of smoke and flame," Clifton told me.

Jerry got three jeeps in succession at eight hundred yards and with some damned good shooting, so I got out of the car very smartly along with Pemberton. After that we were subjected to the indignity of putting up our hands. But the Germans were too busy to pay much

2. Henry Gorrell adds, "One of the armored liaison officers killed in this engagement was the son of Field Marshal Douglas Haig, First Earl Haig, of World War renown. According to eyewitnesses he never had a chance to get out of his tank, which burst into flames immediately after it was struck by an enemy shell."

attention to us, as they were getting ready to handle the long-overdue British armor. At least they took time to tow my damaged jeep away, for they were taking all the light stuff irrespective of its condition. Believe me, I'll give anybody a good advertisement for a jeep. It was the cat's whiskers.

It was now a case of either hiding in a slit trench or carrying on the good work. I managed to return to our line.

Brigadier Clifton has since been taken a prisoner again, this time to remain such.

• • •

On July 26, Auchinleck tried it again. This time South African infantry was the spearhead of the main attack, which took place in the center of the Alamein line. The Royal Natal Carabineers, senior volunteer regiment in the British Empire, were to have the "honor of leading the Eighth Army into the attack." The Australians, at Tel el Eisa along the coast, were to thrust southward, with instructions to take and hold a piece of high ground that later would be used as a springboard for the British armor. Roughly, the plan was to seize a long strip of territory along the coast, thereby forcing Rommel's armor to withdraw from the south, for lack of supplies. In support of the South Africans and the Australians, the New Zealanders simultaneously were to carry out a diversion at the southern extremity of the Alamein line. It was an ambitious plan and details had been kept a close secret, hence it was largely by accident that I became an eyewitness.

• • •

On the morning of the twenty-sixth, I paid a routine visit to the South African infantry in the center of the line. I found the commander of a battalion of the Royal Natal Carabineers who had been in the thickest of the fighting in the past six weeks. They were now asked to make a supreme effort for, as Lt. Colonel Comroy put it to me as he sat with his commanding officers under the fringe of a rocky escarpment in his utility, "If this attack goes over, it will decide the Battle of Libya. Three tank brigades are involved and it is to be a big show."

Lieutenant George Turner of Johannesburg, attached to Comroy's staff, went even further. "It's death or glory for us tonight. Comroy is reconciled to sacrificing half a battalion to push a gap through the German minefield for the armor. It's tough on the colonel, for he knows most of his men by their first names and is acquainted with their families in the Union."

Selected to cooperate with the Royal Natal Carabineers and the

Transvaal Scottish under Brigadier Eric Ponsonby "Scrubs" Hartshorn was the Sixty-ninth Brigade, a composite unit made up of remnants of the famous Fiftieth Division, including the Durham Light Infantry, Green Howards, and certain elements of the Guards.

I shared a bottle of beer with Lieutenant Colonel Comroy and then, pledging secrecy, was invited to return that night to witness the operation.

At 1 p.m. I returned to the press camp behind the line where I watched long columns of tanks, armored cars, and other equipment wend their way westward to take up battle positions. Then I went for a swim. I wished to refresh myself in anticipation of an all-night vigil. Except that the beach was marked by crosses of fallen Allied troops, the peaceful azure background of the Mediterranean made it hard to realize that a war was going on.

I couldn't eat that evening because of my excitement, heightened by the realization that I probably would be the only war correspondent in the desert to witness this attack.

What follows I give to you in diary form:

7 p.m. With an English conducting officer I proceed to the Alamein railroad station, the green cement walls of which are scarred by shrapnel, and then southward along "Springbok Road," a bumpy track littered with broken telephone wires and wrecked equipment, by-passing trucks, tanks, and ambulances all moving up. We drive through gaps in a couple of British minefields and arrive at Comroy's H.Q. He is sitting on a petrol tin alongside one of his officers, eating and saying nothing. His face is tense, for in a few hours his men will be crawling through the enemy minefield under heavy mortar and machine-gun fire.

7:20 p.m. Jerry has recon planes out now. He has noticed the dust along the Alamein track and his 88s begin shelling the South African positions. Comroy's field intelligence officer says that the brigadier is soon to take up his battle position on a ridge just ahead and recommends that I join the brigadier's party.

7:30 p.m. At Brigade H.Q. I meet my old friend Brigadier Hartshorn. I hadn't expected to see him, for he only recently had been appointed to this command. It's a stroke of luck. The brigadier, thirty years a soldier who lost an arm in the last war, immediately invites me to be his guest.

"You can accompany me in my vehicle, Gorrell, and I'll guarantee that you'll have a front-row seat to the fight. Our brigade is proud to take a leading part in this offensive. It's going in first—actually leading the Eighth Army into battle. They are grand boys and their colonel told me this afternoon, 'Don't worry, Scrubs. As soon as you give the word the whole outfit will go in as one man and we'll all be into them with the bayonet.' That's the spirit that will win this battle."

8 p.m. Jerry continues shelling us. Lieutenant Turner looks at the moon and remarks: "I hope the 88s keep off of us tonight."

8:30 p.m. Despite beer with the brigadier and his staff, the roof of my mouth is dry with excitement as the entire Brigade H.Q. starts moving forward. Enemy aircraft are overhead, and the vehicles keep one hundred yards apart. We proceed through a neatly made path in a German minefield to a sort of escarpment, where artillery is ranged behind us. There are hundreds of guns all told and in a few hours they'll open up in unison. The spot the brigadier chooses for field H.Q. is an advanced section of "No Man's Land" and signalers get busy installing telephones. The enemy shelling has now stopped, and in the moonlight as we await "Zero Hour" there is no sound other than that of picks and shovels as the fellows dig slit trenches in the stony ground. The brigadier's driver is enlarging a two-foot shell hole in case things get hot. Trucks laying telephone wires weave back and forth between Brigade Division and Corps H.Q.

9 p.m. The brigadier explains strategy to me, after which there is a period of waiting in which one of the fellows offers me a flask containing South African brandy.

10 p.m. Everybody is keyed up. The British brigadier commanding the Sixty-fifth establishes headquarters nearby and reports his fellows "in battle positions." Brigadier Hartshorn asks me whether I shall mind if in the event things get lively "I ask you to take a running jump?" He tells me that the artillery behind us may provoke German counterbattery action, but as a former journalist he insists that I remain with him in the meantime. An intelligence officer is on the phone checking the positions of the infantry that is going in at midnight and instructs them where to take prisoners. Now Jerry is shelling us spasmodically again and one drops fairly close, but no one pays any attention.

10:40 p.m. Somewhere to the south of us a diversion has started and the Hun answers with streams of tracers. The New Zealanders were on the job.

11:10 p.m. The Aussies have begun their attack southward from Tel el Eisa. Jerry has found them and fires frantically with mortars, artillery, and tracers. In the midst of all this a lieutenant from Durban puts on a captured German pilot's great coat and mimics the Nazi salute. The brigadier, who is sitting in his camp chair yawning, says: "Pretty sloppy salute, George."

German Spandaus snap with rapid bursts resembling a series of whip cracks a few thousand yards distant as the Aussies advance. They are the fastest machine gun I have ever heard. There are a few short busts—Brroop-brroop—after which there is a long rattle of unbroken fire. The brigadier's telephone rings and someone asks, "You can hear them?" The intelligence officer answers, "Yes, we certainly can. We thought they might be firing at you." I notice a flaming beacon to the southwest and am told that it is to guide the RAF.

11:40 p.m. The brigadier is advised that "Your troops are moving southward now with sappers behind them. They are two hundred yards from the trip-wire marking the enemy minefields." So far they have not been noticed by the Germans, who are overoccupied with the Aussies to the right of us and the New Zealanders to the left. The sky is beginning to light up properly now.

11:55 p.m. There are only five minutes to go before "Zero Hour." Several officers attached to South African Brigade H.Q. are lying down on the rocky terrain talking about their girlfriends in the Union. There is heavy mortar fire against the Australians and the shells explode with a deep-throated "whoom whoom," whereupon some of the British guns open fire to assist the Diggers and "keep the Jerries' heads down while they go in with the bayonet." The Hun is really getting excited now and is using 88s as well as four-inch mortars. It is all very pretty up in the sky, but one forgets that when German shells start bursting all around us. Some of them are air bursts from 88s and explode above the ground with black puffs of smoke. There is a helluva clatter and the shrapnel is whistling around our ears, but no one seems to even bother to stoop, so although I'd like to I don't either.

12 midnight: There is an ear-splitting roar as the British artillery opens up behind us, and through it all the brigadier remarks casually: "Gentlemen, the fun has started. Our boys have penetrated the trip-wire and are in the minefield." There is a God-awful row and the fireworks increase in intensity. Someone said, "Christ, that's a barrage." The intelligence officer tells me, "Yes, there are quite a few guns firing. It's a Corps barrage on pinpoint objectives."

12:36 a.m. The brigadier telephones asking for the position of the Carabineers even as German shells crash merrily around us. He has to shout into the telephone because of the noise. "You'd better get a runner out—I want to know where they are." The shrapnel from the shells bursting over our positions sounds like air escaping from a toy balloon with a kid holding onto the mouthpiece, and resembles hail when it hits the sandstone. The Carabineers are well in the minefield and according to the brigadier "are having a thin time, what with the shells, mortars, and their heavy machine-gun fire." They ask for additional artillery support and the British guns lay down a creeping barrage just over their heads. The shells have hardly left the guns before they burst ahead of us with blinding flashes. But the German shells exploding around us are even brighter. The dust they throw up fills your mouth and eyes. I am coughing and cannot see our guns, not even in the bright moonlight. There is only a blinding flash when they fire and they really are dishing it out now.

1 a.m. The Carabineers have now reported they are five hundred yards inside the trip-wire. "Do you think that's enough and should the other outfit get started?" asks the intelligence officer. But General Daniel Pienaar advises them to wait until a South African unit from the second brigade reports progress. An officer asks Hartshorn what our fellows are doing and he answers sarcastically: "They are on their bellies looking for mines and badly tied down by machine-gun fire. Poor bloody infantry. God, how I wish I were with them instead of here egging them on."

1:10 a.m. The brigadier announces that "Our boys are now seven hundred yards in: slap in front of the Jerry pillboxes. We've got to get the general attack started." The brigadier shouts into the field telephone trying to get hold of the commander of the Sixty-ninth and then as his utility is illuminated by the glare of a German star shell, he jumps to his feet and stomps with his foot on the stony sand. He smiles and points to the ground: "That's a scorpion, Hank. It darned near went up your trouser leg." I thanked Hartshorn, for I was intensely watching the fireworks and hadn't seen the creature.

1:15 a.m. British units go forward guided through the gaps by the South Africans. The brigadier tells their commander, "The best of luck to you. We are marking the gaps as well as possible." Shortly after this we hear the urgent fire of Jerry machine guns close by, trying to halt a bayonet attack. Soon, the Germans are reported evacuating their pillboxes and the small-arms fire dies down.

2 a.m. The Sixty-ninth is well into the Hun and Hartshorn urges them on. "Get on with it, boys, for it will soon be daylight." Whereupon he puts down the telephone, and keeping time to the barrage from British 25-pounders, the brigadier whistles the "Song of the Volga Boatmen." The telephone shrills and Lieutenant Colonel Comroy is at the other end reporting his losses to the brigadier, who answers: "Right, Murray. Go on in and stick 'em with the bayonet. Avenge yourselves."

2:30 a.m. We can now hear the clankety-clank of tanks coming up in the rear. The gunners are putting up a helluva row to dazzle the Hun and prevent him observing their approach. Now the first prisoners, including German officers, are reported.

2:45 a.m. The biggest barrage yet. You can hear the gunnery officers' shrill voices above the din, directing the fire. It's a "precise general shoot" and the entire horizon is transformed into a solid sea of flame.

3 a.m. RAF and naval aircraft join in the fray and the Jerries are throwing snakelike coils of tracer into the sky as the bombs shower down.

The infantry has done its job for there is no longer any machine-gun fire. The Aussies have reached their objective but the earth still trembles to the artillery barrage.

3:20 a.m. The infantry reports German tanks approaching, so the brigadier orders the anti-tank guns up, but they are already on the job and the Germans withdraw.

4 a.m. Everyone is dog tired and relieved when the Corps congratulates the South Africans for a good job. A tank major has now gone forward with an engineer major to inspect the gaps in the minefield. More tanks are coming and the show seems to be moving on.

6 a.m. I awaken from a fitful two hours' sleep. The brigadier is nervously pacing the escarpment, for it is now daylight and the tanks have not yet gone in. I hear some expert cursing over the wire as he demands to know the reason why. Some of the South African infantry are in a bad way, for they are deep into enemy territory and are in danger of being cut off if they don't immediately obtain tank support. The Australians in the North are catching hell, for German panzers have closed the gap behind them, and it is now a question of fighting to the death or surrendering.

6:15 a.m. The tanks have not yet moved in and I have only a half hour in which to catch the morning dispatch rider, so wishing Hartshorn the best of luck I return to the press camp behind the line.

• • •

I got the story off, and then went to the Corps Headquarters where I was told that things had not gone according to schedule. The Corps intelligence major, not knowing that I had been a witness to the whole business, announced with a poker face that "This is a local operation and must not be termed an offensive. It is quite possible that we may have to withdraw from positions gained during the night." He said something about the Australians having taken between 100 and 150 German and Italian prisoners, but did not mention the fact that for lack of timely armored support practically an entire Australian battalion had become casualties or been captured in this costly operation.

This spelled failure of Auchinleck's final effort to throw the Hun out of the Alamein area.

That afternoon I returned to South African field headquarters and learned that the British tanks finally had gone in, but that thirteen were immediately knocked out by German 88mm cannon which the infantry, in the darkness, had failed to overrun. The rest of the tanks had withdrawn, forming a cover for the retreat of the Sixty-ninth British Brigade, which had been badly cut up. It seems that in the darkness, the British troops had bypassed several machine-gun nests and 88mm emplacements, and had pressed on with their several hundred prisoners only to be cut off later and themselves become prisoners. In all, the losses of the Sixty-ninth Brigade were about four hundred men.

In justice it must be pointed out that it might have been fatal for the Eighth Army and Egypt, had Auchinleck risked the remainder of his armor, gambling on a breakthrough. After all, further tank losses might have meant the loss of the Nile Delta, for Auchinleck's margin of available tank reserves at the time was indeed thin.

The next evening I eagerly turned on a field wireless set to listen to the BBC news. I was confident that my eyewitness dispatch on the night battle had been at least twelve hours ahead of any other. I was chagrined to hear the announcer in London report:

"THE LULL CONTINUES IN THE WESTERN DESERT."   ·

If I felt bad, how about some of the poor fellows of the South African infantry whom the British tanks had failed to extricate from their precarious positions in No Man's Land? For them, there was every prospect of being "put in the bag" shortly after that BBC fellow got through talking. They also heard London tell them that there was nothing doing in the Western Desert.

Since then I've had drinks with a few of the lucky soldiers who managed to escape "The Lull" with a whole hide.

20

"WINNIE" COMES TO ALAMEIN

AMONG THE MOST ANXIOUS DAYS IN THE WESTERN DESERT were those in August 1942, preceding Rommel's final effort to reach the Nile Delta.

Prodigious losses during the retreat from Mersa Matruh, and subsequently at Alamein, had left their mark. The tired and bruised Eighth Army had fought back, but no matter how game, a boxer who is doubled up after a painful body blow doesn't like to hear the gong for the next round. That's more or less the way the boys felt at Alamein prior to the surprise visit of Prime Minister Winston Churchill to the battlefields of the Egyptian desert. Despite evidence that the German challenger, Rommel, was soon going to plow in again, poised for a knockout punch, "Winnie" had come to Alamein.

The undreamed-of sight of the prime minister, complete with cigar, thumping the ground with his stick as he sidestepped shell and bomb craters in front-line areas skyrocketed Eighth Army morale. The "Desert Rats" popped out of their holes in the sand by the score to cheer him, for he had come to "have a look for himself," and was immediately accepted as one of them.

First to spot the man with the bulldog jaw was the driver of a munitions lorry, jolting along a desert track toward advanced Australian positions along the coast. He saw Mr. Churchill alongside General L. J. Moreshead, looking through field glasses at the famous Hill of Jesus.

"Blimey, its 'Winnie,'" he yelled in amazement.

The cry "Winnie is here" was passed along from one desert outpost to another, together with confident statements of the prime minister made at random to the shirtless, sun-tanned fighting men such as "Empire . . . you have done well . . . great days ahead . . . Victory."

There was something intense about the way Mr. Churchill strode among the troops. He was an impressive, aggressive figure, cigar jutting from jaws that were clamped tight and full of purpose. High-ranking officers who accompanied "Winnie" on his tour of the desert found it difficult to restrain him from walking into the firing line. And when Stukas, attracted by the staff cars in the prime minister's retinue, dived down and dropped their bombs not two hundred yards from where he was sitting at lunch, the old warrior scarcely looked up, but continued flicking the desert flies from his bully-beef like an expert.

After an extensive inspection of infantry positions, Mr. Churchill toured desert aerodromes and personally congratulated commanding officers and the men of the RAF who had flown and fought many times a day, every day for months in support of the land forces.

On the prime minister's return to Cairo there were conferences with South Africa's Field Marshal Smuts, General Wavell, and other high-ranking army, fleet, and air force officers that were to result in complete revision and expansion of Allied plans in North Africa. The new plans conformed to a strategy blueprinted by Churchill and Roosevelt in Washington following the collapse of Tobruk, whereby American and British forces, advancing simultaneously from east and west, were to bottle up Rommel in Tunisia.

These conferences, however, had the immediate effect of speeding up German preparations for a final victory drive into Egypt; Berlin knew that eventually an increased flow of materiel to the Middle East from England and America would turn the tide in favor of the Allies. An idea of what might be expected within the next few weeks was given to war correspondents in Cairo before the prime minister's departure by a high officer of the British Military Intelligence.

"We expect a big and final attack to occur very shortly," said the officer. "Rommel is sixty-five miles from solution to all of his problems, for he has a thickly populated area and a great port in sight. It is indicated, therefore, that he will exert all of his efforts to attain his objectives, which he cannot reach without first destroying the Eighth Army."

He added that this promised to be an "all in" fight and very likely would include repetition of the German strategy used in Poland and the Low Countries; namely, attack by airborne troops coupled with indiscriminate bombing and strafing behind the lines aimed at throwing refugees onto the roads to block retreat of the Eighth Army. He gave us the tenth or twelfth of August as an estimated approximate date for Rommel's next move.

Following this very frank and rather gloomy summary of immediate prospects, I joined several of my colleagues for a series of quick ones at the nearest bar. The next day I returned to the desert, there to await the German thunderbolt.

For an army that within a few days might be fighting again for its life, the men at Alamein certainly had their tails up. "Winnie's" visit had had a magic effect, since on the face of things there was little to justify the cheerful attitude of the fighting men. The sight of Royal Engineers laying out new minefields right up to the outskirts of Alexandria demonstrated the way the wind was blowing. And if this wasn't enough, one only had to stand near the coastal road and watch the long lines of ambulances moving up to handle heavy casualties.

The enemy was sending out strong patrols nightly; prodding the line, seeking its weakest spot. By night the desert trembled to the crash of shells as both sides cut loose with spasmodic barrages that always are indicative of extreme tension.

At Tel el Eisa, where already so much blood had been spilled, there was a steady flow of casualties. Crack regiments of German shock troops had been flown in from Crete to oppose the Aussies along the coast, and they maintained a constant bombardment with mortars.

The "Diggers" reveled in their glory and angered the Germans still more by audacious incursions into their lines in which they would make wide sweeps of several thousand yards at a time, coming up behind the Hun and then running amok with hand grenades and the bayonet. There were cases of Germans and Italians impaling themselves against the Aussie bayonets as, surprised in the darkness and bewildered, they ran at top speed in all directions.

During this period I visited an Australian field hospital in the vicinity of Tel el Eisa and observed the efficiency with which the surgeons operated under fire. One whom I had known on the S.S. *Elisabethville* during the voyage in convoy from the Cape to Suez in May invited me to witness an emergency operation on an officer who had been wounded by a mortar shell as he slept in a slit trench. As orderlies efficiently pumped life-giving blood into the patient's veins from one of many bottles lined up on a shelf in the operating tent, the surgeon emphasized advances in the medical profession that have saved many lives during this war.

"Had it not been for our tabulation scheme," said he, "many of the cases treated here would have died shortly after arrival. Even before our men boarded transport ships in Australia en route to the Middle East, we knew exactly the type of blood that each would require in an emergency, for every man wears a metal disk around his neck on which is printed the number of his blood classification. There are four types of blood. We have it ready in bottles and in case we need any more, all a surgeon has to do is to get it from the walking wounded."

As many as ten transfusions have been given in one hour by these men who operate in the front line. One man was given blood for seven hours before it was possible to amputate his leg. He pulled through.

• • •

A lull in fighting, even though not productive of news, does not mean that men do not continue to sacrifice their lives on the battlefield. There is constant activity, featuring the work of patrols involving from one to a dozen or more men at a time. As newspaper editors back home chafe at the bit, hungry for a "real headline," these men are crawling on their bellies deep into enemy territory, usually under fire, to obtain information vital to the G.H.Q. Before an attack, it is of paramount importance that enemy strong points, particularly gun emplacements, be pinpointed. And in anticipation of an enemy attack, it is equally important to determine where his guns are, so that they may be efficiently dealt with at Zero Hour. The periods preceding Rommel's final abortive effort to reach the Delta and prior to the victorious "Battle of Alamein" late in October provided important lessons in the value of detailed information concerning static positions. It required innumerable patrols and aerial photography. It required that men die.

Many a man who has gone out in the moonlight to obtain such information has either failed to return or has been carried back by his comrades gravely wounded. I've observed several patrols in the Western Desert. It takes guts to do a job of this kind, but invariably the men who were called upon to get the invaluable information walked cheerfully into trouble.

• • •

With the enemy regrouping his positions primary to the final assault at Alamein, it was necessary to take prisoners in various sectors for purposes of identification of enemy forces. Once the South Africans sent out three tanks and three armored cars to get one prisoner, and lost the lot. But they got their man.

"We waded right in and the 'Ities' sprouted like mushrooms with their hands up as their big guns tried to knock out our tanks and armored cars. We could have taken any number of prisoners had we had the necessary transport, but as it was we were lucky to get back ourselves," one of the participants in this raid told me. "Our prisoner? Hell, he was a bloody 'Itie' and not a German, as it had been reported. This is the sort of thing we have to go through to verify rumors. If some big shot hears that Germans instead of Italians are holding certain positions, it's up to us to go out there to find out whether it is true."

• • •

I learned also that some officers tend to get slightly temperamental during a lull. Major "Dickie" Doe, M.C. of Hornchurch, Essex, of the Seventh Artillery Regiment operating in the region of Tel el Eisa, gave me an example.

"Several times a day we're ordered out on the hop to 'smarten up' enemy columns on the move. They've been keeping us pretty busy these days, for Jerry is moving around all over the place." Then he laughed as he described how a few days before, he had organized a human chain of "Diggers" to relay information to his battery necessary to silence an enemy gun that had been lobbing shells onto the doorstep of his colonel's dugout.

> The colonel was mad as Hell, and told me to "stop that damned gun firing or else," so I went out alone on a recoy, dragging two drums of telephone wire behind me. It was a case of personally directing and observing fire from my battery. I got to the edge of that ridge over there under heavy machine-gun and rifle fire but we were just twenty yards short with the damned wire. We were close to the enemy infantry and there was no time to lose, so I got a bunch of Aussies to line up on their bellies one after the other behind me while I edged forward and, in a verbal relay, passed the instructions to the fellow behind him, and so on until the last "Digger" spoke to them into the field telephone to the battery. Twelve "Diggers" helped me to do this job, and my instructions got back slightly garbled because an Englishman finds it hard to understand the Australian lingo, but the boys at the howitzers caught the idea all right and their rounds of fire did the job. They silenced that Jerry gun, and the colonel as well.

Major Doe took me in his Ford armored car beyond the farthest British infantry outposts into No Man's Land and proudly showed me the charred remains of some German Mark III and IV tanks that he had knocked out at sixteen thousand yards with his mediums.

I appreciated his enthusiasm but didn't feel too comfortable when he casually pointed to a German machine-gun emplacement just behind a wrecked Stuka a couple hundred yards distant.

"Stay to the lee of these tanks and Jerry won't bother you," said Dickie, as he continued with his explanation of how he got the panzers.

"Look there, Hank," he exclaimed, pointing to a wrecked Mark IV. "You can see for yourself—the splinters and the twisted tracks. No other shell could have done it. This is one of four tanks I got in rapid order the other day. I watched them from this same armored car, for I was acting as my own observation post, directing the fire of my guns. Another day I was scouting around and saw twelve 88mm guns on the sky line. Our 25-pounder opened up, but the 88s took no notice, so I directed air bursts on them and then ordered rapid fire with the mediums. The Hun sent up a smoke screen, but only eight of the twelve 88s got away, even though we were firing at seventeen thousand yards. There they are, over there, see?"

As I stepped away from the wrecked German tank to look, the Jerry machine gunner yonder, who was becoming annoyed by our extended conversation in No Man's Land, let rip. His bullets ricocheted from the sides of Dickie's armored car as we hopped in. But Dickie laughed and said:

"Oh, don't mind that, Hank. He's only teasing you."

• • •

The air force, which was beginning to receive reinforcements of Boston and Baltimore bombers, as well as Kittyhawk and Hurricane fighters, was also in high spirits.

One of the outfits I liked the most was the famous Australian fighter squadron of Hurricanes under acting squadron leader R. H. "Bobbie" Gibbes, D.S.O., D.F.C. The first time I ever saw Gibbes, he was hobbling about with one foot in a plaster-cast. During a recent attack against superior numbers of Messerschmitts, he had been forced to bail out and had broken his ankle. They wouldn't let him fly just yet, so Bobbie had scrawled in crayon on his plaster-cast: "This damned thing comes off in three weeks!"

As the enemy prepared for his last throw, the flying "Diggers" set a fast pace, carrying the fight deep into enemy territory. Within a few weeks, Number III Squadron of Australians was to shoot down its two hundredth enemy aircraft in the Western Desert. Appropriately, it was Squadron Leader Gibbes who nailed it.

In mixed fighter squadrons, including men from Australia, New Zealand, South Africa, Rhodesia, Canada, and the British Isles, I was pleased to find several American volunteer pilots, including Lance Wade of Tucson, Arizona, who then was acting squadron leader of a Hurricane outfit, and young Pilot Officer Thomas W. Prentice, Jr., of Ponca, Oklahoma, a graduate attorney who had joined the RAF as a volunteer on the day that Athens fell. Prentice, one of the most popular boys in his squadron, told me one afternoon with great enthusiasm that he had just returned "from dive-bombing Rommel's headquarters. You should have seen the panic down there as the big German headquarters' vans were blown sky-high by our 250-pounders. No sooner had we dropped bombs than we went down almost to ground level and strafed the blazes out of them. Just think, perhaps we got Rommel himself," said the curly-haired youngster. A few days later he went out on a "Stuka party" and failed to return. A fine fellow, Prentice. I hope some day I'll meet him again, for there is just a possibility that he became a prisoner of war.

Wade was fast ascending to the status of an ace among fighter pilots in the Western Desert, and had already won his D.F.C. Later, in Tripoli,

I was to see him again, wearing the D.F.C. and bar, earned for shooting down something on the order of fourteen enemy aircraft.

And there was the Fifth South African fighter squadron, flying Tomahawks, that had lost nearly a score of its original twenty-four pilots in combat operations since June 26. Their latest loss had been their Squadron Leader Major Jack Frost, D.F.C. from Queenstown. Not long before, Captain Andrew Duncan, son of the governor-general of South Africa, had been shot down. Yet a stranger would never have known that these boys had been so hard hit, for after a long day's grind patrolling over enemy territory, they would gather around their fiddlers and guitar impresarios and sing at the top of their lungs, as though it was all just a game.

Among my friends in this squadron was Lieutenant John Lindbergh, of Johannesburg, who treated a shell splinter in his neck as a joke. Young John was always the life of the party and a great inspiration to his copilots in combat. I later read in a Johannesburg newspaper that Lindbergh had been killed in action over Tunisia.

For several days I was the guest of the South African fighter boys. I found them plotting how best to spread terror in the enemy lines. Their agile brains produced such novel methods as dropping beer bottles from their diving aircraft, because as they hurtled to the ground they emitted a spooky, spine-crawling shriek. But this wasn't enough. Rommel had boasted that soon he would be drinking beer in Alexandria and Cairo. Therefore, the South Africans bought American canned beer and dropped several tins daily over what looked like headquarter camps, after spraying them liberally with their 50-caliber machine guns. I asked one of the boys what it was all about. He answered:

"Hell, don't you get the point? That's just as good as telling Rommel that the only way he'll ever get good beer around here is if we deliver it to him."

Another trick, finally banned by an order stating that "No more pamphlets are to be dropped over the enemy lines," was the hurling of rolls of toilet paper from aircraft, on which were scrawled such slogans as "Fur der Fuhrer unt der Reich—South African compliments."

Long before Rommel gave the order for his final assault at Alamein, his troops had been roughly handled by bombers of the RAF and the Fleet Air Arm, then consisting largely of Bostons, Baltimores, and night-flying Wellingtons and Albacores. They were always in the air, shuttling back and forth in close formation. Barely had one bomber outfit returned to its aerodrome than others were taking off in the dust churned up by the landing aircraft. The armorers worked day and night without a murmur, their shoulders blistered by the heavy bombs.

I can't see how the enemy got any sleep at all at night, for the roar of the Wellingtons and Albacores flying overhead used to keep us all awake, and they never let up with their bombing. Every night the Jerry lines were brilliantly illuminated as the boys of the Fleet Air Arm, specialists in the use of flares, lighted objectives for the bombers. At first light, just about the time the desert flies were beginning to worry your nose, the day bombers would be out, and the ground trembled to the crash of their salvos, a rude reveille for Germans and Italians to whom Alamein was becoming a nightmare.

Anywhere you turned, there was evidence of an invincible spirit among the fighting men defending the Delta. Just before the big battle early in September, I talked to the crew of a Bofors anti-aircraft battery, with a record of one hundred planes shot down in the desert and seventy in France. Their only complaint was that "Too many fighters are coming in now, and they are taking our job away from us."

This outfit had suffered heavy casualties during many months of desert warfare. I met them when I rushed up to offer my congratulations, after they had brought down two out of a dozen Stukas that had screamed out of the sun and caused me to take an unpremeditated nosedive nearby. They were pleased to have someone express appreciation, for their work was too frequently taken for granted. Among the crew were Sergeant Cyril Elvin, from Parkstone, Dorset, who has commanded one of the guns since July 1940, witnessing the entire siege of Tobruk, and Sergeant Eric Bradbury, from Liverpool, who manned one of the last Bofors guns in action in Dunkirk.

Elvin told me that "Firing at 120 shots per minute, the Stukas are easy meat for our guns. The heaviest raid we had was when a hundred dive bombers came over at a time. We knocked down a lot of them even though Me-109s were strafing us in relays."

Bradbury, who proudly said that the eighty-eighth plane his battery shot down in the desert was a Ju-88, described the last day at Dunkirk.

"We had to break the gun up and leave it, but we did a lot of damage to the Hun planes. Terrific swarms of them came over. I remember Empire Prayer Day, when we were on the beaches of Dunkirk. It was raining and it was the rain that saved thousands of us, for it flooded the enemy aerodromes. Most of all, I remember the Padre who was standing on the after deck of a destroyer leading the prayers as all the men kneeled. It was an inspiring sight."

Having knocked down the two Stukas, the rest of the crew now amused themselves by training their Bofors on Hurricanes from the army cooperation aerodromes they were protecting. It scared the daylights out of the pilots, for it's not funny to have a gun turned on you, even if it's only for practice.

Yes, these ack-ack fellows were certainly full of beans.

• • •

Among those who stuck around to see the next phase of the battle was Major General Charles L. Scott, the American military observer. On July 4 he had told me categorically that he believed Rommel had been stopped. The next time I saw him, he told me that increasing numbers of American heavy bombers were en route to the Western Desert, together with entire groups of B-25 medium bombers and complete All-American squadrons of P-40 fighters.

"If we can hold him this time," Scott told me, "Rommel is through. What we need out here is two to three hundred more bombers, for with them we can bag the Hun lock, stock, and barrel and settle the Libyan campaign.

"Rommel has outrun his supplies and maintenance, and will need a lot of spare parts to regain his full strength in tanks. I wish we had the necessary strength in the air right now. If so, I'd go after him tomorrow morning. All I'd have to do after our bombers had given him the works would be to go in and pick up the pieces."

Scott's prayer was being answered, for late in August more than three thousand American "air support troops" arrived at Suez, presaging active participation of U.S. fighter and medium bomber squadrons in the Battle for Libya.

And as Prime Minister Churchill, in closed session, informed the House of Commons of his conferences in Cairo and his personal tour of inspection at Alamein, great troop transports, including the *Queen Mary* and *Queen Elizabeth*, were nearing the end of their long voyage across the Atlantic and around the Cape, carrying a reserve army, well equipped with tanks and guns from England and America.

It was the beginning of the end for Field Marshal Rommel.

21

"NO RETREAT AND NO SURRENDER"
—MONTGOMERY

I FIRST MET "MONTY OF ALAMEIN" ON AUGUST 25, 1942. A few days earlier, he had taken over command of the Eighth Army from General Auchinleck.

A thin little man of shrewd, foxlike countenance and steel-blue eyes, General Sir Bernard Montgomery, dressed in shorts and wearing a broad-brimmed Australian campaign hat, sat on the steps of his mobile headquarters at Berg el Arab facing about twenty war correspondents. He appraised each of us with a penetrating glance before he spoke a word. Then, carefully selecting every phrase and generally repeating the last word for emphasis, "Monty" told us that the Eighth Army was on the eve of a highly critical defensive battle that might influence the entire course of the war. With a determined snap of his jaw, he gave us his instructions:

"The enemy will attack imminently. When fighting starts, I don't want you to say or write anything—only when I give you the word, for he is looking for information and we're not going to give it to him. History will show that this is a very serious phase in the war. But I am absolutely confident of the outcome—absolutely."

He spoke a few more words, and concluded with:

"You have now had a look at me, and I, at you. That is all, gentlemen." Then he stood up on the steps of his caravan, stretched, and returned to his maps.

We weren't particularly pleased with the army commander's instructions, for what good is it being in the thick of a fight, if you can't write about it? Therefore, the correspondents held a council of war and decided to put everything on paper as it happened, leaving the fate of our dispatches to the army censors in Cairo.

General Montgomery had given us no indication of his plans for the battle, so we had to decide for ourselves what sector might yield the most action. With two other war correspondents I chose the central sector, joining the Thirteenth Corps Headquarters south of Ruweisat Ridge.

There were several days of waiting before the enemy attacked. Rommel, hard up for petrol supplies, anxiously awaited a vital shipment by sea. According to intelligence reports at the time, the enemy had ten days' petrol supply available at Alamein, hence Rommel's plans for attack were on "Blitz" lines. Failure of the initial attack might easily bring disaster.

In the interim, as the Luftwaffe and the RAF fought it out overhead to establish air supremacy, I watched the "new boys" of the Forty-fourth British Division, just arrived from England, sweating blood as they were put through their paces under a scorching sun. In accordance with drastic orders of their former divisional commander, General Montgomery, these men were to be "stretched, pushed to the point of exhaustion, then stretched again, exhausted." The general, a strict disciplinarian, meant business, for as he said, "Our boys must be tougher than the Germans. There must be no rest for them—none whatever!" Already all units in the field, who for days had been on stand-by awaiting Rommel's attack, had received "Monty's" order of the day, calling for "No retreat and no surrender." They knew that the enemy was desperate, and with grim determination stood by their posts.

Things looked bad, for the Germans were reported to have five thousand parachutists and the Italians two thousand. The Thirteenth Corps Headquarters was a hot spot, being frequently bombed and machine-gunned. There was a standing patrol against attack by parachutists, and even our public relations drivers slept with one eye open, tommy guns at hand, while German planes, operating singly, dropped bombs at random, seeking to demoralize the Eighth Army.

As we tried to keep warm in our bedrolls we could hear the German planes coming from the west and it wasn't easy going to sleep at night, especially when they flew right over you, silhouetted against the full moon. If the bombs were going to drop nearby, you could hear them whistle; otherwise, it was a case of trying to relax, waiting for the next intruder.

Usually at first light we were awakened by bomb explosions as the Stukas, out early to avoid interception by the RAF, dropped their ordnance and scurried for cover. There is nothing so comforting as a slit trench under such circumstances, and along with my fellow war correspondents, I became an expert at shallow diving, for usually the Stuka raids were followed with strafing by low-flying Messerschmitts. In three days following the conference with General Montgomery at Berg el Arab, I saw at least half a dozen German dive bombers and fighters shot down by Kittyhawks, Hurricanes, and Spitfires, all within a radius of a mile from Corps Headquarters.

On the evening of August 28, an idea of the tactics to be used in the defense of the Delta was given to the correspondents by General Brian Horrocks, in command of the Thirteenth Corps, who had arrived from England with Generals Alexander and Montgomery. A very tall, thin man of pleasing personality, Horrocks immediately took us into his confidence.

"I am very impressed with the troops of the Thirteenth Corps, which include my old division," said he. "I feel that the arrival of General Montgomery, who in a crisis has nerves of steel, has had a great effect. My old division," he added with a smile, "have arrived from England well equipped with 6-pounder anti-tank guns and artillery, and spoiling for a fight. Additionally, we have the famous Fifty-first Highland Division in reserve. I doubt whether Rommel knows anything about the presence of the Forty-fourth in the desert, and I am fairly certain he knows nothing about the Fifty-first.

"We don't particularly want Rommel to attack us now, for both sides are going to be mauled considerably, and we would prefer more time to prepare a good striking force with which to round up Rommel and settle things once and for all in Libya. The spirit of my troops being as it is, however, Rommel will have a tough nut to crack. I have never fought him before, but feel the tide will turn this time, although we must have a bit of luck—just average luck."

Roughly, the strategy adopted was as follows:

British and Imperial positions at the southern extremity of the Alamein line, toward the Qattara Depression, had deliberately been left weak as a "come on" for the tanks of the Fifteenth and Twenty-first Panzer Divisions, the Ninetieth Light, and the Italian Ariete Division. This time, the Eighth Army was going to fight the enemy on ground of its own choosing. The main British armor was concentrated in the center of the line in the region of "Bear Ridge," and constituted a serious menace to Rommel's flank should he, as anticipated, try a breakthrough in the south.

"If Rommel chooses the southern flank," said General Horrocks, "the going will be bad, and we have a reserve army ready for him in the Delta in his front."

On the night of August 30, when Rommel attacked, there was no need to ask what was happening, for shells from long-range German mobile artillery began crashing around our campsite. They were big fellows and exploded with an oversized bang. The knock-down, drag-out fight had started, and following a preliminary engagement with the British advance guard of armor and infantry in the south, the German panzers swerved northward, looking for trouble.

The next morning, the patrols of German tanks were reported everywhere around us, on armed recoys, and there was a gosh-awful din as entire regiments of British 25-pounders let them have it. The freckle-faced, white-skinned youngsters of the English Forty-fourth Division, most of whom had never fired a gun in anger before, let Rommel know at once that reaching the Delta was to be no easy matter.

"Blimey, what are those things?" the men at the 6-pounders asked in amazement as the snub-nosed panzers approached their defenses.

"German tanks. Take aim and fire when ready."

Before you knew it, the tanks had either been knocked out or had scuttled away. If they were many, the artillery was informed and in a matter of seconds the desert erupted with geysers of sand, smoke, and flame as the shells found their targets. Usually only twisted hulks of burning metal remained when the shelling stopped.

I wasn't surprised to travel several miles northward over the desert on the second day of the battle and learn from an officer of the Forty-fourth that only a couple of hours before, German tanks had approached within a thousand yards of his positions. Those that had not been knocked out had hastily withdrawn when the artillery opened up.

This entirely new method of fighting angered the cocksure German field marshal, and he ordered his Stukas out in large numbers to "remove the nuisances." I watched a battery of 25-pounders shelling a panzer concentration as the Stukas dived. Bombs soon enveloped us in clouds of dust, but the guns never stopped firing. There was such a clatter that it was hard to tell the difference between the bursting bombs and the roar of the cannon, but the shrill voice of the artillery major shouting his orders never faltered: "Raise your sights. Range four thousand. We've got them on the run, men. Synchronize watches and fire fifty rounds rapid at eleven hundred hours."

If a man was hit by bomb fragments, another quickly took his place. Several of the men had been wounded, and wore bandages as they fed the guns.

The Stukas didn't get away with it, for the RAF and the ack-ack were on the job. I saw several Stukas drop like stones and crash in the smoke pall of their bombs.

It was do or die, and there were no fixed defense lines. Each unit, be it armor, infantry, or artillery, had its own little world to defend, usually defined by a few hundred yards of barren, fly-ridden desert. To let the enemy pass would mean encirclement and inevitable death or capture. Corps H.Q. was in an equal fix, and if things went wrong there were excellent chances that we would all be put in the bag. But there was no time to think about that.

Reporting for the first press conference since the start of the battle, we found the Corps intelligence major dusting off his tunic after his umpteenth dive into a slit trench to avoid strafing. Two captured German Stuka pilots stood trembling in anticipation of a raid by their own aircraft as they awaited transfer to base.

Information was scarce, for the battle had been intense with no time for detailed reports.

"Rommel attacked the center of our main armored defenses a few hours ago with about 110 tanks," said the major. "So far he has not gained ground, and many of his panzers have been knocked out. If you fellows want a good story, I suggest you take a shoofty for yourselves. We understand Grant tanks with American crews have been in the action."

That was enough for me. Immediately, I headed toward Bear Ridge.

A division shoot by 25-pounders was going on as we headed south, for air reconnaissance had reported a concentration of thirty-five hundred enemy transport and supply vehicles moving northward. You couldn't hear yourself think for the noise because Bostons, Baltimores, and Mitchells were also bombing Rommel's transports in repeated waves. As we negotiated wired gaps in the British minefields, I had to tie a handkerchief over my nose against the dust of battle.

We found the Americans quickly. Along with the British tanksmen, most of them were stretched out on their backs in the sand, taking a "breather" in between rounds. All around them was a confusion of knocked-out and still-burning British and German tanks. Rommel's panzers had temporarily withdrawn and the 25-pounders and bombers had taken up the fight. Great dust plumes rose in the distance from the divisional barrage as the oven-hot air of the desert echoed to the whistle and whine of scores of shells per minute hurtling overhead. There had been two troops of three American-manned tanks each in the preliminary fighting. "Married" to a British squadron holding the center of the line of Grant, Crusader and Valentine tanks that were half buried in the sand, hull down, they had borne the shock of an attack by eighty Mark III and IV tanks and, with four of the six tanks damaged, had helped to throw the enemy back in confusion. A couple of Americans had been slightly wounded, but morale of the Yanks under Captain William Bailey, from Toccoa, Georgia, could not have been higher.

The fury of the engagement was apparent from the litter of burned-out gear scattered amidst a maze of shell and bomb craters, and the air was pungent with cordite fumes. At every step, one kicked a jagged piece of shrapnel.

I found Bailey tinkering with one of his two undamaged Grants. He was pleased to meet a fellow American, and proud to tell me of this, the first engagement in which men of the U.S. Army Tanks Corps had participated officially since America came into the war.

"See that burned-out tank yonder?" he said, pointing to a huge lump of metal two thousand yards away. "We got that baby. Want to have a look at it?" Thereupon, bouncing along in a jeep, we went up to what had been a Mark IV Special, before it had been hit by an armor-piercing shell from the stepped-up 75 on Bailey's Grants.

As I walked up to it for close inspection, Bailey sat in his jeep, scratching his head, an apprehensive look on his dust-grimed face.

"What's the matter? Have you got sunstroke?" I asked.

"Naw," he drawled. "I was just thinking. See that damned gun? Hell, if I'd known that thing was firing at me I think I'd have been scared."

Then he snapped out of it, and I walked around the remains of the panzer while Bailey fondled one of its broken tracks like a hunter might a duck he had just winged. The shell had broken its left-hand track and gone straight through the tank, killing the driver. The charred remains of the driver's body, and those of another German, in the field gray uniform of the Afrika Corps, were still in the panzer. A swarm of flies hit us full in the face as we prodded around in the tank, and Bailey suggested that we clear out, "Unless you want to pick up a disease."

Before taking a look at another German tank the Americans had knocked out, I picked up a letter in the sand, bearing a Stuttgart postmark. I read the first paragraph in German:

"Dear boy. I am so glad that you are now in beautiful Egypt. We are all waiting to hear of your first visit to Cairo and the Pyramids."

I dropped the letter, without reading further. Presumably, it had been written by the mother of one of the German soldiers whose mangled bodies lay in that mass of twisted steel nearby, attracting the desert flies.

Up to this point, Bailey had been too engrossed in construction details of the wrecked panzer to speak of the engagement. He started to tell me about it as we jolted along in the jeep, but just then ten Stukas leveled out into a dive, and the explosions that followed, though very wide of their targets, abruptly ended the conversation. Bailey stopped his jeep and stood up for a better view as RAF fighters pounced on the Stukas. He might have been an enthusiastic fan at a baseball game, watching the play in the eighth inning with three men on base, as he cheered the British pilots on, waving his arms and smacking his right fist into the palm of his left hand.

"Stick 'em, cowboys!" he yelled. "Go get 'em." And then, as a Stuka plummeted to the ground in flames: "That-a-boy! That'll teach these Fritzes to start something they can't finish!"

Back with his crew, Bailey crouched in the sand, toying with a heavy German armor-piercing shell he was "going to take home as a souvenir." Prompted by the men from his outfit, he told me his story:

The Panzers were in front of us, in the hollow. Suddenly, the big devils with those long guns leading charged our mixed squadron of British and American tanks tasked with holding the center. The orders had been simple: whatever happened, we were to hold the ridge behind us. There was hell to pay as the Germans rushed us, and the whole ridge seemed to be on fire. I was in the turret of my tank, and could see the forms of tanks ahead of us through the smoke, and the bright yellow and orange flashes of high-explosive shells. I was giving orders over the interphone system and could hear my driver yelling out every time he thought we'd hit something. The driver, an Irish man, was a son-of-a-gun. He couldn't see from where he was and every time our 75 fired, he would open the door to see how we were doing. The other boys were raising hell because there was a powerful amount of stuff flying about. We could hear some of it bouncing off our Grant. The armor-piercing shells sounded like a saw snapping into position when they whizzed past. One time four high-explosive shells landed within six feet of my tank. There was a black cloud around us and we couldn't see out of it.

The boys were great. Early in the fighting I saw one of my tanks hit and catch fire. But the crew didn't bail out until they had run out of ammunition. Then six of the boys bailed out under fire. I was praying for them, because Jerry machine-gunners had spotted them and were whipping up the sand all around. They had to wait behind their burning tank, even though it was likely to blow up at any minute, until smoke began pouring out of it in sufficient quantity to cover their retreat.

The other fellows told me they had seen a group of men from a knocked-out British tank scuttling around amidst splashes of flame and bursting shrapnel to disable German tanks.

Staff Sergeant Jesse L. Gilmer from Shreveport, Louisiana, told me how after his tank had run out of ammunition, "We bluffed the Hun by maneuvering back and forth under fire, moving back and forth fifty feet at a time while shells rattled off us like hailstones. Once, a shell blew our sand guards off. Our tank was petering out, the engines were sputtering, the wireless was out and the battery was no good, so eventually we had to pull out behind this tank here that lost its track, and wait to escape, but no one got scared, not even nervous. There was too much going on around us for that."

Sergeant George Gasset, of Hancock, Massachusetts, was firing a gun from his tank twenty minutes after its track was knocked off. The crew asked their commander if they could bail out, but were instructed to hold on until their ammunition was gone.

The Irish sergeant, to whom Bailey had referred, was Alexander Kagan, of Bound Brook, New Jersey. He said he had opened the door of Bailey's tank at times, "Because I was kinda nervous until I saw our gunners hit some of them. Twice, I saw a red flash as well as smoke. You don't see that flash unless your shells have struck steel. After that, I was OK. I was too busy obeying orders from Captain Bailey, who could see when the enemy tank shells were getting close to us from his turret. Every once in a while he would holler over the house-phone, 'Here comes one this side. Back up. Left a bit. Here comes another.'" Bailey explained that in tank fighting, backing up and maneuvering left, right, and forward confuses the enemy range finders.

The American boys were raring to have another whack at the panzers when I left them to visit British tank units. I believe that most of them have since returned to America, for Bailey's unit was sent to the desert to gain experience in actual combat, after which they were to report back to Washington.

• • •

After a battle, you can't go up to a fighting man, pad in hand, and demand that he tell you all about it. He'd freeze up if you did, and anyway, it's hard to reconstruct things in a hurry when you've been toying with death. If a fellow talks at all on the spur of the moment, he'll usually tell you the funny side of it. I guess it's human nature. For example, the first story I heard from a British tank brigadier was that of an orderly who, in the heat of battle, with high-explosive and armor-piercing shells bursting and ricocheting on all sides, had rushed up to his commander's tank and asked him, "Please sir, will you sign the sanitary report for the First Buffs?"

Then there was the case of the RAF fighter pilot who had been forced down as the result of a dogfight and had pancaked into the middle of a British minefield. "We sent a runner up to warn the pilot of the mines," said a tank officer, "and the first thing the pilot told him was, 'If I had known that this ground was so firm and smooth, I'd have put my wheels down.' Our runner told him to stay put and tread softly, laughingly informing him that 'It's a good thing you didn't put your wheels down, for you are in the center of a minefield. Follow me and I'll guide you out.'"

A British tank commander said that, having been forced to bail out of his smashed and burning tank, he rocketed through the turret after the others of his crew and found a bottle of whiskey lying in the sand.

"I felt pretty naked out there in full view of the enemy tanks, with high explosives and machine-gun bullets flying in a thousand directions. It was rather like one of those nightmares you have when you find yourself with no clothes on, in the middle of Piccadilly Circus. But the bottle of whiskey, tossed out by my thoughtful gunner, helped a lot. I passed it around and then we made a break for it. Yet the panzers were withdrawing. Why? A whole regiment of our tanks was coming up to join the fight. The Germans must have realized that what they had been taking on was only a very small corner of our shop window."

• • •

Perhaps the outstanding individual heroes of the battle at the gates of Cairo and Alexandria were a handful of men in an anti-tank company of Riflemen, who, when isolated by the enemy, fought for thirty-six hours, destroying thirty-seven enemy tanks and probably damaging many more.

The story of their magnificent stand was told by Sergeant Charles Calliston, M.M. of Forest Gate, London:

> Our post was a small diamond-shaped ridge. The enemy started machine-gunning us, and sending over mortar bombs. A thousand yards away, I could see the lumpy shape of the leading German tank.
>
> They came rumbling on, starting at once with their machine guns, backed by shells and mortars. There were fifty-odd tanks and a staff car leading them. I let go at 150 yards. You couldn't miss. All our guns seemed to be firing at once. My target burst into flames but came on another 50 yards before halting. Over on my left, one blew up at 200 yards. We were giving them hell but we weren't getting away with it for our position was rather exposed and they let fly with everything they had. They even attacked us with lorried infantry, but the main battle was our guns against the fifty tanks. When they turned and retired we knew that for the moment our guns had won.
>
> Some enemy tanks tried to hide by mixing up with the knocked-out and derelict vehicles, but we were used to most of Jerry's tricks. The crew of one tank tried to repair it on the spot. We picked them off with rifles. All this time the enemy never let up, nor did we. My gun had smashed up five tanks in the first attack, and I only count those that were completely burned out.
>
> The thing that sticks out in my memory is our company commander saying we were cut off and nothing could get through to us. But we had Monty's orders to fight it out. We kept on fighting as long as we had a shell or bullet or bayonet. There was no rest, and when you had the time to listen you realized that we had fewer and fewer guns firing.
>
> Two of my crew crept on their bellies right out into the open under enemy fire to get some ammunition. Then the platoon commander decided to reach a stranded jeep with four boxes of ammunition on

board. God knows how he got to it—they were machine-gunning him all the way.

When the next attack came, the colonel was acting as a loader of my gun. He had taken a nasty one in the head and we wanted to bind it up, but he wouldn't hear of it. Keep on firing, that's what he wanted. When the colonel was too weak to refuse attention we bandaged his head and put him beside some scrub.

With only two rounds of ammunition left, Calliston said he took a line on two tanks and got both of them, after which, removing the breech blocks and sights from the 6-pounders, and carrying the wounded on their backs, they crawled for four hours to reach the British lines.

Later, when word came that the enemy had withdrawn behind his minefields in the south, abandoning his final attempt to reach the Nile Delta, Calliston made a remark typical of all British fighting men in the Western Desert:

"I hope they took time to recover our guns. We still have the breech blocks, you know!"

• • •

There were a few more tank skirmishes ahead as Rommel, with the Delta before him, frantically tried for a breakthrough, but all his attacks crumbled before the determined resistance of the Eighth Army. The Germans and Italians never had an opportunity to use their parachutists, for the RAF had wrested superiority in the air from the Luftwaffe, and they would very quickly have shot transport planes out of the skies. Losses in panzers and troop transports had been considerable as a consequence of bombing and incessant British gunfire. Rommel never got the supplies of petrol that he so anxiously awaited: his oil tankers were sent to the bottom of the Mediterranean.

"No retreat and no surrender," Montgomery had ordered. There was not a man who failed in his duty.

• • •

It was Wendell Willkie, on a visit to the Western Desert as a personal representative of President Roosevelt, who, with the consent of General Montgomery, released the welcome news of Rommel's defeat to war correspondents at Berg el Arab.

"The Boche," said Willkie, "has been stopped on this front, and the danger to Egypt has been removed. This has been one of the significant battles of history, and may well mark the turning point of the war."

Willkie spoke with reason, for the long-awaited Sherman tanks and

105mm self-propelled guns from America had arrived at Suez, and it would now be possible to create a striking force in the desert capable of driving the enemy out of Libya.

Rommel never recovered from this setback at the hands of "Montgomery of Alamein."

22

"MILK RUN" TO BENGHAZI

T HE FAILURE OF ROMMEL'S ATTACK AT ALAMEIN EARLY IN September 1942 gave me a long-awaited chance to visit American and British heavy bomber squadrons in Palestine that, cooperating with the Mediterranean Fleet, had by now virtually closed the eastern Mediterranean to Axis convoys.

By night and day for weeks, American B-24Ds and British-manned Liberator bombers had been pasting enemy shipping at their bases hundreds of miles away, penetrating as far as Navarino Bay, Greece, to the north and to Benghazi in the west. The toll of Italian freighters, tankers, and escorting warships sent to the bottom was rapidly mounting, largely due to high-level precision bombing of the B-24s with their famous Norden bombsight. To great measure, the repulse of Rommel's latest attack at Alamein had been due to the constant hammering of Tobruk and Benghazi, the enemy's principal North African ports of supply. American and British bombers had made the "milk run" to Benghazi practically a nightly affair, even though the mileage involved there and back from their bases in Palestine was comparable to the distance between London and Constantinople.

When I first met the American bomber boys, they were restless and anxious "to get this war over with." You couldn't give them enough work to do, and I was deluged with questions as to future possibilities in fighting on land because, said the pilots, "we want to transfer our bases to the Western Desert so that we are in range to bomb Italy!"

The Halverson group, known as the "Halpros," was headquartered at the time in the Lydda aerodrome in Palestine. They had been the first outfit to arrive in the Middle East and were veterans of fighting in the Philippines, Java, the Andaman Islands, Burma, and China. One of the Halpros' best-known aeroplanes, a Flying Fortress nicknamed "Minnie from Trinidad," had taken part in the evacuation of Java, and had carried forty women and children, packed like herrings, out of Burma. Once credited with sinking a Japanese cruiser off the island of Bali, this relic of the first days of hostilities in the Pacific was now being used as a freight transport, helping in the movement of Air Corps troops to the Libyan front. Newer bombers, with equally colorful nicknames, were now taking the fight to the enemy.

Among pilots who already wore numerous decorations for gallantry in the Far East was Second Lieutenant Milton J. Svoboda from Portland, Oregon. Svoboda won the Silver Star for his participation as navigator on the lead plane in a flight bombing Port Blair in the Andaman Islands on the night of April 1, 1942. This had been the first raid on Japanese-held territory by U.S. heavy bombers based in India.

Perhaps even more spectacular than their part in the dispersal of the Italian battle fleet had been the Halpros' long and difficult raid on the oil fields of Romania. This raid was carried out by personal order of President Roosevelt a few days after America declared war on Germany. With routine matter-of-fact professionalism, the mission had been executed successfully despite temperatures at altitude ranging from 55 to 75 degrees below zero.

• • •

U.S. Army Air Corps regulations at the time did not permit the carrying of newspapermen on any of these combat missions, so, anxious to learn more of actual conditions over the target area, I applied for a flight in a British-manned Liberator. The B-24D Liberators flown by the Americans were an advancement over the Liberators flown by the British. The American planes were equipped with a supercharger, a device permitting high-speed flight at high altitude. The British boys had to carry out their bombing missions at an altitude several thousand feet lower than the Americans, and for that reason their planes sometimes came back badly battered with enemy ack-ack.

It was not a case of partiality. At the time, there were not sufficient B-24Ds in the area to go around, and considering the situation, the British were highly pleased to have the basic Liberator, which they termed a "damn fine aircraft." Nothing short of a direct hit could bring one down, and with their four engines they could fly on indefinitely, even with only two of the four engines running. Thus, compared to some of the British-made bombing aircraft, they were themselves a reliable insurance policy.

I got a berth on a Liberator for a combined bombing of Benghazi by the Americans and the British. The Americans were to take the lead, and I would have the opportunity of seeing the damage they had done to Benghazi Harbor in this dusk attack. My pilot for this mission was nicknamed "Duplex." He was a tough, two-fisted Australian from Campordown, Victoria; one of the most experienced pilots in the squadron. He was an ace who had recently bombed Mersa Matruh alone, in a "sick" Liberator, rather than return to base with his bombs on board. Unable to keep up with the rest of his squadron, he had flown over the target after the other planes had cleared the area. It was an exceedingly ticklish job since a lone bomber, particularly a lame one, is generally easy prey for enemy fighters.

"I wasn't very high," Duplex said, "in fact any fighters could have reached me within three minutes after takeoff, but we picked out our target and let them have it. Our bombs fell right in the target area, blowing up two or three supply barracks. I then started to get the hell out of there, but remembered that we had a camera on board and that if I wanted to prove what we had accomplished, it would be necessary to take some pictures. So, back over the target we went. My heart was in my mouth the whole way. I flew her so low that we were a point-blank target for ack-ack, but they didn't fire. Maybe they thought we were Germans. In any event, we made it back to base without further incident."

Before takeoff the British wing commander jokingly offered each man in his crews ten Egyptian piastres for a picture of a direct bomb hit. Then he said: "Make every bomb count, boys, and keep your eyes skinned for Jerry. And don't worry, Yank, you'll get your money's worth on this trip."

The planes took off at dusk, at one-minute intervals. By 8:15, seated in the aft bomb bay alongside the waist gunners, I began taking notes. I found that because of the altitude, my pen was leaking. Then my teeth began chattering as the mercury tobogganed to subzero temperatures. Occasionally, on instructions from the navigator, one of the gunners dropped flares down a chute. I watched them burst with a brilliant white flash over the sea and then would hear the navigator over the intercom phone: "One degree to port," or "One degree to starboard." It was like being on a ship at sea rocking gently on the waves.

The approach to the target required several hours and proved monotonous, except for occasional remarks over the intercom phone about night fighters. Remembering the mission briefing on the dangers of night fighters, I speculatively looked down the port beam gun, adding my eyes to those of the watchful crew. The pilot told the navigator that he wanted to cross the coast at ten or eleven thousand feet. "The higher the fewer," he said, meaning the night fighters.

We climbed rapidly into a full moon, a moon so bright I could write by its light. At one point the copilot exclaimed: "What a glorious moon! I can think of a lot better things to be doing on a Mediterranean night like this." The pilot answered with a sarcastic: "Aw, why bring that up?" Then there was silence, except for mission-related chatter, as we approached the target.

I called Duplex on the intercom to ask his advice on the best spot in the Liberator from which to see the bombing.

"Stay where you are, in the belly, Yank," he replied. "Incidentally, there'll be no need to advise you when we get over the target. You'll be hearing and seeing plenty."

Promptly at the predesignated hour, we reached Benghazi, guided by a spectacular fire from either a tanker or ammunition ship that had been bombed by an American B-24D. I was so cold my knees were knocking, but I thawed out in a hurry when the fire controller, a Canadian from Vancouver, warned the pilot: "Ack-ack ahead, sir!" A moment later, we rushed headlong into it. Other Liberators were already over the target, and as I looked down into the beams of searchlights sweeping up into the sky I watched bombs from the planes ahead of us rain down on the harbor, creating a modern version of Dante's Inferno below. When the searchlights caught you, their glare was blinding. But because the British sometimes fired their machine guns down the beams of the searchlights, the Italians threw the beams all over the place, appearing just as anxious not to hold anything in their glare as to find it.

Anti-aircraft fire increased in intensity. It was heavy but meaningless, typical of the highly excitable Italians. Tracers and flaming onions (white phosphorus rounds) were streaming into the heavens as well, and the searchlights were turning night into day. Duplex seemed unimpressed. Almost casually he made a couple of bomb runs over the target as shells burst all around us. He might have been driving a rubberneck bus along Riverside Drive on a Fourth of July night instead of bombing Benghazi.

Finally, and it seemed an eternity to me, Duplex made his third bomb run over the target. Brilliant flashes now and then silhouetted the crouching waist and tail gunners intent on their task. Lying on my belly and looking down, I could see frequent splashes of scarlet-blue resembling ladles of molten steel spilling on a concrete floor as the squadron of Liberators did their stuff. Incendiary bombs were racing along the ground like liquid fire.

On the interphone, the pilot talked to the bombardier.

"Can you make out the target, Vick? It looks like Jerry has put down a smoke screen."

"No, it's a ship on fire, and there's a dummy fire over there. Jerry must think we're damned fools."

The fire controller broke in:

"Hullo beam gunner; tail gunner! Fighters approaching! Fire defensively only. Husband your rounds." I was tense, but for this crew it was just routine.

The bombardier took over at this point. "Steady—steady—bomb doors open. Hold her in line. OK skipper, first bomb's gone."

I strained my eyes to see them land, but just then the fire observer shouted:

"Better get out of it, skipper. They're ganging up on us."

You bet they were, but the Aussie pilot merely laughed and seemed to point the nose of the big B-24 straight up into the air. I found myself practically standing on my head as we showed our tail to the enemy. There was another laugh over the interphone and the pilot was asking me:

"How'd you like that, correspondent? That's losing them, eh?"

We made another circuit of Benghazi Harbor for the fourth and final bomb run. The searchlights and the ack-ack were losing ground as the fires were spreading from the effects of thousands of pounds of bombs. I realized again that it was freezing cold, and now that the bomb bay was empty I began thinking only of getting back for something hot to drink.

But it wasn't over. As we approached Tobruk, the fire controller exclaimed:

"Fighter approaching to starboard, sir. It's a Ju-88. Hullo gunners. Range two hundred yards. Hold him in your sights!"

I heard the tail gunner mumble to himself: "If he comes any closer, I'll take him home as a pet!" But the Ju-88 veered off, for the way our pilot was maneuvering it was obvious that the fighter had been discovered, and night fighters rely mostly on surprise. Taking on an alerted Liberator was not a wise course for a fighter pilot wanting to fly another day.

Our Liberator had done its job and plodded home. The ground crews stood by as the pilot brought us in for a perfect landing, and no questions were asked until every man had had his cup of tea. We had been out for ten hours and fifteen minutes. For me it had been a hair-raising experience, and one that I would not have wished to repeat again too soon.

I left Palestine full of admiration for these heavy bomber boys, for what I had witnessed had been mild compared to what they go through without a murmur, night after night. I was convinced that someday soon, having completed the job in North Africa, they would be blowing holes through the roof of "Fortress Europe."

23

THE BOMBING OF NAVARINO BAY

B EFORE RETURNING TO THE WESTERN DESERT, I DID MY BEST
to convince commanding officers of the U.S. Army Air Force in
Palestine that accredited American war correspondents should
be permitted to witness future bombings by the B-24Ds.

It seemed a tough nut to crack. Regulations denying war correspondents
the right to ride in the heavies had originated in Washington, not in the
field. It appeared that so far as the group commanders were concerned,
we could ride in their bombers at any time, but first it was necessary to
obtain the OK of Major General Lewis H. Brereton, commanding all U.S.
Air Force units in the Middle East.

A top-notch American newspaperman by name of Robert Parham,
from Norman, Oklahoma, who recently had been appointed public
relations officer to the Ninth U.S. Army Air Force in the Middle East, with
the rank of major, turned the trick much sooner than we had expected. He
had the backing of General Brereton himself, who agreed that a certain
amount of publicity on bombing missions would not only benefit morale
of the participants but also answer a growing demand in the United
States for first-person, eyewitness dispatches supplementing the terse
and sometimes none-too-revealing war communiqués and official press
handouts.

• • •

One day at Alamein as I conversed with the crews of Sherman tanks
newly arrived from America who were to form the spearhead of General
Montgomery's now-imminent offensive, I received an urgent message
through army signals from Cairo. I was required to report with all haste
at Middle East headquarters of the U.S. Army Air Force.

Bumming a ride on an empty petrol truck back to Alexandria, and then
taking the first available train to Cairo, I arrived puffing and blowing at
Parham's public relations office, only to be told, "I guess you're too late,

because the major has already left by air for Palestine with a group of seven American war correspondents. It's too bad, because this should be really big stuff. Yes, Washington's OK just came through."

Then followed a frantic race to catch up with the other boys, including the Middle East manager of the United Press, Leon Kay, and secure a first-row seat to trouble. Kay had left a message, advising that because of my efforts to promote the trip, he had gone along only to make certain that the United Press would be represented on this first mission, but was willing to relinquish his place to me, were I to arrive in time. I had an even chance of making the grade, for a high-ranking officer in Cairo told me just before my hurried return to Palestine in a DC-3 transport plane that the heavies were loaded up and in "stand by," waiting for a report that the Italian Fleet had put to sea.

Arriving at Lydda aerodrome, I found that the correspondents had long before left for an aerodrome in northern Palestine, preparatory to the takeoff. It looked bad for me, especially since the only way to reach the place was by automobile, and civilian traffic by road after dark was prohibited.

Having already nearly busted my galluses to get this far, I wasn't ready to give in. So with the assistance of an intelligence officer by name of Captain Smith who used to be a professor at Ohio University and knew some of my old friends in Columbus, I prevailed upon an Arab taxi service in Jaffa to haul me to Haifa at a fancy price. No Jew dares to travel the lonely highway through the settlements of northern Palestine by night, so when I stopped at a Jewish café in Jaffa, asking the location of the local Arab taxi stand and telling them my destination, the Jewish proprietor and his wife shook their heads and looked at one another askance.

"You'd better stay here until daylight, for there have been many cases of cars ambushed by Arabs along that road," they said. "And how do you know that your driver is not in league with them?"

I laughed, paid for my coffee, and proceeded to the Arab taxi stand where the owner confirmed my telephone conversation from Lydda. He placed an ancient vehicle complete with turbaned Arab driver at my disposal. I had to pay several pounds in advance, for apparently the taxi fellow didn't trust his own driver. Then we were off, driving at a fast pace in the darkness along the steep, winding road to Haifa. I asked the driver if he could see with his dimmed headlights, and he shook his head. I wasn't sure if he was telling me that he couldn't see or that I should not worry about it. In any event, we rushed headlong into the night.

• • •

It was about midnight when we arrived in Haifa. Before paying off the Arab driver, I went to a Haifa hotel and telephoned the aerodrome, only to be told that the correspondents had gone.

"Gone where? Are they out on a bombing?"

"No, it hasn't come off yet. They've gone to a nightclub in Haifa."

There were nearly half a dozen hot spots in Haifa, and with my Arab friend standing by, I paged them all by telephone. The last number I called produced results. The boys were there and would wait for me.

The nightclub proprietor stared open-mouthed as I walked in, complete with sleeping bag, which I left in the hands of a Jewish hatcheck girl. Then I walked to the correspondents' table, all smiles, only to receive a swift kick in the pants from Leon Kay, who, being on the trail of a first-class story, naturally wasn't overjoyed at my sudden arrival. Nevertheless, he proved a man of his word.

"I didn't think you'd make it, Hank, and it's only by a miracle that you arrived in time," said Kay, "for this afternoon we actually were aboard the bombers, ready for takeoff. But it was a false alarm and the mission was postponed. Don't worry though: I'll hand over my place to you as promised."

We had a drink over it before accompanying the boys to the aerodrome, ready for the mission.

• • •

Next morning, October 3, the mass "correspondents' raid" was on. Seven of us, including Ed Kennedy of the Associated Press, George Lait of the International News Service, and Winston Burdett of CBS, lined up for our issue of fur-lined flying suits and oxygen masks as Major John R. "Killer" Kane, of Shreveport, Louisiana, briefed pilots and crews of his bomber squadron. The Italian Fleet, running true to form, had not come out, so enemy shipping at Navarino Bay, in Greece, had been selected as an alternative target.

As the big, four-motored Consolidated B-24 bombers warmed up for the takeoff on what for the veteran American pilots was a routine mission, but for the correspondents was to be a thrilling experience, I caught a glimpse of Kay's expansive bulk on the runway. He was chewing his lip, and with an effort at a smile, he waved us on to one of the biggest stories of the year.

I got more than my money's worth on that ride. Here is the first part of the story I submitted to United Press, written on my return late that night to the heavy bomber base:

DATELINE AT A U.S. HEAVY BOMBARDMENT BASE IN THE MIDDLE EAST, Oct. 3—(United Press) I returned to Greece with the American Air Force today, roughly retracing the route along which I had retreated with the British in April, 1941.

I saw the enemy draw Yankee blood at Navarino Bay (Pylos) and counted the toll as they paid heavily for it. Two powerful waves of B.24s drove the Germans frantic with an avalanche of 1,000 pound bombs.

Shipping was blown to Hallelujah thousands of feet below as the enemy, resorting to suicidal tactics, attempted to knock the big bombers out of the sky. They failed completely, losing four of five fighters in the attempt.

The military communiqué reporting the mission read simply:

> The Americans bombed two large supply laden cargo vessels from which resulted violent explosions attended by fires.

Here is the whole story, as I experienced it, from the back of a B-24:

Because I had lobbied for a good view, I drew "The Witch," the last plane in the rear element of the B-24 squadron. I don't think I'll be too choosy the next time.

A little dog, "the Duchess," mascot of the crew of another B-24, "Jersey Jerks," was among those that saw us off at the aerodrome. The bitch had done a lot of flying because the boys had picked her up at Lakeland, Florida, but she couldn't go on this mission as there were no oxygen masks for dogs.

I got acquainted with the crew of "The Witch" as the heavy bombers, flying in formation a few hundred feet over the ocean, hammered their way toward Navarino Bay, many flying hours distant.

There was the pilot, blond, husky, square-jawed Lieutenant Glade Jorgensen, from American Fork, Utah, who used to be a professional trombone player back home, and copilot Lieutenant Robert T. Goldberg, from Blooming Prairie, Minnesota. Both had done nine missions in the Middle East and were on their second over Navarino Bay. Jorgensen's ancestors were from Denmark and Goldberg's from Norway. They told me that they wanted to "keep socking the Hun until he's finished because the folks are waiting for us back home."

Then there was Second Lieutenant Peter L. Vlahakes, the Greek navigator from Newark, New Jersey, who thought that his parents "won't mind my bombing Greece because we're not bombing the Greek people— only the enemy ships." He had been born in the United States and was seeing his ancestral country for the first time through a Norden bombsight.

The only married member of the crew was Second Lieutenant Henry M. Sparger, bombardier from Mount Airy, North Carolina, tall, lanky, and slow-talking, but quick on the bomb trigger.

We were flying in loose formation until about an hour before we reached the target. There wasn't much talk, although Staff Sergeant Byrne, radio operator and gunner from Lacrosse, Wisconsin, a short, stubby gent who looked kind of funny with his little wisp of a goatee like *Li'l Abner*'s Paw, reckoned that he'd "like to get back as early as possible, because I want to listen to the World Series over the radio. I think the Cardinals will win this time, don't you?"

Byrne didn't look so funny when the fighting started. Crouching in the revolving top power turret that reminded me of the electric chair in Ohio Penitentiary with all its gadgets, he poured .50-caliber machine-gun bullets into a Messerschmitt-109 like a veteran, although it was the first time he ever had been within shooting distance of enemy fighters. With the tail gunner, Staff Sergeant Donald S. Allen, from New York City, Byrne was given credit for sending one Hun to his grave in flames.

Then there was Frost, the right waist gunner, who after he got a bad one in the right knee shouted in the intercom: "We got him!" And then he fired a dozen more bursts for good measure before collapsing in a pool of his own blood.

The first man at Frost's side was Technical Sergeant Marvin L. Breeding, armorer-gunner from Dallas, Texas, who himself got a bullet splinter in the leg but didn't pay any attention to it until he was sure his pal Frost would pull through.

Technical Sergeant Joseph E. Farmer, from St. Charles, Virginia, who saw the pilot of an attacking Messerschmitt bail out, and then watched the enemy fighter, on fire and smoking like a comet, hit the water, also was hit by shrapnel. Luckily it was only a scratch below the right eye.

• • •

The approach run was uneventful, but as I watched "Snow White," "Jersey Jerks," and the other planes in our element firing practice machine-gun bursts into the water preparing for Zero Hour, I experienced a sense of extreme satisfaction to be going back to Greece for the first time since the retreat from Nauplion, with my own countrymen, in an American bomber.

The calm blue ocean over which we were skimming like monster seagulls had looked quite different a year and a half before when we were being dive-bombed in convoy by Goering's Luftwaffe. I was going to have my revenge now, and the World War song "Over There" with the words "the Yanks are coming, the Yanks are coming" ran through my mind as we neared the Greek coast.

As we approached Navarino Bay and started climbing to oxygen level, the pilot, Jorgensen, ordered us to adjust our life jackets and parachutes. We were climbing slowly several hundred feet per minute in perfect formation. At ten thousand feet, Jorgensen ordered adjustment of oxygen masks. We were still climbing, and as I stood behind the pilots, I was fascinated by the little rubber bulb of their masks inflating and deflating like toy balloons.

Jorgensen broke the spell as he pointed to the shoreline in the haze below. Soon we could see Greece on our right, with its peninsulas resembling long, crooked fingers. We were still climbing, and Jorgensen asked the leading plane, "Snow White," to advise when they were going to drop their bombs so that I could take a photograph. I thought to myself how easy it all appeared, but that was because these fellows were so efficient.

The top gunner now was whirring his turret around, firing practice bursts. A red-hot shell casing clipped my ear and made me jump, but my laugh was only a gurgle in my oxygen mask. Then we were over the target. Major Kane, the squadron commander, had ordered the bombers into close formation for increased protection against fighters. As Jorgensen banked, I could see the ships looking like pencils thousands of feet below. I got my pictures of "Snow White" and "Jersey Jerks" dropping their bombs.

The ack-ack was pretty heavy, but soon the bombardier reported our bombs gone and "The Witch" was leaving the target area.

The squadron commander tuned in for the first time on the interplane radio system, which had been silenced up to that point to prevent the enemy locating our positions.

"Fighters approaching," he warned. That was all.

Jorgensen had already seen them, and as he took avoiding action I got a split-second glimpse of one out of three or four fighters diving on our starboard quarter. They looked like black swallows with yellow noses.

Then, in what seemed an eternity, it was twist, turn, left, right, earth, sky; planes below and planes above, planes upside down and all mixed up with bursts of ack-ack as Jorgensen made a wide sweep around the target area again, performing unbelievable acrobatics with the big bomber to shake the fighters. Pilots Jorgensen and Goldberg were twisting their necks and looking in all directions, the rubber bulbs attached to their oxygen masks inflating and deflating in rapid succession from the extreme tension. So was mine. It was a devilish job to shake the fighters, for they had glued themselves to "The Witch."

Then I heard a shout into my earphones:

"There he is, for Christ's sake open fire!"

All our gun turrets were as busy as Singer sewing machines in a dress factory, and tracers from enemy machine guns were weaving like red thread all around us. Trying to take in everything at once I got myself twisted up in the cord supplying oxygen to my mask. All this time there was land below us, the jagged peaks of the Greek coastline being clearly visible, for we had lost altitude in the course of our evasive tactics. It looked like we had got away from them at this point, but no. Suddenly I saw "Jersey Jerks" alongside us, all of its machine guns firing furiously. Then I saw pilot Jorgensen duck as a stream of bullets hurtled just past his head and across the cockpit. I couldn't hear anything because my earphones had gone dead. Later I found out that in moving around I had pulled out the plug. All I could hear over the noise of the plane was the metallic click of machine-gun casings flying all over the place. I thought Jorgensen was hit, but it had been only a muscle contraction as he reacted to the bullets streaking past his left ear.

I was glued to the spot where I stood behind the pilots, as it wasn't advisable to take off my oxygen mask. We had gained altitude, and a man needs oxygen in the stratosphere. Anyway, there wasn't much I could do as all the guns were being manned. The altimeter read fourteen thousand feet and all of our guns were still going. I replaced the plug in the interphone system in time to hear a shout of exultation from Gunner Frost:

"I got him, sir!"

"You got him—you got that plane?" answered Jorgensen.

Frost's voice was becoming faint, but the reply came back:

"Yessir, I sure did. There he goes now. He's on fire." And then even more faintly, "I've been shot, sir," followed by more machine-gun fire.

Jorgensen anxiously asked over the intercom, "Are you bad hurt, Frost?"

There was a pause and then Frost mumbled, "Yessir, I'm afraid I am. I'm bleeding pretty bad, but we got him, sir."

Jorgensen replied calmly, "Fine business, Frost. Hold tight. I'll come back to help you as soon as I can."

Then I noticed both pilots taking off their oxygen masks. They were no longer of any use, for our oxygen tank had been riddled with bullets and there was no oxygen left. This was my chance to help, and as I ripped my mask off and unfastened my parachute to negotiate the narrow "cat walk" in the bomb bay, I told the pilot that he could remain where he was as I was going to take care of Gunner Frost. The enemy fighters were still about, and it wouldn't do for the pilot to leave his controls. Also, the gunners had plenty on their hands.

The cold was intense as I removed my cumbersome sheepskin coat to reach the waist of the bomber. I found Frost there, lying on his back and bleeding profusely with Gunner Breeding bending over him, while the tail gunner revolved his turret, keeping his sights on the enemy fighters.

Breeding and I cut Frost's trouser leg, unlaced his shoe, and ripped off the blood-soaked sock to apply a tourniquet. My fingers were numb and I fumbled the iodine swabs in the first-aid kit, which were frozen solid, so that I had to breathe on them to thaw them out. As I applied them and dressed his wound, Frost, deathly pale, asked for a cigarette, smiled weakly, and mumbled, "We got him, sir." We managed to stop the flow of blood, trying not to make the tourniquet too painful. Then, after a few minutes, Breeding, who had returned to his gun, said:

"Do you mind looking at my leg, sir? I've been hit, too."

I took a quick look and found a flesh wound in the ankle, to which I also applied iodine.

The engineer, Farmer, who was manning the belly gun, shouted back:

"That-a-boy, Frost. You sure got him. I saw the pilot bail out and the plane hit the sea."

Pilot Jorgensen, leaving Goldberg at the controls, came back and gave Frost a shot of morphine. This done, the wounded man was resting fairly comfortably and there was time to look around in the tail and waist of "The Witch." It resembled a colander. The shot that got Frost had gone through a thick aluminum pipe. Matchwood had been made of the stock of a rifle nearby. I looked to left and right and there were many holes in both wings and in the flaps of the stricken aircraft.

Except for a brief message to tell the leader of the squadron that we had wounded aboard and to obtain permission to go ahead of the rest of the squadron to get medical aid, it was impossible to use the radio. We were deep inside enemy territory. There were several hours more flying over the ocean toward base, and we had become a hospital ship. By sunset "The Witch" had made considerable progress as Jorgensen tried to get more speed out of her. It was difficult, for the two superchargers had been shot away and the automatic steering was out, as was one of the ailerons. Landing wouldn't be too easy as the hydraulics had been damaged and the engineer also believed we had a flat tire. I was able to count at least twenty-five bullet and cannon holes, and perhaps double that number of smaller holes made by splinters inside the bomber.

As darkness fell, Gunner Byrne emerged from his perch in the top turret and explained, "That Hun tried to commit suicide. We got a burst into him at eight hundred yards and another at six hundred. He was smoking, but came in again, and we let him have it at two hundred yards. He was coming level with our tail and it would have been terrible if we had missed."

Gunner Allen said that there were three or four fighters in the last wave.

"One raked us from the side as he side-slipped into the formation. The one Allen and I got fastened on our tail. He must have known he was going west, because he came in awful close to our tail. We couldn't have missed him."

The only thing that saved Allen was the bullet-proof glass in the tail turret, which was scarred by bullets and cannon shells.

I stayed on with Frost most of the time during the return journey and occasionally lit cigarettes for him. He was a game little fellow and nearly always smiling. Afraid that he might pass out from loss of blood, I talked to him for all I was worth to keep him interested. I told Frost that he'd probably be going home soon. Weakly he replied:

"It's no use, sir. They've all got married on me."

There followed three hours of flying in pitch darkness with no break in the monotony. A hundred miles from the aerodrome, Byrne tapped out a wireless message:

"Have medical aid ready."

He repeated it over and over again because the station was jammed.

There was thunder and lightning as "The Witch" came home. Goldberg was suggesting that they should have a crash wagon ready as we might have a flat tire, but Jorgensen was confident that he could land right side up.

• • •

The Haifa searchlights caught us as "The Witch" maneuvered for landing, but Jorgensen gave them the recognition signal and the anti-aircraft batteries held their fire.

At last we were on the ground and an ambulance was rushing alongside to take off Gunner Frost who, according to physicians, would recover. Goldberg slapped me on the back and said, "I guess we're living on borrowed time. But it could have been a darned sight worse!"

The other boys had also had a tough row of it. But I think Major Parham in "Killer" Kane's plane experienced as exciting a time as any. When still over the target area, and in the thick of the ack-ack fire and enemy pursuit, he learned that the bomb-bay doors had stuck, interfering with maneuverability of the leading plane. Taking off his parachute harness and cumbersome outer clothing, Parham, with shrapnel and bullets flying all around, had stepped out onto the "cat-walk" and closed the doors by hand. In addition, the big plane had had technical trouble, and got back with only a trickle of petrol left in the tanks.

"I hope you guys are satisfied with your little trip," said Parham, as we sipped coffee in the pilots' mess.

Leon Kay then revealed that although he hadn't accompanied the mission, he was among the minor casualties. In the excitement attendant to arrival of "The Witch," he had fallen off the running board of the ambulance as it raced to our plane over the soft sand, rocks, and ruts of the desert aerodrome.

"It's not only my tailbone but my nerves," said Kay, grinning broadly and rubbing his backside. "Next time, I'm not going to stay at the base to 'sweat them in' (air force slang for guiding the planes in safely by radio signal). "I'd rather be upstairs with the boys. Waiting around down here is a nerve-wracking experience, Hank."

He then explained what had happened during our absence.

"You guys were already two hours overdue and there was a sandstorm blowing. All we knew was that "The Witch" had casualties aboard and we were worried, for the message had not stated whether anybody had been killed or, if wounded, how badly. A half-hour before you finally turned up we heard the roar of a bomber in the obscurity and as it swung low for a landing we were told that it was a B-24 that had been on another mission and had got lost. This bomber disappeared after sweeping low over the tents and later we heard that a plane had crashed into a mountain in Lebanon. What a night!"

By this time, most of the pilots and crews were trickling off to bed. For them, the "correspondents' raid" was over and forgotten, and tomorrow was another day. Soon, the nearly empty mess echoed to the clatter of typewriters, the seven new initiates having pulled themselves together sufficiently to tell their stories to the world.

24

THE BATTLE OF ALAMEIN

"O NE FORCE. ONE PLAN. ONE! THE EIGHTH ARMY and the air power supporting it are one, not two. One! We are combined. This is our great strength. United we stand; divided we fall." On the eve of the historic battle, General Montgomery, standing alongside Air Vice-Marshal Arthur Coningham, stressed the new spirit of cooperation to the assembled reporters. Fighting as one, the Eighth Army and "Allied Air Striking Force" would combine old and new tricks of warfare with perfect synchronization to crush Field Marshal Rommel's forces.

Air Vice-Marshal Coningham predicted that he would reverse the story of the Greek air campaign. As he spoke, bombers and fighters of the RAF and USAAF, represented in strength for the first time in the Western Desert, roared overhead, engaging in a four-day preliminary offensive against the Luftwaffe. On the night of October 23, 1942, this force merged into a single tremendous effort involving a concentration of artillery and aircraft more powerful than any yet used in this war.

I covered the Air Force for the United Press during the Alamein drive and saw Coningham's prediction come true. Within a few days, the Luftwaffe had been virtually swept from the desert skies, leaving Rommel's ground forces naked in the Egyptian sands, just as the BEF had been in Greece.

More than one thousand enemy aircraft fell into Allied hands between Alamein and Tripoli. Coningham's tactics strangled the Luftwaffe and grounded the famous Stuka dive-bombers of Greek days as hundreds of medium bombers, including U.S. Army B-25s (Mitchells) and British and American fighters and fighter-bombers slashed at enemy aerodromes deep in the desert, destroying dozens of planes in single sweeps.

With a major air victory already won, massed British artillery opened up in a night bombardment reminiscent of Passchendaele.[1] It was the

1. The 1917 Battle of Passchendaele, also known as the Third Battle of Ypres, was one of the major battles of World War I.

most terrifying cannonade I have ever heard. At Zero Hour, 9:30 p.m. on October 23, a deafening crash shattered the tomblike stillness of the desert. Hundreds of 25-pounders and mediums spaced a few yards apart had suddenly released a torrent of splintering steel and fire that leveled everything in its path. For five hours, British artillery, supported by night bombers, kept it up. Montgomery's thunderbolt unnerved crack German regiments holding the center of the Alamein line. They never recovered from the shock.

Few participants could find words to describe the drama of that first night as the infantry foot-slogged it in the moonlight and the glare of their crackling, multitongued shield of explosives. The barrage, according to Lieutenant Colonel G. R. Stevens of the Indian army, "was so exact that our troops felt it to be a part of themselves—a weapon in their hands—just as a pilot feels when the earth has slipped away from him and his engines beat sweet and true and he knows that he has great power in his grasp." A brigadier said, "My men could have leaned against it. The first casualties, and indeed most of the casualties, were men who followed the wall of shells so closely that they became queasy with fumes of the explosives."

As they pressed forward, rounding up thousands of dazed Germans and Italians, the infantry was flanked by silver and red tracers marking their path. It seemed to those who witnessed the spectacle from the air that man-made lava was engulfing the enemy lines in a cascade of multicolored flame. They felt a steady rumble like thunder, sometimes itself drowned out by gigantic explosions throwing sparks high into the air as the British shells and bombs found enemy ammunition dumps.

For ten days thereafter the infantry plodded on, steadily widening the gap for the armor. The desert at Alamein convulsed at the crash of shells and bombs and the pulsating throb of Allied squadrons overhead. There was no telling where Montgomery's spearhead of giant Sherman tanks would break through, for constant pressure was maintained all along the line, and the much-vaunted German field marshal was confused.

From the very beginning, Britain and America were masters of the desert skies. I watched the bomb line steadily moving westward as the battle approached a climax. Between visits to the various bomber and fighter squadrons, and one raid over the battle area to which I was a witness in a B-25, I sat in the operations truck of an RAF Command Fighter Group and saw every detail of the aerial battle. Each move was being recorded on a green baize board resembling a billiard table, with small wooden arrows painted yellow and red. So accurate was the RAF radio location apparatus that it was not possible for the Germans and Italians to put a single plane in the air from any given aerodrome or landing ground within a radius of hundreds of miles without the RAF being aware of it. They could tell almost the exact number of enemy planes that had taken off, and as the total increased or diminished, a close tab was maintained with numbered disks. Strict silence was maintained in the "ops" truck. The radio operators and noncommissioned RAF "scorekeepers" communicated to one another through headsets with mouthpieces attached. Group Captain Carter was always on hand, studying the board intensely with hands cupped in his chin. He ordered his fighter squadrons into the air, according to need.

Translated into words, the arrows on that board gave a running commentary of the battle, somewhat as follows:

"Sixteen-plus Me-109s are taking off at Fuka aerodrome and heading east. Ten-plus are airborne now and appear to be joining others."

The group captain thereupon calmly ordered his fighters, some of them already on patrol over the battle area, to intercept their progress westward as they rushed headlong into close combat being marked by a series of red arrows, depending on their number and direction. It was like playing chess with men and machines as pawns. Suddenly more yellow arrows would appear on the board denoting Stukas taking off from other enemy aerodromes. The Stuka is quite helpless alone against modern fighter planes, and the Messerschmitts were their escort.

"Squadron X, join Squadron Z in interception of enemy aircraft," the group captain ordered into a microphone. "Stuka party!"

After a brief interval the yellow arrows either gradually diminished in numbers as RAF and USAAF fighters reported confirmed victories, or their course was reversed while the enemy aircraft streaked it for home like scared cats. But the arrows were not withdrawn from the board until the enemy aircraft actually had landed again on their own aerodromes. So many enemy planes were destroyed on the ground in Coningham's four-day bomber and fighter-bomber blitz that in subsequent vital days, while fighting on land reached a crescendo, the Germans and Italians sent aircraft out only in extreme emergencies. RAF and USAAF pilots became irritated at the failure of the enemy fighter pilots to accept combat.

"We are patrolling with our fighters right over Jerry's aerodromes, asking him to come up and fight," one RAF pilot grumbled. "But there are no takers."

A bomber pilot revealed that after discharging their loads, RAF bombers were diving practically to ground level, assuming the role of fighters to strafe the Axis ground forces. Such tactics would have been considered suicidal just a few days before.

"The circus on the ground isn't easily described," I was told. "Both sides are firing with their artillery, mortars and machine guns as fast as they can reload and there is a gradually rising cloud of dust over the desert. We have not been able to tell one side from the other, but judging from the bomb line, we are gaining on them."

As though transported at high speed on an invisible endless belt, great formations of B-25s, Baltimores, and Bostons thundered over us, shuttling back and forth in interminable relays to shower as much as 150 tons of high explosives per day on the enemy. Hurricanes, Spitfires, and P-40s accompanied them during the first several days, after which, the opposition being negligible, the medium bombers sometimes went out unescorted. Tank-busting Hurricanes, armed with the heaviest cannon ever installed in aircraft, were also playing a major role in the Allied desert offensive. In one engagement they claimed nineteen hits on fifteen captured British tanks being used by the Germans in defense of their Alamein positions. The tanks were marked with black crosses and carried the red Swastika flag. Three of them went up in flames. The tank busters had been in the desert for six months and in two successive campaigns had inflicted heavy losses on the enemy, with their own losses negligible. At the height of the Battle of Alamein their record included hits on seventy-four tanks, forty-six lorries, eight armored cars, eleven German troop carriers, and three petrol bowzers. The boys called themselves "Flying Can Openers" and their crews had been picked from veteran desert squadrons, including at the time two Americans and several New Zealanders, Australians, Englishmen, South Africans, and Rhodesians.

The Hurricanes were known as 11-Ds and carried two 40mm guns, one under each wing, capable of both automatic and single-shot fire. Their commanding officer, an English wing commander, himself had been credited with more than eight confirmed hits on tanks. The tank busters attacked their targets at terrific speed, sometimes as low as fifteen feet over the ground. They fired a solid-steel shell weighing more than two pounds which generally cripples a tank if it hits its vitals. On impact, the "tank-buster" shells created such friction that a blinding yellowish-white flame resulted.

The Hurricane was the only plane with wings strong enough to withstand the shock of firing the 40mm gun, which was exceedingly effective at several hundred yards. The Americans in the tank-busting unit, the first of its kind ever to go into action, included Flight Sergeant James Smith, from Gainesville, Florida, who once played outfield with the Boston Braves. He joined the Royal Canadian Air Force in February 1941 and was flying Kittyhawks before he joined this unit. The other American was Pilot Officer Dean Jones, from Dessart, North Dakota, who did pleasure flying in Montana, North Dakota, and California before the war. Smith, who joined the squadron on November 15, told me he thought "the tank buster is the answer to tanks from the air point of view. I like the job swell. It's got great possibilities."

The "Can Openers" had lost only one pilot in six months. He was Flying Officer Stanley McPhee, a lion hunter from Nairobi. McPhee, who had a head of hair like a lion's mane, was huge of stature and afraid of nothing. He regarded tank busting from the air as "fine sport." I talked to him the day before he was shot down. Jokingly he referred to the record of a flight lieutenant from London who then was top man in the squadron with twelve Swastikas painted on the side of his Hurricane, denoting that many tanks hit. "I'll beat his record all right," McPhee told me. "I've only got four more to get." I guess the day McPhee was shot down by enemy ack-ack he had been a mite too overzealous. Typical of lion hunters.

"Can Openers" attacked repeatedly, sometimes nine times in succession. The pilots told me that when they were attacking, enemy tanks generally stopped dead in their tracks until they had finished, frantically firing their four-barrel Breda anti-aircraft guns. Ack-ack was the only thing that could ever stop the tank busters, for they hurtled into action at such high speed that it was difficult for the tanks to draw a bead on them with their big guns.

American squadrons of P-40s surprised everyone by setting the pace for consecutive air victories during the three days immediately following the start of the final Battle of Alamein. Never before in combat in the Western Desert, the American squadrons overnight became the toast of all RAF personnel in the Nile Delta. The news of their spectacular victories spread fast, grapevine fashion, and in every RAF mess in the desert there were expressions of admiration for the Yank fliers, such as: "Whizzo!" "Good Show!" "Wizard stuff!" "That'll teach Jerry a lesson!" Commanding officers and flight commanders of crack desert outfits vied for the privilege of being the first to personally congratulate their American comrades.

Uncle Sam's boys first carved their initials in a big way in Jerry's hide on October 25 when the "Black Scorpion" fighter squadron, under Major Clermont Wheeler, of San Jose, California, chalked up its first major victory, bringing down four Me-109s and Macchis in two successive engagements. I was present when the jubilant "Scorpions" returned to their aerodrome, where the Stars and Stripes fluttered merrily atop a tall steel mast in the desert. And I watched Major General Auby C. Strickland, of Birmingham, Alabama, commanding U.S. units at Alamein, ruffle Wheeler's hair with glee as the young C.O. and his officers described their dogfights.

"We saw the fighters coming in and turned into them," said Wheeler. "I saw one of my fellows with a German on his tail and hollered to him to pull out. Then I saw two more. I picked the second one and got a good bead on him. Then there was a puff of white smoke as the Macchi executed a half roll and plunged straight into the deck. Another one fastened on my tail, but I was outdiving him. When I came out of the dive I was only a few hundred feet over Daba aerodrome."

Lieutenant William S. Beck shot down one of the four planes. "He had three of them on his tail but turned around and shot one of them down," said Wheeler. "I saw the plane hit the ground and burst into flames."

Captain Richard E. Ryan, of Worcester, Massachusetts, who only a few days previously had gashed ten inches off the tip of his propeller when he hit a German tank he had been strafing, was credited with bringing down a third plane, while Captain Glade Bilby, from Skidmore, Missouri, got the fourth.

I saw Strickland dig a roll of bills out of his pocket to buy beer for the entire squadron. He repeated it the next day at field headquarters of the "Fighting Cock" squadron, as they returned from another smashing victory. I have never seen fighting men more elated than were the boys of that squadron, which was named after "Uncle Bud," a huge red cock that had been brought by the squadron in the Clipper all the way from America and already had acquired three Egyptian "wives." The squadron had returned to their aerodrome with only one bullet hole in eight aircraft against four Macchis sent crashing to the ground in flames ten miles southeast of El Daba. The dogfight began at ten thousand feet and ended at two hundred feet off the ground as Second Lieutenant Robert L. Metcalf from Hooker, Oklahoma, fired a final burst which sent the last of the four Macchis careening out of control to destruction. The boys kidded "Hooker" because they said he had been so excited that although he had already finished his Macchi and it was out of control, Metcalf kept right on shooting at the plane "to make sure it would crash."

Captain Thomas Clark, of Wetmore, Michigan, led the flight and shot down two Macchis in rapid succession. I heard him tell Strickland that "the first blew up right in front of me into a thousand pieces. Yessir, I got him pretty as you please right in the belly. Then I plowed toward the second Macchi with such speed that I was in danger of crashing with him. But I pulled up in time to watch him make a floundering turn to the right and then crash amidst explosions from his own bombs which he jettisoned as we attacked. I nearly blacked out, turning away from the debris," he said.

Most elated among the American pilots was First Lieutenant Roy E. Whittaker, from Knoxville, Tennessee, who also shot down a Macchi. "It's the grandest feeling in the world," he enthused. "It seems like Christmas to me. This is what we've been training for."

Young Whittaker said he followed Captain Clark down and confirmed his first victory, after which "I turned and saw a Macchi heading southwest toward El Daba. I fired one burst and saw the plane crash and bounce fifty feet into the air before it burst into flames."

The "Fighting Cocks" went out with the "Black Scorpions" the next day on a predawn dive-bombing and strafing raid and caught the enemy with his pants down. When they left there were several big fires, including one huge billow of green flame and smoke where five or six enemy aircraft had been. So surprised was the enemy that they did not even open fire with their ack-ack until after the dive-bombing, when the P-40s hurtled practically to ground level, strafing planes, trucks, and tents in their path. I could hardly hear myself think from the roar of bombers overhead, as Major Art Salisbury, of Sedalia, Missouri, who led the attack, described how "as we jumped them, slinging lead, we could see incendiary bullets burst in great big red balls and ricochet into the sky."

One of the most spectacular air victories of the campaign, however, was scored by the "Black Scorpions" when they destroyed seven CR-42s and Messerschmitts, probably destroyed another four, and damaged three more. It involved a gigantic dogfight over El Daba aerodrome in which one American pilot, Lieutenant Lyman Middleitch from Highland, New Jersey, fought five Messerschmitts single-handed and sent three of them crashing to oblivion. It was Middleitch's fourth victory, and he thus became the ace American P-40 pilot in the Western Desert.

But the boys thought that Middleitch had been shot down, and were mourning his absence when he suddenly strolled into the squadron mess and sat down, looking a bit dazed. Major Wheeler asked him: "What did you do, feller?" In an apologetic tone, Middleitch replied:

"Oh, I got three, sir," after which amidst back slapping he described the uneven fight.

Lieutenant Gilbert O. Wymond, from Louisville, Kentucky, of the "Fighting Cocks," virtually equaled Middleitch's feat, destroying two CR-42s, one probable, and a fourth damaged. When I interviewed Wymond, he told me it was the first time that he had ever fired a gun in action.

"We had dropped our bombs from high altitude and were just leveling off when we saw twenty-five-plus CR-42s," said Wymond. "The Italians went crazy. You could hear them chattering excitedly over their interplane radio, and it seemed to us that they were trying to find out what was going on. We went into them singly and they were swell meat because in the excitement they had split up their ranks."

General Strickland was in the act of buying beer again, when he spotted me on the fringe of the group of pilots.

"When are you going to ride in one of my B-25 bombers?" said he.

"It's a fine chance to see what's going on on the ground."

A few days later I went out on my third bombing raid within a few weeks. It was in a B-25 called "Minnie the Moocher" that kept a date with the German Fifteenth and Twenty-first Panzer divisions in the battle area. She waltzed through the fireworks that the Germans sent up to meet her in fine style, throwing her hips around and slinging her bombs on Jerry with an effort at a high C that would have raised the roof in the Metropolitan Opera House. "Minnie" and her crew made it look easy, but throughout the mission I thought of the remark made by one of the ground crew staff before we took off: "You'd better check your dough with me before the takeoff, boys. You may not need it anymore, and I'm running short."

As we leveled off in tight formation for the bomb run, I caught a glimpse of the flashes of ack-ack guns, followed by black shell bursts around us. The tanks locked in battle far below looked like huge bugs with red tongues, shooting for all they were worth, darting in and out, leaving trails like cobwebs on the sands. There was a thump as "Minnie" got a slug in her backside. Soon, the bomb doors opened. Lying prone in her belly, I could see our bombs slithering down. They were flat at the beginning of their descent and then, in leisurely fashion, they straightened out. When the bombs exploded in the sand amidst the tanks, they threw up what looked like hundreds of small erupting volcanoes. The bombs sprayed the entire battle area, for each of our planes let go their bombs in salvoes at two-second intervals, and on this mission, "Minnie" had brought many friends.

Someone said fighters had been sighted and our escorting aircraft began climbing to meet them. The B-25s hurried home in a fast, steady drive without further incident, and back at the aerodrome I thanked my pilot for a "nice ride."

"You're welcome." He smiled, and added: "It's all in the day's work. All rides are nice when you get back in one piece and land safely with your hydraulics and tires OK. Come back anytime."

In subsequent hours, the desert at El Aqqaqir became a cemetery for Axis armor. The enemy was broken after violent tank fighting, and on the night of November 2-3, El Aqqaqir was captured. It was a thrilling sight as hundreds of fighter planes streamed westward, practically at ground level, in response to an order from RAF H.Q.: "Strafe ho! Rommel is running. Let him have it!" The planes made a shambles of the coast road. It was necessary for the Royal Engineers to clear it of battered enemy transports before supply columns of the Eighth Army could advance.

Rommel's frenzied dash through Tripolitania to the temporary safety of Tunisia was on.

25

ROMMEL PACKS UP

M Y TREK WITH THE RAF ON THE HEELS OF THE NOW fast-withdrawing Axis forces began at 9:30 a.m., November 5, as, pistols in hand, "delousing" units of Royal Engineers exploded mines and booby traps in a desert littered with the debris of retreat.

Rommel was running at such a pace that only fighter aircraft hastily installed in the ruins of El Daba aerodrome could keep up with him. Preliminary intelligence reports attributed the collapse of enemy resistance largely to lack of petrol, oil, and ammunition. As a consequence, scores of panzers had bogged down between El Alamein and Fuka. This emphasized the tremendous impact of the Allied air offensive that had prevented the enemy from adequately supplying his forward bases.

The surge westward was reminiscent of the "land grab" days in Oklahoma, for all desert roads had become a solid mass of British vehicles. Red and green rockets floating lazily into the air were starting signals for the advance. Those who had been slow in dismantling their tents were simply left behind.

Proceeding westward from Alamein, I saw hundreds of German and Italian prisoners on foot and without guards, bucking the tide of the British advance. Good-natured Tommies, grinning broadly, frequently tossed them cigarettes from their vehicles. The prisoners were not all walking. I saw some of them driving eastward along the open desert in their own snub-nosed lorries, bearing the white palm markings of the Afrika Corps. They gave themselves up to amused Red Caps waiting for them in the rear.

Fires dotted the horizon for miles as a good part of Rommel's forces went up in smoke, touched off by his armored rearguard at Fuka. Main forces of the Eighth Army in the north were taking care of the Germans while Greeks and Fighting French had the time of their lives chasing Ities who had been trapped by the thousands in the south. More than thirteen thousand prisoners had been taken already, and they were still coming in. Montgomery had broken the enemy armies.

Rommel began his withdrawal on November 2, the day of the decisive tank battle at El Aqqaqir, where nearly three hundred German and Italian tanks were destroyed. On the following two days the retreat had become general, the Germans in their flight abandoning entire divisions of Italians as they commandeered all available transport. Six Italian infantry divisions were captured almost intact, and half a dozen Italian generals were "in the bag." The Germans, though the first to retreat, left behind eight thousand prisoners. Certainly as many or more had been killed or wounded; the German 164th Infantry Division had practically ceased to exist.

In a pouring rain I was dashing off my first dispatch on this unbelievable spectacle when an RAF intelligence officer came up to tell me, "There are something like four thousand Jerries on the ridge yonder. You can hear our boys shouting at them with a couple of Bren guns. The rain should do the job, and I imagine they'll all be around for a drink of water and some grub before long."

That night I camped in the vicinity of El Daba. There were occasional fireworks as isolated groups of Germans and Italians fired at the bedded-down British convoys, but I doubt anybody got hurt. The offenders were merely expending their ammunition. During the night I had to do my slit trench act a couple of times, for lone night raiders of the Luftwaffe were strafing the road, but it was only a farewell salute by the Hun.

On the morning of November 6 I resumed the march and saw the boys who had been potting at us streaming in, grinning sheepishly and looking very dazed as they watched long columns of what it takes to run an army and air force moving past them to support armor and aircraft at the front.

I had a look at El Daba aerodrome and saw more than fifty German aeroplanes wrecked or stranded for lack of petrol, including at least a dozen brand-new Messerschmitts in their sandbagged blast shelters. Jerry certainly was streaking it westward in a hurry, his main columns now being reported in the region of Halfaya Pass, while a few hundred picked men from the Ninetieth Light Division fought a rearguard action at Mersa Matruh.

Kittyhawks and Spitfires circled low over El Daba aerodrome as Royal Engineers touched off German mines, and then, satisfied that the coast was clear, they landed in a maze of abandoned enemy aircraft. The fighters were maintaining a constant umbrella over the advancing army, protecting the convoys as they chased Rommel. There were, however, no signs of serious aerial opposition. The road westward was strewn with hurriedly abandoned enemy vehicles, guns, and tanks, most of which had been destroyed by fire. I counted scores of the flimsy Italian Mark XIIIs, referred to as tanks but scarcely more than armored cars. In the emergency they had seized up and were abandoned, strewn alongside the road like cigarette stubs. Shell pits and bomb craters for miles beyond what had been our forward positions on the coastal sector were mute testimony of the effectiveness of the Allied artillery and aerial barrage. The enemy left in such a hurry that he had abandoned complete camps, leaving the tents up and failing to salvage his ack-ack guns. We were retrieving many British trucks and tanks, lost during the retreat from Gazala and now marked with the German black-and-white cross.

I met a British pilot who had parachuted behind enemy lines a few days before, bumming a ride to Alamein. He had been hiding from Jerry for three days, and was covered with glycol, oil, and sand, but was grinning from ear to ear. The fellow had landed in the sea, and had had to swim for the relative safety of enemy territory. So many others were not so lucky: mixed up with the litter of retreat were numerous newly dug graves, some containing corpses but not yet filled in.

The downpour continued throughout the sixth of November, but the men were in high spirits. Infantrymen who normally would have had to walk it had deprived German prisoners of some of their vehicles, including motorcycles with sidecars and midget automobiles equipped with tracks. But not even chasing a routed enemy could prevent Tommy from brewing his "cup-a-tea" on the roadside.

At one place I saw a brand-new mosque of concrete construction, recently built by the Italians. Alongside it were several two- and three-story cement buildings obviously being constructed for military purposes, suggesting to me that the enemy had felt there were grounds for precaution against aerial bombing even after their success at Alamein. But that the buildings had been constructed at all indicated the enemy had been feeling pretty sure of himself not so very long ago.

The smell of death was everywhere, emphasized by swarms of flies buzzing over shallow, unmarked mounds in the sand, wetted down by the heavy rain. The German prisoners were the glummest folks I had ever seen, but the Italians were usually laughing. I saw a group of "Ities" having a fine time poking sticks into wreckage of their own trucks alongside the road and waving to the advancing British troops, including one group of Scotties in the rear of a three-tonner who were casually playing cards as they bounced along toward Mersa Matruh. And there was the usual pathetic sight of dogs that had lost their masters, coming up to the troops for scraps of food and water. Generally the boys gave them food, knowing that when hungry critters go wild in the desert they will dig up and eat most anything that war has left behind for them.

The rain had turned the desert west of El Daba into a reddish-yellow muck. Nevertheless, by the night of November 7, the Eighth Army had reached the outskirts of Mersa Matruh, where German suicide squads were still resisting with heavy artillery and mortars. I joined them there, having received a message ordering me to take over coverage of the Eighth Army from Richard McMillan, who was returning to England after having spent more than a year in the desert. I reached the outskirts of Matruh just in time to witness a battle behind an anti-tank ditch on the heights overlooking the coastal town.

It was a desperate fight and could only result in the German rearguard being cut to pieces. Within two hours I saw their 88mm guns and mortars give up one by one before a barrage by British 25-pounders. The Germans, tying white handkerchiefs to the muzzles of their rifles, approached their conquerors with arms reaching for the sky.

I moved up with the armored cars and tanks, bypassing several German gun emplacements and one huge eight-inch gun that the Jerries had sabotaged. Its muzzle resembled a daisy in full bloom and the gunners' kit was strewn about in confusion. There were shell holes from British 25-pounders not five feet from the gun mount. The British tanks and armored cars spread out fanwise along the Matruh escarpment while miles-long supply columns waited patiently to move into the town they knew so well. Shermans, Lees, Grants, and Crusaders flanked by armored cars and Bren carriers threw up waves of dust as they destroyed German machine-gun nests and mortar emplacements in the fading light. German artillery fire was rapidly thinning out as British shells found their mark. Occasionally there was the clatter of machine-gun fire and then a series of loud bangs while the tanks raced toward German pillboxes, shooting rapidly. Then there was silence.

The sun was setting in a crimson glow and scores of German prisoners were picking their way unattended among the British tanks and armored cars, walking toward our lines. They seemed in a trance, stumbling with heads down toward the campfires twinkling merrily in the distance. Behind us, 25-pounders blazed away. It was an awesome picture.

• • •

When I returned to camp, I discovered that a group of six war correspondents, including George Lait of the *International News Service*, Chester "Chet" Morrison of the *Chicago Sun*, Ed Kennedy of the *Associated Press*, and A. C. Sedgwick of the *New York Times*, had got into a mess. As a result, Lait got some shrapnel in his thigh and right leg, and Sedgwick was slightly wounded in the arm. Morrison and Kennedy were unhurt, although a British captain with Chet was seriously wounded by a machine-gun bullet, after which Morrison helped him and came back with blood on his clothes. Apparently, they had decided to follow six tanks on foot along the coastal road late in the evening and had been ambushed by Germans firing mortars and machine guns. Twelve Germans subsequently approached the unarmed correspondents with hands up and surrendered. Morrison, who during the last war was decorated with the Navy Cross and Croix de Guerre, told me there were other Germans making an effort to surrender but they were mowed down by their own troops.

• • •

Before the Germans tossed in the sponge at Matruh, I had a look at a German field hospital on the outskirts of the town that had been abandoned in its entirety, including tents, operating equipment, and medical supplies. I found forty-one patients attended by ten German orderlies still there. The hospital had belonged to the Twenty-first Panzer Division. The Eighth Army also had captured the Afrika Corps telephone exchange and huge quantities of German quartermasters' stores. I was pleased, for having been soaked to the skin by the drenching rain, I felt miserable, and within a few seconds I picked out a German pilots' blue-gray greatcoat that kept me warm during the subsequent advance to Tripoli.

With the suicide squads in Matruh still resisting, we discovered a Jerry sitting alongside the road, with his face cupped in his hands. The boys asked him to what unit he belonged and to our astonishment he replied: "I don't know, I came to Africa three days ago from Greece by aeroplane and was told to wait at this spot for my unit. I've been sitting here ever since as the army retreated."

He pointed to a German glider nearby that had brought him there.

• • •

Even in retreat the Germans were displaying foxlike cunning. They allowed several British vehicles to enter Matruh on the afternoon of November 7 before they opened fire, capturing a ranking officer of the British General Staff. He's now wintering in Italy. Squadron Leader Bobby Gibbes, of the Australian fighter squadron, was permitted to land at Matruh aerodrome before he was fired on, but managed to take off again.

By the next morning Matruh had been overrun and the advance to Sidi Barrani began. In the British column I saw ambulances of the American Field Service patiently edging forward in and out of the wreckage along the road.

The water problem was becoming serious, for the enemy in his retreat had polluted the wells, and rationing was instituted. We covered the distance to Barrani without incident. I hadn't seen a German aeroplane for two days, although some Palestinian machine-gunners just arrived from the south reported they had been strafed on the previous day by two Me-109s. Their officer, an American lieutenant by the name of Bill Durkin, a volunteer from California, had been wounded in the legs. He had joined the King's Royal Rifles in England.

I talked to a young lieutenant of the KRR attached to Bren carriers who laughingly described to me how he had captured General Giorgio Masina, commanding the Italian "Trento" division two days before. The lieutenant, who withheld his name but hailed from Chelsea, London, said:

"The general was in a big Chevrolet staff car when I spotted him. As I got close he switched to a Fiat buggy. My Bren carrier caught up with him and I fired a couple of bursts with the machine gun. The general hopped out. I waved him aside, but drawing himself up stiffly he announced, 'I am the commanding general of the Trento Division.' Then the general's chief-of-staff identified himself, after which we bagged the entire staff."

A Scottish sergeant with the New Zealand Bren carriers said he captured a German officer carrying a wallet stuffed with photographs of civilians hanging on lampposts by their necks.

"One photograph showed a sort of cattle pen," said the sergeant. "On every post there was a human head. The card was postmarked 'Belgrade.' I think I would have shot that German if I'd seen all this before I handed him over."

The sergeant said that he had ambushed seventeen enemy trucks with his Bren and was sending back so many enemy wounded that the doctor at the nearest field hospital sent back a message stating, "If you're going to send back any more, please send them to the Padre and not to me."

Then the sergeant described how an Italian captain had suddenly popped out of nowhere and, saluting, approached the Bren carrier to give himself up.

Whistling like a fellow would to his dog, the captain thereupon made a wide sweep with his arm and hundreds of "Ities" sprouted up from slit trenches all around me. It's sort of a slur on one's character to take Italians these days, but what are you going to do? And the trouble is they're always demanding food. Yesterday in the south a column of enemy trucks loaded with prisoners, mostly "Ities," got bogged down in the mud. There were only two or three Tommies guarding them. I saw a crowd of about thirty "Ities" behind one truck who were supposed to be pushing it. Only about six of them were actually pushing and the rest were hanging on. Whenever the truck moved, two-thirds of them would stop to clap their hands while the others tried to jump onboard. The Germans are completely different: dour and surly. They don't like defeat. Judging from the knuckle-busters and blackjacks we've taken from them, they wouldn't have treated us very nicely if we had been their prisoners. And I've never seen the like of the dirty literature and pornographic photos the Huns carry about.

The carrier boys who were hauling in prisoners by the hundreds, mostly Italians, told me how the Germans in a frantic effort to halt the British advance had laid down minefields, including five-hundred-pound aerial bombs with time fuses. Near Matruh a new German trick was uncovered, in the form of an electrically wired minefield. The Germans allowed our tanks to plunge straight into it, and then set the mines off by pulling a switch. There were several tank casualties.

Pressing on to Barrani, we saw special squads of sappers combing the fringes of the highway with mine detectors on long poles, resembling Hoover carpet sweepers. By now I had lost count of the stranded enemy tanks, guns, and other equipment, although official figures later placed German and Italian losses during the final "Battle of Egypt" at over five hundred tanks and one thousand guns.

The British army was everywhere at once, and the enemy no longer knew where to turn. On the morning of November 10, I awakened in my dew-covered sleeping bag on the sand to find several little groups of Germans within rifle range of our small camp, waiting to be picked up. Had they any fight left, it wouldn't have been very hard for them to rush our pint-sized outfit of one truck and two station wagons. They were a pathetic lot, foodless and waterless except for what they could scrounge from their own abandoned vehicles in the desert. There was no moon during this period, but day and night British equipment, including tanks on multiwheeled American trailers and thousands of supply trucks carrying ammunition, food, petrol, and water, advanced westward in support of the striking forces. In places where the Germans had not had time to lay mines, they had tossed English petrol tins containing Tela mines alongside the road for the vehicles to run over.

The British Army Medical Corps, closely supported by the American Field Service, was doing a wonderful job tending wounded on both sides. British and Imperial casualties had been negligible since the fighting at Alamein; however, immediate attention was being given to the more serious cases, which were handled by flying ambulances operated by the

RAF. These usually arrived on the scene of rearguard battles long before lorried ambulances could get there.

Barrani was desolate, with not even a stray dog about. It's a desert town on the Mediterranean coast, of approximately fifty stone buildings and huge barracks, now roofless and bomb-pitted. Before Barrani, Buqbuq, another excuse for a town on the coastal road, had fallen as British tanks, hedgehog hopping forward on huge trailers, plunged straight through, upsetting emplacements of German 88s and mortars like ninepins.

The formidable Halfaya Pass, where several hundred of the enemy had been bottled up by British flanking advance columns and bombing by the RAF, lay before us. On the evening of November 11 I arrived at the base of Halfaya Pass and learned that at first light it had been stormed and captured by thirty New Zealanders, who for the loss of one of their number killed and two wounded had captured six hundred Italians, opening the way for the victorious advance of the Eighth Army coastwise to Bardia, Tobruk, and Benghazi. I met five of these New Zealanders guarding their prisoners and they told me how in darkness, two half platoons equipped only with rifles and tommy guns had walked up the winding road to the summit of the pass and captured the entire garrison, including twenty lorries, eight field pieces, several anti-tank guns, scores of machine guns, and hundreds of grenades and rifles.

Munching a piece of German army rations gingerbread, a New Zealander sergeant said:

"Thirty of us scaled Halfaya and went over the top before dawn yelling bloody murder. There was a brief exchange of shots and one of our men was wounded. The Ities lay low until dawn and then began waving white handkerchiefs. It seems they had them handy in their caps for it all happened pretty fast. They came over to us with their hands up but then some fired several more shots, resulting in one of our fellows being killed and another wounded. We fired a few bursts with our tommy guns and they gave it up smartly."

I then talked to the prisoners, all except three or four of whom were Italian, mostly attached to the reserve Pistoia Division. One of their noncommissioned officers told me that under command of five German officers, "We were posted at Halfaya three days ago, with instructions to delay the British advance. We knew we would have to give up sooner or later because we had few rations and very little water. Last night our German commanders left us, making a getaway in staff cars and lorries, so we decided to surrender as soon as any troops appeared. When we saw these fellows this morning, we handed ourselves over. We were very surprised that they were only a few dozen."

It appears that the news of the American landing in North Africa, of which we had just learned, had had a lot to do with Halfaya's speedy surrender. I asked the Italian prisoners if they knew that they were in the center of a huge pincer. They answered that they had their portable radio sets in the pass and had been able to keep up with the developments.

Because I was speaking Italian, quite a crowd of soldiers gathered around me. I asked them where Rommel was and a couple of them drew their hands knifelike across their throats. They said they didn't know where he was but if they did, they would . . . etc. It wasn't an act. These Italian soldiers had murder written all over their faces. My deduction was that Rommel was only a fair-weather hero, and even then, only a hero to his fellow Germans.

One of the New Zealand guards told me to tell the prisoners that "in five or six days" the Axis would be wiped out of Africa. There were immediate murmurs of "Good. Maybe the war will be over soon." One Italian went so far as to say that he hoped Italy would sign a separate peace.

"We are not a warlike nation. We are working people," said he, and he displayed anger at the flimsy Italian equipment, compared with the British and American tanks.

There was a general clamor for water. The Italians denied having polluted the watering points, but they were unwilling to prove their point by themselves drinking the water available in these parts. While I interviewed the New Zealanders and their prisoners, an endless column of vehicles moved through the Halfaya Pass, which might easily have held up an entire army for several days, had it been defended by determined troops.

From Halfaya on, the going was easy, and I reached Bardia, a town inside the Libyan frontier, on the evening of November 12. Compared to the pace of the armored columns over the open desert, progress of the war correspondents had been slow due to road blocks along the Balbo highway, enemy mines, and the necessity of doubling back long distances daily to maintain contact with main army dispatch riders. In one instance, we were forced to drive back fifty miles the day before over roads scarred with shell and bomb craters between Sollum and Buqbuq, so that the previous day's story could be handed over for relay by air to Cairo.

The road to Tobruk was now open, and driving on, I met and talked with Italian prisoners struggling back unattended. They told me their instructions had been to join the retreating German forces somewhere in the vicinity of Derna, hence it was evident that no further stand was to be expected before El Agheila, nearly two hundred miles distant.

I camped for the night next to newly filled German and Italian graves on the roadside at Bardia and heard the surprising statement by Rome radio:

"The enemy launched a heavy attack at the frontier today!"

The only attack for some days had been that of the thirty New Zealanders who had accomplished the incredible by taking Halfaya Pass at the point of bayonets. As we listened to the dramatic voice of the Rome radio announcer, advanced striking forces of the British army were at least 125 miles west of the frontier and still going strong.

26
BENGHAZI'S FALL

W E HAD OUTDISTANCED THE MAIN COLUMNS OF THE Eighth Army when I reached Tobruk, in company with Ron Monson of the *Sydney Telegraph,* an old friend of Albanian hill-climbing days. The enemy had left hundreds of mines in the path of his retreat along the coastal road. We traveled the road by automobile, trying to keep up with the pursuing troops who followed the open deserts in light armored vehicles. It gave me the sensation of sitting in the electric chair waiting for someone to press the button. Several vehicles went up on mines ahead of us, and sometimes we were delayed while troops, walking four abreast, prodded potholes in the road with their bayonets.

At Wadi Bardia we had to skirt the most gigantic demolition job I have ever seen in wartime, consisting of a huge bridge that had been blown up by tons of dynamite, leaving the surrounding countryside blackened by blast for several hundred yards. Ruins of the collapsed bridge were still smoldering.

It was a case now of following the middle of the road and trusting to luck, for no British sappers had yet searched the road for mines west of Bardia. For days after we traveled through, army lorries were being wrecked on German mines arranged in such a manner that they would explode only after several vehicles had passed over them and the tarmac had settled.

Between Bardia and Tobruk we saw several graveyards containing hundreds of crosses neatly marked with the Swastika, emphasizing heavy German losses in nearly two years of desert warfare. There were also British and Australian desert cemeteries, relics of campaigns in which Tobruk had changed hands three times.

Before reaching the Tobruk perimeter, an expanse of desert flat as a billiard table defined by multiple coils of barbed wire, we had to take to the fields several times to avoid low-flying Messerschmitts. Once, we got out to inspect a German field hospital that had been afire only a few hours previously and was still smoking. A German hospital tent, in which abandoned enemy equipment had been baited with booby traps, went up in flames from a bare gust of wind and nearly bagged the lot of us.

Armored cars of the Queens Royal West Surreys, whose job it was to occupy and police Tobruk, were about a mile ahead of us as we entered the famous defense perimeter, nine miles from the township. Four miles from Tobruk we slowed down to identify figures on the horizon through field glasses. Converging on the road along the coast, they proved to be South African natives, some of them carrying homemade guitars, and one of them leading a little desert dog at the end of a rope. They greeted us like the Messiah, for we were the first friendly uniformed humans they had seen since their capture with the Second South African Division on June 20. As we pulled up, the blacks who had been helping themselves to the dregs of huge barrels of sour Chianti wine began waving their arms and shouting biblical phrases. Twenty or thirty of them gathered around me, wearing brand-new British uniforms and greatcoats they'd swiped from captured British stores in Tobruk after their German guards abandoned them the night before.

"Gawd bless you. Why did you delay so long, sar?" And, "Almighty God, we helluva suffer. German very bad treat us. Many killed. One man shot German doctor two days ago," were some of their first confused statements. They looked half starved and weak, but eventually I was able to get a coherent story from them.

I learned that the German army had been passing through Tobruk for the previous six days, retreating westward. During the last three days the enemy had been evacuating Tobruk itself, mostly by land, and had done a thorough job of it.

Upwards of seven hundred South African natives had been held in Tobruk as laborers at the docks, out of which there were about two hundred left. Private Abdullah Abrahams, from Capetown, who, because he spoke some German, had been liaison between the Germans and the rest of the prisoners, told me that "Forty-five of our men have been killed on the docks by our own bombs in the past few days. I sneaked out of the prison camp at night and collected their disks from the graves, so am able to identify them all."

Abrahams told me that a German doctor "who was supposed to be treating us for desert sores, etc., and always stayed around our camp, killed one of our men with a machine gun on November 11 because he said the British would be coming back soon." A few days before that, the same doctor had shot another one of these men as they were conducting church services in the prison compound because he was leading them in singing "God Save the King." I pray that God will never give the Germans the power to win anything after the way they treated those poor natives.

Other former prisoners revealed that up to ten o'clock on the previous night, German 88s were still firing from the Tobruk perimeter. "Then our two German guards left us, and said we were free to help ourselves to the British quartermaster's stores." One boy had a guitar he had made with a hacksaw and knife on which he had carved the initials "P.O.W.—Tobruk." The lads gave us a concert with their guitars and mandolins on the side of the road.

• • •

Royal Engineers attached to the Royal West Surreys guided us through German mines at the El Aden–Tobruk crossroad, and we shot ahead into what once had been a dazzling white desert town, but now was a bomb- and shell-scarred ruin. The surrounding landscape was slate gray from bomb blast and the harbor was littered with sunken ships, recalling that next to Malta, Tobruk had been perhaps the most bombed town in this war until the siege of Stalingrad. Bypassing two companies of heavily armed infantry and stretcher bearers walking single file on the road alongside the harbor, and closely following armored cars, we entered Tobruk's main square and had the honor of watching the Union Jack hoisted at the masthead of the Navy House. Not a shot was fired as we entered.

We had expected to find all manner of equipment in Tobruk, but all we got were a few bottles of Italian mineral water, some cans of concentrated Italian tomato extract, and English canned peas and beans. Otherwise there was nothing in Tobruk other than millions of flies buzzing in and out of bomb-smashed buildings. Sanitation did not appear to receive much attention in the Italian army.

I was nearly shot by a South African boy from Capetown as I poked my nose around the wall of the shrapnel-scarred Catholic church near the main square. He had been a military policeman when his unit was captured, and was now patrolling Tobruk on a looted Italian Bersaglieri bicycle. He had jumped off his bicycle and was about to take a shot at me with his German rifle, but when he saw the British uniform he snapped to the salute, and said:

"Praise Gawd, sar. I've shot four Germans this morning, and thought you were another one." He explained that his victims were members of the German rearguard who had been roaming through the town looting, after spiking their guns.

It seems the Germans had been celebrating before leaving Tobruk, for there were many smashed champagne, wine, and beer bottles in the streets.

We continued westward along the coastal road while supply columns of the main army skirted Tobruk along the Trig Capuzzo track; then we passed through the famous Gazala defenses to Timimi, where we saw a huge laager containing more than 150 wrecked German and British tanks, relics of the last campaign. They were a welcome sight, for good metal is scarce these days. There were also huge used-tire dumps, showing that the enemy was also husbanding his rubber. However, on a hasty inspection of other abandoned enemy materiel, I could find no suggestion that the enemy was running short of primary metals. German and Italian hospital equipment invariably was of the finest aluminum, and their machine tools were of excellent iron and steel construction. Neither did the enemy appear to be short of leather, for German cartridge cases were excellent, and would have done credit to a Bond Street pair of shoes.

On the evening of November 18, our party of correspondents reached the village of Giovanni Berta, west of Derna, which had been liberally strewn with booby traps. German mines and booby traps were proving quite a headache. Eventually the reconquered territory would be deloused, but this process took time. Contrivances left behind by the enemy included everything from the soup-plate and plunger mines; the long Italian "N" mines, like a length of rail; the Tela mines buried on the roadside; the paratroops' anti-tank mines, like oversized cups; the death-dealing "S" mines, filled with steel slugs and which exploded at the level of a man's head; and the Italian Bird's Nest booby traps, which nestled like a cocoon on a branch. One didn't dare to use a flush toilet in any of the abandoned modern buildings of towns such as Derna, for to pull the chain might mean that a mine or mines would go off and bring the whole place down on your head. Often booby traps were attached to one or more shells in an ammunition dump, hence these were left religiously alone until inspected by the R.E.s. The South African natives told me they had been forced to help the Germans fashion booby traps made out of such as fountain pens and cheap cameras, which the enemy left behind in the hope that souvenir-hunting Tommies might pick them up and blow their hands off. Never before in warfare have mines and booby traps been used to such an extent as during Rommel's retreat to Benghazi and Tripoli.

It was raining cats and dogs when we reached Giovanni Berta, a pleasant little village in a hollow of the green belt. A few miles ahead of us light tanks of the Fourth Hussars were groping their way forward, dislodging "nuisance" emplacements of German 88s and anti-tank guns left behind to protect Rommel's rear. Fred Bayliss, Paramount News Reel photographer, had returned to Giovanni Berta with his camera smashed and covered with blood. Bayliss, who was taking pictures from the turret of a British tank, was only slightly wounded as shrapnel from a German anti-tank gun knocked the camera out of his hand.

"You should have seen our tanks and 25-pounders go into action," said Bayliss. "A few minutes after the German anti-tank guns had ambushed us, we had destroyed their guns and their German crews were streaking it over the countryside."

Around the village, containing fine modern cement buildings and a pretty little church in which the Italian priest still remained, we found Arabs plowing the red soil (a relief from the bleak sands of the desert) paying no attention to the war going on around them. With their plows, they had to skirt burned-out tanks or stranded German lorries and motorbikes. They would come to us proffering chickens and eggs in exchange for tea and sugar. But we were short of those treasured items, so it appeared that we would have to go hungry because Bedouin Arabs are highly suspicious of money, and the only acceptable currency in this region at the time was the Italian lira.

Monson and I, seeking shelter against the penetrating drizzle, inspected a number of buildings in Giovanni Berta. We took it easy, being suspicious of booby traps. Finally, we found a berth in what had been the post office, where three days before the Italians had removed all the furniture—even the bathtubs and electrical appliances. It appeared that Italian civilians had an argument with the Germans relative to evacuation of their bathtubs, for outside of Giovanni Berta, we found several lying on the side of the road. The only other indications that there ever had been Italians and Germans around here were imprints of hobnailed shoes in the mud, and portraits of Mussolini in his typical pugilistic attitude, steel helmet and all, prominently painted on the white cement buildings. There also were prolific displays of black-lettered Fascist slogans such as "Viva Il Duce—a noi" and "We shall win—Onward!"

As Monson and I tried to get a fire going in the post office to dry our drenched clothing, we were approached by several Italian-speaking Arabs who appeared overjoyed that the British had returned. They said the Italians had treated them very badly and in past months frequently had hanged Arabs for hiding British soldiers and airmen. From the early days of Grazziani's regime, it was said, the Italians had dropped Arab chieftains from aeroplanes into their village squares as punishment for the systematic disappearance of Italian civilians and troops. One little fellow, a Senussi, who had roamed these hills for some months as an escaped British prisoner of war (he had been attached to the Arab Legion) did us a good turn.

"You see these cows and calves around here?" he said. "They are Italian property. As such, you have a right to claim some beef."

Monson and I were ravenous, so we approached the local Arab chieftain and demanded our pound of flesh, so to speak, giving him a receipt for the Italian calf killed and skinned for us in the backyard of the post office. Also, we scrounged a turkey and three or four chickens, all of them abandoned enemy property, and for the next couple of days gorged ourselves royally.

The Italian Catholic priest was the only white inhabitant of Giovanni Berta. Although he had no congregation left, as usual at first light he would toll the bells for morning Mass. There were long rows of deep trenches, apparently meant as graves, in the little churchyard, but they were empty. It seemed they had been prepared in anticipation of a siege, but the Italians had run for it when the village had been outflanked.

At Berta there was a great deal of blood against a wall in the central square, the result of daily executions. It was explained to us that for the past six months there had been a standing military tribunal at Barce with as many as six Senussi Arabs shot or hanged daily on suspicion of siding with the enemy.

• • •

At Martuba, the next town along the road to Benghazi, we were approached by an Arab who came up to us displaying a penciled note. It read: "English pilot with bad ankle five miles away. Appreciate assistance."

The Germans had left Martuba the previous afternoon, so this Arab, who had hidden two aviators of the RAF—one of them American—had come straight to the village to solicit help. After a bumpy ride over the rocky terrain, in and out of wadis and through burned-out German field camps, we came to a little Arab sheepherders' village and were joyfully greeted by the two aviators, who had bailed out of a damaged Wellington bomber a few days before. One was Warrant Officer Bill Fulcher, of Carlisle, Arkansas, who had joined the RAF in Canada, and the other Flying Officer Brian Beattie, of Kempton, Hitchin, Herts, England. They had been bombing Derna on the night of November 12 when their motor failed, and had been forced to bail out in enemy territory. Fulcher lay out all night and nearly ran into a German sentry.

We took the two pilots to the nearest RAF aerodrome and then returned to Martuba, spending all that day and most of the next in a two-roomed shack drying out our kit over a roaring fire constructed from wood we found in bombed buildings. In the meantime, we inspected the little village, through which ran a bubbling brook, and were surprised to see a German soldier emerge with his hands up, followed by Stan, Ron Monson's grinning Australian driver. Stan had found the German lying on his back asleep on a table. At his side was a half-eaten can of beans. The German had quickly put his hands up, and we handed him over to the British M.P.s, after he told us that he had been one of a group left behind to demolish abandoned German equipment. He had carried out his orders very efficiently, for everywhere we turned were smoldering remains of German field hospitals, trucks, and staff cars.

The communications situation was now bad, for we had pushed so far ahead that we no longer were in touch with the army dispatch rider assigned to "public relations," and our rations were extremely low. A redeeming feature of the green belt was that it abounded in good water.

Riding on the back of a truck with Monson, whose Australian army staff car had broken down in Giovanni Berta, we continued along the Balbo highway to Benghazi, which had now fallen. Passing whitewashed Italian colonists' houses along the road, all of them marked with the letters "D-U-C-E" in fresh black paint, we arrived at Benghazi on the evening of November 21. Normally a town of forty thousand people, with modern cement buildings including five-story apartment houses and spacious boulevards lined with palms, Benghazi was now virtually deserted. Monson and I strolled along the moonlit harbor that night to inspect extensive damage done to shipping and harbor installations by British and American heavy bombers, and found one tanker still in flames. It had been bombed about a week before. There had been plenty of time to evacuate Benghazi, which had been wiped clean by the retreating Germans and Italians, although we managed to find a couple of bathtubs in what had been the headquarters of the Italian police. There, before writing my story of the occupation by candlelight, since the electricity was not functioning, I found a document suggesting that not only Mussolini but a member of the Italian Royal Family, presumably the king himself, had visited Benghazi and Derna in midsummer, following the retreat to Alamein. The document contained instructions to the police who were to guard the two exalted personages.

The next morning Ron and I had a look around, but found little of interest, although we were able to purchase fresh vegetables and Italian cheese in the Arab market. The modern military hospital, which apparently had been used exclusively by Germans, judging from medicines and other equipment left behind, was a shambles, for the Arabs had been there before arrival of the British. There was extensive damage to medicines that would have been considered a godsend by any surgeon or general practitioner. Except for a few old women pathetically walking the streets, the entire Italian population had been evacuated.

Visiting another hospital in Benghazi containing British and South African ex-prisoners of war, I heard an astounding story of Italian brutality.

Along with a group of British and South African officers and men, including a Scottish medical captain and a priest, Captain G. H. C. O'Donnell, from East London, told us how South Africans and British prisoners of war had been murdered, tortured, and nearly starved by their Italian captors following the fall of Tobruk. Some had been shot and killed, for no other reason than that they gave the "V" for victory sign. Others had been chained for hours by their wrists to telegraph poles for trivial offenses. The fellow I interviewed told me that treatment at the hands of the Italians was such that for months prisoners were dying in Benghazi at an average of two daily, mostly from dysentery.

The liberated prisoners, all of them emaciated, wore shorts and shirts marked in big red letters with the initials "K.G." for "Krieg Gefangener" (German prisoner of war). They said their rations had been limited to one six-ounce can of German bully-beef and two hard biscuits full of maggots every twenty-four hours, with a very meager allowance of water. They had paid one pound (four dollars) each over the wire to the Italians for such as one tin of jam, three loaves of bread, or one pack of twenty low-grade cigarettes. They testified that if an Italian officer fancied a gold watch or some other piece of jewelry, an interpreter would be sent inside the wired compound—a two-acre tract accommodating fifteen thousand men in which only one ground-sheet and three or four blankets were allowed to an average of every six men—to barter small loaves of brown bread for the desired objects.

All prisoners had seen men shot in cold blood by their Italian guards, or lashed with cat o' nine tails or rifle straps. The Germans, they said, treated them with respect and frequently shared hot food or tossed them cigarettes, whereas the Italians broke every international convention for the treatment of war prisoners, even forcing South African natives at bayonet point to load bombs on aeroplanes and to handle supplies of ammunition at the Benghazi docks.

Nearly all British and Imperial officers captured at Tobruk or El Alamein had been flown to Italy. Most other soldiers had been moved to camps in Tripolitania. A British lance corporal described the visit of Mussolini to Derna, late in June:

"He was just a little runt, about this high," said the corporal, drawing his hand across his chest. "You'd have to put him on a soapbox to make him look like anything. He had a lot of big shots with him. They made us stand at attention as Musso strode about and talked to our fellows. He asked a couple of them in English how the food was and if they were getting water. They told him that the food was rotten and there was not enough water. As soon as Musso was gone, a couple of guards came along and belted us with rifle straps."

Another lance corporal told me he had seen a Maori lashed for giving
the "V" sign. At one time German photographers came to Derna to take
pictures of the prisoners. "We were in an enclosure so small that the men
couldn't sit or lie down," he said. "And some of them had to rest their feet
in ditches used as latrines. Many were afflicted with dysentery and when
they appealed for treatment, Italian doctors gave them purgatives. While
the Germans were taking pictures a couple of fellows gave the "V" sign
and guards promptly fired into the crowd, killing one and wounding
others."

This fellow said that when the Liberators came over to bomb
Benghazi Harbor the British and South African prisoners would wave
and cheer, whereupon the Italians would threaten to reduce their
rations still more.

One soldier described how a party of seventeen men, desperate because
of their treatment by the Italians, had tried to escape after saving up their
rations of water for days. Led by an Australian sergeant, they dug a
channel under a latrine, but at the crucial moment someone coughed and
the lot of them were taken away, never to be seen again. "Some of us were
chained to telegraph poles for as long as twenty-four hours at a time with
weights on our arms. It was horrible, what with the flies buzzing around
our ears and noses and no water."

The boys pointed out that when Italian soldiers hand themselves over
"they grovel and whine like puppy dogs for food, water, and cigarettes,
which they invariably get from us. I guess it's different when these Italian
weaklings are in the driver's seat!"

The Italian war pictorial magazines I found in Benghazi houses
contained highly dramatic photographs and cartoons of the Eighth
Army's retreat to Alamein, featuring columns of South Africans marching
to their prison camps from Tobruk. "Our prisoners" was the caption. No
reference was made to the Germans.

While the navy set to work cleaning up Benghazi Harbor, I had a final
look around. In Benghazi's Catholic cathedral, I found a Dominican
father unconcernedly sweeping and dusting statues of saints that had
been scarred by high explosives. Just across the street, I discovered what
had been the headquarters of the Luftwaffe in Benghazi. It was chock-a-
block with cases of rifle cartridges and stick grenades; also empty bottles
of the finest French champagne marked in red letters "Reserved for the
German Army." Arabs were having their inning in the market square,
charging as much as a shilling (twenty cents) for one egg. I paid two
shillings for a few ounces of Italian Parmesan cheese.

The only going concern I saw in Benghazi prior to my return to Cairo
for a brief rest was an Arab carpentry shop complete with elaborate

wood-working machinery in which they were still turning out coffins. Business in this line must have been good. Perhaps it accounted in part for the Italian treatment of British prisoners of war.

27

THE YANKS BOMB NAPLES

R EMNANTS OF ROMMEL'S PANZERS, FACILITATED IN THEIR
retreat by winter rains, had made good their escape by the
end of November and were entrenched west of Agedabia in
the now famous El Agheila bottleneck, harassed by advance
armored elements of the Eighth Army.

Tripoli lay about three hundred miles west of Benghazi, and due to
exigencies of supply, a pause in General Montgomery's advance was
inevitable. In fact, when I left Benghazi for Cairo looking forward to my
first bath in three weeks, we wondered whether the British and Americans
advancing on Bizerte and Tunis from the west might get to Tripoli first.

I had been in Cairo exactly three days, managing in the meantime
to lose a little dough at the Gezira race track, when Lieutenant Colonel
Parham, of the Ninth U.S. Army Air Force, telephoned me on December 1
to ask whether I was interested in "going on a picnic?" Parham is too good
a newspaperman to wake me up out of a sound sleep for nothing, so I
hustled over to his apartment to talk it over. The last "picnic" to Navarino
Bay hadn't been especially to my liking, but when Parham hinted that
this promised to be an even more spectacular bombing, I at once accepted
transportation the following morning to Gambut aerodrome, in the
vicinity of Tobruk, from where B-24s of the U.S. Army Air Force were
then operating.

With me as we returned to the desert in one of the bombers assigned
to this mysterious mission was Jack Belden, war correspondent in the
Middle East for *Life* and *Time* magazines. Other correspondents were
expected to follow, but it was doubtful whether they would arrive in
time as we learned that the Americans were poised again for a strike
against the elusive Italian Fleet, and the order to take off might arrive
momentarily.

We got to Gambut at midday, December 3, and I met again some of
my old friends from Palestine, including the now Lieutenant Colonel

John "Killer" Kane, who led the raid on Navarino Bay on October 3, and Major Chris Rueter, of Waco, Texas, who had led a devastating American raid on Tripoli a few days before and was to command this mission with Captain Thomas T. Omohundro, of Wagoner, Oklahoma, as his copilot. Captain William Sutton, Langley, Kentucky, was to be lead bombardier, and Lieutenant John Lovelace, Commerce, Texas, lead navigator.

That afternoon American pilots and crews amused themselves by taking pot shots at the Swastikas on wrecked German aircraft littering Gambut aerodrome, using German Mauser rifles and Luger automatics captured during Rommel's retreat. Some of the boys had rigged up crude shower-baths in the sand consisting of washtubs and petrol tins perforated with holes, and treated themselves to a little desert luxury by washing off the sand.

That evening several of the fellows were prevailed upon by gag artists of an RAF outfit to hitchhike to Tobruk approximately twenty-five miles distant "to see the floor show." Tobruk in its best days had never been more than a homely little harbor town, but because its name had been so frequently headlined in the newspapers of the world as a symbol of alternate triumph and disaster, its size had been magnified in the minds of our airmen who were seeing the desert for the first time. They readily fell for the joke.

They got their money's worth on their visit to the desolate ruins of Tobruk that evening, but it was not the kind of show they anticipated. Bombers of the Luftwaffe, operating from Crete, were out early and concentrated their activity this night on Allied shipping in Tobruk Harbor, subjecting it to as heavy a raid as any Tobruk had ever experienced. With pilots who hadn't gone to "the floor show" because they felt that no one could beat the contours of American women, I watched the bombing from Gambut aerodrome and honestly pitied those innocent "Palookas" whose yearning for a glimpse of bare flesh, be it Arab or white, had taken them on an unscheduled visit to Goering's idea of Hell on earth. Most of the Americans had never seen heavy bombing before, and as the British ack-ack batteries of Tobruk bravely fought off an avalanche of German bombers, I heard cracks such as: "Ain't it purty? Gee, I'm sure glad I'm not under that stuff—I'd ruther be over it." This, despite the fact that we saw several German bombers hurtle to the ground in flames. It reminded me of the British submarine officer in Alexandria who after showing me around in his craft, asked with eagerness whether I had ever been in a tank. Replying in the affirmative, although admitting that I had never ridden in one into action, the young naval lieutenant had replied: "Take my advice and don't ever do it. A tank is a death trap. You haven't a chance."

"But what about a submarine?" I had asked. "Aw, a submarine, it's as safe as anything you'll find. I wouldn't ride in anything else. As for a tank, that's out."

The boys who had gone to Tobruk got back just in time the next morning to receive instructions for the day's mission—the bombing of Naples Harbor. The Italian Fleet again had failed to come out, hence General Patrick W. Timberlake decided to send the B-24s in after them. It was to be the first American bombing of Italy, inaugurating the Allied offensive from North Africa.

We started at noon, our orders being to bomb Naples just before sunset. I was one of three newspapermen on that mission, the others being Jack Belden and Russell Hill of the *New York Herald Tribune*.

I rode in "The Chief," commanded by Captain Lee C. Holloway, Montgomery, Alabama, who was deputy flight commander. His bomber had been holed at least seventy-five times but always had delivered the goods. As copilot, we had Lieutenant Darrell R. Sherman, Sutherland, Nebraska, while other crew members were Captain Harold G. Wells, Coscob, Connecticut; Lieutenant John Burger, Minneapolis, Minnesota, and San Francisco; Technical Sergeant B. O. Richey, Fort Wayne, Alabama; Staff Sergeant Carlyle C. Earls, Pearson, Oklahoma; Technical Sergeant Robert L. Rusie, Indianapolis, Indiana; Staff Sergeant Gerald D. Clemmensen and Staff Sergeant Walter Salmon, Baltimore, Maryland. Six of the nine crewmen were married. I made the seventh.

The first hours were uneventful. We were flying low over the water through clouds and a slight drizzle of rain. There was not much talk and everyone was tense, for the task ahead was far from a cinch. We had been warned that there probably would be lots of ack-ack and fighter interception, especially in Sicily and southern Italy.

As we reached stratosphere altitude, I put on my oxygen mask and in doing so spotted a horseshoe hung in the cabin of the plane. I touched it for luck and then noticed Sergeant Richey seated on the floor of the pilot's cabin, reading a pocket Bible. He put it aside as the order came through for him to test his guns. I had heard 50-caliber machine guns firing in actual combat; nevertheless, when Richey suddenly let go it startled me, then nauseating fumes like soft coal filled the compartment. Shortly afterwards, Richey climbed down and resumed reading his Bible. The whole time the plane was climbing, and as the navigator sing-songed the altitude we put on fur-lined flying suits, for the temperature outside now registered 20 degrees below zero Fahrenheit and was still rapidly sinking. Before we reached the target area, the thermometer read 40 below. I thought I was cold over Benghazi and Navarino Bay, but this little trip took the prize.

We couldn't talk much with our oxygen masks on, and soon we were flying in the stratosphere so rare that a man would die in minutes if he didn't wear one of them. I patted the rubber bulb inflating and deflating in front of my chest fondly. It was company, and I felt the parachute on my back contemplatively, wondering whether it would be sufficient protection against fighters' bullets. I had inspected it carefully, as a fellow had told me just before we took off that once a souvenir hunter had swiped his parachute and stuffed the case with a blanket. He wasn't aware of it until several thousand feet up.

I had quite a start when an hour or so from the target, the copilot nudged me and pointed to the sky. I noticed three planes bearing down on us out of the sun with white vapor fumes streaming from their exhausts, and I braced myself for the impact of bullets, but a few seconds later was relieved to see that the planes were ours. I had never seen vapor fumes behind planes before, and had always identified them with German aircraft. For that reason, I believed we were being attacked.

Now the rubber sack dangling from my oxygen mask was packed with "cracked ice" from the moisture and a gunner said his eyelashes repeatedly froze together and he was keeping busy pulling them apart. We were flying over clouds that looked like a solid field of ice and might easily have been over the North Pole. One of our planes in our group— the one with Russell Hill of the *Tribune*—had to turn back because the waist gunner's oxygen mask had frozen up and there was danger of others doing the same. It was tough luck for Hill.

"The Chief" began its descent preparatory to the bomb run, and I saw Mount Vesuvius way below us, like an inverted ice-cream cone vomiting white vapor. I was on the alert because the pilot had said there was a possibility that the bomb-bay doors might fail to open. If so, I was to push hard on the hand-lever.

There were no longer any clouds, and the sprawling panorama of Naples lay below us, bordered by mountains. The town looked very sleepy as the formation leveled out to drop its bombs. Then I saw the pilot motioning frantically to me. Sure enough, the bomb-bay doors were stuck. I pushed the hand-lever so hard that I busted it, and then stuck my head out as a gust of icy wind rushed into the cabin. I could see Naples' dock area thousands of feet below, but it was so damned cold that I didn't care much whether I was over Naples or Timbuktu. Gritting my teeth to stop them chattering, I labored with what was left of the hand-lever and finally the huge bombs, on which most of the boys had written their names and Christmas salutations to Mussolini, plummeted down. My hand was numb on the aluminum lever and I had to use all my strength to close the bomb-bay doors, almost forgetting to look down to see the bombs land, but the pilot motioned to me and out of a side window I observed the effect of tremendous explosions creating clouds of gray-black smoke. Below it was getting dark fast, but the stratosphere was a fantastic orange, red, and yellow glow on the horizon. I could see the flashes of ack-ack guns, and red balls of flaming onions coiling upwards. It was terrific. There was smoke from explosions all over the place, and the ack-ack was wild. There were a few bursts below and behind us and one of our planes seemed to be wading through high explosives.

We had taken them by surprise, and the Italians, as usual, had gone crazy, even firing pom-poms whose maximum range was not more than six or seven thousand feet. Lucky for us, because Italian warships are equipped with some pretty potent guns, only a few of which seemed to be firing. We could see red balls of fire way below us from the pom-poms, and there on the other side of the harbor was the island of Capri, the home of the immortal *Story of San Michele*. I had convalesced from typhoid in Capri six years before and remember the spooning Italian couples and the chorus of larks. The birds there must have all flown away now, because the heavy ack-ack batteries in Capri, not being a target for the American bombs, were really letting us have it. Pompeii and Palermo also were visible down there in the haze, but we hadn't time to rubberneck, and anyway from this altitude, Naples had lost its tourist attraction. The formation climbed again and for a couple of hours the gunners were on the alert, straining their eyes in the darkness for night fighters.

We were heading toward Africa where it would be warmer. Pleasant thought! Then we were out of the danger area and our Pratt and Whitneys were purring away, taking us back for hot coffee. The bombardier returned to the cabin, his face relaxed, and showed me a picture of his wife, saying, "When this ——— war is over, I want nothing more than plenty of fried spring chicken and love. Look at her. Ain't she a honey?" The engines were throbbing evenly, and the engineer, Richey, whose mates say was responsible for saving their lives when they had their hydraulics and landing gear shot away over Benghazi, sat down, and summed up Vesuvius:

"It's a pretty sight, all right," he mused. "It looks something like those battleships when Bombardier Burger drops his bombs on them."

Burger chimed in with: "That's one more show we don't have to go on. Yessir, that's one more bombing nearer home. Our element blanketed the entire area. I believe some of those battleships, cruisers, and destroyers had direct hits."

Captain Wells remarked: "It was a very successful mission. I saw at least two direct hits on ships and a lollapalooza of fire."

We exchanged yarns concerning previous bombing raids, for we had several hundred miles of ocean to traverse, and the fellows recalled one mission over Tobruk when they had fought it out with sixteen German fighter planes. One of them said he reckoned "the reason they didn't tackle us this time is that the Dagos are allergic to 50-caliber machine-gun bullets. We can take care of them every time."

When we got back to coffee and hardtack at Gambut aerodrome after midnight, the complete picture unfolded. All crews confirmed hits or near misses on battleships, cruisers, and destroyers.

From my vantage point I had seen our bombs directly hit or narrowly miss half a dozen Italian battleships, cruisers, and destroyers in Naples Harbor. More than one hundred thousand pounds of explosives were dropped in the dusk attack, and in our wake we left fires raging in shattered powerhouses and ammunition and supply dumps. They had given off huge columns of smoke that all but put famed Mount Vesuvius in the background. Damage of great proportions was inflicted on the harbor itself, which served as a major supply center for Axis forces defending Bizerte, Tunis, and Tripoli.

I had seen a handful of the Consolidated bombers—only a small portion of the total force—drop thousands of pounds of bombs, every one of which hit something at or near the Porta di Massa Quay. In this area, covering approximately seven hundred square yards, there were a number of battleships, cruisers, and destroyers.

I had seen one battleship that had been hit dead center emitting a column of dense white smoke several thousand feet high. In addition there were two large fires spewing hundreds of violet-red particles in every direction. That ship was no rowboat!

From available facts, the first bombing of Naples rivaled the biggest missions carried out previously by American heavy bombers based in North Africa. On this mission, I didn't see one ripple on the water. Our bombardiers pinpointed their targets and socked them from an altitude of several miles.

Major Bob Condon of Larchmont, New York, formerly of Kansas City, Missouri, combat intelligence officer for the bomber group, summed up the mission by saying that the Americans had delivered a "crushing blow against the weaker partner of the Axis."

"If they want any more, they'll get it!" he said.

• • •

I stayed at Gambut that night, and the return trip to Cairo required most of the following day. It seemed that my head, toes, and fingers were still numb, and I lined the pockets of several Egyptian whiskey merchants in the process of trying to thaw them out before writing my story. It took another twelve hours for the yarn to run the censorship gauntlet. On the evening of December 6, forty-eight hours after I had returned from Naples, I ascertained that it was finally on the way to Marconi Cable Company, en route to United Press headquarters in New York.

The raid had been so successful that several crews participating had been granted compensatory leave. Captain Holloway and his crew were among the lucky ones. In gratitude, I shepherded the lot of them to Alexandria, for a round of hot spots before returning to the Western Desert.

28

THE DEATH OF PRIVATE "X"

MY LEAVE IN ALEXANDRIA LASTED ONLY A FEW DAYS. On December 13 I was hurriedly recalled to the front because Rommel had suddenly pulled out of his formidable defensive position in the El Agheila bottleneck. I rushed to Cairo and boarded the first available plane bound for Agedabia, some twelve hundred miles distant. The trip required three days, with two night stops, giving me an opportunity to mingle with the fellows who had recently arrived from America. In three short weeks these men were to transport nearly two and a half million pounds of vitally needed supplies, chiefly petrol, to the forward areas.

On my first night at an American aerodrome in the desert I found myself in a meditative mood. In my mind I mulled over events of the past two years. I had had a ringside seat to nearly every phase of the war in the Mediterranean areas, more often being mixed up with reverses than successes as I chronicled the gallant battles of the unsung, hard-fighting, and never-yielding Tommy on land, sea, and air. No man could ever give him sufficient credit for what he had done, and the extent to which he had suffered to preserve freedom. He never knew when he was beaten and always came back for more. But Tommy had grown weary in the days following the withdrawal from Alamein. Countless times I had been asked, "When are the Yanks coming, Gorrell?" And each time I had declared that the Yanks were coming. They were coming with their planes, tanks, bombs, and shells. I assured these young fighting men that the Yanks were coming, and in numbers that would turn the tide.

Well, the American boys had arrived, along with Sherman tanks and complete squadrons of B-24 bombers and P-40 fighters. They had played a dominant role in the recent defeats suffered by the Afrika Corps. Now these Americans, some so fresh they were still removing tags from their recently issued army shirts and pants, were to be part of the final phase of Montgomery's triumphant campaign. The drive, enthusiasm, self-assurance, and businesslike attitude of these young men was like a fresh breeze blowing from the Mediterranean after a suffocating Khamsin. Victory was in the air.

Rommel was stumbling back from El Agheila as thousands of U.S. Army Air Forces personnel flooded into the Western Desert. I saw hundreds of American-built aircraft, ranging from fighters and medium bombers to converted Lockheed-Douglas planes, some of which used to carry passengers between New York, Chicago, and San Francisco. All were piloted by boys from the U.S.A. who had arrived in the Middle East looking for a fight and anxious not only to kick the Hun out of Africa, but to follow through with an invasion of Italy and the Balkans.

Christmas was fast approaching and the morale of our boys was high. I saw a sign in the operations room of the aerodrome reading: "Only nine more shopping days to Christmas!" Whoever wrote that had quite a sense of humor. One couldn't get a decent drink of water out here, let alone buy a beer. But nothing could get these Americans down. I spoke to a fellow who told me that he had been ten years in the army, having "started by shoveling horse manure with the cavalry and ending up with the air force." Returning from a long walk over the desert "in search of a Christmas tree," in disgust he had hung up a stocking outside his tent that his leg-pulling pals promptly filled with sand. In a world of change, humor in the face of adversity remains a constant.

I completed my hurried dash to Agedabia in a DC-3 transport plane piloted by Lieutenant Walter Nelson of Savannah, Georgia. As we skimmed the tops of the wadis and telephone poles as a precaution against low-flying enemy fighters, Nelson frequently waggled the wings to show the American Air Forces star to Tommy anti-aircraft batteries below. I sat on one of a number of huge petrol drums, contemplating what might happen were a Messerschmitt to swoop down and plug us full of incendiary rounds. This thought made me fully appreciate what these American lads were doing. Technical Sergeant Roscoe Best, from Maryville, Tennessee, pulled me out of my mood by handing me a set of earphones and asking if I'd like to listen to some swing music. He had tuned the aircraft's radio to a London station and apologized about the static. He added, "I was able to tune in some good stuff a while ago, but the trouble is the atmospherics are funny and we can't hold a station very long."

Nelson landed his plane without mishap on a very bumpy landing ground. No sooner had his craft been unloaded than stretcher cases from the front lines were hoisted in to be rushed to hospitals in the rear area. Obligingly, Nelson accepted a hurried dispatch I had written on Rommel's spectacular and entirely unexpected pullout of El Agheila, promising to post it as soon as he could. I then left him to his task and proceeded to scrounge transport to the army public relations headquarters up forward.

• • •

The next day, in company with my army conducting officer, I inspected the recently abandoned El Agheila defenses. We got there after a tough ride over a road sown with "S" and Tela mines. The former were nicknamed "Jumping Jimmies" by the army boys because when you step on one of them it jumps into the air and socks you in the chin before exploding and plugging you with steel pellets three times the size of ordinary buckshot. Quite deadly. These mines were just as effective against light vehicles, since if you drove over them, the explosion would be level with a driver's head and they had a range of about one hundred yards. That same day, another conducting officer had run over a Tela mine and was injured so badly both his legs were amputated. When I heard this, I insisted that we take the extra precaution of filling up sandbags and laying them on the floorboards of our utility truck before we began our journey.

The El Agheila bottleneck was a nightmare of mines and booby traps interspersed with barbed-wire defenses and abandoned trenches. Mines left by the enemy were retarding the Eighth Army's progress substantially, and by night as I lay under the stars battling Italian fleas, I could see British sappers groping forward by moonlight looking for the infernal devices. Warning of the mines were such signs as "Can your parents replace you? Mines!" or, "Go west, but canny!" In some cases, booby traps had been attached to German and Italian corpses to explode in the faces of our fellows as they turned them over preparatory to burial. But the sappers were working fast, making way for thousands of vehicles and hundreds of tanks moving up and preparing for what promised to be a decisive battle for Africa somewhere in the rocky wadis southeast of Misurata.

At Marble Arch aerodrome just west of El Agheila, we came across an entire RAF fighter wing. Complete with ground equipment and personnel, three whole squadrons of fighter planes had been transplanted overnight by American and British transport planes. These planes were now landing virtually every hour, delivering petrol and parts to keep these fighters operating deep into enemy territory. To make this possible, more than six hundred German mines had had to be removed from the aerodrome by Royal Engineers who were on the scene hours after the last Germans had pulled out.

Following the advancing British army into Nofelia and Sirte, thence to Buerat where Rommel had retired behind another formidable defensive line prepared long months previously as a last barrier before Tripoli, we had to retrace our course several miles to look for our rations truck, which had fallen behind. Eventually we came upon it, in a "safe lane" marked by sappers alongside the road. Driver Dennis, a veteran not only of most of the desert campaigns but also of the BEF retreat from Greece, grinned at me as he crouched over a flat tire.

"It's a good thing you came back for me," he said, "for with all this traffic and approaching darkness I doubt whether I could have caught up with you. When there's mines around, I'm in no hurry at all. You see, I'd rather be late, than *the* late Mr. Dennis!"

• • •

Things were tough for us all in this desert. At night it was bitterly cold, and no sooner would we finish playing hide-and-seek with the fleas than we'd have to fight the hordes of flies and mosquitoes that dive-bombed us in relays. The mosquitoes were so aggressive that even if you were lucky enough to have a net over your camp bed, you need only touch it from the inside with the tip of your finger to be bitten two or three times. Those without nets cowered under their blankets, but inevitably awoke with red bumps all over their bodies. The water situation made our discomfort worse. Water was both scarce and polluted. We were allowed only three mugs a day for drinking, bathing, and shaving. Unfortunately, the "Bill Harris" worm, more properly called "bilharzias," was prevalent in the area. This nasty bug breeds in polluted water and can cause extreme intestinal distress and, if untreated, death.

• • •

I spent Christmas Eve on the coast near Sirte. The weather was lousy. It was raining and blowing a gale, and our mouths were constantly gritty with sand. I was amused, however, watching our driver-cook struggle to make the bully-beef and canned American potatoes more palatable for our Christmas Eve dinner. That night we got a good laugh from the Christmas edition of *Crusader,* the Eighth Army weekly newspaper, outlining the charms of Tripoli. A paragraph that caught my attention stated: "Very refreshing after the wastes of Cyrenaica will be the sight of the Tripoli girls. Dark eyed and lush figured, many of them are daughters of Italians who married Arab women before the Fascists forbade mixed marriages. There are many beautiful Italian and Maltese girls, too. None of them are stand-offish!" This remark was illustrated by a luscious dame wearing a flimsy brassiere and a nearly transparent skirt, shaking her hips vigorously.

The only other compensation for the drab and dreary day was a magnificent golden, red, and orange sunset casting a final warming glow over the seashore. Even the waves, hurling themselves angrily against the rocks, became a beautiful gray-green and milky white backdrop. And as though an omen of peace that would prevail on the Christmas Day to come, little sand thrushes came timidly up to our makeshift table on the beach in search of crumbs.

To the accompaniment of sappers touching off mines, we were treated that night to a light show of white and green signal rockets fired by British troops whom not even Rommel could prevent from celebrating. When the moon rose it became our only other source of light on that dark night, and served as a reminder that we were still of this Earth. Everything else around us was so completely unfamiliar that it would have been easy to believe that we were millions, not thousands, of miles away from home. Except for the sound of trucks maintaining the vital link between front-line troops and base supply depots, we seemed completely isolated from the world we knew.

We certainly came to appreciate the efforts of the British army truck drivers, many of whom were killed by mines before they reached their destinations. For although our Christmas had been a dreary one, two days later an elaborate rations camp had been established near our site on the coast. We were amazed to be issued with such as freshly baked bread, a variety of canned vegetables, cigarettes, and even Canadian tinned bacon and herring. A veritable marketplace had sprung up in the desert wastes. I recalled a statement made by the German General Ravenstein when, after being captured by the Eighth Army, he described a tank battle as a "game of surprises" that is a tactician's paradise but a nightmare for the quartermaster. It occurred to me that it is the quartermaster who contrives mobility, making the "game" of mechanized warfare possible, for only through his determined efforts could the Eighth Army have advanced this far.

My frame of mind having been somewhat improved by a full stomach and the first cigarette in several days, I decided to have a look at Rommel's right flank. The trip promised to be interesting since German panzers had just pulled out of a strong defensive position at Wadi Tamat and were digging in for a final stand behind Wadi Zem-Zem. Reports that Italian infantry units were being hurriedly evacuated to the rear, in German troop carriers, provided a touch of humor: Rommel had become a bus driver, with Mussolini breathing down his neck. It was quite understandable. The Italians were wary after having been stranded between El Daba and Alamein. They therefore had forced the Germans to use their available troop transports as a sort of bus service between the wadis southeast of Sirte and Tripoli.

On the main road west, before turning off into the open desert, I met several German prisoners who had been left behind specifically to place new mines on the roads after British sappers had cleared sections of highway. Luckily for us, they were no longer able to do so; they would spend the rest of the war as P.O.W.s. They perhaps thought themselves lucky, too, as they stared open-mouthed at the tanks and trucks loaded with supplies rolling westward. These Germans were thin, weary, and hungry, and it was hard to get much out of them in the way of a news story. All of a sudden one of them, the youngest, began talking as if to himself. He was a blond boy in his late teens or early twenties who, I was told, had had one of his toes frozen off during fighting in Russia. He had arrived in North Africa during Rommel's retreat from Alamein. He mumbled:

"Die menge tutes—Amerika," or "It is the quantity that does it—America." Then, pointing at the trucks, he added: "We can't compete against this!"

The remark struck me as indicative of what might be in the minds of thousands of other Germans as they retreated toward Tripoli.

• • •

Approaching Wadi Kabir we joined up with a supply column flanked by armored cars equipped with anti-aircraft guns to protect against Messerschmitts and Stukas. The trucks were spaced widely apart, scattered over a substantial area. When enemy aircraft were sighted, they created quite a scene: expertly, like cowboys rounding up cattle on the open plains, the protecting vehicles would herd the supply trucks in and out of the sand dunes, making them zig-zag to confuse the aeroplanes. The attacking pilots could see a supply convoy moving along the sand just as easily as they could spot a line of merchant vessels at sea. And in fact, the armored cars would mother the convoy much in the same manner as escorting warships do in a convoy of merchant ships. In any event, when traveling with a supply convoy, there was no mistaking the fact that you were a choice target.

After one such attack, when the convoy had shaken off a mob of Stukas, I went up to the driver of the nearest truck and offered him a cigarette. He thanked me profusely, observing that it wasn't often that he had a chance to talk to anyone while on a job of this sort.

"Even my best pals in British fighting units won't have me these days, what with Jerry planes acting up," he said glumly. "It was only yesterday that I stopped next to some fellows I knew. They said to me, 'Glad to see you, chum, but please do us a favor and get that truck the blazes out of here. Don't you know there are aircraft about?'"

Driving a truck in a supply convoy was no snap in wartime. These "B.

Echelon" boys often suffered more casualties than did the dug-in infantry and armor.

We reached the Wadi Kabir without further incident, although en route we'd seen several cars and trucks burning. They told their own story of the dangers of Stukas and low-level strafing. We camped that night next to an Arab burial ground in the wadi. The following morning at first light a long-dead Arab chieftain named Zidon did me a very good turn. Stukas had just bombed elements of our armored brigade, and as their escorting Messerschmitts came down to strafe, they themselves were attacked by Spitfires. I was standing next to the chief's tomb with its dome of rock, intensely watching the dogfight, when I realized that the bullets from the German and British planes were kicking up sand too close for comfort. With a start, I dived into the tomb and was instantly protected by thick stone. I was out of danger, although I found myself tangled up with bits of white rag that the Arabs in this region have a habit of hanging with string over their graves. They also pile a dead man's belongings around his grave, figuring that he might need them in the world to which he is going. This fellow Zidon must have been a big shot, because the tomb contained the rotting remains of ten wooden plows and dozens of folded tents. Had he been alive, I'd have gladly bought old Zidon a drink for providing me shelter when I most needed it.

Our party of correspondents remained in the sand seas of Wadi Kabir for forty-eight hours since it was reported that Montgomery's armored attack was imminent. We were kept on the hop, though, for there were repeated Stuka raids.

• • •

On New Year's Eve, I was reconnoitering the wadi with Captain Murphet, searching for a camping ground not quite so spooky as the area around Zidon's tomb and possibly affording even better protection against bullets and shrapnel. As we drove along the base of the dried-up bed of a prehistoric lake, I spotted a British ambulance with huge red crosses on its sides crawling down an escarpment. Suddenly, it lurched to a dead stop, its wheels churning the soft sand. The driver didn't need to ask for help. Men simply went to his aid: it's the code of the desert. British soldiers who had been laboriously drawing water at a well nearby rushed over to assist. In a jiffy they had truck and driver back on firmer ground. The Cockney driver's chatter to his rescuers, plainly audible at some distance across the Kabir bowl, summed up news and tidbits collected on his travels over the past few days:

"Not much doing around here," the little fellow said. "We've driven a couple of hundred Ities out of Fort Bungum." (He spoke of a Beau

Geste–like fort located between Wadis Kabir and Zem-Zem.) "Set the place on fire, we did, and they ran like Hell. Nothing much else. Had a bit of a shoofty and knocked out four Jerry tanks. Smartened them up a bit, we did, so he's giving us a spot of bother with his Stukas and MEs [Messerschmitts]. Got a fellow in here with a busted jaw. Shrapnel. Must get him to the M.O.," he added matter-of-factly, referring to the medical officer. Then he put the ambulance in gear, and with a jaunty wave of his hand, shouted, "Happy New Year to you, chaps!"

He never saw the New Year.

I heard the aeroplanes approaching. The distant drone of engines deepened into a full-throated roar, followed by a whine that the huge bowl of the wadi, acting as a sounding board, magnified a hundred times as a dozen dive-bombers leveled out for their bomb run. There was a high-pitched moan, ending in a shriek as the bombs hit all around us. The Stukas were getting out of it as the anti-aircraft guns in the wadi blazed away, but the escorting fighters were not. They came at us, criss-crossing fifty feet above the sand, spitting bullets like mad. When it was over, the ambulance was a blazing funeral pyre, with the Cockney driver still at the wheel. They got him out, somehow, but not the fellow with the busted jaw. He didn't need the medical officer now.

Later, in the strange serene silence that returned to Wadi Kabir, I stood bareheaded as an American field serviceman and three British truck drivers lowered the Cockney driver to his last resting place among the graves of Arabs. Those old graves could hardly be discerned now, except for the slight mounds of sand and rock, some with wooden bowls and wicker baskets on top, all rotting away and becoming part of the anonymous desert. As the soldiers shoveled sand over their comrade's body, an army padre read the Scriptures and marked his tomb with a wooden cross, reading: "Private 'X' - - - - Field Ambulance Unit. December 31st, 1942."

So ended 1942 for a London boy.

But it was not long before his death was avenged. Not a half hour after he had been buried in the indescribable bleakness of the Libyan desert, another wave of Stukas and Messerschmitts came over. RAF fighters were waiting for them. The Germans never had a chance to do other than jettison their bombs. There was a rattle of machine guns as Spitfire went after Messerschmitt and Kittyhawk took on Stuka. I saw two enemy planes burst into flames as the sun set on the newly dug grave of Private "X," the English boy now resting with ancient Arabs. As the enemy aircraft hurtled down and exploded, huge columns of smoke rose into the sky, marking this place of death.

Two Stukas for Private "X."

29

THE "LADIES FROM HELL" ATTACK

B ETWEEN NEW YEAR'S AND JANUARY 14 WHEN MONTGOMERY fought the last major battle before Tripoli, we had a dreary time of it in the desert.

The water situation had become serious, and night after night I crawled into my "flea bag" with a raving thirst, for there was nothing but salty water to drink. We made tea of it three times a day in an effort at camouflage, but it made no difference. Adding to our trials, it was necessary to return to Sirte because one of the P.R. vehicles in our party had broken down and we would have to lay up for several days while army mechanics tinkered with the engine.

I believe that following my forced sojourn in the Arab quarter of Sirte, I could give valuable advice to any scenario writer concerning ingredients necessary in construction of a true "shanty town," for this fly, mosquito, and flea-ridden dive on the windswept sand dunes facing the Gulf of Sirte, abounding in tin cans, broken bottles, old tires, the remains of wheelbarrows, and skeletons of dead cats and dogs—with a few old shoes thrown in for good measure—must have beaten them all. There were millions of fleas in the tumble-down Arab huts, covered with odd bits of petrol tins and scraps of rusting corrugated iron, so we pitched our leaky Egyptian-made tents in the open as though we had outsmarted the insect populations. There was no need to worry much about the war, for the Luftwaffe was taking time out and only dropped occasional bombs at night to tell us they were still around. I had found a German "bivvy," something like a sausage skin made of canvas, and just long enough to accommodate a fairly tall fellow, but so low down on the sand that getting up inside the damned thing in the morning was something like the antics one performs in the upper berth of a New York–Chicago sleeper. The thing was pretty warm, and easily hoisted and dismantled. But its warmth was also very much appreciated by Mr. and Mrs. Flea, who trooped in at nightfall with hundreds of their relations. I don't

277

know which was worse, the alternate sand and rain storms during those agonizing days in Sirte while the army mechanics tinkered away, or the bugs. Of a morning, after an all-night itch-fest, I could only halfway put my pants on in the bivvy, and had to finish the job outside, prodded along by my uninvited bedmates. I nearly froze my "fanny" in the attempt, and even the salty tea was a welcome tonic. Most of the next day was generally spent in delousing, but the fleas were always gaining on me, and in between rounds the flies would worry my nose, probably hired to keep me busy by Mosquito and Company.

The Arab urchins remaining in much-booby-trapped Sirte cautioned us not to step into the main square, the place being thoroughly mined. They usually spoke some Italian, having been sent to Italian schools. The little beggars had managed to remain in the town by running into the desert when the Italians had pulled out, herding along with them the entire Arab population, together with all of the livestock in Sirte. Their argument had been that when the British entered they would shoot all residents of Sirte and then steal their belongings. These kids were pathetic sights, garbed in rags even worse than those I had seen worn by the half-starved peasants of Persia. The morning, four days later, when we pulled out of this ash bin, we saw these children dive hungrily for holes in the sand where we had buried our tin cans. On extricating the cans they would run their fingers along the inside edges, then suck them as a kid in the States does when his mother has finished making a chocolate pudding.

We were much better off in our next camp, south of Buerat, just out of range of heavy artillery massed by the enemy in salt marshes along the coast, in anticipation of Montgomery's final attack. Along the shoreline there were pretty little desert flowers of all colors, one specimen having the aroma of jasmine. We sat it out there in improved weather, watching the incessant supply traffic along the main road. When we saw scores of Sherman, Grant, and Crusader tanks roll up on multiwheeled trailers, we knew the British attack was imminent, for tanks generally are not ordered up much before an action, being too valuable to remain in forward areas, exposed to aerial attack.

• • •

By the tenth of January, the Luftwaffe began widespread dive-bombing, devoting particular attention to the big headquarters camps, including Main Army H.Q. along the coast. The RAF soon would put a stop to it, but as yet, like the tanks, they had not moved up in force, so my hands became bruised from frequent efforts at out-diving the Stukas and Messerschmitts. This waiting business, in between attacks, can get pretty dull, especially if you are out of cigarettes, and our party was down to smoking stubs broken up and rerolled into bits of newspaper. We used to play bridge on the folding table of our station wagon to pass the time, and usually carried on until an hour or so after dark. Just before Montgomery's big push, with the Hun distinctly nervous, I was playing bridge with a couple of fellow reporters and our conducting officer. As I recall, the bidding had reached three no trump. Suddenly there was a clatter as of thousands of firecrackers going off. German night fighters were at it again, strafing the roads and coastal camps. We dived for our slit trenches as red tracers plowed the sand on all sides of us. Needless to say, the bidding that night never went higher.

January 14 was a big day for me, for as I called at the camp of the public relations dispatch riders on the coast road preparatory to Montgomery's night attack at Buerat, I was handed a cable, already four days old, announcing that my wife had given birth to a bouncing baby girl in Johannesburg. Never have I gone into an attack in better spirits, despite the fact that the previous night had been a sleepless one as German planes showered us with anti-personnel bombs, which burst on a level with the sand, and whose shrapnel is effective at a hundred yards. I had been the whole night in a slit trench, unable to sleep because at every move, sand trickled down my neck and into my eyes and ears.

We had been advised that the Fifty-first Highland Division was to make a frontal attack in the center of the strongly entrenched Buerat line, while armored divisions of the Eighth Army were to attack southwestward, in an outflanking move. I could not cover both drives, for they would be simultaneous, and anyway in a blitz action of this type, unless you yourself are advancing in a tank there isn't much to see except tremendous clouds of dust. I chose to go in with the Highlanders.

It was to be a night infantry attack to bridge the enemy's main defenses and clear the road to Misurata, Homs, and Tripoli. Reaching the Highland positions, we could hear six-inch shells crashing with nervous irregularity on the rocky undulating ridge ahead as the infantry made ready for Zero Hour. Following their commander's instructions, forward patrols of the Highlanders scuttled about and popped their heads in and out of their slit trenches on the ridge, for they had been instructed "to show yourselves occasionally and draw enemy fire, as we want to make certain that the Hun is still there when we go in tonight."

Fritz and Vittorio yonder were trigger-finger nervous. The double thump-thump of their mediums, and the less frequent but more spectacular croomph—croo-oomph of the Big Berthas on that ridge with their attendant clouds of dust and showers of rock proved it. And just in case the deliberately clowning steel-helmeted human targets in front of us didn't make sufficient show of it, our fighter bombers—sometimes twenty at a time—periodically dived out of the sun and dumped bombs along the entire sector to keep Jerry on the jump. Except for a few well-dispersed command vehicles nesting in the wadis where a few days ago army officers had traded tea with Arabs for eggs, there was nothing much to indicate that anything unusual was scheduled, except that the skirl of bagpipes wafted over the barren desert slopes. Highland bagpipers had also played day and night at El Agheila, making the Hun so nervous that he had pulled out before the Scotsmen could have a go at him with the bayonet, and leaving behind not only thousands of mines and booby traps but also straw-stuffed dummies with tin helmets and all, in a gesture of Teutonic mockery.

These Scotsmen were tough babies. They chafed at the bit as they polished and repolished their already glistening bayonets while the enemy artillery banged away. The Scotties had heard that Mussolini's "Young Fascists" were among the troops facing them at Buerat. And they knew that at Zero Hour they would face not only heavy enemy gunfire but also a complicated network of mines featuring the fearsome "fish-hook" or "S" mines, which don't give one much of chance when he steps on them. Said one Scot to me:

"If I get my hands on any of those 'Young Fascists' I'm going to make them walk ahead of me into their own mines to clear the way!"

Before the attack I met a young tough from Glasgow, with his red tasseled Tam o' Shanter over one eye. I exchanged a few words with him and could hardly make out his reply, so acute was his burr.

"The water and food," said he with a growl, "have been vurra bad. If they don't make it up to us in Tripoli there'll be a rotten row!"

With the bagpipes shrilling "A Hundred Pipers and All" and other famous ditties, surely making cold shivers run up and down the spines of the enemy, I walked to a mobile signals headquarters and heard Eighth Army armored cars reporting on dispositions of the enemy as they also kept him on the hop, weaving in and out amidst shell fire. To me it was a meaningless dribble, such as "Harry moving to William—over; guns blocking William; can't reach him—over."

• • •

Adding to the apparently peaceful scenery of this spot, which in a few hours was to become a historical battleground, were camels, sheep, and goats pasturing on scrub growth. But British guns, infantry, and tanks were also very much here—scattered over an area several miles square. Awaiting nightfall and the signal to advance, I exchanged jokes and cigarettes with steel-helmeted Scotties resting in slit trenches. It was to be their second major engagement since Alamein, and ambulances plowing the dust along the desert tracks testified to the grimness of the occasion.

Highland Divisional H.Q. was pleased when air reconnaissance, just before sundown, confirmed that apparently Jerry was going to make a fight of it here with his back to the last major town in the Italian Empire. By this time the field hospital that was to take care of the anticipated heavy casualties moved into the front line. I visited it as orderlies adjusted resuscitation apparatus consisting of a Primus stove with air vents fashioned from petrol tins, designed to give warmth to the seriously wounded. They were banking the big operating tent with sand, to keep the surgeons' instruments clear of dust.

At sunset I watched the sappers shock troops moving to the starting line, trudging slowly, widely scattered along the ridge, carrying bayoneted rifles and packs containing one blanket each. They were joining other battalions that had hugged that shell-battered ridge throughout the day, awaiting the order to go over the top. Lorried infantry reserves were to arrive at moonlight, and we now learned that Zero Hour was set for 10:30 p.m. Meanwhile, motorcycle couriers roared along the powdery tracks, their faces grayish-yellow masks from the dust.

The nerve center of the battle was to be a hole in the ground in No Man's Land where the divisional general and his brigadiers equipped with headphones were to direct operations. The attack must go through and the High Command was taking no chances of being outdistanced by their own troops. As night fell, a cold wind was blowing, creating a suffocating dust storm. The enemy's defensive gunfire became more intense. It usually does when darkness sets in.

Under the first pale light of the moon, what had been a pasture land for sheep and goats was transformed into a scene of teeming activity, with gun carriages drawn by armored cars moving southward and staff cars and jeeps racing about herding in scores of lorry loads of troops who cheerfully hummed songs of the Scottish Highlands as they prepared for battle.

The correspondents' little camp beneath the eucalyptus trees in a tiny oasis had become Information Headquarters and Intelligence H.Q. It was the usual prebattle bustle with tension increasing as the time passed. German aircraft flew over, dropping flares several miles southeast of us followed by bomb explosions, but somehow they had missed our beehive of activity.

No sooner had the infantry been off-loaded than the men were set to digging slit trenches, but RAF night fighters were faithfully patrolling, keeping the Luftwaffe at bay. I thought of the troops hugging that ridge with only a blanket to shield them from the cold winds and marrow-chilling desert dew. Everyone around me appeared to be consulting his watch.

Finally, there were 10 - 5 - 3 - 2 and 1 minute to go.

On the split second of the predesignated hour there was a rending crash as scores of guns opened up and the horizon became a sheet of shimmering flame. There was a steady roar like the unbroken rumble of thunder, reminding me of Alamein. British artillerymen, stripped to the waist, were sweating freely in the cold as they fed the guns. No one spoke a word. The orders had been given and everyone knew them. I saw a rocket float lazily into the night sky, fired by the brigadier from his hole in the ground, and as one man, the kilted "Ladies from Hell" went in with leveled bayonets. The sky was criss-crossed with tracers and one could barely discern the crash of the enemy's replying mortar fire and grenades, such was the intensity of the British barrage. German "Big Berthas" had ceased firing and we now had it all to ourselves. Somehow, as I heard the notes of the bagpipes floating in from the battleground I couldn't help thinking of the sleepy "Young Fascists" tugging on their trousers in slit trenches, for 10:30 p.m. in the Tripolitania desert is equivalent to the early hours of the morning in any town, and it's a nasty hour to be attacked by a mad crowd of shouting Scotsmen lunging at you with the bayonet.

We moved forward with the infantry and could hear Tela and "S" mines exploding ahead followed by cries of distress and then: "Stretcher bearer!" Walking wounded began coming back. They were surprisingly cheerful and puffing at the inevitable cigarette. Readily they replied to our queries.

"The attack? It's going fine. 'A' company is fifteen hundred yards into him. Not much opposition." And so it went.

The Germans and Italians, unnerved by the bagpipes and the fury of the Highlanders' attack, had offered only token resistance. Most of the casualties had been wounded on "S" mines or by stray machine-gun bullets. The enemy was pulling out of his rock and sandstone trenches fast, not even firing back with his artillery for his guns also were retiring, goaded along by a creeping barrage.

At midnight, I returned to the medical dressing station and watched surgeons operating on the more serious cases, the operating tables lit by shadowless lamps. There were not many casualties considering the scale of the attack and such was the organization that only a few hours after it had started, blood for transfusions had arrived by aeroplane at a spot a few hundred yards from the starting line. By 1 a.m. gunfire was practically nil and we were advised by Divisional Operations H.Q. that the infantry were plodding on through enemy minefields with tanks closely supporting them, mopping up stray machine-gun nests and mortar posts. By early morning on January 15 we heard that the Highlanders not only had created a bridgehead but had broken through the center of the Buerat line, and the chase of the defeated German and Italian armies was resumed. The conducting officer, Captain Murphet, rushed back to Sirte with our dispatches, and waiting for him to rejoin our party, I strolled to the wired compounds in search of prisoners. To my surprise, they were practically empty. A burly Scots sentry, guarding the compound, cupped his hand to one ear as I repeated my question several times.

"Prisoners? You'll not be finding many here, laddie. Why? Well, furrst of all Jerry ran too fast, and second of all, don't you know that this is the Highland Division?"

• • •

By morning, complete silence had returned to the scene. Camels and sheep were still grazing in the vicinity, and desert thrushes trilled in the trees over our tents. The silence was broken on only one occasion, by the furious rattle of machine-gun fire and the scream of fighter planes twisting and diving in battle overhead. I looked up to see the American star on the glistening wings of a P-40 that was hurtling headlong after a fighter plane marked with the black cross. Other planes bearing the American star were handing out similar medicine to a dozen or more Messerschmitts. Judging by the pace at which they scurried back to their aerodromes, they must have been sorry they ever stuck their yellow noses out. Before the dogfight was over two Messerschmitts had crashed in flames.

With a tidal wave of infantry and armor closing in on him on all sides, Jerry was stumbling back to Tripoli like a punch-drunk boxer who is unwilling to give up yet is fairly certain that he is going to be K.O.'d in the next round. He had received a bloody nose from his opponent, an Irishman by the name of Montgomery, who was throwing ten punches to Rommel's one.

I followed Highland troops through the strongest defensive positions I had ever seen, with row upon row of winding trenches three-quarters of a mile in depth, blasted out of the rocky countryside. A member of the Black Watch who participated in the attack told me most of the trenches were already deserted when he and his comrades had rushed up for a little bayonet practice. The Buerat line as I saw it was even stronger and more involved than the famous El Agheila defenses. Picking my way through the tangle of trenches, I found among other things that Jerry's trainer had made the mistake of trying to pep him up with Hennessy and Cointreau before the final bout.

That night after an exciting surge northward toward Misurata, we pitched camp near the coast road in the open desert, next to a group of several hundred Itie prisoners. Figuring that if Jerry got knocked out and lost them Tripoli they should have to start from scratch again on this Fascist Empire business, these Italians had taken a few pot shots at the advancing Highland columns with their battery of 210s. While I wrote my story for that day by candlelight inside our truck, the prisoners were glumly munching British biscuits and trying to get used to American four-engined bombers flying over them without being shot at as they shuttled on to Tripoli to drop General Montgomery's visiting card. One of their officers told me that an Italian general had ordered his battery "to hold the British at all costs and give us time to organize defenses further back."

Throughout Sunday the fifteenth we had been advancing through the desert virtually parallel with Germans and Italians retreating northward along the Buerat-Misurata road. In six consecutive hours of tedious driving, we had covered about fifty-six miles over a bumpy, rock-bound, sandy track, and even as I pounded away at my portable, the Highlanders were again on the move with only forty more miles to go to Misurata. The advance had forced the enemy out of half a dozen airfields in the Buerat-Misurata-Homs triangle; therefore Jerry could only send his long-range bombers over to try to figure out where we were. Occasionally they dropped their bombs in the light of flares, but that sort of thing didn't worry anyone. Anyway, all of our vehicles were widely dispersed and it would simply be a bad piece of luck were they to score a hit. I felt, however, that there might be a spectacular bit of fireworks were one of the stray Hun bombs to connect with one of hundreds of cases of Italian shells stacked up around our one-night stand. Most of the Itie artillery had withdrawn in such a hurry that they forgot to take their ammunition with them and they had left enough behind to blow up Rome. Other stuff abandoned by the enemy ranged from empty bottles of Cointreau to unwashed cooking pots and dried lemon extract in glass containers bearing the words in Italian: "For increased Vigor!" In the course of the chase I found all sorts of odds and ends lying about in the desert suggesting that the enemy had barely got away, ranging from shoes, socks, shirts, and underwear to deck-chairs, entire field kitchens, and hand cameras.

The Scots were not bothering about small pockets of enemy resistance to the left and right of us. And it was a peculiar sensation to be rushing northward parallel with the Balbo highway on which the enemy was still retreating. Occasionally we got reports such as: "B. company by-passed enemy transport. Saw rockets fired," or "Hurricane flying over the main road has been shot down by enemy ack-ack. We haven't time to investigate." Those ack-ack crews would not be firing much longer. They were already far behind us, cut off from their main forces.

Long-range enemy fighters, getting in a final lick before they moved on, had inflicted a few casualties on the Highland columns. At one place along the track they were burying three or four fellows of a Scottish cook-house staff who had "bought it" from machine-gun bullets a few minutes previously. That goes to show you that not even the cook is safe these days. No, this had been no picnic!

Where there are tragic episodes in warfare, there are also plenty of comical incidents to balance them. Speaking of cooks, we were bouncing along looking for Tactical Division H.Q. far ahead of us when a fellow waved us down, saluted, and said:

"Excuse me, sir, but could you help me? You see, sir, I'm the cook for Main Division H.Q. and I have their rations for tomorrow with me. Can you tell me where they are, please?"

No, we didn't know, and in turn asked the cook if he knew were Tactical Division was. He didn't answer us. Scratching his head, he walked off mumbling something about the general's breakfast. And he didn't bother to salute again!

On another occasion we had stopped to get our bearings from an armored-car commander who it appeared at the same time was querying an officer of an artillery wagon on the same subject. Waiting to get a word in, we heard the following conversation:

"Do you know where we are?"

Answer: "No, I don't."

"Where is so-and-so?"

Answer: "Damned if I know."

"Any mines about?"

Answer: "I believe not—anyway not many."

The querying officer laughingly said: "Thanks for the information. One mine is enough for me!"

But by nightfall everyone had more or less found one another. On an occasion like this, especially when the enemy has beetled off in such a hurry, there are times when fellows in the rear are not quite sure what is what. But one thing was certain: we were going to get to Tripoli, and the distance to the big town was diminishing with every hour.

30

THE FALL OF TRIPOLI

WITH LESS THAN 130 MILES TO GO, THE EIGHTH ARMY had broken the back of the Tripoli defenses on reaching Misurata, where there was drinking water in abundance thanks to artesian wells and viaducts constructed by peacetime Italian prisoners.

Entering the Tripolitanian green belt was a dramatic occasion, for only an hour before we had been debating whether we could afford a mug-full of water each for washing and shaving, having shared our dwindling supply with the thirsty crew of a Bren carrier.

We thought we were witnessing a mirage when, in the distance, there suddenly appeared the dazzling picture of the little colonial town of Giuda, with its fine cement buildings and an Arab mosque glittering like diamonds in the sun. As though to avoid a collision, our driver lurched to an abrupt stop, and shouting—"WATER!"—dashed pell-mell to a viaduct nearby where the life-giving fluid was trickling in quantities on fertile ground. Following the driver's example, I also tumbled out and practically threw myself into the shallow viaduct. I came up out of breath, spluttering, but refreshed, and the opening words of Kipling's famous poem "Gunga Din" came to my mind:

> You may talk o' gin and beer
> When you're quartered safe out 'ere,
> An' you're sent to penny-fights an' Aldershot it;
> But when it comes to slaughter
> You will do your work on water,
> An' you'll lick the bloomin' boots of 'im that's got it.

Just like the "arf-a-pint-o'water green" that Kipling's "Regimental Bhisti" had given his wounded master of the field of battle in India during Queen Victoria's reign, so was this water we found in Tripolitania "green and crawlin." Nevertheless, we were all grateful for it.

Were I a student of verse, I might have attempted a poem marking this memorable occasion when water became plentiful for the dauntless and long-suffering troops of the British Army of the Desert. Not only had the Eighth Army scattered Rommel's Afrika Corps, but it had won a crucial battle with the elements. No longer was it necessary to send vitally needed vehicles back hundreds of miles to fetch water in German petrol tins. The petrol problem also was solved, for there would be more than sufficient to reach Tripoli. As for rations, due to a splendid supply organization the shortage never had attained serious proportions and now, if necessary, the army commander could commandeer what was needed in Italian villages along the Tripoli highway.

• • •

When we reached Misurata there were more armed Italian police than British soldiers on hand.

We barged into Misurata township with few thoughts other than how we were going to have our eggs cooked when before us appeared half a dozen of the enemy in olive drab, armed to the teeth. Our car screamed to a stop again, and the driver instinctively reached for his tommy gun. The sentries turned out to be Italian carabinieri who were expecting us. Presenting arms, they gave us direction to the Misurata Prefecture, adding that His Excellency the Prefect was waiting for us. They must have thought one of us was Montgomery himself! Anyway, we followed the policeman's directions and arrived at the elaborate governmental palace, where we were received with honors by the prefect's personal bodyguard and ushered in.

I exercised my Italian on the short, fat, bemedaled prefect and got the low-down on the current situation.

It seems the Italians were glad that we had arrived because the Arabs in Misurata, a sizable town on the coast, were getting ugly, and the local Italian population were trembling in fear of their lives. The prefect, Brigadier General Amedeo De Caro, said he had received orders from Rome through General Bastico to remain in Misurata with the entire administrative staff of the district to protect remaining Italian civilians against Arabs. He assured us that the entire police force was at our disposal, whereupon I hastened to explain that we were merely war correspondents and that the Eighth Army was too busy chasing the Hun to indulge in social calls, but we would see what we could do to calm the nervous civilians. The prefect, flustered, began hemming and hawing, saying that he had expected that at least a colonel would call on him.

The prefect was most imperial in his bearing, making a big show of his importance as he talked to us. The Roman Eagles were embossed in silver on his epaulets. He had a double row of ribbons and was constantly addressed as "His Excellency" by his flunkeys. There were three sub-machine guns lying on his divan along with two or three blankets. It looked as though he had spent a sleepless night while Bedouin Arabs walked in and out of evacuated houses carrying off such items as beds, tables, chairs, and linen.

Normally there are over a thousand Italians in Misurata, a pleasant colonial village complete with blocks of white cement flats and scores of buildings including a church, all of modern construction but scarred with silly Fascist slogans such as: "We shall shoot straight. To us, O Duce!"

I talked to Italian Franciscan friars in the Misurata church. They said the British army had been expected for a long time, adding that at Tripoli we wouldn't be likely to find much except evacuated civilians, because Rommel was pulling out fast with the sole intention of joining hands with General Walther Nehring's forces in Tunisia.

I spent a night beneath clean sheets in the Misurata Hotel, and before continuing to Homs, I plowed into a couple of fine omelets garnished with Parmesan cheese. However, there being no wine to go with the eggs, I went across the street to bargain for a few bottles of Chianti. There was a crowd in the wine shop, including several Italian policemen, and I heard the following heated conversation between a policeman and an Arab youth. The policeman, displaying his revolver in a huge holster, said:

"Do you see this gun? Well, the English aren't going to take it away from me. The Italians are still policing this place, and if you do anything wrong we shall shoot you."

Whereupon the Arab answered, "Yes, but we've done nothing to warrant your shooting us and henceforth we are taking orders only from the British. Italy is not running Tripolitania anymore."

Several excited Italians joined in the argument, after which it was explained to me that most of them regarded the British as savior "because if you had come a few hours later the Arabs would have sacked the entire town and killed the lot of us."

I asked some of the people how they felt about things. They answered that they were not to blame for the war:

"There is only one man to blame—Mussolini! We are poor people and not interested in politics. One government for us is as good as another, and we are ready to change right now. By the way, do you think there will be any more bombing? We've had enough."

• • •

The Highlanders were now in scenic county abounding in greenery including stately palms and olive trees. Even though their columns were making a mess of plowed fields and the vast burial ground surrounding the holy city of Zliten, the Arabs displayed extreme friendliness. Arab urchins frenziedly shouted the traditional "Saida" and waved eggs they wanted to barter for tea and sugar, but the Scottish motorized infantry, driving at a fast clip, was stopping for no one. The village of Zliten capitulated without a shot being fired, the Italian military police remaining there surrendering under a white flag to the first Scottish vehicle.

Thereafter for the first time in weeks, vehicles that had been struggling through sand seas and muck went onto the macadam highway toward Homs. It was a fine road which the Germans and Italians had blown up in places to delay the Eighth Army, but otherwise in splendid condition. The Highlanders were in high spirits; they joked and sang as their division moved up in the moonlight through the palm trees. It was great to see a victorious outfit on the move with their artillery, including big guns from America, advancing almost in parade array, with no opposition from the skies. The bulk of enemy aircraft now were well west of Tripoli.

Three days before the fall of Tripoli we rested with the Scotties near Homs, slightly west of the ancient Phoenician town of Leptus Magna, with its ruins and tombs projecting from the sand, while Italian artillery shelled us from a distance in a desperate effort to delay the fall of Tripoli. Amidst shellfire, I could see the infantry advancing toward Homs, mopping up Italians at bayonet point. While cooks attached to Divisional Headquarters "brewed up" to the accompaniment of bagpipes, German and Italian prisoners were brought in for questioning.

At 10 p.m., January 20, the order to continue the advance was given and we passed through Homs, where resistance had been broken by an infantry charge, resulting in the seizure of a hill fortress dominating the main road to Tripoli. Under the first light of the moon the Highlanders found their way blocked by an anti-tank ditch twenty feet deep and wide and stretching as far as we could see through the hills and to the sea. To complete the barrier, the enemy had blown up the macadam highway, making it necessary for the tired infantry, who had been on their feet night and day since the start of the final offensive at Buerat, to fill it in with picks and shovels. I saw their general personally directing the job, with troops working in relays of several score at a time. They slaved away well over an hour filling in and leveling the gap. It was an inspiring sight. More than once the general himself grabbed a shovel to set an example while RAF night fighters circled overhead protecting the snakelike column of guns, tanks, ammunition tracks, and lorried machine-gunners and infantry against enemy bombers.

Since the enemy had not chosen to make a determined stand in the hills immediately behind the huge ditch, it appeared they had pulled out altogether, possibly spurred by reports that Montgomery at the head of the British armor had broken through the Gebel Nefesa from the southeast in an outflanking move. To complete the illusion there was utter silence, accentuated by the rhythmic scraping of Scottish picks and shovels.

The general in his jeep was first to cross over the ditch, immediately followed by light equipment, after which the guns were manhandled over the obstruction and soon the entire column was moving on in the silent night. We had been so anxious to push on to Tripoli that our truck had maneuvered into a leading position, but the good-natured Scottish general had waved us back with a "No, no. We've got to win the war first! You'll have to wait for my advance guard to go through."

It was lucky that we waited, for as it was we three correspondents were well in the lead column which a few miles further walked into a hornets' nest. It was an ambush, and we seemed to have dived headlong into a cauldron of flame. There were mortar bombs exploding all around, punctuated by the sharp, whiplike crack of anti-tank guns. Several tanks ahead were hit; also some trucks carrying sappers. Scottish artillery hurriedly ranged on the exact spot and began rapid fire. Their shells whistled and crashed in quick succession and we could hear calls for stretcher bearers ahead. The general raced his jeep into the thick of it and personally sorted things out, ordering leading trucks in the column to turn around as the tanks deployed in battle formation on both sides of the road, firing their guns along the lines of tracers from Fiat and Spandau machine guns. So quickly had the artillery gone into action that for a while we couldn't tell the difference between our own shells and those of the enemy. At the height of the row, ambulances nosed down the macadam road, illuminated by green and white flares. Verey lights vied with the flares and the now bright full moon trying to turn night into day.

The enemy had carefully prepared this ambush, which was a final gesture by a rearguard unit of the famous German Ninetieth Light Division. They knew that advancing British troops, armored cars, and tanks would be silhouetted along the crest of the hill overlooking their positions, so on spotting the first vehicles they sprayed the hillsides with mortar shells whose explosion was many times magnified by the rolling countryside.

As though it were all in the day's work, the Highland Infantry piled out of their lorries and marched single-file into the darkness with rifles and Bren guns at the ready. Two companies of machine-gunners from a London regiment, who had fought it out all the way from Alamein, rushed up in light lorries with their Lewis guns, and soon tracer was ricocheting in cascades as Lewis and Bren guns sought out the quick-firing Spandaus and the more leisurely Fiats among the rocks. Bullets spluttered around like bacon frying over hot coals, glancing from the boulders with a sickening whine. The enemy being well dug-in, what followed became one of the most dramatic and hardest-fought infantry actions of the entire African campaign, wherein the Ninetieth Light Division strove to uphold their reputation for valor. This miniature battle in the foothills of Gebel Nefesa, forming a natural barrier before Tripoli, sealed the fate of the last town in the Italian Colonial Empire.

Through the anxious hours that followed as a few companies from the "Seaforth Highlanders" fought it out with the Hun, I was able to record the enemy's gradual retreat by the position of his flares and Verey lights. Having tried to take Tripoli ahead of the army and then thought better of it, with two English colleagues I withdrew to what looked like a likely spot a few hundred yards to the rear to watch the fireworks. Around 2 a.m., there appearing no immediate prospects of continuing, I laid my Jerry pilot's greatcoat on the ground and went to sleep. At the time Highland artillery had been firing from well behind us but as the Germans retired they had moved on. At about 5:30 a.m. on the morning of January 21, I was awakened by a tremendous crash right behind me. It was the signal for a concentrated barrage. There were several batteries of 25-pounders within a few hundred feet of where I was sleeping and I decided not to move, although there was a terrific rumpus and even though I kept my eyes shut, the gun flashes blinded me. They fired rapidly—1, 2, 3, 4—1, 2, 3, 4—and it seemed as though I was sitting amidst a tremendous array of gigantic kettle drums. Then the enemy began his counterbattery work. German shells looking for our guns crashed ahead of us, then behind us, then slightly to the left. It wasn't part of my job to sit there waiting for the center shells, so I scrambled to my feet and dodged behind the wall of a crumbling Arab hut, just as the German 88s completed their bracketing. But the Scottish gunners never faltered. If anything, they speeded up the rhythm of their fire, and my peaceful nook reeked with smoke and fumes from the 25-pounders and bursting enemy shell. It was only a gesture on the enemy's part lasting about fifteen minutes, but it was one of the longest fifteen minutes I have ever experienced. I then realized why the infantry had started digging slit trenches around us.

Hastily writing my story of this rearguard action, I rejoined the advancing troops, taking time out, however, to inspect the battleground ahead.

In the words of one Scottish infantryman, this had been a tougher fight than the Alamein infantry attack considering time elapsed and intensity of the engagement. It appeared to me from the manner in which the Germans had entrenched themselves in this spot about ten miles west of

Homs that they had determined not only to make things difficult for the Eighth Army but at the same time to stage a demonstration that might tend to appease their already grumbling Italian allies, before bidding farewell to Tripolitania. (Between Zliten and this spot, hundreds of Italians had been left flat-footed by the Germans, who in some instances had even laid minefields between themselves and the Italian "rearguard," making the latter's capture a certainty.)

The enemy had been too well entrenched and dispersed for the artillery alone to oust them from their ambush, hence the commanding general of the Highlanders decided on an outflanking move by infantry. Silently the Seaforths, backed by London machine-gunners, had crept stealthily through hills reminding me of my home state of New Hampshire and, making a wide sweep, had come in on the entrenched Germans from the left, with two pimples dominating the highway their main objective. Covering the final few hundred yards on their bellies, they had dug themselves slit trenches with their trench tools while some burrowed into the dirt with their hands, awaiting the signal to attack.

I roamed the battleground while stretcher bearers were still carrying in dead and wounded and was deeply impressed by the drama of the thing. I saw grooves where infantrymen had lain in wait with their rifles and machine guns, resting on newly dug sandy soil; also empty packs of cigarettes they had smoked chain fashion awaiting Zero Hour. Then there were hobnailed marks somewhat similar to those left by sprinters leaving the starting line in a footrace, representing the final scramble toward the enemy as the Scots charged into deadly fire with bayonets fixed. In some places there were pools of blood marking the spot where men had fallen, not to rise again. The ground was criss-crossed with tank tracks and wheel marks. The tank tracks were ours and the wheel marks those made by lorries of the Ninetieth Light as they withdrew. In patches there were olive groves where the Germans and Scots had fought it out, and every tree trunk and branch was scarred by shrapnel from shells, mortars, and grenades. The ground was strewn with bright bits of shell and grenade fragments that had made this place a living Hell for a few brief hours. In contrast, however, as I retraced the battleground at leisure, the countryside was serenely peaceful, with lizards wriggling in and out between shell holes and lilies growing among the abandoned heavy equipment in a background of imprints of hobnailed boots. Mountain larks were singing and crickets were chirruping.

In six hours of furious fighting, the infantry had systematically weeded out nests of Spandaus and mortars, tracking down their opponents by following the line of tracers from their machine guns. The Scots seldom got close enough for their favorite style of fighting with the bayonet. The

Germans were not having it and fired thousands of rounds of bullets trying to wipe out the men of the Seaforths. Tanks had come up in support, but most of them had got stuck in a gorge of yielding reddish clay and still the infantry had hung on.

I met Maltese Lieutenant Albert Dinech, who joined the Seaforths looking for a fight to avenge ordeals suffered by his parents in Malta. He had been wounded six times. He gave me his impressions of the fight:

"Take my runner and batman, for instance," said Dinech.

> They wouldn't leave me. The runner was caught by the explosion of a mortar shell as he walked at my side tracing down a Spandau. He fell seriously wounded but I was unhurt and carried on. There were snipers all around us. My sergeant major, who himself was killed later by German treachery, fought like a mad man. Once I heard him shout "Musta. Come here and see how a swine is shot." Thereupon he stood up and put a bullet from his rifle through the head of a German sniper who was on his knees aiming at one of our boys. A group of Germans came toward us with their hands up. I told our fellows not to shoot them. Then we saw a Bantam German caterpillar troop carrier with three aboard, rattling in our direction with two Germans running alongside. It was a ruse. We had gained our objective, and they desperately were trying to eject us. The next thing we knew the Germans from the caterpillar were hurling stick grenades. They caught us like rats in a trap and killed my sergeant major and several others.

Nearby, wounded men lay on stretchers waiting to be removed to hospitals in Homs, and a detail was burying the dead, marking the graves with crude little crosses. There were tanks shielded from the view of aeroplanes by the scarred olive trees. On the ground were bandoliers, steel helmets, and soldiers' packs. But if anyone had been driving along the highway later on and hadn't seen the wounded men and the burial parties and sought out all these things, they'd perhaps have never known that this ground had been consecrated by the blood of these fine fellows from the Scottish Highlanders who went into the attack against greatly superior odds, and won.

Tanks of an Armored Brigade that had been transferred to the coast road for a triumphant entry into Tripoli were roaring past as I stooped to pick up a blood-stained Tam o' Shanter and pay book not far from the main highway. Thinking it had been mislaid by the stretcher bearers, I took it back to an M.D.S. captain enquiring for the owner. The captain consulted the pay book and waved his arm in the direction of a freshly covered grave.

"There's your man, Jock," said he. "He won't be needing his Balmoral any longer. I suggest you keep the hat badge as a memento of one of the toughest fights in the history of this regiment."

I did so, and I have it with me now. I shall treasure it all my life. It reads: "Sans peur"—"Without fear."

• • •

Ambulances were removing the casualties as I continued westward, when suddenly five Me-109s swooped down strafing the road. Miraculously, no one was hurt. Had the Germans timed their attack a few seconds earlier, they might have nailed General Montgomery himself, for he had only just passed in his automobile to inspect the road ahead. With the campaign nearing an end, Montgomery seemed to be everywhere. Invariably he returned salutes of the cheering infantry. Sometimes pacing alone, in open fields with tanks and cannon as a background, and his aides at a respectful distance, the sight of Montgomery reminded me of pictures of Napoleon.

The next forty miles were covered without incident as tanks of the Armored Brigade bowled along, dragging light vehicles and cannon after them through obstructions. Behind them, sappers and engineers were repairing great craters along the winding road through the mountains, clearing the way for the victory parade. One of these craters was the work of a single infantryman wearing the uniform and gaiters of the Ninetieth Light Division, whose body I had seen lying on the roadside as we passed. I learned that half an hour after Scottish sappers had defused German charges under a bridge, there had been a tremendous roar as the bridge went up. This German soldier had replaced the charges and gone to certain death to uphold the honor of his division. He was killed by machine-gun fire while making an effort to escape.

In their headlong retreat the German rearguard had not even bothered to bury their dead or pick up their wounded, some of whom lay on the roadside moaning for "Wasser."

Rolling along at high speed closely behind forward scout patrols of armored cars, I saw Italian peasants who had spent the night under the stars, returning to their farm houses with blankets in hand. Frequently, they waved at us. Again there were all manner of Fascist slogans on the white cement road houses such as: "The Fascist regime is a regime of Justice," and "Vinceremo!" meaning "We shall win." Alongside these buildings, grinning broadly, were Scotties cleaning chickens with huge dirks. Squatting nearby were Italian prisoners who had been out in the fields and begun converging on the main road while British tanks clattered past. The Ities waved to us in childish glee.

On the evening of January 22 we were only twenty miles from Tripoli, which was now visible in the distance as a white rambling city along the coast. General Montgomery squatted Indian fashion alongside his personal tank while 25-pounders and 75s from thirty-ton Sherman tanks were blasting the Germans from a road barrier just ahead. I could see the glow of great fires on the outskirts of Tripoli, confirming air reports that the scorched-earth policy was being applied to barracks and munitions dumps.

Had the army commander been in a hurry, the town would have been occupied that night, but it was preferable to await daylight.

At dawn on January 23, exactly three months to the day since the start of the Battle of Alamein, Montgomery's victorious army entered Tripoli, meeting with no resistance, for the defeated armies of the Axis already were many miles to the west, streaking it for the temporary safety of the Tunisia frontier.

When I reached Tripoli's main square, quite a crowd had gathered on the sidewalks to stare open-mouthed at dust-grimed drivers of Crusader and Valentine tanks, who were calmly shaving to the accompaniment of catchy Highland ditties rendered by red-faced Scottish pipers. The pipers' facial contortions suggested that their lungs might burst at any moment.

The men of the Eighth Army had seen crowds before and were not particularly interested. But along with them, I was all eyes when a gorgeous little creature in the white uniform of the Italian Red Cross appeared on a bicycle and began throwing lovely smiles in every direction, as she expertly weaved in and out amongst the flabbergasted troops. When the little siren had left, the spotlight shifted to the center of the square where two fellows, one a British officer and the other a uniformed Italian, were gesticulating and gradually raising their voices. I stuck my nose into it when I heard an aggravated voice demanding:

"Does anyone around here speak Italian?"

It was a captain of the British provost marshal's staff who had been trying to make himself understood by a uniformed Italian police officer.

"I do, what's up?"

"I'm in a hurry," said the captain. "They tell me this fellow is the Italian chief of police. Ask him the location of police headquarters and City Hall, and tell him to be quick about it, for the British army is taking over."

I turned to address the uniformed Italian, but before I could open my mouth, he was talking to me.

"Well, well, well!—If it isn't my old friend the giornalista Gorrell.— Don't you remember me—Vecchioni?"

No, I didn't, and anyway the British captain was beginning to lose his temper. Again I demanded to know where Tripoli's police headquarters were, so that the British Red Caps could take over.

"Oh," said he in mockery. "The giornalista Gorrell doesn't remember Vecchioni?"

With that, pausing after every phrase, and mimicking the voice of doom—something like the judge on the bench passing judgment on a criminal at the dock, he exclaimed:

"Rome—September, 1936—you were expelled from Italy—I, Vecchioni, had the honor—the privilege—of carrying out Il Duce's orders!"

Then this pompous fellow, whom I now remembered as the man who had read me Mussolini's expulsion order in Italy seven years before, clicked his heels, raised his hand in the Fascist salute, and with a half bow, placed himself through me at the disposal of the British conquerors of the Italian army.

Corporal Jim Hart, Red Cap from Bournemouth, was among Vecchioni's escort, as with long military strides, the Italian took the lead toward the Tripoli Police Station. Hart loitered behind sufficiently to ask me:

"I say, who is this bloke anyway?"

Briefly I filled him in, whereupon Corporal Hart inflated his chest and laughed triumphantly. Starting off at a fast clip to catch up with the party, he threw back over his shoulder:

"Don't you worry, Yank. Jim Hart will keep an eye on this fellow from now on!"

31

CONCLUSION (BUT THE WAR GOES ON)

Cairo, April 1943

AT THE PRESENT WRITING, I'M WONDERING WHETHER THE censors will complete their perusal of my first effort at a book before I receive orders to move on with the Allied armies of invasion.

I had hoped to return to the U.S.A. for the first time in four years, if only to inspect the roof on an old New Hampshire farmhouse, but things have been happening too fast for that. So I'm back in Cairo again, and I've a feeling that although it's going to be a tough trek, with lots of the boys falling by the wayside, all of us will soon be marching again—through Hitler's backyard. And speaking of roofs, it looks as though the one over the "Fortress of Europe" is leaking pretty badly already, for it is being bombed day and night. What's the use of a fortress without a roof, Adolf?

I'm not at liberty to go into details at present, for in so doing I'd be rendering valuable service to the opposition. It's no secret, however, that the Mediterranean coastline, from Gibraltar to Suez, Haifa, and Beirut, is crawling with Allied troops and aircraft. And I have permission to add that although we face several score German and Italian divisions scattered throughout the Balkans, Italy, the Greek and Italian islands, and Southern France, the Allied High Command is confident that at the proper time it can apply superior forces at selected points. That alone is sufficient to give the enemy the jitters.

Except for hundreds of troops enjoying a final fling before the main act begins, life in Cairo and Alexandria hasn't altered much. You'd never guess from the faces of Egyptians, for example, that there'd been a major victory in Tunisia and that all of Africa was now in Allied hands. The expressions of Egyptians are no different from those that greeted me two years ago when I arrived from Greece with the BEF, for the children of the

Sphinx look upon the doings of men of the Western World through a veil of fatalistic indifference.

Perhaps on closer examination, certain facts will emerge. You'll find first of all that Egypt is a huge arsenal—bigger than ever before. Second, behind the mystic shroud of Oriental indifference, a dramatic game is in progress. There's always been a game of sorts around here, frequented by diplomats, intrigue artists, and spies of all nationalities. This new game is entirely one-sided, the croupiers being trusted servants of John Bull and Uncle Sam. As for the dice, they're loaded, and when they stop spinning there's serious trouble ahead for those fellows who anxiously await the verdict within their leaky fortress across the Mediterranean.

Take a trip east or west for a few miles, if only so far as Suez or Tobruk, and you'll see plenty more, but with the possible exception of tremendous activity in the air, you mustn't mention it. So here I'll leave a gap to save the censor trouble. I've never known "security" to be so strictly applied in the Middle East.

For nearly a month, the strategic air offensive in the Mediterranean has been increasing in momentum, the Italian islands dominating the Sicilian Narrows being bombed around the clock with an intensity and destructive effect never before equaled even by the great artillery bombardment of the Western Front in 1918. They say it's only a sample of what's coming, but it's not a bad start since Sicilian and Sardinian aerodromes are already virtually impotent. Additionally, the Italian navy has lost valuable bases, with the result that only the other day a convoy of eighty-odd ships reached their port of destination, having negotiated the Mediterranean without incident.

It's a time-tested formula, this bombing, applied in ever greater dimensions. The "Battle of Alamein" began the same way, Rommel's forces wilting before the land fighting ever started under concentrated bombing and strafing by the Western Desert Air Force. The procedure was repeated in even more spectacular form in Tunisia, where hundreds of Allied bombers pounded the docks at Bizerte and Tunis to a pulp, cutting off General Hans-Jürgen Von Arnim's supplies, while equal numbers of planes "kept the enemy's heads down" at Mareth, Sfax, and El Hamma. Under a protective screen of bombs and shells, the Eighth Army moved forward, linking arms with General Eisenhower's American, British, and French forces to stage the grand squeeze that so dramatically ended the North African campaign. In the two days preceding the occupation of Tunis, more than three thousand bomber and fighter sorties were carried out. Such a display of air strength had no parallel, even in Poland when the Luftwaffe was at the zenith of its strength.

Recent raids by American Liberators against Italy have equaled any daylight assaults ever launched from Britain. Successes of the B-24Ds have been striking. In a raid on Naples Harbor, they destroyed twenty ships. In a raid on Ferryville, in Tunisia, they put the docks completely out of commission. In an assault on two Sicilian landing grounds, the Americans destroyed seventy-three aircraft on the ground. Later, at the Sardinian naval base, they accounted for Italy's only two effective heavy cruisers. Current day and night raids on Italian islands and southern Italy by the RAF and USAAF from North Africa involve bombers in the hundreds. Simultaneously, the Bomber Command offensive against Germany has attained such proportions that fifteen hundred tons of bombs can be dumped over a single target in one night.

"This is only a start," they repeat. Hundreds of bombers and fighters, just off the assembly lines in England and America, are standing by ready for the signal to lash out and smother resistance to Allied landings in Europe under an avalanche of high explosive. We are creating an air force in North Africa vastly superior in numbers and tactics—an air force such as Germany failed to pit against Britain in 1940!

Well, I'm glad I'm not the other fellow. For my part, I wouldn't wish to experience anything worse than the bombings to which the BEF were subjected by Goering's Stukas in Greece and Crete, even if that type of bombing is "out of date." Yep, that's what they tell you. The Stuka is way behind the times now, having given way to fighter-bombers and the American "Battleships of the Air."

Certainly so far as air strength is concerned, we're going in with the upper hand. We also pack a terrific wallop in other lines, but that's the sort of thing I'm not allowed to talk about. If the enemy is nervous, it's because he knows we have his measure. Experience has taught us, for instance, that:

1. There is no longer any reason to regard the Hun as a "superman," all arguments by Goebbels to the contrary. Some time ago, along with our Russian allies, we discovered that "Blitzkrieg" is even more obsolete than the Stuka, applying only when the opponent is weak and unprepared. More recently, we knocked the Germans silly in North Africa. From now on, it's just plain slugging, and let the best man win.

2. The secret of victory lies in coordination of effort. In other words, all branches of the services must be trained and utilized together. We learned this lesson at a price, at Dunkirk and Nauplion, and at the cost of many lives during the first year of conflict in the Western Desert. The result was the first major victory for British arms at Alamein when General Montgomery demonstrated what can be done through synchronization of effort on land, air, and sea by smashing Rommel's Afrika Corps. "Ike" Eisenhower's brilliant victory in Tunisia was a crowning test. The use of

air power in the North African campaign will go down in history as a classic of perfect coordination and cooperation with the land forces.

3. Broadly speaking, allowing for changes in climate and terrain, all original basic principles of warfare have been confirmed. Alamein and subsequent assaults against "impregnable" positions in Tunisia proved conclusively that the infantry, even in modern warfare, must lead the attack. It was different during the "Blitzkrieg" days in Poland, the Low Countries, and France, where the enemy was taken by surprise and German panzers plunged through their lines and ran amok. More recent engagements against prepared positions have demonstrated that largely because of the development of the anti-tank gun, tanks alone cannot always achieve a breakthrough. Alamein was a case in point, for there the infantry slugged it out for nine days before Montgomery saw fit to send his armored divisions through the gap they had created, for the kill. This might have been any attack in the Battle of the Somme, preceded by short, intense artillery preparation. In consultation with experts in the Middle East, I have concluded that bombers are extremely effective in "softening" enemy resistance and paralyzing his communications and supply lines prior to an attack, but the air force has by no means displaced artillery. Aircraft are incapable of laying down a prolonged barrage, even though they considerably lengthen the artillery's range. However, at the psychological moment they can assume a vital role by laying down a deluge of bombs on concentrated points, as was the case in the final assault against Tunis.

4. Except for the land mine, which Rommel used in his retreat from Alamein to Tripoli to an extent heretofore unknown, this war has produced no outstanding weapons. This explodes the myth of the "secret weapon," another brainchild of the German propaganda machine. Tanks, planes, artillery, and guts are still the major ingredients of warfare. The mine has multiplied many times the effectiveness of barbed-wire entanglements, and also has been found exceedingly effective in covering a retreat. That being the case, we can expect the Germans to use mines for some time yet.

• • •

That the dictators don't like the look of things is self-evident. None other than my "old friend" General Franco spilled the beans immediately after the collapse of Tunisia when he began bleating about this war having "reached a dead end" and offering himself as a "neutral mediator" to the warring nations. Odd, isn't it, that the man who was first to benefit materially from the Axis schemes for world conquest should be the first to scream for peace when he gets a good whiff of what's in store for him.

Perhaps Franco's mentor, Mussolini, put him up to it. I believe that in his shoes, I might also have enquired concerning prospects of calling the whole thing off.

Look at a map of the Mediterranean, and you can take your choice of any number of possible objectives for the impending Allied offensive from North Africa. Perhaps by the time this is published, we'll already have been given the answer. I cannot provide it now.

Wherever it hits, the springboard for the attack will pack a considerable wallop, for Allied forces now massed along the southern shores of the Mediterranean have become bloodied, veteran troops, confident in themselves, their leaders, and the vast resources and capabilities of the administrators and supply machinery supporting them.

Counterbalancing the great difficulties of an overseas invasion against strongly fortified and resolutely defended positions (and it would be a great mistake to underestimate the determination of any troops who are fighting to defend their own homelands) must be weighed the fact that our armies may also be expected to include "homecoming" troops, i.e., French and Greeks who will have that enormous inspiration to spur them on. And just as Franco had his "Fifth Column" in Madrid and Hitler had his professional minorities to help him disrupt defenses in the Balkans, so can the Allies rely on abundant help from imprisoned populations. Axis nervousness over prospects of an invasion in the Balkans is reflected by the reported presence of about seventeen Italian divisions in Yugoslavia, Dalmatia, and Montenegro (no doubt they are being kept busy by Draza Mihailovich's patriots), supported by at least half a dozen German divisions farther inland. In Greece alone, there are upwards of twelve Italian divisions at present, and four German. The defenses of Crete were brought up to strength some time ago, with one and a half German divisions reported in the islands. From my previous experience in the Balkans, I would judge that there are millions in Greece, Romania, Yugoslavia, Czechoslovakia, and even in Hungary who would quickly flock to the United Nations standard were they given sufficient incentive. The potential repercussions of a successful invasion are unlimited, for we must also take into account the burning flame of revenge kindling in the hearts of the people of Poland, Norway, the Low Countries, Belgium, France, and even Spain, where Franco straddles a very shaky stool.

However much the underbelly of Europe is softened by bombing and propaganda, it is bound to be the scene of desperate battles, disappointments, and casualties on a vast scale. We have no illusion about walking into any country in Europe without first having to fight hard for a foothold. That is one of the lessons of Tunisia, where even the Italians, sensing an immediate threat to their native land, fought with credit. The future involves an operation unprecedented in history and must be approached with becoming gravity. As I complete this book, it is even considered possible that the Axis may attempt a mad-bull rush at the Allied fence in the Black Sea area as a desperate throw to disrupt our plans. Failing that, the "Battle of Europe" is not far distant.

Henry Tilton Gorrell
April 1943

Abrahams, Abdullah, 253
Abyssinia, 15, 148, 149
Acre Armistice Convention (1941), 127
Africa, 59, 146–51. *See also* Egypt; South
    Africa
Afrika Corps, 106, 146, 152–53, 165, 176,
    181–82, 189, 242, 246, 269. *See also*
    North Africa; Rommel, Erwin
Airedale (destroyer), 155, 162
Air Medal award, 4, 144, 145
Alamein, Egypt: Allies' air force at,
    204–7; anti-tank company of
    Riflemen at, 216–17; Auchinleck's
    forces at, 176, 187, 189–98; casualties
    at, 186–91, 199, 211, 213, 238, 239;
    Churchill at, 199–201, 207; first battle
    of, 185–87; Gorrell at, 189–98, 208–18,
    224, 240–41; information-gathering
    activities at, 202; Italian forces at,
    209, 210, 217, 235; lull in fighting
    at, 202–7; Montgomery's defeat of
    Rommel at, 10, 10n2, 208–18, 234,
    235, 299, 300; prisoners of war from,
    235; Rommel's final defeat at, 234–41,
    298; Rommel stopped at, 176, 181–87;
    Royal Air Force (RAF) at, 235–36;
    tricks played on Rommel's troops at,
    205; U.S. forces at, 204, 207, 212–15,
    234–41
Alan, Lance Corporal, 184
Albanian campaign, 8, 9, 70, 80–84,
    87–88, 92, 93, 139
Alcazar siege, 25
Alexander, Harold, 210
Alexander the Great, 126
Alexandria, Egypt: attitudes of residents
    of, 152, 174–76, 297–98; evacuation
    of, 176–81; firing over, 174, 176–77;
    Gorrell in, 106, 162, 165, 168, 174,
    176–81, 268–69

Alfieri, Dino, 18
Ali, Rashid, 107–8, 114, 115
Allen, Donald S., 228, 232
Allen, Larry, 177
Allenby, Sir Edmund Henry Hynman,
    126
American Field Service, 169, 174, 182,
    246, 248–49
Anglo-Iranian Oil Company, 107
Antonescu, Ion, 76, 79
AP. *See* Associated Press
Arab Legion, 256
Arabs: and Allied advance to Tripoli,
    256–58, 261–62, 277–78, 289;
    assistance to RAF aviators by, 257–58;
    Axis propaganda aimed at Muslims,
    107–8; Bedouin Arabs, 115, 256; in
    Benghazi, 261–62; cemetery for, in
    Wadi Kabir, 275–76; Damascus as
    capital of Arab world, 124–25; and
    desert heat, 130; execution of, for
    siding with the Allies, 257; farming
    and livestock tending by, 130, 256;
    German prisoners of war compared
    with, 186; in Giovanni Berta,
    256–57; Italians' treatment of, 256;
    marriage between Italian men and,
    272; mosques of, 125, 286; sale and
    provision of food by, 124, 256, 258,
    260, 288; Senussi Arabs, 256, 257; in
    Sirte, 277–78; and Syrian campaign,
    119; taxi service provided by, for
    Gorrell's trip from Jaffa to Haifa,
    225–26; as Trans-Jordan frontier
    police, 115; transportation for Arab
    girl to Jezzine, 124; in Zliten, 289. *See
    also* Middle East
Aranjuez fighting, 32–33
Asensio, Jose, 28, 37
Associated Press, 32, 34, 73, 106, 128, 177,

226, 245
Athens, Greece, 83–84, 88–98
Auchinleck, Sir Claude, 146, 152, 176, 187, 189–98, 208
Australian troops: Army Medical Corps of, 103, 106; and Benghazi bombing, 220–23; in Greece, 95, 101; in Middle East, 106, 115–24, 126–27; in North Africa, 168, 185–87, 189, 192, 194–95, 197, 201, 203, 204
Austria, 9, 58

B–24 bombers, 219–24, 226–33, 262–69, 299
B–25 bombers, 234–37, 240–41
Badoglio, Marshal, 14, 52
Baghdad, Iraq, 129–30, 135–36
Bailey, William, 212–15
Baillie, Hugh, 64
Balkan Peninsula: Albanian campaign, 8, 9, 70, 80–84, 87–88, 92, 93, 139; British forces in, 94–95; espionage in, 81–82, 84–92; German occupation of Romania, 78–80; German plan for, 71–73, 301; German troops in plain clothes in, 72, 80, 94–95; Gestapo in, 74–75, 81, 84–92; Gorrell in Bucharest, Romania, 75–80; Gorrell in Budapest, Hungary, 9, 67, 70–75; Gorrell in combat situations in, 84, 100; map of, 69; Soviet invasion of Bessarabia in, 70, 76, 77, 80. *See also* Greece; and other specific countries
Baltimore (bomber aircraft), 205–6, 212, 237
Barry, Bob, 66
Barry, Dennis, 66
Basrah, Iraq, 128–29
Bastico, General, 287
Battle of Britain, 181
Bayliss, Fred, 255–56
BBC, 117, 148, 198
Beattie, Brian, 257
Beck, William S., 239
Bedouin tribes, 115, 256, 288
BEF. *See* British Expeditionary Force
Beirut, Lebanon, 122, 126–27
Belden, Jack, x, 262, 264
Belgium, 74, 301
Benghazi, 146, 219–23, 258–61
Berlin bureau of United Press, 77
Bessarabia: repatriation of German residents from, 78, 80; Soviet invasion of, 9, 70, 76, 77, 80

Best, Lieutenant Commander, 102, 169, 174
Best, Roscoe, 270
Bethan-Green, R. P., 170
Bilby, Glade, 239
Bir Hacheim, 152, 174–75, 182
Black Shirts, 11
Blamey, Sir Thomas Albert, 126
Blitzkrieg, 8, 49, 299, 300
Boer War, 150
Bofors guns, 206–7
Bolshevism, 39, 52, 55–56, 61, 67, 107. *See also* Soviet Union
Booby traps. *See* Mines and booby traps
Boris, King (Bulgaria), 77
Boston (attack aircraft), 204–5, 212, 237
Bowers, Claude, 35, 36
Bradbury, Eric, 206
Breeding, Marvin L., 228
Brereton, Lewis Hyde, 4, 144, 156, 224
Briggs, H. F., 170
Britain. *See* Great Britain
British Army Medical Corps, 248–49
British Expeditionary Force (BEF): evacuation of, from Greece, 92, 96, 97, 148, 150, 174, 272; in Greece and Crete, 234, 299; at Halfaya Pass, 106; and Iraq revolt, 108–10; retreat of, ·Belgium, 74
British Intelligence Service, 92, 97–103
Brown, Stewart, 17–18
Browning salvos, 163, 163*n*1
Bucharest, Romania, 75–80
Budapest, Hungary, 9, 67, 69, 70–75
Buerat and Buerat line, 279, 280, 283, 289–90
Bulgaria, 71, 72, 77, 80–82, 93, 94
Buqbuq, Egypt, 249–50
Burdett, Winston, 226
Burger, John, 264, 266
Burgess, William, 112
Burma, 219
Byrne, Gunner, 228, 231
Byron, Lord Gordon George, 8*n*1

Cairo, Egypt: army censors in, 208; attitude of residents of, 152, 176, 297–98; Churchill in, 200, 207; food costs in, 152; Gorrell in, 102, 128, 146, 152, 157, 224–25, 262, 297–98; United Press bureau in, 146
Calliston, Charles, 216–17
Cantoupoulos (censor), 83
Capri, 266

Eritrea, 15, 125, 148
Espionage: in Balkans, 81–82, 84–92,
    97–102; during Spanish Civil War,
    51–54
Ethiopian War, 11, 14, 15, 17, 52, 53, 59
Executions, 26–28, 51–52, 54, 257

Farmer, Joseph E., 228, 231
Fascism, 8, 14–21, 55–59. *See also* Hitler,
    Adolf; Mussolini, Benito
Field hospitals. *See* Hospitals and
    medical care
Fifth Column, 53, 96, 100–101, 135, 150,
    301
Finland, 67, 70, 76
Fleas, 271–72, 277–78
Florence, Italy, 16–17
Flory, Harry, 38
"Flying Can Openers," 237–38
Food: for Albanian campaign, 87; in
    Benghazi, 258, 260; Christmas Eve
    dinner near Sirte, 272, 273; cost of,
    in Cairo, 152; in Giovanni Berta,
    256–57; Gorrell's lack of appetite, 57;
    Highlanders on, 280; in Italy, 14–16;
    in Madrid, 22–23, 29, 43–44, 46, 53, 57;
    in Misurata, 288; for prisoners of war,
    259, 284
Fort Bungum, 275–76
Forte, Aldo and Ralph, 18, 20
Fort Victor Emmanuel, Eritrea, 125
France: anti-aircraft defenses of,
    during early World War II, 68; and
    appeasement of Hitler and Mussolini,
    39; attitude in, during early World
    War II, 68; blitzkrieg against, 300;
    and Maginot Line, 65, 67, 68; Paris
    bureau of United Press in, 43, 48–49;
    surrender of, to Germany, 74, 150. *See
    also* Paris; Vichy French
Franco, Francisco: advance against
    Toledo and Madrid by, 22, 23, 25, 37;
    air superiority of, 51; and Aranjuez
    battle, 32; and Axis defeats, 300–301;
    and expulsion of Gorrell from
    Spain, 10, 34–36; and Fifth Column,
    53, 301; and Guernica battle, 49;
    Italian and German support for, 8,
    31; and Madrid siege, 43–44, 48, 52;
    newspaper coverage of, 61; radio
    spokesman for, 38, 39; and Roosevelt,
    58; spies for, 51–54; supporters of,
    50; victory of, in Spanish Civil War,
    55–56. *See also* Spanish Civil War

Free French troops, 106, 118, 124–25
French Revolution, 26
Freyburg, Bernard "Tiny," 168, 175, 181,
    183–85
Frost, Gunner, 228, 230–32
Frost, Jack, 205
Fulcher, Bill, 257

Gas masks, 65–66
Gasset, George, 214
Gazala, 152, 165, 181, 255
Gazala–Bir Hacheim line, 152
Gebel Nefesa, 290–94
Genghis Khan, 130
George II, King (Greece), 97
George VI, King (United Kingdom),
    10n3, 42
German-Soviet Non-Aggression Pact, 67,
    70, 80
Germany: aerial bombs of, during
    Spanish Civil War, 23; attack against
    Soviet Union by, 70; and Balkan
    Peninsula, 70–80; and Battle of
    the Mediterranean, 158–64; and
    blitzkrieg, 8, 49, 299, 300; bombing
    of, 299; bombing of Beirut by, 122;
    declaration of war against Soviet
    Union by, 126; division of Poland
    between Soviet Union and, 67; and
    German-Soviet Non-Aggression Pact,
    67, 70, 80; German troops in plain
    clothes in Balkans, 72, 80, 94–95;
    and Gestapo, 74–75, 81, 84–92; and
    Habbaniya battle, 110–11; invasion
    of Austria, Czechoslovakia, and
    Poland by, 9, 58, 63–64, 73; invasion
    of Belgium by, 74; invasion of Crete
    by, 9, 108, 112–14, 150; invasion of
    Cyprus, Syria, and Palestine, 112;
    invasion of Denmark and Norway
    by, 72, 73; invasion of Greece by,
    72, 92–102; invasion of Netherlands
    by, 74; invasion of Romania and
    Yugoslavia by, 9, 72; and magnetic
    mines, 66; and Middle East, 103,
    106–16; and Spanish Civil War, 8–9,
    23, 27, 37, 47, 49; surrender of France
    to, 74; timetable of, during World
    War II, 70–71, 106–7; and U-boats,
    66, 159, 161. *See also* Hitler, Adolf;
    Luftwaffe; North Africa
Gestapo, 74–75, 81, 84–92
Gibbes, R. H. "Bobbie," 204, 246
Gilmer, Jesse L., 214

bombing in, 226–33; Russian fighting in, 70; and United Nations, 301. *See also* Albanian campaign
Green Shirts, 76–77, 79
Guadalajara, Battle of, 9
Guernica, battle of, 49

Habbaniya, battle of, 108–11
Haifa, Palestine, 122, 225–26
Haig, Douglas, 191*n*2
Halfaya Pass, 106, 243, 249–51
Hammer, Lt. Col., 185–87
Harding, Jerry, 183
Hart, Jim, 296
Hartshorn, Eric Ponsonby "Scrubs," 193, 194, 196
Harwood, Henry, 162
Hasey, Jack, 125–26, 126*n*1
Hasty (destroyer), 155, 161
Heineman, Harold, 172
Hemingway, Ernest, ix, 46–48, 51*n*1
Hermione (cruiser), 155, 161
Herrero, Emilio, 27–29, 43
Highland Division, 188, 210, 279–94
Hill, Russell, 264, 265
Hitler, Adolf: appeasement of, 39, 63–64; attack against Soviet Union by, 70; and division of Poland between Germany and Soviet Union, 67; Gorrell's great-aunt on, 66; invasion of Austria, Czechoslovakia, and Poland by, 9, 58, 63–64, 73; and minorities in the Balkans, 301; and Mussolini, 8, 15, 21; occupation of Romania by, 9, 72; propaganda by, 55–59, 61, 66, 107; and Spanish Civil War, 8–9, 23, 27; timetable of, during World War II, 70–71, 106–7; war against Jews by, 39. *See also* Germany
Hogan, J. S., 186
Holloway, Lee C., 264, 268
Homs, 289
Horrocks, Brian, 210
Hospitals and medical care: air transport for, 270; and ambulance driver, 275–76; and American Field Service, 246, 248–49; in Benghazi, 258; and British Army Medical Corps, 248–49; in England, 63, 65; German field hospitals and hospital equipment, 246, 253, 255, 258–59; Gorrell in, 146; in Greece and Albania, 84, 92, 97; in Homs, 293; and Navarino Bay bombing, 232–33; in North Africa,

168, 169, 171–72, 183, 201, 246, 253, 255, 258–59, 275–76, 281, 282, 293; and nurses, 15, 132–33, 182; in Spain, 46
Humor in wartime reporting, 171–72, 205, 215–16, 270, 285
Hungary: attitude in, toward World War II, 71–72; German railroad right-of-way through, 80; German troops in plain clothes in, 72; Gorrell in Budapest, 9, 67, 70–75; reports of German troops massing on Hungarian frontier, 73–74; and United Nations, 301
Hunting, 57–58, 147–48
Hurricanes, Hawker (fighter aircraft), 97, 204, 206–7, 209, 237
Hürtgen Forest, Battle of, x, 2

India and Indian forces, 142, 187, 220, 235, 286
Indochina, 149
Ingersoll, Ralph, x
International Brigade during Spanish Civil War, 37–38, 44, 50, 52, 59, 99
International News Service, 226, 245
International Telephone and Telegraph Company, 79
I.R.A. *See* Irish Republican Army
Iran, 107, 127–37
Iraq, 106–12, 115, 127, 137, 140
Iraq revolt, 106–12
Irish Republican Army (I.R.A.), 65
Italy: and Albanian campaign, 8, 9–10, 70, 80–84, 87–88, 92, 93; anti-British feeling in, 15–16; artillery practice around Viareggio, 17; and Battle of the Mediterranean, 154–55, 159, 161–64; Black Shirts in, 11; bombing of Naples in, 262–68; and casualties of Albanian campaign, 84, 87, 88, 92; collapse of Italian Empire, 8, 10; Communists in, 17–18; creation of Italian Empire, 14–15; entry of, in World War II, 76; and Ethiopian War, 11, 14, 15, 17, 52, 53, 59; fascism in, 8, 14–21; food in, 14–16; Gorrell's birth place in, 16; Gorrell's expulsion from, 7–8, 11, 18–21, 296; and Greco-Italian war, 80–91; League of Nations' economic sanctions against, 14, 15, 17–18, 59; and Misurata, 287–88; Mussolini's Corporate State in, 16–17; and North African campaign, 209, 210, 217, 235, 243–44, 247–48,

250–51, 273; and prisoners of war, 258–61; secret police in, 15–16, 19–21; and Spanish Civil War, 8–9, 18, 23, 27, 32–33, 37, 47, 52–53; United Press Rome bureau in, 17–18; U.S. raids against, 298–99; Whippet tanks of, 32–34, 37. *See also* Mussolini, Benito

Japan, 137, 146–51, 220
Java, 219
Jeffreys, Norman, 125–26
Jerusalem, 114–15, 118, 126
Jews, 39, 52, 55, 79, 108–9, 114–15, 225, 226
Jezzine, Lebanon, 123–24
Jones, Dean, 237–38
Jorgensen, Glade, 227, 229–32

Kagan, Alexander, 214–15
Kane, John R. "Killer," 226, 229, 232, 262–63
Kansas City, Mo., *Journal-Post*, 20
Kay, Leon, 225, 226, 233
Kazvin, Iran, 132–35
Keen, Ed, 42
Kennedy, Ed, 106, 128, 129, 226, 245–46
Kenya, 147, 148
Kidnapping, 79
Kippenberger, Howard K., 183–84, 190
Kirk, Alexander, 19, 19n1
Kittyhawk (P-40), 152, 204, 207, 209, 237–38, 240, 269, 276, 283
Knickerbocker, H. R., x
Korizis, Alexandros, 92n1, 96
Kornhuber (Gestapo member), 74–75
Koutsakous, 87

Lait, George, 226, 245
Laming, Hugh, 123
Land mines. *See* Mines
Lawrence of Arabia, 115, 126
Laycock, Harold, 118, 123–24
League of Nations, 14, 15, 17–18, 31, 59
Le Gentilhomme, Paul Louis, 118, 124, 126
Libya: Italian forces in, 10, 10n2; South African forces in, 149, 168. *See also* Tobruk, Libya
Libya, Battle of, 192, 207, 210, 218
Life magazine, 56, 262
Lindbergh, John, 205
Lippmann, Walter, 56
Lloyd, Lord, 187
Lloyd George, David, 67

Lodge, Henry Cabot, 181
London: gas masks for civilians in, 65–66; German blitz of, 102; Irish Republican Army in, 65; preparation for war in, 63–66; United Press bureau in, 18, 37–39, 62–67. *See also* Great Britain
London Daily Mail, 82
London News Chronicle, 34, 82
Lovelace, John, 263
Luftwaffe: in Alamein, 234; in Alexandria, Egypt, 174, 177; and Battle of the Mediterranean, 153, 154, 158–64, 168, 228; bombing of King Peter's plane by, 97; bombing of Matruh, Egypt by, 169; and British retreat from Greece, 99–101; in Greece, 97; in North Africa, 278–79; in Poland, 298; and Tobruk battle, 169–70
Lupescu, 76, 78

Macedonia, 93, 94
Madagascar, 149, 151
Madrid: executions in, 26–28, 45, 54; food in, 22–23, 29, 43–44, 46, 53; Franco's advance on, 22, 23–24, 37–38; Hemingway in, 46–48; Hotel Florida in, 46–47, 53; imprisonment of Natacha in, 45–46; Natacha in, 30–31, 45–46; Palace Hotel in, 23, 30; siege of, 43–53; social life of Gorrell in, 30–31; Telefonica in, 30, 44–45, 47–49; United Press bureau in, 22–23, 28–30, 43–45, 53. *See also* Spanish Civil War
Maginot Line, 65, 67
Malaria, 103, 106, 146
Malega, battle of, 53
Malta, 153, 154, 156, 162
Malta convoy, 153–65
Maniadakis, Konstantinos, 84, 90–91
Maoris, 175, 183, 184, 260
Martuba, Libya, 257–58
Matruh, Egypt, 168–69, 171, 174–76, 182, 184, 189, 245, 246
Mauldin, Bill, 10
Maydon, Lynch, 163–64
McClure, Rev. Donald, 147–48
McManus, John C., ix–x
McMillan, Richard, 97–99, 101–2, 153, 180–81, 245
McPhee, Stanley, 238
Medical care. *See* Hospitals and medical care